SOCIAL CONSEQUENCES OF MODERNIZATION
IN COMMUNIST SOCIETIES

SOCIAL CONSEQUENCES OF MODERNIZATION IN COMMUNIST SOCIETIES

EDITED BY MARK G. FIELD

THE JOHNS HOPKINS UNIVERSITY PRESS
BALTIMORE AND LONDON

Manufactured in the United States of America

The Johns Hopkins University Press, Baltimore, Maryland 21218
The Johns Hopkins Press Ltd., London

Library of Congress Catalog Card Number 76-169
ISBN 0-8018-1786-2

Library of Congress Cataloging in Publication data
will be found on the last printed page of this book.

This book is dedicated to the social scientists of communist societies, with the hope that someday we may discuss the consequences of social change around the same table.

CONTENTS

Preface

This book is the result of a lengthy process of gestation, described
in some detail in the Introduction. It is based on a selection of papers prepared for and presented at a symposium sponsored by the American Council of
Learned Societies, under the general auspices of the Planning Group on Comparative Communist Studies of the ACLS. The symposium was held at Schloss
Leopoldskron, Salzburg, Austria, between 5 September and 10 September 1972.
The symposium, which I chaired, was organized by a committee consisting of
Talcott Parsons, Alex Inkeles, Ezra F. Vogel, T. Anthony Jones, and myself and
brought together twenty-one social scientists at Salzburg. Three social
scientists who were unable to attend sent papers. The presence of three persons from Eastern Europe (two from Poland and one from Yugoslavia) helped give
a more balanced perspective to the discussions. We had hoped that more
colleagues from Eastern Europe and the Soviet Union might attend, but this did
not prove a realistic expectation. A complete list of the participants at the
symposium and the names of our two rapporteuses will be found in the back of the
volume. Not every participant prepared a paper, and the papers submitted varied
from a set of hypotheses or ideas to be explored to highly developed presentations. In all, nineteen papers were prepared for the symposium, and they too
are listed in the back of this book. Because of space limitations, only a selection of the papers most centrally relevant could be included here. An editorial
committee which I chaired, consisting of R. V. Burks, Zev Katz, Alex Inkeles,
and Ezra F. Vogel, had the delicate and often painful task of making the final
choice. As it turned out, only ten papers, that is, half of those prepared for
the symposium, are included.

In the Introduction which follows, I will specifically acknowledge my
intellectual debt to the Planning Group on Comparative Communist Studies, ACLS.
But in an enterprise of this type, the credit in essence belongs to all those
who participated in it; it belongs to those who informally "got around a table"
and began discussing areas of research and work that needed to be done; to
those who took it on themselves to draft early documents outlining the specific
areas to be investigated; to those whose knowledge of the literature and of
scholars around the world suggested books, articles, names; to those whose
task was to make possible the coming together of papers and persons in Salzburg.
To all of these, I want to express my sincere thanks and gratitude; my apologies
for the delay it took to publish this volume; and the hope that this book is
but one small link in the endless chain of our imperfect knowledge of human
societies.

Finally special thanks are due to Francine Miller who helped edit
the first version of this book, to Barbara Roos who did the Index on short
notice, and particularly to Stephanie Vendetti who, under most trying
circumstances, typed and re-typed this work.

Introduction

Mark G. Field

What kind of social structure has emerged (or is emerging) in communist societies, and how does such a structure compare with that of noncommunist industrial societies? These broad questions are the central focus of the essays in this book and of the symposium where they were first presented and discussed. This volume, as incomplete as it is in its coverage, is an attempt to contribute to our understanding of comparative communism and of comparative social structure, particularly that of modern industrial and urban society. Comparison is, indeed, at the heart of social analysis and understanding. As Durkheim stated in his pioneering study, Suicide: "Only comparison affords explanation."[1] The time has come, as is shown below, to add communist societies to the roster of modern (or modernizing) societies available for analysis by sociologists and by social scientists in general. I hope that such an addition will help us in understanding not only communist societies but modern societies, and that the contribution will be at both the empirical and the theoretical level.

Comparative studies of communist societies are not new in the West. The effort presented here is linearly related, for example, to the book edited by Donald W. Treadgold, Soviet and Chinese Communism: Similarities and Differences (Seattle: University of Washington Press, 1967), or to the even more recent Change in Communist Systems edited by Chalmers Johnson (Stanford: Stanford University Press, 1970). The Johnson volume grew out of a seminar that was sponsored and supported by the Planning Group on Comparative Communist Studies of the American Council of Learned Societies. The same group supported our symposium, and I want to express here my own gratitude, as well as that of all the participants in the symposium, for the intellectual and material support provided by the Planning Group members and the American Council of Learned Societies.[2] But implicitly, and at times explicitly, the interest of the symposium's organizers went beyond the framework of communist societies to encompass other modern societies and to determine which major characteristics these societies might share and which ones they might not.

The organizers of the symposium also hoped that our effort would serve to stimulate some of our sociological colleagues (particularly younger scholars) to direct their attention to communist societies. It is indeed paradoxical that at the very moment when increasingly sophisticated sociological studies and more detailed statistical data are becoming available from the communist countries, there is a dearth of sociologists interested in such studies. It is almost as if, in a perverse fashion, communist societies held more interest for social scientists when they were cloaked in mystery, when visits there were practically impossible, when sociology in these societies did not exist, when the statistical data were scarce and suspect. Partly in the light of these considerations, the organizers of the symposium hoped that it would be a thrust in a revived effort of social scientists to examine modern communist societies. The symposium was sparked by a small group of scholars based primarily at the Russian Research Center and the East Asian Research Center at Harvard, who convened a meeting at Cambridge in May 1970 to assess the state of the field, to present papers, and to discuss further plans and directions. This meeting echoed in some way the concern expressed earlier by Marshall Shulman about the state of Soviet studies in the United States:

> Perhaps the most important gap is in sociology. For a
> long time it has been the case that the difficulty in
> conducting systematic sociological studies in the Soviet
> Union, and the attractions--including financial--of other

sociological investigations made it difficult to recruit
qualified students in this field. But the need is more
urgent, and the moment is perhaps more propitious than it
has been. The beginning of sociological investigations
in the Soviet system, and the hopeful beginnings, all argue for renewed efforts in this direction. There is no
doubt but that, despite the remaining difficulty of doing
intensive field investigation in the Soviet Union that is
normal elsewhere, sociologists could make the most single
exciting contribution to Soviet studies today.[3]

The essays presented here are only the beginning of what we hope will be more
systematic studies by social scientists of contemporary communist societies.
As these societies gradually lose their mystery, they should become grist to
the sociological mill. Their incorporation as legitimate objects of sociological discourse and inquiry, as I mentioned earlier, not only will permit
better knowledge of these specific societies, but should contribute to
comparative sociological theory and understanding.

Social Change Under Communist Rule

        The purpose of this section is to present some of the basic
theoretical considerations and issues that underlay the symposium and the
essays themselves.

        Our intention was to explore in depth some of the sociological and
systemic consequences of social change under communist rule. This social
change we subsume under the shorthand term of "modernization," a term that is
not without its ambiguities, as we shall see later. But the issue that
initially intrigued us was that we were dealing with societies where a process
of guided or directed or managed modernization existed. This could be compared, by implication or explicitly, with the more spontaneous or more organic
or less-directed process of modernization that takes place in noncommunist
societies, in what is called the Western industrial world and Japan. The
directing, the managing, the administering of social change is a central
feature of communist societies and the undisputed responsibility of an organization or agency-the Communist party or its functional equivalent under a
different name. Thus, the existence and the central role of that agency, with
its wide-ranging and quasi-total power over the entire society, is the major
structural element differentiating communist from noncommunist systems. The
political aspects of this process of forcible change in the communist world
are relatively well-known, perhaps because they are the most striking and
visible manifestations of it. And although we certainly were interested in
the sociological aspects of that process--for example, in its preconditions, in
the peculiarities of the diffusion of the major aspects of a process developed
elsewhere (such as industrialization)--our main concern was the sociological
consequences of this development and the degree to which these differed from
what one could see in the noncommunist world. These consequences have been
much better documented and discussed for noncommunist societies, if only
because the information has been much more readily available, published, and
disseminated. Indeed, the secretiveness with which communist regimes veil
their operations and their results and control the flow of information is what
has often lent a "strangeness" to these societies, has been the despair of
social scientists trying to deal with them, and has contributed to discouraging
students from entering this area of investigation.

It should furthermore be noted that with a few possible exceptions, the regimes with which we are concerned took over and retained power in essentially underdeveloped or developing societies. Thus, from a strictly classical Marxist viewpoint, these revolutions or seizures of power occurred prematurely, in the sense that capitalism was not allowed to do its historically assigned task: to produce an increasingly large, conscious, overexploited, alienated proletariat and a mature system of industrial production and technology. This system, once expropriated after a revolution and managed by the proletariat, would then yield the fruits of abundance and banish human misery to the museum of history. Communist regimes have thus been modernizing regimes, eager to catch up to and surpass the West and, with the exception of China and Cuba (so far), sacrificing almost everything else for that purpose. The classical, alliterative, and masochistic litany voiced by Stalin in 1931 about the beatings that Russia suffered at the hands of her enemies throughout her history because of underdevelopment set the tone for the mystique of development, industrialization, and modernization:

It is sometimes asked whether it is not possible to slow down the tempo somewhat, to put a check on the movement. No, comrades, it is not possible!....To slacken the tempo would mean falling behind. And those who fall behind get beaten. But we do not want to be beaten. No, we refuse to be beaten! One feature of the history of old Russia was the continual beatings she suffered because of her backwardness. She was beaten by the Mongol khans. She was beaten by the Turkish beys. She was beaten by the Swedish feudal lords. She was beaten by the Polish and Lithuanian gentry. She was beaten by the British and French capitalists. She was beaten by the Japanese barons. All beat her--because of her backwardness, military backwardness, cultural backwardness, political backwardness, industrial backwardness, agricultural backwardness. They beat her because to do so was profitable and could be done with impunity. Do you remember the words of the prerevolutionary poet? "You are poor and abundant, mighty and impotent, Mother Russia." Those gentlemen were quite familiar with the words of the old poet. They beat her, saying: "You are poor and impotent," so you can be beaten and plundered with impunity. Such is the law of the exploiters--beat the backward and the weak. It is the jungle law of capitalism. You are backward, you are weak--therefore you are wrong; hence, you can be beaten and enslaved. You are mighty--therefore, you are right; hence, we must be wary of you..... We are fifty or a hundred years behind the advanced countries. We must make good this distance in ten years. Either we do it, or we shall be crushed.[4]

It was thus the lot of most of these regimes (beginning with Stalin) to do to their societies what the capitalists were not given a chance to do, and in that process they acted as capitalists (i.e., as state capitalists) reproducing in their own societies many of the same general phenomena that Marx and Engels had observed and criticized in British manufacturing and mill towns. These included the exploitation of labor; the wholesale use of piecework; absolute and ferocious discipline (backed by the full power of the state); the reduction of workers and peasants to the status of soldiers of production--or slaves, as Solzhenitsyn has recently reminded us; and huge inequalities in power, incomes, and styles of living. A Stalin might dismiss these phenomena as part of the dialectic of history, as the necessary price for the communist society that eventually was to emerge from that travail, or similar rationalizations. But in fact such an approach created a specific type of society that acquired a momentum of its own, that exhibited some elements common to nonsocialist industrial societies, and which, once established, evolved a structure that had hardly been anticipated or intended by the founding fathers, including Lenin and Stalin themselves.

The symposium was thus part of an effort to incorporate communist societies into the sample of modern societies, to subject these societies to the same kind of inquiry whenever possible, and perhaps to demystify them, at least in the sociological sense. Not too long ago many Westerners found it difficult to accept the notion that the Soviet Union, a socialist state, was not a homogeneous society of equal citizens (or comrades) but was a highly differentiated and stratified society. Today, sociological studies from the Soviet Union point to this type of stratification and show, for example, that one's life chances are associated with one's family social position and that workers and collectivized farmers stand far from the top of the stratification pyramid. Thus, even in communist societies today the wise child chooses his parents well!

At a time in the industrial West when so much attention, questioning, and ambivalence attach to modernization and progress, it is proper and legitimate to ask whether modernization, carried out under the aegis of communist parties, produces (or re-produces) some of the same general phenomena. An analysis of communist social systems thus should permit us to further our comprehension of modern, and particularly modern industrial, society around the world, and to address ourselves in a more informed fashion to the question of the "costs" of such social change. (The term "costs" is meant here, of course, in much more than a strictly economic sense. Indeed, philosophers and moralists have raised in one guise or another this age-old problem about the nature of human action, about man's willingness to pay a "price" [including in a Faustian sense his soul or essence] for some glittering bauble of no intrinsic worth.) The dehumanizing and profoundly alienating aspects of modernization as industrialization, mostly under private capitalism, are what so profoundly shocked Marx and Engels in the nineteenth century and impelled them to seek an explanation and a resolution of the many contradictions they saw in that process. How was it, they asked, that a development that had originally been hailed as liberating mankind from drudgery, misery, and toil had actually led to its most cruel form of enslavement? For the Marxist vision of the future did not reject material abundance and well-being per se except of course for "commodity fetishism." Quite the contrary. It saw this as the guarantee of an order in which the production of commodities and the physical wants of all people would cease to be problematic, thus allowing them to devote themselves to higher, more dignified pursuits, without the antagonisms and the envies that inequality inevitably causes in the fragmented capitalist class society. If a shorthand phrase for that utopian vision exists, it is the Garden of Eden with the fruits of advanced industrialism. And the disquieting aspects of society's transformation from traditional to modern are what have kept so many social analysts, particularly sociologists, from the nineteenth century on, focused on the nature of human relations in the industrial (or industrializing) world. This concern is often expressed in Tönnies's classical distinction between the Gemeinschaft type of social order and the Gesellschaft--the shift from the primary to the secondary group, the decrease in personal contacts and the rise of the impersonality of the marketplace, the move from status to contract, the sense of a loss, estrangement, and isolation of the anonymous urban centers of the industrial world. This is epitomized with some poignancy today by the gradual decrease and eventual disappearance of the small shop in France, replaced by the chromium-bright, hyperefficient supermarket, where to be sure prices are lower and shopping can be done with a fraction of the time and effort required earlier. But what of the small amenities and familiarities, the sense of belonging, the ability to exchange greetings? The small personalized rituals of such human contacts are all but lost in almost every field of human endeavor, through the application of rationality, calculability, accountability, technology, and science. In medicine, to take another case--in that humane practice par excellence--science and technology have multiplied the effectiveness of intervention in illness and trauma and helped retard death. On the other hand, the increasingly "scientific" physician is seen by his patient as cold and unfeeling, resulting in what has been described in the Soviet Union as the "veterinarization" of medicine; that is, an approach centered on organs or organ systems and not on the patient as a sentient human being with anxieties and affect. And the functionally dictated evaluation of people by what they can do rather than who they are makes them consider themselves "cogs in the machinery" caught in the "rat race" and leads either to countercultures of the types that sporadically arise in industrial society or to deviant escapes into certain kinds of crime or addiction.

Social scientists should thus examine the nature of modern society under communist regimes to see whether these societies are qualitatively different from noncommunist ones and, if so, in precisely what aspects. But in addition to the comparative aspect, important in any sociological inquiry, this concern fits quite directly with sociological attempts to describe and analyze the nature of modern society in general. What are the preconditions for its appearance? What are its basic structural features? What are some of the general trends or directionalities it exhibits? And more centrally (at least for this symposium), what kinds of effects does it produce? For example, is the destruction of the environment and the pollution of soil, water, and air the product only of nondirected spontaneous modernization dictated by profit considerations, or does the modern industrial society, regardless of how it was brought about and is now governed, obey certain laws or regularities that transcend space and ideology? That industrial managers in both Soviet and American societies often find it more expedient and economical to pay fines for polluting air or water than to install filtering mechanisms is revealing. And the existence of a socialist regime in the USSR is not likely to save Lake Baikal from the spoliations of industry.[5]

This brings me to the controversial question of the "convergence" of modern industrial societies. Briefly stated, this hypothesis (which will be discussed at some length in the paper by Jones) holds that the functional prerequisites of an industrial order are such that they tend to create a type of society and culture that is fairly uniform wherever it arises, regardless of both historical antecedents and contemporary forms of governance or ideological commitments. Or, to put it another way, given the prerequisites for industrialism, the number of options is limited and tends to become increasingly so as the society matures. Thus the factory as a mode of production tends to exhibit universal organizational and managerial demands (for example, the alienation of the workers from the means of production) and to require the same general structure (need for discipline, time orientation, punctuality, etc.). It generally places the worker in roughly the same hierarchical order (which then spills over into most spheres of nonfactory life) wherever a factory system is instituted. Minor variations may exist, but the overall pattern has more elements in common than dissimilarities. The word "convergence" must be interpreted in a flexible way, as the expression of certain tendencies moving toward a fairly common pattern. As we shall see later in the discussion by Jones, this may well include a gradient of elements that are more or less susceptible to moving toward convergence--thus the economic-productive component, because of universal technological factors, may show much more convergence than, let's say, the political structure. But as the paper by Lowenthal cogently argues, the impact (or the implication) of modernization on the polity is far from negligible, particularly if that polity is concerned with its level of productivity--that is, its national power compared with that of other contemporary polities.

In communist countries, however, the very notion of convergence tends to be emphatically rejected, primarily on ideological grounds, for it implies that essentially modern societies tend to be (or to become) structurally similar and thus removes that very distinctiveness that communist regimes claim. This might explain why none of the five Soviet social scientists invited to participate in the symposium accepted (or was allowed to accept) the invitation. These

societies see the party as the only agency capable of bringing about the positive elements of modernization and controlling, if not suppressing, the
negative by-products seen in the capitalist world. According to this view, the
party, with its almost total control over most human and economic resources
(including public opinion, which it mobilizes in support of the regime), will
produce a less traumatic, more humane, more coordinated, more rational, more
planned, smoother mode of transformation than societies where no such body
exists. At least this is the claim of the party. But social reality, unfortunately, does not always conform to ideological dogmas or theoretical
dicta, as is well documented from a reading of the history of communist
societies and is also evident from the essays which follow. The process of
modernization apparently has produced in communist societies many of the same
consequences as in noncommunist ones. But another fascinating phenomenon is
worthy of some attention: the complex of consequences of modernization for the
very agency that set it into motion in the first place--the Communist party.
Indeed, if one follows an evolutionary and even Marxist and dialetic approach
to that development, one might argue that in the early phases of development
after the party takes over, it is objectively a progressive force in removing
the shackles of the past and releasing the frozen energies of the previous
social order. It manages this, as we noted earlier, by mobilizing control over
most of the resources. But once the breakthrough or takeoff has been accomplished, once the economy has reached a certain degree of maturity, once the
society and its people have become more "modern"--more educated and sophisti-
cated--and once they operate in terms of that modernity, then what becomes of
the party? How does its role change? What are the factors that push in the
direction of that change, and to what degree is the party able to retain control and adapt to the new conditions, which as Lowenthal has pointed out,
would logically mean a decrease in the functionality and legitimacy of the
party according to its original, self-appointed mandate? For example, to what
degree do the self-adjustive mechanisms of a market economy (albeit limited)
make the party's functions of control obsolete? To what extent does the
party's insistence on an ideological screening of scientific or even artistic
activities actually impoverish society? To what degree does this pervasive
kind of political power actually obstruct the society's mastery of the environment and reduce its ability to compete with other societies?

The reader increasingly will find that this volume has only scratched
the surface, and that this symposium and its product should mark not an end but
the beginning of a more systematic attack on the range of problems inherent in
all modern societies, East or West, socialist or capitalist, or mixed. I shall
refer to some of these problems toward the end of this essay.

Modernization

The word "modernization" tends to be difficult to define. In addition, it mobilizes all the doubts and ambiguities with which the process
itself has been associated, and particularly brings to mind the "costs" entailed by that process. Indeed, before the symposium the Planning Group on
Comparative Communism of the American Council of Learned Societies discussed
whether the term was meant in a normative sense--that is, as something desirable, or intrinsically good--and whether the West (and particularly western
social scientists) was not guilty of naive ethnocentrism in using Western
advanced societies as the reference point, as the model, against which the
modernization process in communist societies was to be compared and judged.
In this symposium the term is used as descriptive shorthand for a process
and a product of the transformation of society from traditional to nontradi-
tional--from the Gemeinschaft to the Gesellschaft type of social worder.

No judgment is intended on the moral value or the desirability of that process, or at least none was directly implied. As such, the issue of modernization raised four basic questions that were discussed at some length in the early phases of the symposium:[6]

1. The question of the necessary preconditions for modernization both in the West, where it arose as a "sociocultural invention," and in societies that adopted and applied that invention for their own purposes. Thus the communist societies attempted in their own ways, to implement or adopt (and adapt) a process of social change that had already taken place elsewhere. This is, of course, an important question historically, though perhaps not central to the symposium except that some of the prerequisites for the transfer of a pattern developed in the West to communist societies must be identified. Some participants, for example, held that only the development of law and contracts permits modernization to proceed, and that the absence of these and of procedural mechanisms will hamper the further modernization of communist societies.

2. The definition and the nature of "modern" society, "modern" culture, and "modern" man which received a great deal of discussion. This question also incorporated the problem of transfer or diffusion of modern patterns of social organization and techniques to developing societies, and the social, cultural, and psychological strains or costs attendant on that process.

3. The nature and structure of modern or industrialized communist-type societies, and particularly the nature, the role, and indeed the necessity and the "functionality," of the party. This included an examination of the changing nature of that role at different stages of modernization, each one with its central problems, and an attempt to look into the future of that role--indeed the future of the party.

4. Finally and centrally, the visible and empirically verifiable consequences of the modernization process in communist-type countries, with a rough attempt to delineate the degree to which these consequences resemble or diverge from those visible in noncommunist societies, for example, social differentiation and deviance.

Jones provides a most useful review of the concept of modernization. He points out that the study of communist societies so far has tended to be relegated to area specialists rather than to sociologists. He argues that such societies are not esoteric, sui generis, but belong to the general type of industrial (or industrializing) social systems undergoing a process of more or less forcible change and adopting patterns, many of which have been developed outside these societies. Furthermore, observers of these societies have tended to become mesmerized, so to speak, by this political nature--an important feature to be sure, but one that has led inevitably to underemphasis, if not almost complete neglect, of their sociological aspects. No doubt the political focus, with its dual aspects of decision-making and decision enforcement, has often provided the most dramatic contrast between communist and noncommunist societies. The control, the terror, the concentration camps, the muzzled press, the ideological dictation, the instrumentalization of human beings are areas in which sociologists unfortunately have not been particularly interested. At the same time, the lack of sociological work in these societies has deprived the scholar of much data needed for comparative work. Nevertheless, the process of development in these societies must be seen as a sociological as well as a political phenomenon. It is thus important to conceive of socialist societies as "modernizing" societies but, of course, modernizing within the framework of their particular political formation.

The Nature Of "Modern" Man

Inkeles's paper deals with a quite different aspect of the process of modernization, namely, its characteriological or psychological aspects. More precisely, Inkeles examines two elements: first, an inventory of the kinds of human traits that develop as part of modernization or accompany it, and which seem to be universally associated with that process regardless of its cultural or historical setting. To put it another way, What kind of personality structure fits best, or is best adapted to cope with modernization, and indeed to implement it? The second element, directly related to the first and perhaps even more germane to this book, is the following: Given the traits that fit best with the needs of a modernizing society, what have been the deliberate efforts of both the Chinese and the Soviet regimes to bring about these traits among their populations? As Inkeles points out, this is primarily the function of the school and the educational system in general. This takes the form of exhortation and the inculcation of certain values and attitudes. Inkeles is dealing with nothing more than a deliberate and concerted effort to convert traditional man into modern man.

What then are the traits that Inkeles identifies as part of making man modern?

1. A shift in allegiance from traditional authority (family, small community, church, etc.) to leaders of government, public affairs, trade unions, and so on. This signifies the loosening of ascriptive ties of solidarity.

2. Increased interest and participation in local affairs and activities.

3. A broadening of the individual's horizon beyond local and parochial concerns to encompass interest in national affairs.

4. An openness to new (i.e., nontraditional) approaches in all spheres of life, whether natural, mechanical, or interpersonal.

5. Belief in the efficacy of knowledge in general and science in particular to master nature and solve problems--rejection or passivity, resignation, and fatality.

6. Awareness and mastery of time, of planning, of regularity and discipline--that is, an orientation toward the future.

7. Maximization of opportunities for personal development, increase in skills, and job mastery together with a concern for improving opportunities for the education of one's children.

The significance of Inkeles's paper is that it brings developments in the communist world into line with those in other advanced industrial countries around the world. He points to the general congruence of modal personality types in the modern world, whether communist or noncommunist. During the discussion of his somewhat controversial paper at Salzburg, Inkeles took pains to insist that his inventory of traits that, in his mind, characterize modern man were not "normative." That is, they were not necessarily "good" or "desirable," or even conducive to happiness, but that he had difficulty in conceiving of the existence and the functioning of a modern industrial society without them.

Modernization In Communist China

In his paper, Vogel deals with modernization and development as they
have taken place, since 1949, under communist rule in China. In particular,
Vogel stresses the characteristics that differentiate China from other societies, whether communist or noncommunist. He points out that the Chinese communists have established, for the first time in the twentieth century, effective
control over their national territory, then adds that they had accomplished
considerably more in political and social modernization than in the economic
realm--that is, in industrialization. China is, of course, at a very early stage
of modernization; for example, 80 percent of her population is still rural. In
contrast to what happened in the Soviet Union and Eastern Europe, the communist
leaders in China seem more concerned about the rural than the urban sectors of
society, although this did not appear true in the beginning when Soviet influence was strong. Indeed, in the first decade after 1949 there were no
indications that the Chinese pattern would diverge significantly from the
Soviet model; Chinese leaders also aimed for modernization and development.
But by 1961 clearly a high level of development and industrialization was a
long way off, and this realization led to the decision to slow down or even
reverse the trend toward industrialization and urbanization. This does represent a significant departure from the standard development patterns of communist societies. Vogel summarizes the characteristics of the contemporary
Chinese approach as: (1) firm administrative control; (2) low level of capital investment; (3) state administrative and technical advice; (4) intensive
utilization of labor; (5) local coordination; and (6) decentralization and low
level of specialization. The paper by Frolic also emphasizes the differences
between the Soviet Union and the People's Republic of China regarding urbanization (certainly one of the hallmarks of the modernization process).

The significance of the Chinese case should be stressed. For here is
a communist society widely differing in its approach to modernization (after
having begun by imitating the Soviet pattern). If anything, the Chinese
pattern reveals the diversities of the modernization process. It reminds one,
for example, of the decision of the Yugoslav party to seek its own special path
to socialism and modernization. But the question is whether these divergences
will continue.

Modernization In Other Communist Societies

Speaking about North Korea at the symposium, Hong also emphasized industrialization, political development, and changes in life patterns and traditional belief systems. But he noted the pejorative overtone given the term
"modernization" in Southeast Asia, where it stands for the exploitation of
underdeveloped nations by imperialist societies. Pusic pointed to some of the
salient elements in Yugoslav history after 1945 and singled out for his comments
the concept of self-management. He traced the cultural antecedents of self-
management to the importance of local autonomy and local loyalty in the face
of foreign occupation and domination and to the need to resist the encroachments
of an alien power installed in Belgrade. Comparing the development of Yugoslavia and of Poland after World War II, Wesolowski isolated the common and
not so common features of the two societies (for example, the ethnic homogeneity of Poland compared with the multiethnic nature of Yugoslavia). In
Poland the issue of centralization versus decentralization is also being
debated. The discussion at Salzburg ranged over a variety of issues and of

societies, including the Soviet Union and Cuba.

Political Aspects Of Modernization In Communist Societies

The papers by Lowenthal and Jowitt focused the discussion more cen-
trayly on the political aspects of modernization in communist countries, though
with strong sociological overtones. As I noted earlier, Lowenthal deals primarily with the role of the ruling party in the "postmobilization phase." The
party, through its mobilization efforts, has brought about the modernization of
society. Can it then continue to operate as it has in the past? How will it
cope with the consequences of the processes it originally set in motion? Lowenthal accepts the Parsonian concept of the internal differentiation of society,
and questions whether in the future a differentiated society can be ruled and
operated by a single party. He believes this is impossible or, if possible,
done only at the great price of a loss of efficiency, particularly in the economic realm. Indeed, Lowenthal holds in accord with Parsons that at certain
stages of development, nothing can substitute for democratic associations and
procedural forms. He thus rejects George Fischer's hypothesis of a monistic
system relying on the development of professionally competent apparatchiki.
Lowenthal's analysis also deals with large functional problems: (1) The
ability of the system to solve problems of economic efficiency, particularly the
development of technological rationality. In this regard he notes, for example, the strategic importance for individuals of certain basic rights such as
the right to criticize and disagree without being punished--that is, the "right"
to be wrong." (2) The question of interest groups and their articulation. It
is true that the party hears conflicting views and arbitrates or chooses among
them, but it is not put under pressure by those groups. Sometimes, however,
surprises can result from inadequate communication (as in the riots in Poland
in December 1970). (3) The question of legitimacy. In general, communist
regimes (with the possible exception of Czechoslovakia) have achieved some
legitimacy via a consensus of values; but the party essentially engages in
self-legitimation. It claims that its task is to coordinate, integrate, and
keep society together. But it rejects the idea that a mature society could
exist without a guardian. Lowenthal feels that real legitimacy must be institutional and procedural--that there is no alternative. The party, furthermore, can attract good technicians but only mediocre politicians, so that in
the long run, the system must either become more pluralistic (and multiparty)
or regress.

Lowenthal's paper provoked, as might be expected, a great deal of
discussion at Salzburg, centering particularly on the functions performed by
the party (some of which may not be easily apprehended by outsiders). Field,
for example, questioned the ability of the party and its ideology to provide
answers to the question of "meaning" as used by Max Weber--that is, in terms
of ultimate values. Another participant countered that Soviet society was
basically stable and that he did not see any evidence of a possible breakdown
within the next fifteen to twenty years. Indeed, he went on, the problems
faced by Soviet society are not any more serious (though they are different)
than those, for example, of American society. He added that the case of
Eastern European societies was, however, less clear. In his rejoinder,
Lowenthal pointed out that he was making no short-range predictions, that
the problems in the West were of a different kind, and that Western democratic society was more flexible and better able to cope with its problems
than that of the one-party states.

Jowitt's presentation focused on the political nature and functions
of Marxist-Leninist regimes and on the questions not only of modernization but

of what he calls transformation and consolidation. Jowitt defined as modern those societies in which the dominant institutions are characterized by relational rather than command capacities; in which authoritative definitions (social, cultural, political, economic, and ideological) are open to critical analysis; and in which tasks are formally conceived and executed in terms of impersonal rules and schedules. The nature of these characteristics is what permits an examination of the evolution of traditional societies toward modernity, as well as analysis of the implications of the above criteria. This includes the price that modern society pays for modernity (for example, an overemphasis on instrumental rather than expressive behavior, and the reaction toward romanticism or other types of countercultures). Socialist societies are concerned with three tasks: transformation, consolidation, and modernization, and these are sequential. The change from one stage to another is associated with different types of personality and styles of leadership. Jowitt emphasized that in the last five years (prior to 1972) some socialist societies have confronted a series of problems and challenges arising from the modernization process itself and its implications for the party, and this has led to a reemergence of some of the "mobilization" characteristics of Leninism. Jowitt, among others, argued that it is imperative to distinguish between the universal characteristics of modernization and the distinctive historical expressions in concrete societies that provide them with sociopolitical substance.

Stratification And Mobility In Communist Societies

Among the consequences of modernization hardly anticipated by men like Lenin or Stalin, the growth of social differentiations, inequalities, and differential access to opportunities for power and economic goods certainly occupy a prominent position. The presentations by Katz and Matthews dealt with these questions.

Katz reviewed his recent examination of the social stratification that has developed in Soviet society, particularly the relationship of this stratification to power. He used the concept of "class" as a social grouping fulfilling a series of functions (economic, political, social, cultural) and described the class of nachalniks (a term for people endowed with power) that has arisen in the Soviet Union as a result of modernization and industrialization. He concluded that the nachalnik class (which includes different levels of power) is bound to, and dependent on, the regime.

The discussion that followed Katz's presentation at Salzburg touched on many areas: the special legal position of the peasant, who is fixed in his class position (through the internal passport system) and cannot move without permission (the same, incidentally, was true of Soviet workers between 1940 and 1956); the increasing degree of egalitarianism (at least in wages) as a result of the rise in the floor below which people were not allowed to sink, the smaller number of power-wielders in Soviet society compared with the nachalnik class identified by Katz; the need to differentiate between power (the ability to use coercive sanctions) and influence (the ability to play an important role); the tradition in Russia of creating classes by political decisions, and the fact that perhaps the classes resulting from modernization constitute interest groups more autonomous than the party would like to see. Thus another Russian historical pattern may possibly repeat itself: that is, the binding and unbinding of classes. Inkeles commented on the durability of the Soviet class structure, which still conforms to the contours he had outlined in the late forties. He felt that the concept of a nachalnik class as outlined by Katz was too broad. One must, he stressed, continue to bear in mind the symbiotic relationship between one who wields power at the top of the political pyramid and the specialist or intellectual below him who provides the necessary knowledge.

Matthews deals in his presentation with the relationship between school and society. The educational system is affected by the wider process of social differentiation at work in Soviet society and begins to resemble, in several respects, that of "bourgeois" societies. There is increasing pressure for a differentiated school system that will accommodate the wishes of the middle class: special schools for gifted children; more admissions to the vuzy (higher educational institutions); the use of private tutors to facilitate such entrance. As Matthews says, "Education bends to social demands." At the same time, there is increasing discrepancy between the aspirations of students and the opportunities for employment, particularly for those who have received a complete intermediate and higher education. As in the West, the children from the intelligentsia are overrepresented in higher education. Indeed, Khrushchev's reforms (now largely dismantled) were partly intended to draw more proletarian children into the intelligentsia and to subject every student to the experience of working with his or her hands.

The discussion following presentation of the Katz and Matthews papers included some comparisons with the experience in China, where until recently openings in the universities have been limited to children of peasants and workers. Recent changes, however, make it possible for children of the intelligentsia to enter universities provided they work for two years at manual labor. Also, Chinese universities have recently reintroduced entrance examinations having eliminated them for several years.

Certain salient features in Soviet education were also pointed out during the discussion. For example, applicants to the universities are of two types: those who come directly from secondary schools and those sponsored by groups, agencies, or institutions, who have had some work experience, and who then must return for several years of service to the recommending agency (kolkhoz, army unit, etc.). This must be seen as an attempt to "democratize" access to educational opportunities. Nonetheless, children of the intelligentsia still dominate the student body at Soviet universities.

In reviewing Soviet educational patterns in the last fifteen years, that is, from the time of the reforms introduced in the late 1950's under Khrushchev and associated with polytechnicalization, Rosen pointed out that these patterns were consonant with the traits of modern man outlined by Inkeles. Khrushchev's reforms addressed themselves to the major problem of preparing students to fit more closely the roles in the economy. Thus, to some degree these reforms (particularly entrance examinations) helped to stratify the population. Polytechnicalization was not a great success: it prepared students for a relatively narrow range of skills; it led to a decline in the quality of training in traditional academic subjects; and managers of industry were more interested in meeting their production quotas than in devoting time, personnel, and materials to training apprentices. The reform program has been greatly modified and revised since the mid-sixties. The Soviet Union also faces a still unresolved major problem in the low quality of education in the rural areas. Thus the fit between the educational system and the demands of a modern society is less than adequate.

Urbanization In Communist Societies

Frolic's paper turns to another important element in modernization: urbanization. His essay is of particular interest because it compares urbanization policy in China and in the Soviet Union. The two societies exhibit, at least at the present historical stage, rather different approaches to the city. The Soviet view, classically Marxist in this respect, is that the city is important and provides a favorable environment for man; the Chinese view, influenced by Mao's personality, is that the countryside is preferable, or that at least a better balance between city and rural life should be struck in China. Frolic concludes that the two social systems are sufficiently different that their urbanization processes are not identical.

The discussion that followed Frolic's presentation was wide-ranging, and against the background of urban development returned to several of the issues and problems examined earlier. What, for example, is the relationship of increasing urbanization to deviance and crime? Is the city criminogenic? What are some of the problems associated with the shift of the economy toward the service sector, and away from extractive and manufacturing industries? What is the implication of the difference between private industrial firms disposing of their profits as they see fit, and governmental units disposing of tax funds for public services? In the discussion Katz also pointed to little-known aspects of stratification patterns in Soviet urban areas: the residential address itself may reveal the social status of the individual (as it often does in the West); there are secret Soviet cities not on the map, whose existence is known only by a postal number; housing in the Soviet Union is one-third privately owned, one-third in the hands of local Soviets, and 8 to 10 percent cooperative, the last usually the best type of housing.

The paper by Konrad and Szelenyi, who were unable to attend the symposium, presents a rare insight into the process of urbanization as it is taking place under communist rule in Hungary. The two authors point out that the rate of urbanization lags behind that of industrialization, resulting in a situation they call "underurbanization." Urbanization is not controlled by a supply and demand market mechanism but is the result of administrative decisions. As a result of these decisions, the ability to reside in an urban area has become a special privilege, reserved to certain groups of the population; it has, according to the authors, beome a "feudal right." And this has created a new category of workers who work in the city but live in the countryside.

Deviance In Communist Society

Connor's paper covers another important consequence of the process of modernization: the increase in nonpolitical deviance and social disorganization, particularly alcoholism, juvenile delinquency, and crime. Connor feels that there is a great deal of similarity between the Soviet and Eastern European experience on the one side and that of Western Europe and the United States on the other. He sees one of the causes of such a phenomenon in the mass transfer of (mostly male) populations from the countryside into poorly integrated or organized industrial and urban centers, where social controls are few. This increases the opportunities for deviant behavior of all types, as seems to be borne out by the evidence in both communist and noncommunist societies. The statistical evidence must be considered (in all societies) as suspect and deficient,however, since the "counting" of crimes or other deviant behavior is never accurate nor complete; indeed, a great deal of it never comes to the attention of the reporting agencies. In the discussion, Field pointed to a reverse phenomenon in statistical counting in the West: the "increase" in mental illness that apparently accompanies industrialization and urbanization, which is largely the result of better detection, diagnosis, and reporting rather than an increase in mental illness itself. Tucker noted the constancy of the alcoholism problem in Russia (so that it could not all be blamed on modernization). It was also pointed out that the sale of alcohol makes an important financial contribution to the state treasury in the Soviet Union, so that the state is unwilling to pass up this sort of revenue.

Research And Development In Communist Society

Solomon addresses himself to the following question: What accounts for the poor Soviet performance in research and development? His paper focuses, in essence, on the relationship between science and modernization. After surveying the history of the relationship of science to the economy and to the polity, Solomon argues that the Soviets view science as instrumental--that is, not as an activity to be supported for its own sake, but as one that will yield economic benefits via technology. Reasons for the relatively poor Soviet performance may be found in the institutional system, particularly in the separation of research from production (especially under Stalin). Even today many elements in Soviet society discourage innovation. One should also contrast the Soviet approach (with its heavy emphasis on borrowing) with that of the Japanese, who tend to buy licenses and improve on them rather than merely copy them.

A point that emerged in the discussion that followed is that the Soviets are much more innovative in noncivilian technology (military, aerospace), because they promote competition between research teams. This suggests that Moscow is not unaware of institutional arrangements that encourage technological innovation, but that it is unwilling to introduce such arrangements in the civilian sector for political reasons. In the USSR, Burks pointed out, the civilian manager who innovates also takes the risk of not meeting his immediate production targets. Rather, he is rewarded for failing to innovate. This contrasts with the situation of the American manager, for example, who is likely to be penalized for falling profits and summarily dismissed if he does not introduce cost-reducing processes or attractive new products. In consequence, the Soviet economy may continue to lag and suffer reverses compared with market-type economies in the West (failure to go to the moon, the need to purchase huge amounts of wheat abroad, etc.). Thus, in the competition between East and West, the East may well suffer because its institutional arrangements are such that they slow down the process of innovation. According to some discussants, the importance of this lag is in fact recognized by the Soviet leadership in the establishment of science-cities, far from the centers of political power, where innovative work is encouraged. The discussion also turned to the different approaches taken by Japan and the Soviet Union, and some implications in this area for Chinese development (conflict between national pride and the need to borrow foreign technology).

Field's paper addresses itself to the preservation and the conservation of human resources through the health system. His point of departure is the functional significance of the ability to perform social and occupational roles, and the importance of medicine and the health system in mitigating the incapacitating aspects of illness. He views the health system as a social mechanism that transforms generalized inputs or resources into specialized services and commodities important to maintaining health and treating illness, as well as preventing premature death. Almost from the time of the Revolution, the Soviet Union has paid a considerable amount of attention to this question, and has established a comprehensive and socialized health system at the national level. The Soviet government has looked upon health as an important national resource, worthy of the investment of sizable funds and large numbers of personnel. A comparison with the health system of American society indicates that although the two systems are quite different institutionally, in essence, in functions, and in claims for resources they may have more in common than is generally assumed, and in the future they may well tend to converge toward similar structural patterns.

This concludes the examination of the highlights of the essays contained in this volume and of the discussion evoked by these essays and the papers that, for a variety of reasons (mainly space) could not be accommodated within this book. I invite the reader now to turn to the essays themselves. Some general conclusions and consideration on "Where do we go from here?" will be found in the Postface.

Notes

1. (Glencoe: Free Press, 1951) p. 41.

2. Donald L. M. Blackmer, Richard V. Burks (Chairman), Frederic J. Fleron, Jr., John Lewis, Robert C. Tucker (former Chairman), Gordon B. Turner, ACLS.   ,

3. "The Future of Soviet Studies in the United States," presented at the American Association for the Advancement of Slavic Studies, Columbus, Ohio, 26 March 1970, p. 6 (mimeographed).

4. J. Stalin, Problems of Leninism (Moscow: Foreign Languages Publishing House, 1953), pp. 455-56.

5. Marshall I. Goldman, The Spoils of Progress, (Cambridge: MIT Press, 1972).

6. The discussion that follows is based on the following: (1) The papers presented at the symposium and published (in a revised form) in this book. Usually I refer to these in the present tense. (2) The papers presented at the symposium but not published here for a variety of reasons (mainly space and central relevance). I usually refer to these in the past tense. (3) The discussions that took place at the symposium, also referred to in the past tense.

PART ONE

MODERNIZATION

Chapter 1.

MODERNIZATION THEORY AND SOCIALIST DEVELOPMENT

T. Anthony Jones

1

It is a strange paradox that sociological discussions of social change
in industrial societies have until very recently ignored that third of mankind
living under socialist forms of government.[1] What makes this inattention paradoxical is that socialist societies provide an excellent opportunity for studying attempts at directed social change, for looking at the consequences of trying to plan both industrialization and a specific form of social structure at
the same time. Sociologists have, however, been reluctant to study socialist
societies and have generally relegated their consideration to the nontheoretical
status of "area studies." Furthermore, even where socialist countries have
been analyzed, there has been a pronounced emphasis on political structure
rather than social structure. In part this has been the result of political
bias, but it has also been a consequence of attempts to construct models of these
societies as distinct types. Of all the socialist societies, most attention has
not unnaturally been given to the USSR, since it is the longest-lived one to
date. Unfortunately, studies of the Soviet Union have been rendered sociologi-
cally inadequate because researchers have given too much attention to a search
for the basic, defining characteristics of a "Soviet type" society, and have
shown too little interest in cross-national comparative analysis.[2]

The search for such basic models of Soviet society has been a constant
preoccupation of scholars since the early days of the Bolshevik Revolution.
Opinions have ranged from the blindly eulogistic, such as Sidney and Beatrice
Webb's vision of Soviet Russia as a "new civilization," to the utterly defama-
tory, with references to "Red Fascism." Transparently, the political values of
the writer have been a not inconsiderable factor in the type of model chosen.[3]
Sociological, as opposed to political, models of Soviet society have been far
less frequently attempted, and even when they are attempted there is little
effort to integrate them into the sociological theorizing which goes on concerning social phenomena in general.[4] Indeed, there has been a striking failure to
apply existing theory to the analysis of Soviet society, or to alter that theory
in the light of such analysis. This is less true of political science, which
began increasingly to apply general theoretical concepts to Soviet politics in
the 1960s, although even this development was a relatively late one.

Since the death of Stalin, patterns of change in Soviet society have
forced students of Soviet affairs to reappraise their conceptual tools.
Especially, during the 1960s this took the form of a largely sterile debate regarding the extent to which the USSR had moved beyond the bounds of totalitarianism, and consequently what type of label could be put upon post-Stalinist
Russia. While some were reluctant to admit that any far-reaching development
was either taking place or even possible,[5] others sought to capture the "essence"
of the new stage of Soviet society in a single concept, such as that of "the
administered society."[6]

From this debate, however, there has emerged a growing emphasis on two
areas of concern, the consequence of which has been to increase the role of
social-structural, as opposed to political, factors.[7] First, it is clear that
the Bolshevik Revolution was not only a political revolution (in the sense of
building a new political system), but also a modernizing revolution. As a
result, Soviet leaders are seen as having certain problems in common with
leaders in other developing societies; for example, the development of a viable

industrial base and a system of social organization adequate to the task of utilizing and further developing such a base. As Inkeles has reminded us in this regard, the Bolsheviks saw this as their major goal, the Soviet self-image being above all the image of the developing society.[8]

Second, there are the consequences of the Soviet leaders' attempts to modernize-namely, the emergence of a highly developed industrial society and the qualitative changes in social structure which attend such a transformation. In discussing the Soviet Union as an industrial society, politics is no longer seen as "the sole, nor indeed the universally determining force operating; nor is the fact of political development the central problem. Instead, this approach stresses such things as size, complexity, forms and levels of such social realms as education, social mobility, mass communication, and the like. In the industrial society perspective, we see all these as having a pattern of effects on the social order not mainly because of but often regardless of the political system which prevails."[9]

The adoption of this approach has been consistently advocated by Inkeles and his former students during the last two decades, but only recently have there been any systematic attempts by other sociologists to incorporate the patterns of Soviet and other socialist societies into theories of industrial society.[10] Pursuing this program necessarily presents certain conceptual and methodological problems, solutions to which have yet to be devised.

2

Any model of society necessarily involves the systematic neglect of certain alternative forms of structure. It is now widely recognized that the assumptions underlying any given model, which determine both the elements included and the form of their interrelations, represent particular values which have their origins in various personal and sociocultural foci. This is no less true of models of socialist societies, which have in general been grounded in Western-centered political biases, a fact too obvious by now to need demonstration. As we have moved toward new models, these biases have also changed, becoming in the process more like those underlying social-science theorizing in general. Concretely, this has entailed a movement from models of "totalitarianism" to models of "industrialism," although a considerable element of overlap still exists.[11]

Both the early and more recent models, however, are imprecise. If we look at the voluminous literature on totalitarianism, for example, it is difficult to find a definition of the concept that is at all rigorous. For the most part, writers have either used the term as if no definition were necessary or have merely given a list of defining traits, most of which have been rather ambiguous. Moreover, there has been a general failure to empirically test the viability of the underlying assumptions. It is almost as if earlier writers have been so impressed by the appearance of Soviet Russia and Nazi Germany, and so convinced of their similarity, that any need to test their generalizations about these societies seemed superfluous. As a result, most efforts were aimed either at trying to discover how these "pathological" cases arose in the first place or at trying to find reasons for their impending collapse.[12] If one examines the list of the defining traits of totalitarianism, it is clear that the concept is almost exclusively concerned with political power. From this perspective, the direction in which influences flow is not seen as at all problematic: they flow from polity to society. As a consequence, the necessity of looking at the social structure as a source of change or stability of the total system is automatically ruled out.

Many problems are involved in attempting to apply the totalitarian model[13] in current conditions: its failing to consider the sources of social support for the regime, its neglect of the degree of development of Soviet society, and its failure to include the idea of experimentation.[14]   Its decline, however, did not begin until account had to be taken of the changes that followed the death of Stalin, which "undercut the two elements central to the totalitarian model: 1) the permanent purge and the concentrated use of terror, and 2) monolithism within Soviet society."[15] These changes necessitated an essential reconsideration of totalitarianism, since terror and monolithism had earlier been taken as critical and defining characteristics. For some writers, moreover, the crucial characteristic of totalitarianism lies precisely in the unlimited power of a single leader, particularly a "pathological" leader. According to this view, the major change in Soviet society was the death of Stalin himself.[16]

Western writers' search for new models after these changes has generally included some attempt to take into account the effects of the industrialization process in Soviet society. The models which resulted can be broadly classified into two types, which may be referred to as the liberal-democratic and the administrative-technocratic.[17] The liberal-democratic models tend to stress the degree to which industrialization is incompatible with totalitarianism, offering predictions that economic development will inevitably lead to political democracy, if only for the sake of efficiency. Less dogmatic writers leave the possibility of noncollapse open, but declare that the only alternative to liberalization is stagnation and decay. Thus, Parsons maintains that the totalitarian form of organization "will prove to be unstable and will either make adjustments in the general directions of electoral democracy and a plural party system or regress into generally less advanced and politically less effective forms of organization, failing to advance as rapidly or as far as otherwise may be expected."[18] The problem with this position, however, is that it assumes that "efficiency" is tied to "democracy," and the history of many West European societies during this century shows that the relationship is by no means a necessary one. In a slightly stronger tone, Brzezinski maintains that "if the party rejects a return to ideological dogmas and renewed dogmatic indoctrination, it unavoidably faces the prospect of further internal change. It will gradually become a loose body, combining a vast variety of specialists, engineers, scientists, administrators, professional bureaucrats, agronomists, etc. Without a common dogma and without an active program, what will hold these people together?"[19] He goes even further in maintaining that "the effort to maintain the doctrinaire dictatorship over an increasingly modern and industrial society has already contributed to a reopening of the gap that existed in pre-revolutionary Russia between the political system and the society, thereby posing the threat of the degeneration of the Soviet system."[20]

A decade earlier Labedz had claimed to notice the same phenomenon: "there is a growing discrepancy between the maturing Soviet social structure and fundamentalist ideological prescriptions. The gap is steadily widening, and the legitimacy of the system is therefore under constant threat."[21]

An opposite point of view is taken by writers in the administrative-technological perspective, who maintain, in the tradition of St. Simon, Weber, and Michels, that industrialization leads not to political democracy but to domination by bureaucrats and specialists. The assumption here is that totalitarianism and industrialism are essentially compatible, with industrial technology even aiding the institutionalization of totalitarian forms of organization.[22]

In moving from the totalitarian model to those models which include social structural as well as political elements, we begin to confront certain problems that are common to all developing societies. These problems include such questions as developing a system of national administration, mobilizing the population, institutionalizing innovation in science and technology, increasing the agricultural surplus, raising the educational level of the population to meet the growing need for specialists, developing a national identity, and so forth.

So far, the new models have not replaced the totalitarian model so much as they have directed attention to domains that the latter ignored. This is partly because the totalitarian approach was concerned with the principles of organization of power in the society at large and not with the context within which these alleged principles operated. The use of an industrial society model does provide such a context, and is therefore potentially capable of taking into account the available resources of power and the constraints under which it operates. In this refocusing process, however, we should be careful not to assume that certain consequences automatically flow from viewing the Soviet Union as an advanced industrial society. We need to demonstrate what the linkages are between industrialization and the organization of political power. It would be foolish to assume either complete determinism, toward which both the liberal-democratic and the administrative-technocratic camps veer, or complete nondeterminism, which would assert that industrialization has no systematic effect on totalitarianism. The middle path is far more difficult, however, for it involves specifying the relationship involved, and this can be done only through careful conceptualization and research.

This approach, however, cannot proceed on an ad hoc basis. We need a few simple models which direct our attention to certain sets of relationships rather than others. The materials for these models, moreover, will have to come from two sources-from a theory of industrialization and from a theory of the principles of socialist political organization. What follows is an attempt to suggest some of the bases upon which such a program may rest and to indicate some of the problems which will be encountered in pursuing it. I hope that this will go some way toward correcting the assumption made by some writers that the adoption of an industrial society model automatically provides a solution to some of the many difficult problems involved in analyzing socialist societies.

3

When theorizing about social change, sociologists show a strong tendency to see it as exhibiting direction, as showing a progression of some kind. This is seen most clearly in the work of the nineteenth-century theorists, but it is also evident in the return by some contemporary sociologists to a modified form of this perspective under the rubric of neoevolutionary theory. The philosophical underpinning of these developmental theories is that change involves an element of cumulation or progress,[23] whether in terms of degree of complexity, degree of rationality, or level of personal options.[24] Although the ideological nature of these assumptions has been frequently noted, analyzed and challenged,[25] it is difficult to see how a theory of social change could entirely avoid some assumptions regarding direction; indeed, if change were entirely random, a theory to account for it would not be possible at all.[26] The problem, therefore, is to determine the major directions of change and the nature of the cumulative processes they entail.

The concepts with which theories of cumulative social changes are most directly concerned are those of development, modernization, industrialization, and industrialism. Unfortunately, the precise meaning of these terms is far from self-evident, and the loose manner in which they have been used has provided the basis for a fierce academic debate during the last two decades. Apart from producing an extensive literature on the subject, though, the results have been at best inconclusive and at worst confusing.

The lack of consensus with regard to concepts such as modernization and industrialism involves more than just a problem in semantics, for it reflects a basic underlying uncertainty as to the precise nature of those large-scale processes of change that have been in operation during the last few centuries. Where some consensus does exist, it is on the consequences of such change as may be observed, but the processes which brought about these consequences, and the

degree to which these processes are common to all societies, have yet to be adequately specified.

Since the literature on this subject is so vast and so ambiguous, it
would be neither practical nor, in all probability, fruitful to attempt to summarize it here.[27] At this stage, it may be more useful to outline some of the
general characteristics of and problems underlying modernization theories, giving
particular emphasis to their implications for the study of socialist societies.
To anticipate my conclusion, I think it is clear that there is at present no
theory in so-called modernization theories, and that the likelihood of developing
adequate theory in this field will remain remote until: (a) instead of characterizing total societies in terms of an ad hoc checklist of attributes, a less
holistic approach is adopted which systematically deals with carefully delineated
sets of relationships between variables; and (b) the analysis of socialist
societies is firmly incorporated into general theorizing.

One of the basic difficulties is that notions of development, modernization, and so on, represent slightly different perspectives on the same
phenomena, resulting both definitionally and practically in a large degree of
overlapping, the terms often being used synonymously.[28] Theorists are at their
most vulnerable when trying to define each term so as to clearly differentiate
it from the others, and the futility of the exercise becomes apparent when they
then proceed to ignore their own definitional distinctions.

The most general term that may be used for cumulative social change is
development, for since it lacks the culturally more specific contents which are
present in terms such as modernization, industrialization, and industrialism, it
may in principle be applied to all historical periods. The concept of development
is central to the notion of biological evolution, and although it is not without
difficulties, it has proved to be a useful device. Unfortunately, those who advocate its use in sociology have yet to show clearly how its application to
societies can satisfy the criteria entailed in its use in biology. According to
Nagel, for example, in order to be able to apply the concept of development to any
system, the changes observed in it must be cumulative and irreversible. Furthermore, "those changes must in addition eventuate in modes of organization not previously manifested in the history of the developing system, such that the change
acquires an increased capacity for self-regulation, a larger measure of relative
independence from environmental fluctuations."[29]

These are extremely dubious assumptions to make about social systems or
societies as a whole, and in any case they are propositions which need to be subjected to investigation rather than accepted by definitional fiat. It would seem
preferable at this stage, therefore, to avoid using the term development in the
strict sense mentioned above, in favor of terms which avoid such tenuous assumptions as increasing self-regulation and irreversibility.[30] In principle, at
least, concepts such as modernization, industrialization, and industrialism may
be used as explanatory devices in a way in which the concept of development may
not. The coexistence of these concepts, however, raises certain difficulties.
One of the most frequently encountered is the question of the interrelations between these concepts; whether one is a prerequisite for another, whether one can
occur without the other, whether one is a subset of another, and so forth. The
relationship between industrialization and modernization presents just such a
problem.

Broadly speaking, theories of social change fall into two types, those
stressing differences in degree between historically earlier and later societies
and those stressing the differences in kind between them. The former theories
typically take a long-term perspective on modernization; the best example is the
work of Levy, who has defined both industrialization and modernization in terms
of the extent to which members of a society utilize inanimate sources of power,
tools, or both. According to this definition, all societies except the most
primitive contain industrial elements, and the differences between societies is

the extent to which technology is present or absent, extensive or limited. This gives us a typology which distinguishes between relatively modernized and relatively nonmodernized societies.[31]

A similar approach is taken by Moore, who accepts the conventional approach of considering modernization partially in terms of economic growth. "In fact," he asserts, "we may pursue the convention further and speak of the process as industrialization. Industrialization means the extensive use of inanimate sources of power for economic production, and all that that entails by way of organization, transportation, communication, and so on."[32] The major problem, of course, is to discover exactly what is referred to by the phrase "and all that that entails," and then to explain why it is entailed. In very general terms, there is a wide area of consensus that the concept of modernization is concerned with historical trends of increase in such things as the level of popular literacy, the percentage of urban population, the predominance of secular values, and the extent and spread of communications. There is also agreement that industrialization refers to the increasing use of productive technology. What is not made clear, however (and this issue is evaded altogether by defining modernization and industrialization in the same way, as do Levy and Moore), is the degree to which these processes are interdependent or independent of each other. For example, if one takes industrialization to refer to the events and consequences of the so-called industrial revolution in eighteenth-century Western Europe, then modernization may be seen as a consequence of industrialization. Once one extends the meaning of industrialization to include any historical increment of tools or inanimate power the relationship becomes more problematic, and each can be seen as a dependent or an independent variable according to the particular problem in hand. Within the concept of modernization there are many factors which may be related to the level of industrialization to different degrees, some of which may be only indirectly related, and others which may be to a large degree independent of industrialization. One cannot even raise this question, though, if the concepts are seen as interchangeable.

An example of that school of writers which sees modernization and industrialization as separate, albeit historically related, processes may be found in the work of Kautsky, who suggests that although the concept of modernization may include industrialization, the concept of industrialization does not include all of the elements of modernization. Further, "Industrialization always involves modernization, an industrial society is always a modern society.... On the other hand, modernization does not always involve industrialization; at least the beginnings of modernization can appear without industrialization."[33]

Thus, some elements of modernization are postulated as being independent of industrialization, whereas industrialization is seen as being dependent upon some degree of modernization. Kautsky then goes on to pose the central problem that while we "can see some elements of modernization quite clearly as the consequences of industrialization, others can be associated with industrialization only retrospectively as its preconditions. One might say that modernization can be not only an effect but also a cause of industrialization."[34] The question still remains, however, of which element of modernization are dependent on, and which independent of, industrialization and vice versa.

When one turns to the sociological literature on the consequences of industrialization to find a solution, one is impressed more with its extent than its theoretical rigor. Not only is there a general vagueness about the relationship between industrialization and its supposed social, political, and cultural effects, but some sociologists doubt that it has any effects at all. Thus a writer like Blumer may take such an extreme position as to state that "industrialization, by its very makeup, can have no definite social effect. It is neutral and indifferent to what follows socially in its wake."[35]

Most writers on industrialization, however, agree that there are certain clearly definable social effects of industrialization, even though they may

not agree on the actual list of items involved or have a systematic theory to account for those they do include. Most sociologists in what may be called the
determinate school of theory in this area take industrialization as the independent variable, then set out to specify a series of dependent variables which are
said to be related to industrialization. Unfortunately, the terms used are often
deliberately vague, and writers use words like "accompany," "are concomitants of,"
"are consequences of," and "are related to," instead of squarely facing the
issue of whether direct or indirect causation is involved, or whether it is
rather a case of historical correlation not necessarily related to industrialization per se. Whatever the particular checklist of traits that is offered, however, they are generally regarded as an operational definition of "modernization"
or "industrialism."

Virtually any trait, structure, or statistical aggregation which is present in a society whose major form of production is of the industrial type but was
not present in that society before the adoption of industrial production is a
potential candidate for being considered a consequence of industrialization. The
long lists of such consequences which some writers provide lead one to suspect
that they have in fact included every potential item, perhaps in a mistaken attempt
to be comprehensive. It is obvious, however, that there is no a priori basis for
assuming that any item is caused by industrialization, although clearly some are
more plausible than others.

There is little point in reiterating here the large number of lists of
what are considered to be the social consequences of industrialization, since
these are easily accessible in the general literature,[36] and, more important, differences between them are more a matter of the authors' opinions than of any close
theoretical consideration. There are, however, a number of what are considered
core items consequent on industrialization upon which there would be more general
agreement. A relatively representative version of this view may be found in the
collaborative work of Kerr, Dunlop, Harbison, and Myers, whose Industrialism and
Industrial Man attempts to specify systematically the social consequences of
industrialization.

According to Kerr et al. industrialization may be taken as referring to
the actual course of transition from a traditional society toward industrialism.
During this transition there is an increasing complexity of technology, whereby
the production process becomes more highly differentiated. The changes in technology and its associated economic organization create new problems of human organization, putting continual pressure on the system of social relations. The
sum total of the social consequences of industrial forms of production Kerr et al.
call "industrialism," a term used to refer to "the concept of the fully industrialized society, that which the industrialization process inherently tends to
create."[37] This rather vague and circular definition does not apply to any
specific industrial society, however, but approximates an ideal type.

Industrialism is defined in terms of several characteristics which are
seen as essential, insofar as they are functionally related to the alleged "needs"
of the productive process. To begin with, industrialism is characterized by
continuous change--science and technology are closely linked, and "the continuing changes in science and the technology and production methods inherent in
industrialization have a number of decisive consequences for workers, managers,
and the state and their interrelations."[38] The changing nature of technology
creates the need for a wide range of skills and professional competency within
the work force, which in turn makes it necessary to recruit and train personnel.
"The industrial society requires continual training and retraining of the work
force; the content of an occupation or job is seldom set for life as in the
traditional society. Its occupational mobility is associated with a high degree
of geographical movement in the work force and with social mobility in the
larger community both upwards and downwards."[39] Thus, social mobility is seen
as a consequence of the rate of change of technology, and impediments to this
mobility must be either removed or modified. Thus, "the industrial society

tends to be an open society, inconsistent with the assignment of managers or
workers to occupations or to jobs by traditional caste, racial groups, by sex
or by family status. There is no place for the extended family in the industrial society; it is on balance an impediment to requisite mobility. The primary family constitutes a larger and more mobile labor force."[40]

But mobility in the industrial society is not random; it comes to be
organized and governed by a complex of rules. Associated with this complex of
rules is the educational system, for "industrialization requires an educational
system functionally related to the skills and professions imperative to its
technology."[41]

Within the work force, rewards and an individual's degree of subjection
to authority come to depend upon the functional importance of the individual's
skills and responsibilities.

> The variety of skills, responsibilities and working conditions at
> the work place of enterprises requires an ordering or a hierarchy.
> There are successive levels of authority of managers and the managed,
> as well as considerable specialization of function at each level of
> the hierarchy of the work place. There is a related differentiation
> according to compensation; enterprises establish a wage and salary
> schedule which differentiates groups of workers and managers. Job
> evaluation and salary plans symbolize the ordering of the industrial
> work force by function and compensation.[42]

At the same time, the differential evaluation of occupations according to their
functional contribution to the production process and the overall scarcity of
skills and talents leads not only to differential rewards, but also to different styles of life.

> Above all, industrial society is an urban society. This has conse-
> quences for the existence of widely differing subcultures in society, for dif-
> ferences tend to be reduced by the effects of mass communications and rapid
> transportation. Agriculture becomes simply another industry and ceases to be a
> value in its own right, and "the industrial society frees itself from its agri-
> cultural antecedents."[43]

The need for coordination of the complexities of industrial society is
said to result in increasing government control, and with this complexity rules
of conduct proliferate. The elaborate hierarchy of authority and the degree to
which different aspects of society are interdependent make this web of rules imperative. Moreover, "cultural and national differences are less significant to
the web of rules the further a country is along the road toward industrialism."[44]
Kerr et al., however, proceed to assert that "the industrial society, as any
established society, develops a distinctive consensus which relates individuals
and groups to each other and provides a common body of ideas, beliefs and value
judgments integrated into a whole."[45]

In sum, therefore, the industrial society is seen as "an open community encouraging occupational and geographic mobility and social mobility . . .
it is pluralistic, with a great variety of associations and groups and of large-
scale operations; the individual is attached to a variety of such groups and
organizations".[46]

What Kerr et al. have done is to suggest some general characteristics
of industrial societies which are explicitly, albeit rather vaguely, related to
the hypothesized functional needs of advanced industrial technology and are also
the core of elements common to most theories of modernization. Although various
other writers differ in language, emphasis, and degree of specification, there is
nevertheless a relatively high level of consensus on these points outlined by
Kerr et al. in spite of the many criticisms that have been leveled against this

work during the last thirteen years or so.[47] The most contentious areas on which there remains most disagreement are those of the degree of openness to mobility, the extent of the decline of ascriptive criteria of recruitment, the degree of consensus on values among the population as a whole, and the whole question of political pluralism.

Kerr et al. have recently reconsidered their earlier work in the light of subsequent data and criticisms and have amended some of their central propositions.[48] In particular, they give more stress to the increasing professionalization of management strata, as the professionals become more highly trained technically; in addition, they assert that the "technostructure" is taking over more of the managerial functions in industrial society. Two major changes in the authors' position are worthy of note, however, since they are symptomatic of certain theoretical changes among other social scientists since the publication of their earlier work. First, they retreat from their earlier stress on the ultimate convergence of industrial societies, although they still assert that this is a major "tendency" of industrialization. Second, and more important, they have attempted to specify more explicitly those areas of society that are most closely determined by technology and those that are least affected. Thus, the impact is seen as being greatest in the occupational structure and the relative ordering of incomes, in the standardization of household and consumer spheres, and in the structure of communications and transportation. The impact is said to be less in the general educational system, still less in higher education (especially in those areas not directly concerned with scientific or technical skills), the character of urban areas and urban policies, and the activities of the growing stratum of intellectuals.[49] As we move from areas of greater determinance to areas of lesser determinance, therefore, we would expect to find differences attributable to such factors as differing elite decisions, different initial cultures, traditions, and so forth. The end result of industrialization, however, is still seen as "pluralistic industrialism," with no clear sovereignty for any one group; the emphasis is on mixed sovereignty, "and there are many possible mixtures."[50] However, since any situation short of total domination by one group is pluralistic, this statement is not very helpful.

Although many writers would give greater emphasis to some points, or add others such as the growth of planning, the increasing concern with welfare and social service provisions, and so forth, this overall view can be taken as fairly representative of mainstream theorizing. A more recent survey of the literature by Faunce and Form confirms this impression, for apart from some differences in emphasis on various factors, their list of consequences is very similar to that of Kerr et al.[51] Unlike Kerr et al. in their later works, however, they do not face the problem of specifying which areas are most closely and which least closely related to industrialization, and this still remains one of the major prerequisites for fruitful theory construction.

Obviously, if we are to build theories regarding the consequences of industrialization, the first task has to be to develop some sort of hierarchy of determinance for various aspects of social structure. The problem at present, however, is that some items are still being treated as consequences of industrialization which are only indirectly, or not at all, related. Nor can we rely on some intuitive sense of plausibility, since this may prove equally unreliable. A case in point is the assumption that there is more openness to social mobility in industrial than in nonindustrial societies, for there is some evidence that when you hold occupational demand constant there may be no significant difference between societies.[52] Similarly, there is now some doubt whether the striking similarities between occupational prestige hierarchies are specifically due to industrialization.[53] Both of these relationships are highly plausible, and yet they have turned out on closer inspection not to be related in any clear-cut way to industrialization. One could also cite other cases where the same reevaluation has occurred.[54]

As we begin to distinguish between those aspects of industrial societies
which are closely related to industrialization and those which are the consequence of other factors, the possibility of developing theories should increase.
It is clear, however, that this can result only from comparative studies, both
among industrial societies and between industrial and nonindustrial societies.
The inclusion of the industrialized socialist societies in this endeavor is
clearly of the utmost importance if we are to avoid the problems of the past, and
it is in this area of sociological theory above all that the comparative study
of socialist societies can make the greatest contribution.

4

The possibilities for comparative analysis involving socialist societies are now better than they have ever been. Not only has the growth of
sociology in Eastern Europe and the Soviet Union provided an enormous amount
of valuable research data,[55] but there has been an ongoing debate in these
countries regarding the basic, concrete characteristics of socialist societies
as distinct types. Under the impact of sociology a number of competing perspectives on the social implications of industrialization have developed. Although
there has been nothing comparable to the enormous amount of energy Western social
scientists have expended upon building models of industrialization and modernization (indeed, there has been a denial that such an enterprise is useful), there
has been a gradual disenchantment with the rigid formulations of official Marxist-
Leninist social thought.[56] Although the idea of modernization as a universal process is rejected, the idea that industrialization produces certain limited consequences regardless of the political system within which it occurs has become
more acceptable. These would include such things as increasing levels of urbanization, the growth of education, and the shape of the occupational profile. At
the same time, however, the implications of these factors for social relations
and modes of personality are said to be different in socialist societies, basically because of the socialization of the economy in the latter.

In socialist societies industrialization is still seen as leading inevitably toward communism, by a process of increasing homogenization of the
population. In this process major distinctions between sectors of the population,
such as differences between manual and nonmanual work and between town and country, continually decline. These consequences are said to be already in evidence
in those societies which have reached the level of developed socialism,[57] even
though homogenization has not as yet reached an advanced level. Within capitalist economic systems, however, industrialization is said not to involve increasing
homogeneity, since differences in property relations continue to exist.

Although this recognition of the continued existence of social differences by theory is an advance upon previous perspectives, it still involves a
more restrictive evaluation than has been advocated by Soviet sociologists.[58]

Many Soviet sociologists have given a great deal of attention to the
role of differentiation, especially as it concerns social relations related to
changes in the occupational profile. To a large extent, they have been successful
in changing the emphasis from that of class to that of occupation, both as the
basic unit of analysis and as the major determinant of social relations.[59] Such
differences as are analyzed, however, are still seen as being mainly nonantagonistic, Soviet sociologists having been more reluctant than those elsewhere in
taking the step toward developing a political sociology.[60]

Nevertheless, Soviet sociological thought has become more like that in
other countries, for, as Yanowitch and Fisher have recently noted,

it is clear that the conceptual apparatus of Western stratification
studies has begun to permeate Soviet Marxists perception of their

> own social structure. A conception of social structure as embracing
> a hierarchy of occupational strata differentiated by income,
> prestige, cultural levels, value orientations and power has now
> become--implicitly or explicitly--part of the normal discourse of
> Soviet social thought. . . . The Marxist approach to social
> structure is now regarded as encompassing "all that is positive"
> in Western stratification studies.[61]

As a result, comparisons between socialist and nonsocialist societies have become much easier, although certain differences in the classification schemes used
still present difficulties.

While recent developments within Soviet and East European sociology
provide a valuable basis from which to develop an empirically based theory of
modernization, socialist sociologists have themselves been no more successful
than those in other countries in creating such a theory. When there have been
attempts to provide a sociological, as opposed to official Marxist-Leninist,
model of the consequences of industrialization, one is struck more by their
similarity to Western models than by their differences, in spite of the different
terminology used.

About a decade ago Jan Szczepanski pointed to the need for sociologists in socialist countries to move from describing social processes to developing theories to account for them. While stressing that such theories would have
to rest upon the analysis of both political and economic factors, he himself
tended to give rather more emphasis to the latter.

> An examination of the social effects of the function of the economy
> is of decisive importance to the construction of a general theory
> of the process of emergence of socialist societies. The establish-
> ment of a network of political administrative and economic insti-
> tutions only creates the base of that society. Whereas its
> characteristic features, its unique collective image, differentiations
> and stratification, its distinctive groups, patterns of behavior,
> social relations, systems of values--all this begins to take shape
> as a result of the socialized and planned economy. In a certain sense,
> the formal processes occurring here are comparable to those shaping
> capitalistic formations: the capitalistic enterprise, the functioning
> of its economy, the opportunities created, the chances of promotion
> and degradation latent in the economy. These contributed to the
> formation of the structure characteristic of that society--its cultural
> patterns and personality types.[62]

The functioning of the economy, Szczepanski went on to note, is closely
related to industrialization processes, and since these are present in capitalist societies as well, the questions of whether and to what extent the consequences of industrialization have to be faced are the same. While acknowledging
certain formal, structural similarities, Szczepanski stresses that the socialist
political system affects the manner in which these consequences are institutionalized, influencing both their content and the relations between them. From
this point on, Szczepanski's argument merely reiterates conventional Marxist-
Leninist assertions regarding increasing homogeneity and the simultaneous
creation of a new socialist type of personality. This latter assertion,
though, raises several important questions for sociology. For example, if one
looks at the content of this new personality, many of its dimensions are at
variance with virtually all of the theoretical predictions in Western sociology
during the last hundred years regarding the consequences of industrialization
for the value-orientation of personality. Thus, "the traits of this personality
are basically the following: subordination of personal interests to social ones,
recognition that the growth of social property is the basic motive for personal
economic participation, acceptance of the values of the socialist state as one's
own, and the direction of personal behavior in accordance with that system."[63]

Personality traits such as these have generally been thought of in the West as associated more with societies at a very low level of social different-iation than with industrial societies. This highlights a central contradiction (at least in Western sociological terms) which has always existed within socialist social thought, namely, that one can create Gemeinschaft social relations within a structure which seemingly necessarily involves Gesellschaft relations.[64] Al-though I do not wish to entirely rule out this possibility, there is little evidence that such a process is occurring in socialist societies, and in fact much of the evidence points in the opposite direction.[65] On the other hand, however, the idea of a socialist modal personality type does raise the theore-tically crucial question of the mediation processes of the consequences of in-dustrialization, affecting not only the form of their institutionalization but their cultural content as well.

Not all socialist sociologists would agree with Szczepanski that economic factors are the best starting point for developing a theory of socialist society. Another Polish sociologist, Wesolowski, has provided an alternative focus from which to begin--the role of the state in determining the development of social structure. Wesolowski concludes his argument in favor of a basic dis-tinction between capitalist and socialist societies--that in the latter the form of social stratification is a direct consequence of political decisions regarding the allocation of resources and rewards, whereas in capitalist societies it is more a consequence of class relations. This difference, Wesolowski claims, has important consequences for the structure of interests and conflicts in socialist societies.

> In socialist society the uneven distribution of goods in high
> demand is mediated by the mechanism of government decisions. The
> general system of wages is determined by the government, as is the
> income of the individual citizen. Contradictions of interests may
> occur here on two planes: one is the plane of contradictions between
> groups with different incomes, the other is the plane existing between
> these groups and the "general regulator" represented by the government
> (in a wide sense of the word).

> The government's role as a direct regulator accounts for a
> peculiar psychological situation. People with discrepant incomes
> tend to blame the government (as a regulator of their income) rather
> than the better off groups. This tendency is much less common and
> much less explicit in the capitalist system. There, interest contra-
> dictions are chiefly conceived as contradictions between different
> social groups. This difference between the two systems is of
> tremendous importance for any discussion of conflicts of interests.[66]

In this passage, Wesolowski has provided precisely the means for developing a model relating industrialization processes to political contexts, something which is lacking in the approach of Szczepanski. Not only does the state act as a mediator between the consequences of industrialization and their eventual institutional form, not only does it effect their organizational and stratificational patterns, but it at the same time structures social interests and defines the lines of social conflict. The crucial importance of this ap-proach should be immediately clear, not only for the development of theory for socialist society, but for the development of a comparative model of industrial-ization and modernization. What Wesolowski rightly claims to be a central characteristic of socialist societies is daily becoming a more central aspect of all industrial societies, namely, the increasing role of the state as a regu-lator of resources and a determinant of both social structure and its direction of change.

Whatever validity earlier views may have had regarding the difference between "socialist" and "capitalist" societies in terms of the role of political factors in the industrialization process,[67] the maintenance of this distinction is now very much in doubt, and is likely to become even more so in the future. Whatever the reasons for the growth of the state in advanced industrial societies,[68] its power to determine the social structure of a society in general, and its stratification system in particular, is everywhere increasing. Any attempt to develop theories of social change in industrial societies, therefore, must rest upon a close analysis not only of the manner in which industrialization processes influence social structure, but also upon a careful consideration of the manner in which those who control the political decision-making system recognize, aid, hinder, or remold pressures for change emanating from industrialization.

One problem this approach would have to consider is how political decisions might affect the way the industrialization process itself develops, since at some level there has to be a compatibility between political decisions and the functioning of the economy. Since economic growth continues to be a major preoccupation of all industrial societies, political mediation is necessarily constrained by what are perceived as necessary concomitants of such a goal. The question here is to what degree social structure elements of industrial societies are necessary for and determined by the existence of the industrialization process.

Theorists differ widely in their assertions about the degree of determinance involved in industrial societies, ranging from those who see a high level of determination in all spheres (providing a closely knit system) to those who see it in a limited number of spheres only (giving rise to a loosely knit system). As Feldman and Moore have noted,

> virtually no one rejects the notion that industrial societies share a core set of social structures that together provide a kind of extended operational definition of industrialism itself. This core would include the factory system of production, a stratification system based on a complex and extensive division of labor and hierarchy of skills, an extensive commercialization of goods and services capable of filling the various niches in the occupational and stratification system. If one goes much beyond this list, the degree of requiredness or variability becomes distinctly controversial.[70]

Even within this list, however, there is no specification of the closeness of fit which is thought to be necessary between the industrial process and the structure of the society within which it occurs. One implicit notion is that there is a minimum of correspondence which is necessary to the maintenance and development of the industrial system, but the relative degree of autonomy of any of the elements is left open. Thus, within this core set of structures there is a whole range of possibilities. In spite of these problems, some writers have continued to stress that the further along the path of industrialization a society goes, the more its form will approximate that of other advanced industrial societies--and this brings us to the notion of "convergence."

5

One of the unfortunate consequences of sociology's failure to develop a viable theory of industrialism has been the emergency and subsequent decline of what came to be known as the convergence thesis. The form the thesis took was unfortunate not only because it was one further means by which social science was drawn into the ideological cold war, but also because its patent oversimplifications and the lack of theoretical sophistication among its most vociferous advocates brought the whole notion of determinate processes in modernization into disrepute. Consequently, a valuable opportunity for serious theoretical debate was lost. It is now time, however, to reconsider the whole notion of convergence and its implications for socialist and nonsocialist societies alike and to attempt to specify more clearly the degree to which various aspects of the social structural concomitants of industrialization are determinate. The convergence thesis, therefore, needs to be reappraised and recast rather than entirely abandoned.[71]

The idea that there may be a process of increasing convergence between industrial societies has its origins in the very beginnings of sociological theory, especially in the long-term perspectives of such theorists as St. Simon, Marx, and Spencer.[72] Contemporary theories of convergence have been formulated on a somewhat less strictly deterministic level than the classical theories, yet their underlying assumptions are very similar, being based on the premise that as industrial production becomes more developed, more and more areas of life come under its domination.

One of the most systematic statements on increasing similarities between industrial societies is that of Levy, who is quite unequivocal in his support of the idea of convergence: "As the level of modernization increases, the level of structural uniformity among relatively modernized societies continually increases regardless of how diverse the original basis from which change took place in these societies may have been. In other words, the more relatively modernized societies become, the more they resemble one another."[73] This is carefully qualified by the statement that convergence "does not imply that they are all becoming more like any particular relatively modernized society at any given point in time."[74] Levy's formulation, therefore, differs from those of cruder convergence theories in that it avoids the ethnocentrism involved in taking Western social forms as the norm by relating convergence to forms which have yet to appear.

In a different vein, Duverger has suggested that convergence may occur through a gradual mutual movement toward socialism, achieved by the growth of liberalization in socialist societies and an increasing socialization in Western societies.[75] This prediction is based on the premise that there is greater efficiency in centralized planning and control, and on the assumption of an increasing dysfunctionality of the principles of capitalism. Taking issue with these assertions, Aron has argued that Duverger's version of the convergence thesis rests upon the abuse of certain ideal-types or simplifications: "The first simplification consists in the concentrating on three specific fields-- economy, politics and ideology--and especially on the system of values associated with the first two. A second simplification consists in deciding on some option in each field which we consider as being either inherently decisive or decisive in relation to what our particular interests are."[76] In other words, in the absence of a theory which would systematically direct our attention to certain spheres rather than others, the choice of items which are seen as decisive in patterning future changes is relatively arbitrary.

Aron, who has been among the more cautious advocates of the convergence thesis, rejects it entirely with respect to the political system. Thus, we find him stating in The Industrial Society: "supposing the technical-administrative substructures in both types of society became increasingly similar, supposing even that the Soviet planners . . . instituted a form of market economy, would this inevitably bring the one-party system and the ideological monopoly to an end? I have no hesitation in giving a negative answer."[77]

In other respects, Aron accepts a limited degree of convergence as a possibility, in particular with regard to the regulation of resources as the socialist countries adopt more aspects of the market mechanism. In terms of the ownership of the means of production, however, Aron rejects the possibility of convergence and likewise the notion of increasing homogenization of income as state control and planning increases. With regard to the latter, Aron argues that this possibility is complicated by societal differences in the meaning of income differences, that is to say, of collective versus individual supply of goods and services. Moreover, a decline in income inequality as state control increases rests on the assumption that state decisions are determined by the functional need of the economy for a particular pattern of wage differentials, and there is no evidence that this is the major factor in these decisions.[78]

Insofar as convergence is based upon the idea that there are functional requisites to the utilization of advanced industrial technology it is a feasible concept; but, as we have seen, the "logic of industrialism" is itself rather indeterminate. Its strongest claim to our attention lies in the assertion that the more advanced industrial technology becomes, the stronger becomes the pressures on the social structure to conform to the functional exigencies of this technology. This is similar to Durkheim's notion that an increasing dependency of parts occurs in societies of the organic solidarity type. Thus, as technology advances, social elements not immediately related to this technology come to have consequences for its functioning. This may lead to attempts by groups and individuals both to reduce any dysfunctional consequences of these elements and to influence them so that they may become positively functional.

In spite of this tendency, however, there is a limit to the extent to which the consequences of industrialization may extend through the society.[79] Moreover, it is also essential not to forget that as well as influences coming from industrialization, there are also always influences of time and space--that is to say, historical factors.

All industrial societies have had different historical positions initially, and this may in many ways influence the way a given society experiences the modernization process. This raises the problem of the relative importance of historical factors as against the logic of industrialism. In order to assess the probability of convergence, therefore, we have to take account of both the preindustrial social structure and the route, or trajectory, of industrialization. Thus, as Kerr et al. were themselves forced to recognize, "the culture of a nation and the degree of continued adherence to that culture . . . affect worldwide diversity in the process of industrialization."[80] Also, because of the special character of the basic resources and the central industries, "no two cases of industrialization can be expected to be identical."[81] Furthermore, one constantly has to keep in mind that societies coexist in time and in space, more often than not competing with each other, and for the sake of expediency sometimes adopt each other's solutions or practices.[82]

The importance of preindustrial elements which are inconsistent with industrialization is that, as Feldman and Moore have suggested, they do not just disappear: "Rather, if industrial development does continue, they become attenuated, partially suppressed, partially adapted to changes in the core structure. By their persistence, they constitute a continuing source of tension, a focus of social problem solving....[Moreover], the solutions are always partial, and always have further consequences that in turn provide new sources of tension."[83] One might also add that the original, preindustrial culture often provides an important anchorage point and a source of "cultural identity" for societies in the throes of rapid sociocultural change. Examples of this in socialist societies include the "Russian priorities" campaigns in the USSR, the revival of traditional medicine in China, and the persistence of ethnic identities in Eastern Europe.

In addition to variations stemming from different historical starting points, another important process which may affect patterns of development is cross-cultural borrowing. Latecomers to industrialization can now exercise some choice regarding the means they may adopt, for industrial societies already exist which provide them with living models of alternative forms of organization.

This important difference between first and subsequent worlds of development poses the vital question of how the historical era in which a society modernizes influences the form a society takes. One implication of the existence of differing contexts of modernization is that the target of industrialization is of necessity always historically relative: "The effect of this 'historical era',

that is, the effect of a vast and ever-changing body of knowledge about industrialization and industrialism, is to introduce a kind of 'double dynamic' into
the processes that together make up industrialization. First, industrialization
means change away from some pre-industrial social structure. Second, industrialization now means constant change in what is perceived to be the destination."[84]

There is another basic ambiguity in the standard formulations of modernization theory which further weakens the more simplistic versions of convergence.
Although advocates of convergence invariably state that industrialization is not
totally standardizing but rather sets limits within which diversity can occur,
they noticeably do not solve the problem of specifically defining these limits.
Admittedly, this raises the problem of conceptualizing different levels of
functional efficiency in organization and level of output; but to continue to refer to "industrial needs" and "functional correspondence" in terms of very general
and vague criteria can neither prove nor disprove the thesis. Casting the argument in favor of convergence in the form of statements about ultimate, long-run
developments does not solve the problem either, but instead makes the thesis
practically untestable.[85]

Feldman and Moore have shown one possible way out of this difficulty by
shifting the emphasis from functional determinants to the analysis of situational
possibilities within fairly well-defined limits. They propose that we view societies as subsystems of a worldwide system, each subsystem being seen for our
purposes as a tension-management system. Thus, if we take "system" in its most
limited sense (in terms simply of a set of interrelated elements), we can see that
we have to take into account changes within more than one subsystem. This statement underscores the fact that industrialization is a worldwide phenomenon and
does not occur in a series of discrete, unrelated systems. Such perspective has
both positive and negative consequences for the possibilities of convergence.

A negative aspect of this stems from the fact that since industrialization is continually changing, each society enters the process at a different stage
of world development, as well as with a different culture and social structure.
This means that there is no necessity for each society to go through the same
developmental sequence as the earliest industrializing societies, so that this
stage presents the newly industrializing societies with different problems. The
solution of these problems may necessitate different forms of social organization
in each society.

There is also a positive aspect--since each society enters an already
industrialized system, the available models, techniques, and knowledge will tend
to limit the degree to which the industrializing process within a given society
can diverge from the types already in existence. Also, the fact that some societies have already solved a number of their problems will in itself be an incentive to emulate these solutions. Thus, convergence may occur not because of any
ironclad logic of industrialism but because one model is taken rather than another.
This does not entirely vitiate the functional perspective, but rather is an additional consideration. One might call this convergence by emulation instead of
convergence by evolution.[86] Elements of emulation should therefore be expected in
cases of guided industrialization; and socialist societies occupy a central position among societies in this category, since perhaps more than any other societies
they have consciously sought the goal of industrialization. Bauman has noted that
economic growth by industrialization in socialist societies has resulted from "the
conscious efforts of the organized centers of political and economic decision; and
it must be so in the modern world, where the spontaneous birth of an industrial
pattern . . . has become almost logically impossible, but where the same industrial
pattern emerging as the result of organized and planned action is practically
inevitable."[87]

There is thus a tension between the alternatives posed above, the first
one pushing societies toward divergence, the second tending toward convergence.
The important point, however, is that both processes are influenced by the

requisites of the industrialization process, and that these remain to be specified before more restricted predictions can be made.

One methodological way out of the current impasse would be to build analyses around limited sets of problems faced during the modernization process, for by focusing on problems we can see how functional and historical factors interact. We can also see how solving one problem can influence the solving of future problems. An example of this is the ways the United States and the USSR solved the problem of labor shortage in industrialization: "both societies were faced with a similar problem--the recruitment of an industrial labor force; each, however, experienced this problem in a somewhat different form--absolute vs. relative scarcity; each adopted different although perhaps equally appropriate solutions, each now experiences dissimilar strains from solving the same problem."[88]

The problems themselves can be seen as deriving from the interrelation between the exigencies of industrial organization (in its widest context) and the historical conditions of the industrializing society. The importance of this perspective is that change is seen as both continuous and structured. It may well be, therefore, that in predicting the future course of industrial societies, "less is likely to be gained by fitting out an equilibrium model--the kinds of structures that are functionally consistent with industrialism but 'still' incompletely developed--than by direct attention to the sources of continuous change. Although some further development of similar structures may be expected, these may arise less from essentially static 'consistency' demands than from attempted solutions to common dynamic problems." [89]

By focusing on problems in this way we can also escape one of the major pitfalls of the earlier versions of the convergence thesis, the tendency to use holistic units of analysis such as the total society, the polity, and the stratification system. Much of the debate proved to be sterile because conflicting tendencies can always be found within such units, and so evidence could be marshaled both for and against a particular form of convergence. Also, the approach advocated by Feldman and Moore is consistent with our earlier discussion regarding the central role of the state as a "problem-solver" and as an increasingly important determinant of social structure in industrial societies.

One of the consequences of the growth of the state is a process of increasing bureaucratization of the society, and some social scientists see this as a major factor making for convergence.[90] It is not just the fact of bureaucratization that may bring about convergence, however, but rather what one might call "the bureaucratization of life-chances" which increasing state control implies. One of the consequences of this development is to alter drastically the forms of conflict in a society, so that conflict between classes is gradually replaced by conflict between interest groups and the state. There are many who would agree with Meyer, however, that property differences between societies still operate to produce differences in social structure,[91] and that this limits the possibility of convergence. At the same time. it must be realized that as the industrial state has developed more and more, the role of private property has declined relatively.[92] For example, the concept of a just rate of profit has now reappeared after an absence of three hundred years or so, thus restricting rather severely the freedom of use of private property in production. If this trend continues, and there is much evidence that it may, then convergence may occur as a result of each society's developing a form of what one might call "neomercantilism," under which economic, political, and social relations within the society will be almost entirely regulated by the state.

6

Having briefly looked at some of the problems involved in constructing theories of modernization and at the areas of possible convergence of industrial societies, let us now turn to the question of how the study of socialist societies may be more closely integrated into sociological theorizing.

Clearly, the current confusion in terminology will have to be removed before socialist societies can be adequately analyzed as industrial societies. The difficulties inherent in current theories can be reduced to three general problems. One is that concepts are only vaguely defined, and even where they are more carefully defined they are often difficult to operationalize empirically. All too frequently they are used more as descriptive devices or mere labels than as units in a formal theory. The second source of difficulty, as we have seen, is that there is still a great deal of confusion about how the concepts are related to each other. This is due for the most part to the large overlap between them, each containing many elements of the other. Last, with regard to the contents of these concepts, there still remains a large element of ethnocentrism regarding what is actually entailed in the processes of industrialization and modernization. By tying the contents of modernization to the Western experience, the whole discussion becomes circular, making the development of viable theory impossible. It also prevents us from ever disentangling the factors involved in the development of particular items, since it then becomes impossible to separate industrial from cultural and historical factors. At the same time, any attempt to build a typology of industrial societies becomes a crude "them" and "us" exercise, diverting attention from the fact that within each of the categories of "Western" and "socialist" societies there is a high degree of variation, making them as unhelpful as units of analysis as the equally vague concept of "Third World" societies.

Given the enormous problems present in the various types of modernization theory, one can understand why some writers suggest that terms like modernization be avoided altogether. In spite of the difficulties, however, it is unlikely that these concepts will be dropped from sociology, and there has been no shortage of new definitions. For example, Dore has suggested two uses of the term modernization, which he refers to as the transitive and the intransitive versions. The transitive form refers to "the transformation of the economic, political, legal, social or cultural life of a nation in accordance with models derived from other contemporary societies thought to be more 'advanced.' It is a use of the term which implies nothing specific about the content of this transformation, its goal or its methods."[93] The intransitive form on the other hand, refers to "a process of social change including and contemporaneous with industrialization, which has already been taking place for decades or centuries in the industrial societies and which is now starting to a greater or lesser degree in the developing societies."[94]

Dore himself prefers the transitive use of modernization, thus removing it from its current connection with industrialization, which would be the intransitive use. The problem with the transitive form, however, is that it renders modernization devoid of historical content and thus makes it completely relative—that is, entirely dependent on what a given society chooses to define as "more advanced." The problems this raises for comparative analysis are obvious.

I suggest that giving historical content to concepts of large-scale social change is more profitable, at least at this stage, than making them highly abstract; and so I urge the intransitive use of modernization. The scope of this concept, however, should be drastically reduced to include only those social forms which can be shown to be a direct consequence of, or caused by, industrialization in the narrow sense (i.e., as referring only to the use of industrial technology in either producing or consuming capacities).[95] Cumulative trends that cannot be shown to be caused by industrialization could then be referred to as development, even though they may prove to be reversible at some future time. Industrialization would then refer only to the process of increasing use and extent of industrial technology, and the term industrialism would no longer be necessary.[96]

If these uses are adopted, the content of the concepts of modernization and development can only be determined by systematic comparative analysis, not

by definitional fiat. A first step toward this goal would be to begin to specify
a hierarchy of aspects of industrial societies in terms of the degree to which
they are determined by the presence of industrialization. One immediate consequence of such a listing would be to enable us to predict and watch for convergent
trends in those aspects most closely related to industrialization, which in turn
would be a further way of testing the strength of the relationship. Particular
care would have to be taken, however, to make sure that observed convergence was
not due to one society's emulating another.

At the same time, more attention should be given to developing large-
scale models showing how the social elements become interrelated to form a system. This is as important as specifying a hierarchy of determinance, since predictions for individual societies must be based upon their particular systemic
qualities. To begin with, of course, these models will have to be highly simplistic, since only a limited number of factors can be dealt with at a time. Within
such single-society models, it is also necessary to build a hierarchy of elements; only here the criterion is not the degree of determinateness in relation
to industrialization, but rather the degree to which these elements have a determining influence on other factors within that society. These factors may be
cultural, political, social, or economic, depending upon which values gain
primacy within the society. This is an important task, since, as Buckley has
noted, "systems theorists have long recognized that just because a number of
variables are interrelated in a systematic manner does not necessarily mean
that each is of equal weight in producing characteristic states of the system;
any systemic variable may run the gamut from insignificance to overwhelming
primacy."[97]

Once we have begun to build models of how elements in specific societies combine to form a system, the task of developing a typology of industrial
societies will become easier. The question of a typology of industrial societies
remains to be seriously addressed by sociologists, who at worst have continued to
speak of industrial society as a single entity and at best have worked with a
simple division into "capitalist" or "Western" and "communist" or "socialist,"
an approach also adhered to by Soviet social theorists. One of the few writers
even to raise the question of a typology has been Aron, but even he has continued
to adhere to this dichotomous categorization.[98] The problem with this approach is
that it ignores important differences between socialist societies. Even within the
capitalist category, it is equally doubtful whether such societies as Japan, the
United States, France, Germany, and Britain really constitute a single type.

Allied to the question of a typology of industrial societies is that of
the existence of distinguishable stages or phases through which industrial
societies pass. Many of the assumptions found in current writing on stages are
prefigured in Sombart's early typology of capitalism, which he separated into
early, full, and late stages.[99] Underlying this sequence of stages is the assumption of the increasing importance of the state, with its attendant bureaucratization, increasing economic calculation, and impersonality of social relationships
and the displacement of purely market mechanisms in favor of conscious planning.
If we add to this list the increasing importance of science, we have most of the
elements contained in those perspectives which see the logic of advanced industrialization as having led to a qualitatively different type of society.

Almost invariably, writers have chosen to designate this new type of
society by the term "post" something or other. Some of the contenders include
such terms as postcapitalist, postindustrial, postbourgeois, postmodern, and
even postcivilized.[100]

Although each of these terms has questionable connotations, they all
claim to point to the emergence of certain trends in industrial societies that
are of such a magnitude that it is possible to speak of a qualitatively new type
of society. It is being alleged that science and knowledge (or "information")
have now replaced industry or "the means of production" as the main source of

change within society, and coinciding with this change is a change in the basic social structure of society. It is doubtful, however, that this new monocausal approach is any more realistic than the older approaches which relied on various forms of technological determinism. There is little doubt that science has become a source of continued innovation in society, both directly by creating new occupational roles, making new forms of social organization and communication possible, altering longevity, and so on, and indirectly as a source of innovation in productive technology. That science is an increasingly important factor in social change, therefore, is certainly true, but trivially so. What is being asserted, however, is something more--that science has become (or is becoming) such a multivalent determinant that it has resulted in the emergence of a new type of society, one that goes beyond the characteristics of the industrial society.

This notion of a new level of development has found surprisingly widespread acceptance in both capitalist and socialist societies. In spite of their rejection of concepts such as modernization and convergence, social theorists in socialist countries have now developed their own form of the postindustrial society concept, the concept of "the developed socialist society." A comparison of the descriptions of developed socialist and postindustrial societies reveals a remarkable similarity, even though the terminology chosen and the implications drawn are different. Thus, the developed socialist society is characterized as having reached a stage where science has become the major determinant of industrial production, where high levels of education and knowledge have radically changed the character of labor, and where the rational planning, calculation, and organization of resources have become the major focus of governmental action.[101] This stress on greater rationality has resulted in "scientific management" assuming ever-greater importance, and in the growth of interest in such activities as cybernation and sociological research in order to make the management of social processes more rational.[102]

In a wide perspective, similar processes can be seen to be at work in socialist and nonsocialist industrial societies. The major problem, however, is that of discovering whether these processes have the same implications or consequences for a given range of phenomena in these societies. For example, increasing occupational specialization and the growing complexity of social organization involve higher levels of structural differentiation, and for some writers, this is taken as a definition of modernization. This is the process expected to create the most significant long-term changes in socialist societies. Although it is undoubtedly true that industrialization does involve a trend toward increasing differentiation, it does not cover all aspects of society (for example, sex-role differentiation appears to be decreasing). Also, it would be wrong to assume that certain political or social consequences automatically flow from increasing differentiation, or that it has to take the form observed in nonsocialist societies. Generally, socialist societies exhibit lower levels of differentiation, but it would not be correct to conclude from this that they are at a lower level of modernization than other societies, or that they will necessarily "catch up" at some future time.

Nettl and Robertson have suggested that socialist societies exhibit a specific type of differentiation, which they call "compressed."[103] In these societies, differentiation occurs

under intensive and extensive elite surveillance . . . in other words, whilst the members of the political elite assume and/or directly control strategic, frequently multirole, positions in all "key" areas of a society, this does not mean the proliferation of specialized political and economic tasks does not continue apace. Nor does it mean that concrete organizations cease to multiply. It may well be argued, for example, that in accordance with such a definition of compressed differentiation, contemporary Britain in some respects is more akin to the Soviet Union than conventional wisdom suggests.[104]

It is partly because of the compressed nature of socialist structural differentiation that the political predictions of Western theorists have been vitiated. At the same time, the pattern of change in socialist societies clearly shows that liberal democracy is neither a necessary consequence of industrialization nor, indeed, a necessary prerequisite for continued industrialization. One of the lessons to be drawn from the experience of socialist societies is that increasing specialization of functions provides the <u>potential</u> for structural pluralism, but that such potential may be realized only under certain conditions. Social differentiation occurs along many dimensions and to varying degrees, and <u>the role of industrialization should be seen as involving tendencies toward forms of differentiation which may or may not be institutionalized according to conditions prevailing in any given society</u>. Thus, in socialist societies, many roles and institutions are multivalent to an extent not found in nonsocialist societies, so that the increasing potential for relative autonomy of various parts of the society as specialization increases may not occur.[105] This is not to deny that interest-group formation may occur in socialist societies, but rather to suggest that in the long run the extent of development and activities is under no apparent necessity to assume the same form as in nonsocialist societies.

Although we are now more aware of the existence and activities of various interest groups in socialist societies, this is still not the same as claiming that in all industrial societies the occupation-based system of stratification "generates interests, represented by formal associations which engage in conflict."[106] Industrialization may be a necessary condition, but it is obviously not a sufficient condition. Although there does appear to have been an increase in awareness of group interests on the part of various groups in socialist societies, interests are operative only insofar as they are recognized and allowed expression by the Party.[107] Also, these interests do not follow clear-cut lines of group boundaries, but cut across boundaries according to systems of patronage.

The party's recognition of spheres of interest appears to depend upon the degree to which those interests are seen as relevant to the regime's goals of growth and control. Thus, scientists are able to gain a degree of autonomy, while writers are not. An intermediate solution to the polar extremes of "repression" or "autonomy" is to incorporate interests into the Party as information bearers, as is the case with industrial and economic specialists and groups such as lawyers. The degree of immunity from "administrative measures" various groups have is also related to their status as "autonomous," "incorporated," or "bought off"; thus, a top scientist may openly dissent without dire consequences, whereas an ex-general or a writer may not.

The general system of control in socialist societies operates within the context of the pattern of stratification and interests just mentioned. Thus, the solutions adopted to deal with groupings directly affect the organizational controls that are developed. The party remains the most important part of the machinery of control and has attempted to retain control (in the absence of terror), of groupings within the machinery by what Fleron calls "adaptation." In the longer term, however, there may be a conflict between <u>partiinost'</u> (party-mindedness) and technical ability, thus creating severe problems of recruitment for the party. A further problem involves how specialists' skills are to be integrated into political goals without allowing the specialists to usurp the definition of these goals.[108]

As I stated earlier, the elements of a viable model of socialist societies will have to come from a theory not only of modernization, but also of the principles of socialist political organization. The future path of socialist societies will clearly depend upon the interaction of these two elements, and it is on this relationship that our research should be more systematically focused.[109]

Several areas for investigation may prove fruitful in developing such an approach. For example, as long as the party controls access to decision-making, it is possible for groups to emerge from increasing differentiation without becoming either autonomous or effective in influencing decisions. What we need to know, therefore, is which elements of the stratification process are most likely to create pressures for widening access to decision-making. Allied to this is the question of which groups can gain access to decision-making by influencing or controlling formal organizational institutions in either the state or party hierarchy. Outside of this, there is also the possibility that various groups can influence decisions by opening up informational bypaths such as samizdat, using the press and specialist journals, and using other means of influencing decisions via "public opinion," either national or international.

Given that planning and scientific management involve intricate problems of control, a way has to be found to incorporate various information-bearing groups into the overall organization.[110] We then need to know what factors are operating to determine which strata or groups will be "administered," which will be "bribed" in various ways, and which "coerced" into compliance with decisions. The way these questions are settled will have important implications for the types of group and public awareness which develop, thus influencing the world view of the population regarding strata-state relations.

The solutions adopted to deal with these and other problems which occur as the level of industrialization increases will depend not only upon the exigencies of industrialization, but also upon the world view of the political elite which makes the major decisions. Since the way problems are perceived and decisions are considered depends upon the existing world view, we need to know which factors are involved in determining, supporting, and changing this view. At the same time, there are influences which stem from generational changes and changes in patterns of recruitment, and the outcome of these factors also depends upon the mechanisms of socialization and control which are developed to protect the prevailing world views.

Given the importance of the principles of socialist political organization for the way the consequences of industrialization are influenced and institutionalized, we need to know not only the degree to which such principles are common to all socialist societies, but also the extent to which they differ. This question necessitates the systematic comparison of socialist societies with each other, the methodology for which has been given increasing attention in recent years. At the same time, greater efforts must be made to integrate the analysis of socialist societies into our efforts at building theories of modernization. The questions raised above regarding the relationship between industrialization and social change, the impact of political decisions on the institutionalization of such change, and the mechanisms whereby elements of stratification and the political center are articulated with each other are coming to apply just as much to nonsocialist as to socialist societies. Consequently, it has been my aim here to suggest that it is to these questions that we must address ourselves if we wish to develop an empirically based theory of modernization. It is clear that to continue to ignore the experience of socialist countries would be not only intellectually inexcusable but theoretically disastrous.

Notes

[1] A socialist society is here taken as referring to any society with a communist form of government. The term socialist is used in preference to communist, since the societies in question claim to be at a socialist rather than communist level of development.

[2] The most notable exception is the work of Inkeles, who has consistently

advocated not only the analysis of the Soviet Union as an industrial society, but also systematic comparison between it and other industrial societies.

[3]See, for example, Alexander Dallin, "Bias and blunders in American Studies on the USSR", Slavic Review 32 (Semtember 1973): 560-76.

[4]Strangely enough, little interest has been shown in developing a sociology of communism. The work by Monnerot (1953), although entitled Sociology of Communism, has in fact very little that is sociological about it, being mainly a polemic in the totalitarian tradition, and I am not aware of any other attempt to develop such an enterprise. Jules Monnerot, Sociology of Communism (London: Allen and Unwin, 1953).

[5]See, for example, the collection of articles edited by Zbigniew Brzezinski, Dilemmas of Change in Soviet Politics (New York: Columbia University Press, 1969), in which the general feeling is that Soviet totalitarianism will "degenerate" rather than "evolve" under the impact of post-Stalin changes. An argument in favor of retaining the concept of totalitarianism in the analysis of Soviet society can also be found in Paul Hollander, ed., American and Soviet Society: A Reader in Comparative Sociology and Perception (Englewood Cliffs, N. J. : Prentice Hall, 1969).

[6]See Allen H. Kassof, "The Administered Society: totalitarianism without Terror," World Politics 16 (July 1964): 558-75. This perspective forecasts a rationalization of totalitarianism rather than a liberalization or democratization. The same position is taken by Paul Cocks, "The Rationalization of Party Control," in Change in Communist Systems, ed. Chalmers Johnson (Stanford: Stanford University Press, 1970).

[7]As Meyer has aptly noted, before the death of Stalin "any scholar who would have suggested that there was not only a social structure, but one that might be described in terms of interest groups or of a stratification pattern comparable to that of the United States, would have appeared ridiculous and politically suspect." Alfred Meyer, "Theories of Convergence", in Change in Communist Systems ed. Chalmers Johnson (Stanford: Stanford University Press, 1970), p. 315.

[8]Alex Inkeles, "Models and Issues in the Analysis of Soviet Society," in Survey, July 1966, p. 8. It would be incorrect to infer from this that industrialization is the only goal, for as Lowenthal has recently remarked, "in Marxist ideology, the ultimate goal that gives meaning to all communist effort is not the modernization of a particular country, but the attainment of the classless society on a world scale." Richard Lowenthal, "Development versus Utopia in Communist Policy," in Change in Communist Systems, ed. Chalmers Johnson (Stanford: Stanford University Press, 1970), p. 39. However, we should also not forget that in the interim enormous resources are devoted to the task of achieving modernization, and success or failure in this endeavor is a major impetus to policy-making.

[9]Alex Inkeles, "Models and Issues in the Analysis of Soviet Society," pp. 9-10 (emphasis added).

[10]Recent attempts to incorporate socialist societies into theories of stratification include F. Parkin, Class Inequality and Political Order (New York: Praeger, 1971); D. Lane, The End of Inequality? Stratification under State Socialism (Harmondsworth, England: Penguin Books, 1971); and S. M. Lipset and Richard Dobson, "Social Stratification and Sociology in the Soviet Union," Survey, summer 1973, pp. 114-85. A lengthy critique by a Soviet sociologist of the work of Lipset and others on stratification in socialist countries may be found in V. I. Staroverov, "Sotsialnaia struktura SSSR v burzhuaznoi kritike ili

otkroveniya Seymoura Martina Lipseta," Sotsiologicheskie issledovaniya, no. 1 (1974), pp. 141-49.

[11] Soviet theorists, however, would claim that the theory of industrialism and convergence in fact merely represents the anti-Soviet thrust of bourgeois sociology. See, for example, the articles in N. B. Mitin, Sovremennye burzhuaznye teorii o sliianii kapitalizma i sotsializma (Moscow: Nauka, 1970).

[12] Examples of such attitudes may be found in the symposium edited by C. J. Friedrich, Totalitarianism (Cambridge: Harvard University Press, 1954). Nowhere in these articles do we find a systematic definition of totalitarianism, the authors often taking as axiomatic precisely that which needs to be demonstrated. The sole exception was Timasheff, who made a distinction between totalitarianism as a trait of state functions and totalitarianism as a type of society, although this distinction was not taken up by any of the other contributors. In his later writings, Friedrich has maintained his view of the Soviet Union as a totalitarian society, although Hannah Arendt has come to agree with those who see it as a post-totalitarian stage. See the discussion of this in Lowenthal, "Development vs. Utopia in Communist Policy."

[13] Strictly speaking there is no model of totalitarianism, for the relationships between the alleged elements of totalitarianism were never clearly specified.

[14] Inkeles, "Models and Issues in the Analysis of Societ Society," pp. 4-5.

[15] F. J. Fleron, Jr., Communist Studies and the Social Sciences (Chicago: Rand McNally, 1969), p. 123.

[16] Robert C. Tucker, "The Politics of De-Stalinization," World Politics, July 1957.

[17] J. Azrael, Managerial Power and Soviet Politics (Cambridge: Harvard University Press, 1966). Other typologies have been suggested, such as that of Jerry F. Hough, "The Soviet System: Petrification or Pluralism?" Problems of Communism, March-April, 1972.

[18] Talcott Parsons, "Evolutionary Universals in Society," American Sociological Review 29 (June 1964): 356.

[19] Brzezinski , Dilemmas of Change in Soviet Politics, pp. 28-29.

[20] Ibid., p. 30

[21] Leo Labedz, "Ideology: The Fourth Stage," Problems of Communism, November-December 1959, p. 10.

[22] C. J. Friedrich and Z. Brzezinski, Totalitarian Dictatorship and Autocracy, 1956

[23] For an early analysis of this see J. B. Bury, The Idea of Progress (London, 1921).

[24] The concept of development is closely associated with the evolutionary per-

spective in sociology as put forward by nineteenth-century theorists. The reaction against this perspective, which set in after about 1920, was based on the
rejection of the assumption that development is cumulative and unilinear, and
that the "stages" of development are universal. Also, it was clear that there
had been a failure to specify the systemic characteristics of societies and institutions and to delineate the processes whereby one stage gave way to another.
See S. N. Eisenstadt, "Social Change, Differentiation and Evolution," American
Social Review 19 (1964): 375-86.

[25]See the summary in Robert I. Rhodes, "The Disguised Conservatism in Evolutionary Development Theory," Science and Society 32, no. 4, 1970.

[26]Strictly speaking, of course, it may well be that a theory to account for what
we perceive as directional change may prove an impossibility; but this does not
mean that we need not search for such a theory in the meantime.

[27]The most systematic statement remains that of Marion J. Levy, Jr., Modernization and the Structure of Societies (Princeton: Princeton University Press,
1966). Also see Talcott Parsons, "Some Principal Characteristics of Industrial
Societies," in The Transformation of Russian Society, ed. Cyril Black (Cambridge:
Harvard University Press, 1960).

[28]The problem of definition is a major one in the modernization literature, and
there is a wide range of opinions concerning the content of concepts. Many
writers use these terms in a commonsense and often ambiguous manner, making
integration of their work difficult. What follows here is a sampling of some of
the more accepted usages in sociology.

[29]Ernest Nagel, "Determinisms and Development," The Concept of Development, ed.
D. B. Harris (Minneapolis: University of Minnesota Press, 1957), p. 16. For a
debate on whether development involves innate tendencies or preordained sequences of change, see Harris, The Concept of Development.

[30]In fact, a better case can be made for the claim that self-regulation of a society decreases with increasing structural differentiation. See the persuasive
argument by S. F. Nadel, "Social Control and Self-Regulation" Social Forces 31
(March 1953): 265-73 regarding the self-regulatory characteristics of
"primitive" societies.

[31]In the Structure of Society, Levy defines industrialization in terms of systems of production utilizing inanimate devices and sources of power, and then in
his later work Modernization and the Structure of Societies uses precisely the
same criteria to define modernization. It should be remembered, however, that
Levy's work has provided an important corrective to those perspectives which
stress a dichotomy between "traditional" and "modern" societies. For a critique
of these models see S. N. Eisenstadt, "Social Change, Differentiation and Evolution," pp. 375-86, and R. Bendix, "Tradition and Modernity Revisited," Comparative Studies in Society and History 9 (1967): 292-346.

[32]Wilbert E. Moore, Social Change (Englewood Cliffs, N. J.: Prentice-Hall, 1963),
pp. 91-92.

[33]John H. Kautsky, The Political Consequences of Modernization (New York, John
Wiley, 1972), p. 20. One writer, Norman Jacob, has gone so far as not only to
define modernization and industrialization as independent, but also to claim that
modernization can occur without development. He achieves this strange result by
defining modernization as the capacity for innovation of a society sufficient to
maximize the potential of that society "within the limits set by the goals and

the fundamental structure (or forms) of the society"; development is defined as the maximizing of potential regardless of specific goals--that is, the capacity for continual as opposed to goal-specific change. Norman Jacob, Modernization without Development: Thailand as an Asian Case Study (New York: Praeger, 1971), pp. 9ff. By these definitions, the USSR would be modernized but not developed, and it may seriously be doubted whether any society can be termed developed according to such criteria. A more serious theoretical problem, however, is that it is difficult to see how one could operationally determine whether or not a society is maximizing its potential for change, even were we given the benefit of long-term historical hindsight.

[34]Kautsky, Political Consequences of Modernization, p. 21.

[35]Herbert Blumer, "Early Industrialization and the Laboring Class," Sociological Quarterly 1 (January 1970): 5-14.

[36]The summary by William A. Faunce and William H. Form, Comparative Perspectives on Industrial Society (Boston: Little, Brown 1969), is fairly representative of such lists.

[37]Clark Kerr, J. R. Dunlop, F. H. Harbison, and C. A. Myers, Industrialism and Industrial Man (Cambridge, Mass: Harvard University Press, 1960), p. 3.

[38]Ibid., p. 34

[39]Ibid., p. 35

[40]Ibid.

[41]Ibid., p. 36

[42]Ibid., p. 38.

[43]Ibid., p. 40

[44]Ibid., p. 42

[45]Ibid.

[46]Ibid., p. 46.

[47]In his critique of the Kerr thesis, Bendix, "Tradition and Modernity Revisited," pp. 292-346. agrees with other writers who challenge the assumption that the logic of industrialism is unstoppable, and not contingent upon successful institutionalization.

[48]Clark Kerr, J. T. Dunlop, F. H. Harbison and C. A. Myers, "Postscript to 'Industrialism and Industrial Man'," International Labor Review 103 (June 1971): 519-40.

[49]Ibid., pp. 19ff.

[50]Ibid., p. 16.

[51]Faunce and Form, Comparative Perspectives on Industrial Society.

[52]R. M. Marsh, "Values, Demand and Social Mobility," American Sociological Review 28 (1963): 565-75. The effect of industrialization on social mobility may well be to increase it by creating new occupations rather than to increase mobility by removing structural barriers.

[53]R. M. Thomas, "Reinspecting a Structural Position on Occupational Prestige," American Journal of Sociology 67 (1962): 561-65. Marsh, "Values, Demand and Social Mobility," pp. 565-75.

[54]For evidence on the family, see Peter Laslett, The World We Have Lost (New York: Charles Scribner's Sons, 1965). As a further example, it is now well-known that high levels of urbanization can occur without extensive industrialization

[55]Sociologists in socialist countries began systematic comparative research in the late 1960s, the most ambitious being the joint Soviet-Polish research reported in Jan Szczepanski and G. V. Osipov, Sotsialnie problemy truda i proizvodstva (Moscow: Mysl; Warsaw: Ksiazka i Wiedza, 1969), and in M. N. Rutkevitch, W. Wesolowski, V. S. Semyonov, M. Jarosinska, and V. V. Kolbanovski, Transformations of Social Structure in the USSR and Poland (Moscow and Warsaw, 1974). The literature on sociology in Eastern Europe is now quite extensive, but a good idea of the level of development in each country may be found in Rudi Supek, Sociologija i Socijializm (Zagreb: Znanje 1966), for Yugoslavia; Andreas Hegedus, Sociolgues hongrois: Etudes, recherches, (Paris: Editions Anthropes, 1969), for Hungary; Peter C. Ludz, Soziologie und Marxismus in der Deutschen Demokratischen Republik, (Neurvied and Berlin: Luchterhand, 1972), for the German Democratic Republic; and Jan Szczepanski, ed., Empirical Sociology in Poland (Warsaw: Polish Scientific Publishers, 1966), for Poland.

[56]This has gone furthest in Eastern European sociology, particularly in Poland. The most critical sociology, however, remains that of the Praxis Group in Yugoslavia. See, for example, Rudi Supek, Humanisticka, inteligencija i politica (Zagreb, 1971), and Svetozar Stojanovic, Between Ideals and Reality: A Critique of Socialism and Its Future (New York: Oxford University Press, 1973).

[57]The Soviet concept of the developed socialist society is discussed later.

[58]For the amended official view, see G. Glezerman, Socialist Society: Scientific Principles of Development (Moscow: Progress Publishers, 1971).

[59]See Zev Katz, The Soviet Sociologists' Debate on Soviet Structure in the USSR, Paper I, Sociology of Soviet Audiences,(Cambridge: Center for International Studies, MIT, 1971) and the introduction in Murray Yanowitch and Wesley Fisher, Social Stratification and Mobility in the USSR, (White Plains, N. Y.: International Arts and Sciences Press, 1973).

[60]A leading Polish political sociologist, Jerzy Wiatr, while defining politics as "the area of struggle for power and its utilization," also adds the important qualification that "we should remember that 'utilization of power' includes in socialist countries several activities traditionally regarded as 'non-political' which greatly enlarges the scope of this concept"--Jerzy J. Wiatr, Socialist Industrialization and the Political System (National and Local)," in Empirical Sociology in Poland, ed. J. Szczepanski, (Warsaw: Polish Scientific Publishers, 1966), p. 101. A tentative Soviet approach to the question of power may be found in an article by Volkov in Yanowitch and Fisher, Social

Stratification and Mobility in the USSR.

[61]Ibid., p. xiii.

[62]Szczepanski, Empirical Sociology in Poland, pp. 145-46.

[63]Ibid., p. 149. A standard account of the orthodox position on socialist personality may also be found in A. I. Afanas'eva and A. A. Nurullaev, Kollektiv i lichnost (Moskva: Mysl, 1965).

[64]An account of similar tensions between development and utopianism in socialist societies may be found in Richard Lowenthal, "Development versus Utopia in Communist Polity," in Change in Communist Systems, ed. Chalmers Johnson (Stanford, Calif.: Stanford University Press, 1970).

[65]As Kassof has noted in a different context, "If the experiences of the more advanced industrial nations are a guide, the absorption of emotional energy in the pursuit of personal and family consumption is likely to be antithetical to the high level of public commitment and self-sacrifice which the system has traditionally sought to generate and upon which the maintenance of a mobilizational atmosphere depends." Allen H. Kassof, ed., Prospects for Soviet Society (New York: Frederick A. Praeger, 1968), p. 503.

[66]W. Wesolowski, "Social Stratification in Socialist Countries," Polish Sociological Bulletin, no. 1, 1967, p. 29.

[67]For those social groups which bear the burden of providing the costs of industrialization, it probably makes little difference whether the process is politically directed or a result of laisser-faire capitalism--in either case the suffering is very high. The only difference may be that they have different people to blame for their miseries.

[68]A good case may be made for seeing this as a result of the increasing interdependence between societies within a growing world system. In such a situation unregulated processes are seen as potential sources of national and international disruption, and so attempts are made by the state to bring them under its control.

[69]The beginnings of a model relating government to social stratification may be found in David Apter, Some Conceptual Approaches to the Study of Modernization, (Englewood Cliffs, N. J.: Prentice-Hall, 1968), especially pp. 23-47.

[70]Arnold S. Feldman and Wilbert E. Moore, "Industrialization and Industrialism: Convergence and Differentiation," Transactions of the Fifth World Congress of Sociology, Washington, September 1962, 2: 156.

[71]For a recent summary of some of the literature on convergence, see Alfred Meyer, "Theories of Convergence" in Change in Communist Systems, ed. Chalmers Johnson (Stanford: Stanford University Press, 1970).

[72]For a review of the history of the concept of convergence, see Ian Weinberg, "The Problem of the Convergence of Industrial Societies; A Critical Look at the State of a Theory," Comparative Studies in Society and History, January 1969, pp. 1-15.

[73]Marion J. Levy, Jr., Modernization and the Structure of Societies (Princeton:

Princeton University Press, 1966), p. 709. The same position is taken by Apter, who argues that industrialization produces sufficient structural and organizational uniformities as to "render obsolete certain once-powerful distinctions, such as those between capitalism and socialism or between private and public property--particularly as organizational types"--Apter, Some Conceptual Approaches to the Study of Modernization, p. 334.

[74]Levy, Modernization and the Structure of Societies, p. 709.

[75]Maurice Duverger, Introduction à la politique (Paris, 1964), p. 367.

[76]Raymond Aron, The Industrial Society (New York: Simon and Schuster, 1967), p. 108.

[77]Ibid., p. 123.

[78]Ibid., p. 112. See also Wesolowski, "Social Stratification in Socialist Countries," pp. 22-34.

[79]What is involved here is the question of the relative autonomy of system parts. See Alvin Gouldner, "Reciprocity and Autonomy in Functional Theory," in Symposium on Sociological Theory, ed. L. Gross (New York: Harper and Row 1959).

[80]Kerr et al., Industrialism and Industrial Man, p. 280. The most influential analysis of the impact of different starting points on the path of industrialization of a society has been that of Alexander Gerschenkron, Economic Backwardness in Historical Perspective (Cambridge: Harvard University Press, 1962).

[81]Kerr et al., Industrialism and Industrial Man, p. 46.

[82]For example, the Soviet interest in Taylorism in the 1920s and the more recent interest in American management techniques and organization theory.

[83]Feldman and Moore, "Industrialization and Industrialism: Convergence and Differentiation," 2: 158.

[84]Ibid. (emphasis added).

[85]This is true of functional theories in general, however.

[86]Chalmers Johnson, ed., Change in Communist Systems (Stanford, California: Stanford University Press, 1970), pp. 23-24.

[87]Z. Baumann, "Economic Growth, Social Structure, Elite Formation: The Case of Poland," in Class Status and Power, ed. R. Bendix and S. M. Lipset (London: Routledge and Kegan Paul, 1966), p. 535. An excellent discussion of this question may be found in Wiatr, "Socialist Industrialization and the Political System (National and Local)."

[88]Feldman and Moore, "Industrialization and Industrialism: Convergence and Differentiation," 2: 160.

[89]Ibid., p. 166. (emphasis added).

[90]This is the position taken by Meyer, "Theories of Convergence."

[91]Ibid., p. 339.

[92]This is not to deny the continued existence of social classes, but rather to stress their relative decline as a potential determinant of social structure. What appears to be occurring is that new bases of social class are developing as a result of the growth of the state, with a mixture of political decisions and economic constraints replacing the former importance of property. This does not imply that the state is in any way a "neutral" force, since the degree to which various sections of society are able to either control or influence its decisions will determine the degree to which it favors one section rather than another. Whether the resultant groupings should be called "classes" or "interest groups" is a moot point at this time, although I would favor the former, since the connotation of interest group does not sufficiently stress the unequal distribution of power between groups. Although the growth of the state was seen as a consequence of industrialization by Kerr et al., they did not see it as implying a modification to their prediction of increasing pluralism.

[93]R. P. Dore, "On the Possibility and Desirability of a Theory of Modernization," Communication Series, University of Sussex, Institute of Development Studies no. 38, October 1969, p. 4.

[94]Ibid., p. 4

[95]The definitions suggested here are similar to those adopted by Apter, Some Conceptual Approaches to the Study of Modernization. I disagree with Apter's reification of modernization, however, when he refers to modernization as creating more complex systems of roles, for in my usage this is part of modernization itself. The problem stems from looking at the impact of relatively modernized societies on those which lack an industrial base. Whereas Apter treats this as a case of modernization, I would prefer to see it as a case of cultural transfer, since according to my definition the institutionalization of modernization can occur only in a society which has undergone industrialization.

[96]One of the most central problems with this definition is that one has to decide how direct a consequence of industrialization an item has to be in order for it to be considered an aspect of modernization. In principle, however, it should be possible to decide on a cutoff point in terms of the degree to which the item is subject to wide variation owing to the influence of nonindustrialization elements.

[97]Walter Buckley, Sociology and Modern Systems Theory (Englewood Cliffs, N. J.: Prentice-Hall, 1967), p. 67.

[98]Raymond Aron, The Industrial Society (New York: Simon and Schuster, 1967).

[99]See the brief discussion of this typology in D. Bell, "The Post-Industrial Society: The Evolution of an Idea", Survey, spring 1971, pp. 102-286.

[100]See the survey of these and other terms in Bell, "The Post-Industrial Society."

[101]Descriptions of the characteristics of the developed socialist society may be found in B. Sukharevsky, "Ekonomika SSSR--ekonomika razvitogo sotsializma," Kommunist, no. 18 (December 1971), pp. 58-72; and M. T. Yovchuk, "Nekotorye aktualnye problemy obshchestvennykh nauk v svete itogov 24 syezda KPSS," Filosofskiye nauki, no. 5. (1971), pp. 3-15. The impact of the scientific and technological revolution on socialist social structure has also been extensively analyzed by Radovan Richta, Civilization at the Crossroads (White Plains, N. Y.: International Arts and Sciences press, 1969). What is described in this work is

essentially what the Soviets call developed socialism. To the Western reader, however, there is a striking similarity between the changes outlined for social-ist countries and those occurring in Western societies.

[102]An analysis of the way in which Soviet sociology is linked with planning and management needs may be found in P. Hollander, "The Dilemmas of Soviet Sociology," Problems of Communism, November-December 1965, pp. 34-46; and G. Fischer, Science and Politics: The New Sociology in the Soviet Union, (Ithaca, N. Y.: Center for International Studies, Cornell University, 1964). The upsurge of interest in management theory in the Soviet Union during the last decade has also led to in-creasing interest in Western theories of management. See for example, D. Gvishiani, Organization and Management: A Sociological Analysis of Western Theories (Moscow: Progress Publishers, 1972).

[103]This lower level of differentiation was earlier remarked upon by Mark G. Field, "Soviet Society and Communist Party Controls," in Soviet and Chinese Communism: Similarities and Differences, ed. D. Treadgold (Seattle: University of Washington Press, 1967), although he referred to it as relative undifferentiation.

[104]J. P. Nettl and Roland Robertson, "Industrialization, Development, and Modern-ization," British Journal of Sociology 17 (1966): 282-83. The strategic im-portance of overlapping elites is also clear in many nonsocialist societies. For example, see Zbigniew Brzezinski and S. Huntington, Politics: U.S.A.--USSR, (New York: Viking Press, 1964); and C. Wright Mills, The Power Elite (New York: Oxford University Press, 1956).

[105]The question of the degree to which specialized roles become fused into a dual executive status has been dealt with at length by Fischer, Science and Politics: The New Sociology in the Soviet Union.

[106]Faunce and Form, Comparative Perspectives on Industrial Society.

[107]See H. G. Skilling and F. Griffiths, eds., Interest Groups in Soviet Politics, (Princeton, N.J.: Princeton University Press, 1971); and M. C. Lodge, Soviet Elite Attitudes since Stalin (Columbus, Ohio: Charles E. Merrill Company, 1969).

[108]In highly industrialized societies, the political center becomes crucially dependent upon the effective upward flow of information for its efficacy. This involves a tendency for there to evolve what Apter, Some Conceptual Approaches to the Study of Modernization, calls a reconciliation system. A limiting factor, however, would be the degree to which instrumental values become a dominant con-cern of those at the political center.

[109]A model integrating pressures from industrialization with the process of de-cision-making in the state political system is also, as we noted earlier, becom-ing increasingly crucial in the analysis of nonsocialist societies, making the distinction between models of socialist and nonsocialist societies as distinct types less and less meaningful.

[110]Fleron, Communist Studies and the Social Sciences, Chap. 11.

Chapter 2.

THE MODERNIZATION OF MAN IN

SOCIALIST AND NONSOCIALIST COUNTRIES

Alex Inkeles

Statement of the Problem

One element in the ideology of every social movement is a conception of the character of the people as they are and a vision of what they should be like. In those movements which seek to transform the religious order, concern for such characteriological issues often lies at the very heart of the movement.[1] But even in movements oriented mainly toward transforming the economic and political order, ideas about the nature of man and his social relations are always decidedly central concerns. If, therefore, we are to comprehend the processes of social change induced and guided by the revolutionary communist parties in the countries in which they have taken power, it is indispensable that we discover and understand their conception of man's social character as it is and as it should become.

In this paper I hope to advance the idea that the leaders of the two great communist revolutionary movements of our time--those of Russia and China-- sought to bring about a transformation of human character and social relations having much in common with the more spontaneous process of change which has characterized other developing countries.[2] No doubt in the socialist countries the process of modernization has been more self-conscious, the goals more explicitly stated, and the resources employed to attain those goals more massive. Nevertheless, it is my position that, far from being a unique historical process, the struggle to create a new type of "socialist man" has been only a special case of the more pervasive concern to convert people who express traditional values and act in traditional modes into men and women who in attitude, value, and action may be called modern.

Two Models of Man In Social Movements

In radical movements, we may distinguish two main perspectives on the issue of character and human relations. One of these I will designate the populist, the other the elitist perspective; neither term is to be taken as an evaluation, let alone as pejorative.

In populist movements, the elite views itself and its immediate class associates as embodying qualities which are decadent, corrupt, even evil. These must be extirpated, and a new set of personal characteristics and patterns of human relations must replace them as the social ideal and, indeed, as the daily norm. Generally these new qualities are considered not so much new as lost or atrophied. Followers of the movement assume that the lost virtues can be found still alive and vitally expressed somewhere among "the people"--usually this means in the traditional village or among simple, unsophisticated working folk who, precisely because they have been out of the mainstream, bypassed by history, are seen as having preserved in pristine form sterling qualities of character and noble patterns of human relations which should now become the standard for all. In varying degrees this orientation characterized the Narodniki in Russia, re-emerging in a peculiar variant in the Zionist movement; it was the basis of much of American Midwestern populism; it was built into Ghandism in India; and it makes up a substantial element of the contemporary American youth's counterculture.

In the elitist orientation we turn over the coin. Rather than believing that the masses embody the most valued characteristics, the elitist perspective considers the personal qualities of the rank and file precisely the main problem obstructing the progress of the historical movement. The masses are passive when they should be active; they are accommodating when they should be uncompromising; they forgive when they should be unrelenting in the pursuit of vengeance; they diffuse their energies when they should be highly organized under tight discipline; they are carried away by passions about trivial matters when they should concentrate their attention exclusively on the really basic structural issues. In this view the masses cannot hope to fulfill their historical mission unless their character is transformed; that is, until they are made over into a new model of man. And, mirabile dictu, the embodiment of this new model is already at hand in the very person of the revolutionary vanguard. That vanguard has only to bestir itself, to expose the masses to the possible, and the masses have only to learn from and emulate the vanguard, to insure that reeducation is essential to achieving the desired revolutionary transformation of man and society.

No doubt this typology, like all schemes of this kind, is crude and exaggerated. Yet it seems to me that these two very general polarized models define a dimension along which we can, without great distortion, locate any radical political movement, whether of the left or of the right.

In the case of Marxism-Leninism I would argue that although the movement incorporated some elements of populism, it was in general decidedly weighted toward the elitist pole of the dichotomy.

The populist element in Marxism-Leninism is found mainly in the mystique which surrounds the conception of the proletariat. In Marx's view history had assigned this class the unique role of transforming capitalism into communism, bringing man to his highest stage of social development. The proletariat was considered able to fulfill this historic mission because its relation to the means of production had schooled it in the organization and rationality essential to running an industrial civilization. Since postcapitalist society was to rest on the principles underlying modern industrial production, the anticipated transformation was inevitable and the role of the proletariat as its guide was a historical necessity.

Yet there was a catch. Apart from the propensity of the outmoded ruling classes to use force to prevent change, there existed an additional impediment to the otherwise inevitable transformation of capitalist society. The obstacle lay in the unhappy fact that large segments of the proletariat did not, in fact, incorporate in their persons the qualities which, theoretically, their class membership should have conferred on them. "False consciousness," especially as embodied in religious belief and practice, widely diffused throughout the proletariat living in even the most advanced capitalist countries a set of historically inappropriate and politically undesirable values, attitudes, and modes of interpersonal relations.

Marx never resolved the issue of what to do about false consciousness. He seemed to assume either that it would in time erode under the impact of the increasing impoverishment of the proletariat or that it would not matter when weighed against other historic forces which would engulf the capitalist systems and lead to the institutionalization of socialism. Lenin, however, confronted the issue head-on. Lenin's special contribution to communist theory lay precisely in his instinct for the jugular in this matter. He broke the impasse into which the element of populism in Marx had led the communist movement by decisively reorienting it in the direction I have designated as elitist.

Lenin's position first became unmistakably apparent in the pages of

52

<u>What Is To Be Done?</u> With great force he argued that the revolution could not be expected to develop spontaneously because the masses lacked a revolutionary consciousness. History therefore required a small, dedicated, tightly organized band of professional revolutionaries to carry the movement forward. Lenin argued that one of the central tasks of this movement was to instill in the masses qualities which were lacking, to teach organization and discipline, to heighten awareness, and to stir consciousness. The model to be emulated was provided by the devoted professional revolutionary, who brought this image to the masses "from outside." This "outside" was, as a gesture to the founding fathers, given sanction by insisting it was actually a part of the proletariat, only that part which was the more conscious, developed "vanguard." Despite Lenin's resort to this rationale, however, I see no way in which we can correctly read Lenin's argument, and his early practice in guiding the party, other than by recognizing that he had moved Marxism, or at least his branch of it, decisively to the pole which I have labeled elitist.

The Soviet Approach to Individual Modernization

When they came to power in 1917, Lenin and his cohorts faced some problems unique to their situation, and others certainly rather distinctive. Nevertheless, many aspects of the situation they confronted were similar to those which have faced the leaders of many less developed countries over the past two or three decades. These problems were not all economic, political, or military, but also included as central elements a set which may be designated psycho-cultural. They found that the **character of the population--in particular its modes** of living and interacting with nature, man, and society--was not such as to maximize the people's integration into the new and more dynamic social order the Revolution sought to establish.

Some of the indicators of Soviet Russia's underdevelopment were the obvious ones of low levels of literacy and inadequate development of schools; limited diffusion of the means of mass communication; high birth rates coupled with high mortality rates; overwhelming concentration of the population in village agriculture, and concomitant low levels of industrialization. These objective conditions were, inevitably, linked to subjective factors. One segment of the population in Czarist Russia was already over the threshold of psychological modernity by 1917; but this group constituted a very thin stratum of society, limited to part of the intelligentsia, some segments of the industrial and commercial middle class, and a very modest portion of the small urban industrial labor force. The rest of the society, in varying degree, expressed the proto-typical orientations of tradition-bound men.

In our research on individual modernization we have established that there is a set of personal qualities which cohere as a syndrome empirically designating a type of man we may properly call modern.[3] The use of the term modern to characterize this syndrome is justified on two grounds. The first, purely theoretical, justifies this usage on the basis of face validity. That is, the content of the questions used in the scales fits our theoretical concept of individual modernity. In addition, use of the criterion method also justifies designating this syndrome as modern. The men manifesting it are more often found among those with more formal schooling, and among users of the mass media, urban residents, and, most important, persons who work in industry or other parts of the modern sector of the economy.

Each element in this syndrome has its analogue in the agenda that Lenin, Stalin, and the entire Communist party program developed for transforming the Soviet population into a mobilized, industrialized, centralized, and bureaucratized nation. To make the point clear, I have presented below the main components of the modernity syndrome as we developed it on the basis of men in six noncommunist developing nations--Argentina, Chile, East Pakistan, India, Israel, and Nigeria. The description of each element of this model of modern man is accompanied by a brief indication of how the theme is relevant to the official conception of the ideal Soviet citizen.[4]

Before we present these juxtaposed models, however, it is essential to sound several cautionary notes. First, the qualities of the modern man as described below should be recognized as relative rather than absolute. Thus, when we say that modern men have shifted their allegiance to leaders of public as against more primordial associations, we mean that this is true only by comparison with more traditional men in the same culture. This definition does not require that to be modern a man must have cut all, or even most, of his ties and allegiances to leaders of primary institutions. Second, one must realize that any general model must be used selectively and with discernment when it is applied to a concrete historical situation. Thus, in the Soviet context an intensified reaffirmation of primordial ties with one's ethnic or religious group may be, in certain exceptional situations, characteristic of the most modern rather than the less modern men. This appears to be the case, for example, among Soviet Jews who have attained scientific eminence. Such special cases should not, however, mislead one as to the applicability of the model in most situations. Third, we should note an important difference in the degree to which the two models juxtaposed below can qualify as empirical reality. The model of modern man has been tested empirically, and extensively so. The model of the ideal Soviet citizen, by contrast, remains a mere construct formulated by students of Soviet affairs through an analysis of programmatic utterances found in official sources.

Element 1: The modern man asserts increasing independence from the authority of traditional figures like parents and priests and shifts allegiance to leaders of government, public affairs, trade unions, cooperatives, and the like.

The continuous and continuing preoccupation of the Soviet regime with shifting individual loyalties from primal groupings to other objects, most notably to the Communist party and the Soviet state, is of course one of the most extensively documented features of Soviet history. Its most dramatic manifestations were in the early campaigns against the influence of the "bourgeois family" and the Orthodox church. At later stages in Soviet development, increasingly intense efforts were focused on developing strong loyalty to the Soviet state, a campaign which from outside has often seemed, to put it mildly, intensely nationalistic.

Throughout, of course, the idea of devotion to the Communist party and absolute commitment to support of its leadership, summed up in the idea of partiinost', has been vigorously indoctrinated. Indeed, over the decades from 1930 to 1950 the intensity of this effort, especially in the form of extreme concentration on the theme of loyalty and devotion to the person of Stalin, earned it the Soviets' own designation as "the cult of personality." Since Stalin's death, of course, the situation has been normalized. At the same time, the long-term objective has been attained. In some isolated regions of the Soviet Union loyalty to extended kinship networks, to tribe, or even to local religious leaders may still take precedence over allegiance to the Soviet state. On the whole, however, by the end of the Second World War, certainly by 1970, it could be said, with regard to this first component of the syndrome of individual modernity, that the overwhelming majority of the Soviet people had almost entirely and rather solidly established themselves on the modern side of the line.

Element 2: The modern man shows a strong interest in and takes on active part in civic and community affairs and in local politics.

Meeting this particular requirement of individual modernity in the Soviet context has involved some ambiguity, and at times has been fraught with considerable tension. In the Soviet Union active participation in local civic and community affairs does not mean participation in an autonomous role as an individual or group organized around self-determined objectives. Rather, it means participation in the tasks of building socialism as those tasks are identified, and the means for attaining them specified, by the Party leadership. Within those limits, however, this element of the syndrome of individual modernity has been decidedly emphasized in the model of the Soviet citizen favored by the system. Actively working in the local party organization, serving as an agitator, participating in the special campaigns of the trade unions and other collective organizations, and writing letters to the editor are some of the activities the Soviet citizen is expected to undertake as an active participant in the larger program for building socialism.

Element 3: The modern man strives energetically to keep up with the news, and within this framework prefers news of national and international import to items dealing with sport, religion, or purely local affairs.

The persistent Soviet concern with achieving the fullest development of the media of mass communication, and the fullest involvement of the population in the diffusion of a new world view is so well documented as to need no elaboration. News and information concerning the process of national development and, to a lesser extent, news of foreign affairs have been the almost exclusive ingredients of Soviet mass communications. Religious events are of course not reported at all, and sport news plays a very minor role indeed.

Element 4: The modern man is open to new experience, to new ways of doing things in his orientation to nature, to mechanical things, and to interpersonal relations.

The Soviet system has not, of course, encouraged the notion that one ought to experiment with politics, and has not permitted its people to entertain the idea that any system other than that based on the absolute and exclusive leadership of the Communist party is worth serious consideration. In a great many other respects, however, the Soviet system has a long history of experimentation with new forms of social organization in the family, in the school, in agriculture, and in industry. One of the objectives of the regime has always been to train citizens in the ready acceptance of such innovation, especially as it might apply to technological change--as in the introduction of new machinery, new techniques, or new ways of relating the labor force to its tasks in production.

Element 5: The modern man believes in the efficacy of science and medicine and in general eschews passivity and fatalism in the face of life's difficulties. He believes that men can learn to master their environment. In brief, he expresses a sense of both personal and social efficacy.

The commitment to transform nature and society to make them conform to man's conception of the good is at the heart of the communist world view. Its particular Soviet form is manifested in the concept of "building socialism," and its concrete expression is in all the vast works of construction which are so typical of Soviet economic activity. The role of the Dnieper Dam as a kind of shrine of the secular religion of constructionism and the later near-deification of the first Soviet cosmonauts provide relevant illustrations. Passivity, let alone fatalism, is in the Soviet context treated almost as a cardinal sin. To be a Bolshevik is to be one who can overcome all obstacles. Training in the assertion of "will," especially the will to build and to accomplish, is an essential ingredient in the curriculum at all levels of Soviet education.

Element 6: Closely related to the theme of efficacy is the modern man's concern with the mastery of time, the institution of routines dominated by the clock, which orientation is itself only a special case of a larger concern with planning things in advance as a basic component in both personal and national affairs.

The struggle of the Soviet regime to discipline the sense of time of the Soviet population, and especially of the new recruits to industry who flocked in from the countryside, is by now legendary. The struggle was, of course, greatly complicated by the fact that individuals had great difficulty in securing home conditions sufficiently stable to enable them to respond to the imperatives of the clock at the factory and office. The problem was further complicated by the unreliability of the system of urban public transportation. By the end of the Second World War, and certainly by 1970, these issues seemed largely to have been resolved.

So far as planning is concerned, little need be said. The emphasis on planning is perhaps the single most distinctive feature of the Soviet political-economic system, and the efforts to involve the entire population in commitment to plan fulfillment are widely known.

Element 7: The modern man expresses an interest in maximizing his personal opportunities to achieve education, to acquire skill, and to improve his personal condition, and he particularly holds high aspirations for his children's educational and occupational attainment.

This element of the syndrome of individual modernity is in some ways an extension of the finding that the modern man is efficacious rather than passive or fatalistic. He does not accept his station or condition in life as given or fixed, but rather strives energetically to improve it. In the modern industrial milieu, acquiring additional education and skill and excelling in production are among the main channels for the expression of such ambitions. In the Soviet case the elimination of private enterprise and the sharp restrictions on the accumulation and use of private property lead people to concentrate their efforts to improve their condition almost exclusively on acquiring additional education or skill, except for that minority which prefers the path of power within the framework of the party apparatus.

The Chinese Case

The unfolding of Chinese communism has in certain important respects been distinctly different from Soviet development. Nevertheless, certain broad features of the challenge which Mao and his collaborators faced upon consolidating their power in mainland China were very similar to those confronting Lenin and Stalin in their efforts to modernize Soviet Russia. The qualities the Chinese leadership wishes to inculcate in its citizens are clearly reflected in the guidebooks for teachers and in the readers prescribed for children in the early grades of school.[5] From an analysis of these readers and guidebooks, it is apparent how thoroughly the concern for qualities we have identified with the modern man permeates the educational process in communist China.

For example, the teacher is charged with "fostering the child's constructiveness, capacity for planning, and creativity". (p. 46). Instruction under the rubric of "life guidance" has as its prime objective "the cultivation of the child's capacity for self-awareness and autonomy, his revolutionary ideology, and his spirit of patriotism and internationalism". (p. 49). To attain these objectives the teacher is urged to adopt "the methods of competitions and challenges in order to elevate the children's initiative and enterprise". (p. 50). As the basic principle of "communist morality" the child should be taught "to oppose all oppression of man by man; to struggle for the liberation of all workers irrespective of race or nationality from every form of exploitation". (p. 54).

The objectives sketched for educators in their guidebooks are reflected in the main themes of the stories in children's readers. These readers include a heavy component of information, ranging from descriptions of the general social organization of communist and traditional China, the Communist party, and the People's Liberation Army, through rudiments of scientific knowledge, to matters of simple personal hygiene. These stories of course teach that the old society was virtually all bad and that the new society is decidedly all good. Of particular importance to us, however, are the beliefs and values about daily life which are taught, the personal orientations fostered, and the individual qualities favored by the materials presented in the readers. Thus, under the heading of "beliefs about work" the analysis of readers shows that they encourage the belief that: "Any goal can be achieved by hard work"; "A scientific approach to problems ensures their solution"; "Nature can be conquered by study of natural laws and hard work."

Moreover, the personal characteristics which the readers treat as especially praiseworthy and deserving of emulation include being a person: "industrious in work and study"; "diligent and persistent, especially in the face of hardship"; "achievement and goal oriented, desiring to achieve"; "dedicated to the building of the 'new' society"; "prudent and with foresight" (pp. 191-92).

In this agenda for child socialization one may clearly discern most of the themes we earlier identified as characterizing the modern man: allegiance to national and supralocal organizations; active participation in civic affairs; personal ambition coupled with initiative and autonomy; interest in keeping informed about public affairs; belief in science; a sense of personal and social efficacy; openness to innovation and new experience, and so on.

To point up this broad congruence between the elements of our model of the modern man and the mold in which the Chinese leadership seeks to cast its youth is not to deny that there are important differences in emphasis between the Soviet and Chinese cases, and between each of them and countries that have developed, or are developing, under conditions of capitalism or with mixed economies. For example, the Chinese model places exceptionally heavy emphasis on qualities important to being a good farmer, and on the related theme of frugality, whereas the Soviet ideal citizen is much more either the highly skilled industrial worker or the scientist-professional. Moreover, both the Soviet and the Chinese models approach the theme of individual expression and personal autonomy quite differently from the way that theme is expressed by modern men in noncommunist countries. The former give much more emphasis to group goals, to collective interests, and to communal rather than to individual progress.

Nevertheless, there is an unmistakable congruence between the model of the modern man as he emerges from the study of the less developed nations in the noncommunist world and as the Soviet and Chinese systems define the qualities of their ideal citizen. This similarity in emphasis, so far transcending the limits of time, geography, and culture, suggests that there are common problems faced by all developing countries in shaping their populations to a new standard of value and conduct meant to suit them for fuller and more effective participation in the emerging urban industrial order of society.

Vicissitudes of Individual Modernization

Our models of the process of individual modernization are, of course, too abstract. We draw a line from traditionalism to modernity, and then place individuals along it as we might move the pieces in a game. A is so far along the continuum on this dimension, and B on that. In so doing we gloss over the conflict, the struggles, the dilemmas, and the costs of individual modernization.

Take, for example, the shift of primal loyalty from the tribe, the sect, and the family to the nation, the state, the party, the commune, or the trade union. In the novels of Achebe we have an exceptionally revealing and sensitive account of the strains men experience as they struggle with the conflict of loyalty to clan and family in a modernizing Nigeria.[6] The grim history of the efforts to break the hold of the Orthodox church on the allegiance of the devout and faithful in the Soviet Union are not soon forgotten. Comparable accounts from China's experience are still largely kept hidden from us; but we can easily imagine the strains that must have been created by the demand of total devotion to the commands of the state and its local commune in a culture in which the Confucian cannon defined obligation to family and devotion to parents as the supreme duty.

The contradictions are of course not limited to those between the demands of the traditional and the requirements of the modern. Indeed, many of the most interesting tensions are those between conflicting elements within the definition of the ideal modern man. Thus, the modern industrial order requires a man who takes initiative--is autonomous, self-starting, and self-directing. Yet it also requires him to relate to, and to adjust his activities to, the complex patterns of interdependence which modern large-scale organization fosters and rests upon. The balance between these elements can at best be a delicate one, and at many points one must expect an outright clash of principles and requirements. Moreover, the problem is likely to be particularly acute in systems like the Soviet and the Chinese, which are so strongly oriented toward collective goals that cannot easily be rendered compatible with high degrees of individual initiative.

Postmodern Man

The Soviet Union is no longer a less developed nation. By some point after the Second World War it had moved decidedly into the category of those societies which qualify as developed. It came, in the process, increasingly to share the problems and concerns we identify more with postindustrial society. In this stage of national development, the modernity of average men is no longer statistically problematic; yet issues relating to individual modernity may be a major problem for the system.

In accord with the principle that for each stage of socioeconomic development there is a characteristic type of man, the postindustrial society must reckon with the postmodern man. We are thus entering on a whole new era in the interrelations of personality and social structure. And again we may expect that in some respects the personal qualities which come to the center of attention will in part be shared across the boundaries which divide socioeconomic systems, and in part will bear the distinctive imprint of one or another of these systems. For example, one may see in both the Soviet Union and the United States an increasing discontent and even revulsion with overbureaucratization, and a profound feeling that individuals must be given more control over their own lives. In both societies there is also a widespread tendency to question the logic of unlimited growth and to argue vigorously for stemming the attendant destruction of delicately balanced ecological structures.

In other respects, however, the two systems seem to generate emphases in the postmodern man which are at considerable variance with each other. For example, the postmodern tendencies in the noncommunist countries include a strong interest in communalism; romantic glorification of poverty and of the life style of the uneducated and economically disadvantaged; patterns of dress and hair style which are archaic, symbolic, or otherwise distinctly expressive; and rejection of logic and a search for transcendental experience. None of these manifestations is particularly evident in the counterculture manifested in the Soviet Union. That movement is conservative in its approach to personal dress and morality, is logical and practical rather than glorifying feelings and sensations, and insists on the literal implementation of legal and constitutional guarantees rather than emphasizing an apocalyptic or transcendental vision.

Notes

[1] In radical religious movements central importance is often also attached to transformations in ritual life. Closer examination will, however, reveal that the focus on ritual itself expresses an underlying concern for how ritual embodies or reflects values and interpersonal relations.

[2] My failure to include the other socialist countries, especially those of Eastern Europe, should be understood as a matter of convenience rather than of principle. At the moment when the Communist party came to power in Russia and China, both were in major degree "undeveloped." Although this was equally true for some of the other communist countries--let us say Albania and Bulgaria--others, such as Czechoslovakia, were among the most industrialized and modernized national states in Europe at the time they came under communist rule. To encompass the whole range of resultant types is beyond what is possible in as brief a paper as this must be.

[3] For the evidence of the Harvard Project on the Social and Cultural Factors in Development, see: Alex Inkeles, "The Modernization of Man," in Modernization: The Dynamics of Growth, (New York: Basic Books, 1966) ed. Myron Weiner; Alex Inkeles, "Making Men Modern," American Journal of Sociology 75 (1969): 208-25, and Alex Inkeles and David H. Smith, Becoming Modern (Cambridge: Harvard University Press, 1974). For reports of other efforts to measure individual modernity, see: J. L. M. Dawson, "Traditional versus Western Attitudes in Africa," British Journal of Social and Clinical Psychology 6 (1967): 81-96; Joseph Kahl, The Measurement of Modernism, (Austin: University of Texas Press, 1968).

[4] There is, unfortunately, no single source known to me in which one can find a comprehensive discussion of the official conception of the ideal Soviet citizen. Forays in the appropriate direction will be found in: Alex Inkeles, Public Opinion in Soviet Russia (Cambridge: Harvard University Press, 1950); Margaret Mead, Soviet Attitudes toward Authority, (New York: McGraw-Hill, 1951); Raymond A. Bauer, The New Man in Soviet Psychology (Cambridge: Harvard University Press, 1952); Jules Monnerot, Sociology and Psychology of Communism (Boston: Beacon Press, 1953); Carl J. Friedrich, ed. Totalitarianism (Cambridge: Harvard University Press, 1954); Raymond A. Bauer, Alex Inkeles, and Clyde C. Kluckhohn, How the Soviet System Works (Cambridge: Harvard University Press, 1956); H. Cantril, Soviet Leaders and Mastery over Man (New Brunswick, N.J.: Rutgers University Press, 1960); Alex Inkeles, Social Change in Soviet Russia (Cambridge: Harvard University Press, 1968); Gayle D. Hollander, Soviet Political Indoctrination (New York: Praeger, 1972). Some of the sources cited above supplement their description of the ideal Soviet citizen with discussions of the often contradictory model encouraged by actual official behavior. For a more explicit statement of this model see Nathan Leites, The Operational Code of the Politburo (New York: McGraw-Hill, 1951). A more contemporary account may be found in numerous publications summarizing the samizdat materials appearing clandestinely in the USSR.

[5] We are particularly fortunate to have available a detailed and highly competent analysis of Communist China's elementary school readers. These books were prepared under the direction of the People's Education Publishing House in Peking

and used in Shanghai and Peking between 1958 and 1964 to instruct children in grades one through five of the Chinese elementary schools. See Charles P. Ridley, Paul H. Godwin, and Dennis J. Doolin, The Making of a Model Citizen in Communist China (Stanford, Calif.: Hoover Institution Press, 1971).

[6]See Chinua Achebe, Things Fall Apart (New York: McDowell, Obolensky, 1961); idem, Arrow of God (London: Heinemann, 1965); idem, A Man of the People (London: Heinemann, 1966).

Chapter 3.

THE CHINESE MODEL OF DEVELOPMENT

Ezra F. Vogel

Economic planners are increasingly aware that a high national growth rate does not necessarily prevent increasing poverty, unemployment, and social malaise. It is a matter of some interest, therefore, to consider the experiences of a country that has given a high priority to reducing inequalities and decreasing unemployment and has nonetheless achieved a respectable growth rate.

At the outset, it must be frankly acknowledged that we do not possess the level of information about China that we have for other developing countries. The Chinese have not engaged in detailed public discussions of strategies, program planning, and program evaluations. Accurate aggregate statistics have been virtually unavailable since 1958. Nonetheless, the published documents from China, combined with accounts by foreign visitors (including myself) and former low-level officials from China, make it possible to outline the basic approach to development and, within broad limits, to evaluate the success of various programs.

The Internal Development Program

The core of China's development program has not proceeded from the more developed countries to China but from the more developed parts of China to the less developed parts. The gap in standard of living between the east coast centers and the backward areas of inner China is almost as great as that between the more developed and the less developed countries, and the scale of internal developments is comparable to the efforts of modern Western countries to assist in the development of most of the rest of the world's less developed countries. The Chinese rural population of about 550,000,000 approximates the combined populations of the late-developing countries in Africa, South America, and Southeast Asia. Chinese economic planners, industrialists, and technicians are overwhelmingly from the more developed and sophisticated east coast urban and industrialized centers. While continuing to develop modern industry in east coast areas, they have endeavored to reduce the gap by building up the backward areas of inner China.

Like the impact of Westerners on less developed countries, the impact of Chinese urbanites on the Chinese hinterland has been far greater than their narrow technological role. In the course of introducing elements of more sophisticated urban world culture, they have enhanced the hinterland's awareness of their relative deprivation. While initiating fundamental improvements in health and standard of living, they have also aroused the resistance of local people who because of traditional attitudes or vested interest resent the intrusion into their local social fabric.

But because the Chinese aid program takes place within a single country, the Chinese have many advantages over developed countries endeavoring to assist less developed countries. Because of the small scale of foreign trade, the Chinese economy is affected little by international economic forces inconsistent with the development program. Because of the long historical unity of China and

the common threads of culture throughout the country, the hinterlands have less
basis for unified resistance to the efforts of the national leaders. Because of
a unified political infrastructure, backed when necessary by force, Chinese
leaders are within broad limits able to implement measures they consider good
for the whole country in spite of local resistance. These advantages reduce but
by no means eliminate the tensions and problems inherent in the confrontation
between the developers and the developing.

Like many countries undergoing rapid development, China has both a modern sector with heavy industry, high technology, large-scale commerce, and professional administrators and a premodern sector with handicraft industry, low-
level technology, small-scale commerce, and part-time administrators. The
Chinese have adapted different forms of socialist organization to the two parts
of the structure. The modern sector is incorporated into the state structure,
subject to state planning, with allocations coming from the state budget, and
with standardized organizational procedures. The premodern sector has, in
socialist theory, a lower form of socialist organization, the cooperative, with
budget dependent on sales and salaries dependent on profits. Like private
business in the West, the cooperative is subject to state regulations, but it is
not directly administered by the state.

The modern sector is administered at varying levels of government.
Local levels of government are directly under the higher levels, and the specialized branches of local government concerned with finance, commerce, transport,
specialized industries, and the like are directed by corresponding branches at
higher levels. But each industrial, commercial, or even educational institution
is assigned primarily to one level of government. The largest industries,
especially those involved in defense, are administered directly by organs of the
central government. Somewhat smaller industrial and commercial operations are
administered by the province, and still smaller ones are administered by municipalities and counties. Communes usually contain some branches of the state
system, but also contain some cooperatives.

In the rural sector, communes are further divided into brigades and
brigades into teams. All are organized as cooperatives, with salaries paid on
the basis of profits after produce is sold to the state organization.

Chinese leaders would like to bring a larger portion of the economy
into the modern sector of state organization but are restrained by the difficulty of managing such diverse tiny enterprises directly with standard planning
and by the problem of motivating local groups without leeway for profit.
Because pricing and allocation of materials favor state enterprises, many co-ops
would be willing to give up the autonomy of internal operation and become part of
the state sector. But the dual structure and the dual pattern of organization
are not likely to be easily changed in the foreseeable future.

Chinese planners have by no means had a single clear-cut model for development which they have applied with perfect uniformity. They have had numerous
starts and stops, and one can still detect changes in response to changing circumstances, both external and internal. Yet since the early 1960s the Chinese
programs have achieved sufficient consistency and constancy that one can meaning-
fully talk of a model of development. For want of a better term, I shall call it
an "Intermediate Development Model."

Before considering this model it is useful to outline major changes in
strategies before the early 1960s. When the Chinese communists came to power in
1949, they initially concentrated their efforts on controlling inflation, gaining
information on the nature of economic activity, and increasing the relative
power of state firms over private firms. In 1953, they began their First Five-
Year Plan, which concentrated resources on large modern industrial and construction
projects and relied on assistance from the Soviet Union. In the course of the
First Five-Year Plan, the leaders nationalized all large-scale industry and

organized handicraft workers and farm laborers into cooperatives. In the Second Five-Year Plan, they endeavored to achieve a "Great Leap Forward" by devoting more attention to backward areas and mobilizing the population for mass labor projects. In the course of the Great Leap Forward, rural co-ops were combined into large communes, averaging about 20,000 persons. Local masses were mobilized, but without detailed planning. In the early 1950s, the leaders had hoped to achieve a dramatic breakthrough in industrialization in as little as three five-year plans, but in 1958 they tried to complete the basic breakthrough in only three more years.

Although economic development proceeded rapidly until 1958, by 1960 excessive mobilization, inadequate planning, and bad weather created a crisis in agricultural production, confusion in the supply network, and disruptions in industrial production. By 1961 it was clear that a high level of industrialization would not be achieved for several decades. The leaders therefore cut back on industrial plans, gave more aid to agriculture, made concessions to private marketing, and decentralized commune powers. Concessions made for private marketing were later tightened, and by the mid-1960s the expansion of light industry, electrification, and improved irrigation were having an impact on the countryside. Increased agricultural production in turn provided the raw materials for the continued expansion of light industry. New efforts would later be made to preserve political purity, to simplify bureaucracy, and to simplify and purify education; but the thrust of development policy enunciated in 1961 has not been basically changed. This approach combined many of the perspectives of the Great Leap Forward: decentralization, emphasis on backward areas, and intensive use of labor. But in 1961 the perspective was that it would take several decades to achieve industrial breakthrough, and that it was therefore necessary to posit a long intermediate stage. Compared with the Great Leap Forward, hasty mobilization thus gave way to more systematic planning and coordination. The commitment to rapid industrialization remained, but all aspects of the basic development program were geared to a long stage of intermediate modernization.

The Intermediate Model

The basic approach to development is to compensate for a low level of capital investment with a high level of administrative and technical advice and intensive utilization of labor. Central guidance is matched with administrative decentralization and a low level of territorial specialization. The social program endeavors to provide a basic level of security for all citizens, and a strenuous effort is made to reduce inequalities. The entire effort is undergirded with firm administrative control.

Firm Administrative Control. Many features of the Chinese model are widespread in other developing countries, but one of the distinguishing features is the extent to which the party organization is able to mobilize the population.

The determination of the Chinese leaders and the strength of party organization are products of decades of ferment and mobilization. Chinese who entered adulthood from the 1920s through the 1940s were preoccupied with the question of how to strengthen and enrich China, a question which acquired even greater urgency during Japanese occupation in World War II. Despite the cleavages between Chinese communist leaders which erupted into public view during the cultural revolution, all leaders share this commitment to strengthening China under the direction of a strong party organization. The party had almost 20,000,000 members by the beginning of the Cultural Revolution, and in 1973 it was announced that the reconstituted party organization had a membership of 28,000,000. Membership in the party is a privilege earned by years of hard work, study, and proved loyalty. The party organization had developed gradually during

World War II and during the Civil War from 1946 to 1949. The major new programs of the 1950s, such as land reform, collectivization, and communication, have been preceded by determined party-building. Membership in the party provides fraternal solidarity centered on high commitment to the nation, and the criticism of uncooperative or lax party members in rectification campaigns helps to maintain a high level of responsiveness to central policy. The party organization is thus a reliable instrument for managing and supervising the infrastructure throughout the country.

The party leaders have in turn relied on a continuing propaganda campaign to mobilize the support of the population. The essence of the propaganda effort is to inspire the people to work for the good of the Chinese people and to give them the informational base they need to achieve this. The most common sources of inspiration are the Thoughts of Mao Tse-tung and stories of individuals and groups who willingly risked their comfort or even their lives to accomplish something for the good of China. The effectiveness stems in part from the success of party leaders in articulating outrage toward Kuomintang leaders who tried to exterminate the communists, toward Japanese who occupied China, toward Americans who surrounded China with military bases, toward Russians and Indians who invaded Chinese territory, and toward Chinese bullies who exploited ordinary people. The leadership thus publicizes its role in fighting enemies as well as in eliminating filth and degradation and raising the standard of living.

To convey the message, the government uses not only newspapers, magazines, radios and loudspeakers, and traveling movie-projector teams, but the more personal approach of mass meetings, traveling drama and song troupes, and smaller groups.

Everywhere in China, people are organized into small groups through their place of work, their neighborhood, or their membership in a production team. Although many of these groups have multiple purposes, one purpose is to make the citizenry aware of national goals. These small groups are linked to higher levels of organization through their leaders and sometimes through other members as well. Within the group, the members are expected to engage in mutual criticism, giving approval to those who work for national goals and applying pressure to those who pursue their own goals too intently. All members are expected to express their commitment to the ideals, and they must publicly evaluate themselves and their peers in accordance with how well they live up to their stated ideals.

Although group discussion centers on inspiring talk and rational arguments rather than threats, it is perfectly clear to all citizens that if they deviate from these standards they may be subject to severe sanctions. The sanctions are commonly applied in the course of rectification campaigns, held every two or three years, when the small groups meet much more frequently and some of the groups select targets for large assemblies where they are denounced by all their friends. People are reluctant to defend a target person directly, for fear that the target and his defender would be considered a plotting clique and therefore subject to even more thorough criticism. Some targets of criticism have been subjected to indefinite periods of "study" and physical labor in special camps, and in some of the more severe campaigns, sizable numbers have been shot or have committed suicide under pressure.

Over the years, as small groups lose their crispness, some participants may mouth commitments without great emotional involvement. Indeed, the Chinese communist press frequently criticizes such failings. But with the combination of patriotic fervor, inspiring messages, and the implicit fear of sanctions, there is a high degree of civic responsibility. Because of the strong civic sense, robbers, work evaders, spoilers of state property, and personal profiteers are quickly reported to authorities, to be dealt with "by the masses."

With this high commitment by party cadres and ordinary citizens, the government is able to implement programs which involve considerable constraints over the population: rationing, plain living, transfer of workers from urban to remote rural areas, and limited expression of opinion. The government can therefore implement a thoroughgoing program of development not possible in countries with fewer official personnel.

Low Level of Capital Investment. The Chinese state has maintained a modern industrial base in Shanghai, Manchuria, and elsewhere, especially in sectors related to national defense. But the major national effort has been to encourage local areas to support their own industrial development at a level they can afford. The key motto is self-reliance (zi li geng sheng).

Local leaders passionately want to bring modern industry and large-scale construction projects to their areas. Modern factories and construction projects have symbolic connotations of progress and success even beyond their instrumental value. The constraints come from local budgets and local capacities. Despite dramatic progress since 1949, the material level of the Chinese countryside remains low compared with that of the developed countries, and the capital generated   local savings is not adequate to support large-scale, capital-intensive projects. Local officials lack the funds to purchase and transport large quantities of modern machinery or to produce these goods on the spot. Even if they had the funds, they probably would not get permission from higher officials, who want to ward off visionary projects beyond local means.

The ongoing effort to mechanize the countryside has enjoyed considerable success, but "mechanization" thus far means not the most advanced technology but simple machines which can be produced locally without heavy investment of capital: plows, rakes, cultivators, irrigation pumps, and the like. Large tractors are used more for transport than cultivation, and hand tractors are only beginning to be introduced in suburban communes. The current level of mechanization eases the physical burdens without removing the need for intensive labor.

State Administrative and Technical Advice. Although the central government apparatus does not provide a high level of funding for local areas, it does play an important role in training local people, in introducing new technology and administrative practices, and in rationalizing, within the limitations of scale and available capital, the local use of labor power. Since the late 1950s, when sizable numbers of technical and administrative workers were available, the government has carried on a large-scale program of sending them down to the countryside and out to the hinterlands. Some of those are sent down to perform manual labor, but sizable numbers are assigned specific administrative and technical tasks. By concentrating state aid in the form of administrative supervision and technical advice, the state hopes to achieve advances which do not require huge inputs of capital.

At each level of administration, revolving around this core of party leaders are specialized personnel responsible for supervising and upgrading education, public health, irrigation, rural electrification, agronomy, agricultural technology, crop management, and the like. Some of these officials themselves go out from their offices to perform the technical work, and some supervise the work of others at still lower levels.

In the educational sphere, for example, educators sent to the countryside have trained local teachers and supervised local schools and special literacy classes as well as teaching directly. The result has been a rapid improvement in educational standards. Although many adults have not remained in classes long enough to become literate, most—but not all—rural youth of elementary school age are now receiving minimal literacy training. Even though only a small percentage of rural youth continue formal educational programs beyond elementary school, elementary school graduates are able to read the simplified newspapers and directives which come down from higher levels.

In addition to the flow of personnel down from higher levels, lower-level personnel are sent up to special training courses. Because many rural youths trained in the urban areas during the 1950s were reluctant to return to the countryside, in the 1960s the effort has been to provide all schooling within the commune. Rural youth therefore have no opportunity to become too attached to the urban way of life. Nonetheless, local rural personnel already assigned to specific jobs in the countryside are frequently sent up to higher levels for special training or refresher courses. Above the county but below the provincial levels of administration is the special district. County personnel are frequently sent up to the special district level for extended meetings or short training courses lasting from a few days to a few weeks to get new directives or new information in such diverse fields as medicine, public health, engineering, agriculture, teacher's training, politics, and propaganda. County officials may hold similar meetings and training programs for commune level officials, and commune officials in turn hold meetings for brigade and production team officials.

A variety of experimental and demonstration centers are also established at various levels of government, often manned or at least supervised by administrators from higher levels. Experimental stations are especially widespread in agriculture, as each level of government from commune up usually has its own experimental plot. These plots are designed to test various seeds and fertilizers under local soil and climatic conditions, with machinery or draft animals available locally. Personnel at that level of government or from lower levels are invited to observe and study these experimental plots for their own guidance.

Each level of administration also selects one unit of the next lower level as a model for other units, and it administers the model unit directly. A special district directly administers a model county, and when special district personnel do their turn at manual labor or lower-level work they are most likely to be sent to this model unit. A county similarly selects a model commune which it administers, and a commune in turn administers a model brigade. These model units provide examples of how new inputs of management and know-how can improve efficiency and production. These model units are then publicized and visited by representatives of other units at the same level so that others may emulate the new techniques.

In short, although the state does very little to make capital available to local areas, it carries on a very extensive program in advising, training, retraining, applied experimentation, and demonstration which insures rapid testing, distribution, and absorption of new administrative and technical practices.

Intensive Utilization of Labor. Unemployment and underemployment have been serious problems for Peking; however, the problem has been not excessive manpower in general, but excessive manpower in the cities. The traditional channel for mobility has been from the countryside to the city, and with the continued existence of urban-rural disparities, large numbers of migrants have continued to flow into the cities in search of an easier way of life with a higher income. Economic growth in the cities has not been rapid enough to absorb the new migrants. They come in greatest quantity when economic problems are more severe in the countryside, when new opportunities are created in the cities, or when administrative surveillance to reduce migration grows lax. The problem of excessive migration was especially severe in 1956 and in 1960. In 1956-57 migration increased because many rural dwellers were trying to escape collectivization. In 1960-61 many urban dwellers who had found jobs in 1958, when capital investment in urban areas was expanded, were without jobs because of industrial retrenchment, and peasants were flowing into the cities to escape the rigors of commune labor projects and, in some cases, food shortages.

Ever since 1949 the communist leaders have systematically attempted to reduce the rate of rural-urban migration, to relocate recent urban migrants in the countryside, and to place urban school graduates in the countryside. In part this is to assist in modernizing the countryside and to avoid the added strain on transport facilities required to get rural produce to the cities. But, in addition, the regime has been concerned lest rootless unemployed and underemployed in the cities, the "vagabonds" (liu mang), cause unrest.

In the urban areas, personnel with lower levels of skill and education are not automatically assigned by the state to needed jobs. To a considerable extent, lower-level workers are free to approach handicraft co-ops, construction crews, rural production teams, and so on, to find their own work. However, local governments do have a personnel branch which assists people seeking employment. Although the state does not ordinarily take the initiative in finding openings for unskilled laborers, it does occasionally check through local neighborhood organizations for unemployed people, especially "vagabonds." If there are any, they are likely to be rounded up and settled in the countryside.

Many so-called factories, especially those formed in 1955-58 as part of socialist transformation, are in fact consolidated handicraft shops without modern machinery. Some are little more than repair shops and hand-assembly plants which require intensive inputs of labor. These factories are labor-intensive not because of the intentions of economic planners or factory managers, but because more advanced machinery is still not widely available.

There is no indication that the government has held back the modernization of industry so that it will absorb more manpower. On the contrary, where rural labor is plentiful communes make an effort not only to provide more intensive cultivation and reclaim land but to start new handicraft shops. About 80% of the population lives in the countryside, and in two model counties where data is available (from Jon Sigurdson's data, unpublished) only about 3% of the working population is employed in industry. A deliberate slowing down of modernization to absorb more manpower in industry could not at this point make a meaningful dent on the absorption of manpower. Although some urban factories and offices are overstaffed by Western standards, the basic approach for dealing with excessive manpower in the cities is to relocate people in the less modern sector--that is, agriculture.

The relocation of urbanites in the countryside is a massive movement which takes a variety of forms. All administrative cadres and all students at higher schools and universities are expected to spend part of each year engaged in physical labor, usually in the countryside. Periodic campaigns for "simplifying administration" are designed to clear offices of unnecessary staff and, when possible, to send them to the "production front," often in the countryside. Other rectification campaigns, aimed primarily at correcting political deviations, have the effect of reducing the number of office personnel and keeping them occupied in labor and "study" projects.

All graduates of higher technical schools and universities are given job assignments by the state after they graduate. They are assigned where they are needed, and this often means the countryside. When universities were reconstituted after the cultural revolution, only people who had spent several years in production or the armed forces were eligible for admission. Some graduates are assigned to the nearby countryside, but many graduates, along with some skilled workers and administrative cadres, are sent to northern and western China, where they may work opening up frontier areas. As in other frontier areas, new railroad and highway centers require administrative and technical personnel and serve as base areas for prospecting teams, construction crews, and other crews helping to upgrade more remote areas.

Following traditional Chinese patterns, soldiers are expected to spend part of their time in productive labor--raising some of their own food as well as assisting civilians in harvesting, flood or drought relief, and special construction projects. In border areas some troops and discharged veterans earn their own keep through farming and industry, but they remain available in case of military outbreaks.

In the countryside, local administrative units endeavor to find appropriate projects to make full use of available labor power. In areas with surplus
labor, efforts are made during the regular growing season to plow more deeply,
plant seeds more closely, and plant second crops between rows of the first crop.
Once crops are in the ground, more time is spent transporting water, and if production team members have time, they weed more frequently or collect more soil
from river bottoms and more greens from mountains and marshes to be used for fertilizer. In 1958-59, when some of these programs were first introduced on a
massive scale, they sometimes had not been adequately tested for local conditions,
and labor was misallocated from regular crop management. The results were sometimes disastrous, but by the early 1960s these projects benefited from more
adequate testing and more regard for other ongoing projects.

If food products are more than adequate to meet local needs and to fulfill state quotas, production teams are encouraged by higher levels to replace
food crops with industrial crops like cotton, flax, hemp, oil-bearing crops, and
so forth, since they not only maintain agricultural employment but help create
new openings in light industry.

Probably the greatest efforts to absorb labor in the countryside are
focused on extending the growing season and creating projects for peasants in the
slack season between crops. As much as possible, single-crop areas have been converted to double-crop areas and double-crop areas to triple-crop areas. Many
rural handicraft shops, food processing industries, and repair shops are created
or expanded in the off-season.

The most dramatic efforts to make use of excess labor in the slack between seasons are the mass labor projects. Local peasants, sometimes in coordination with urban personnel sent out to work on specific projects, are organized to
reclaim mountainous, rocky, or marshy land. In areas not profitable for regular
crops, peasants are encouraged to develop orchards, tea groves, or grazing land.
In still other areas, peasants plant trees to prevent erosion or to expand forest
reserves. Some help build dikes, dams, and reservoirs or extend irrigation
channels, others work on road or railroad construction projects. In most cases
the laborers have little machinery and use simple digging tools or carrying poles
and baskets. The projects thus make use of an inordinate number of laborers.

These varied projects for absorbing excess labor are organized at a
variety of levels. At the lowest level, production teams organize planting,
weeding, and fertilizing for ordinary peasants, but they may also organize older
or younger people to help with orchards or tea groves, to look after animals, or
to gather firewood or herbs for traditional Chinese medical practitioners. In the
slack season, the production team might also organize small-scale irrigation or
land reclamation projects within walking distance from their fields. Larger-
scale projects are organized by the appropriate administrative unit, whether it
be the brigade, commune, or county. A common method of organizing these projects
at higher levels is to requisition a number of workers from each production team.
Thus, higher level units are not required to expend additional salary inputs except for eating and housing expenses on the project sites.

More than 90 percent of the rural population is organized into communes,
with salaries paid mostly by the production teams. The production team functions
like a cooperative, selling its produce to the state and distributing the profits
to the members. However, in mountainous areas, frontier areas, and other areas
which cannot be operated profitably for some years, the co-op type of organization
is replaced by a state farm. Workers on state farms are not paid according to the
profits from their collective labors, but are given set salaries or at least
supplied with minimal necessities. State farms may be organized by the military
or by the state administrative apparatus for cadres sent for more labor experience or to correct their political thinking. The state farm is usually more
formally structured than the production team, and it is also well adapted to
geographical and climatic conditions which are inappropriate to ordinary stable

family agriculture where income is determined by profits after produce is sold to the state.

In short, the Chinese communists have adapted a variety of techniques to increase the effective utilization of labor power for large-scale projects not touched by modern machinery. It is difficult to estimate the underemployment of administrative staff organizations or of urban construction workers awaiting new assignments or underemployment among peasants where opportunities for mass labor projects are not readily available. Occasional accounts in the Chinese press make it clear that the problem of underemployed urbanites has not disappeared, but the accounts of foreign visitors support the view that these various programs have kept unemployment and underemployment low enough so they are not a serious problem.

Chinese plans are not as precise as plans in other countries in presenting accounts of capital, machinery, and personnel needed. Rather, plans represent quotas, with general estimates of the inputs required to meet these targets. If a plan is running behind schedule, administrative pressures are brought to bear and input adjustments are made to increase the likelihood that quotas will be met. Beyond the annual targets which guide local economic development there are projects designed to increase production in the long run by expanding acreage, improving irrigation, and controlling droughts and floods. The effort to keep everyone actively employed is not so much a function of precise economic planning as of a politically guided effort to increase productivity in general and to reduce social unrest.

Local Coordination: Decentralization and Low Level of Specialization. In the early 1950s central government ministries were given considerable power in coordinating economic activities, but by 1957 it was clear that these ministries could not directly supervise the range of specialized economic activities in the provinces. In part the difficulty stemmed from the inadequacies of transportation and communication, the lack of uniformity of machinery and products, and the exaggerated production reports that were sometimes sent to higher levels. But in part it stemmed from the red tape of a large bureaucracy overloaded with responsibility for directly administering the whole economy. Therefore many powers were handed down to local administrative units, under the direction of their party committees. Local plans and budgets must now be approved at higher levels, but as long as each local unit meets its economic target for goods and taxes to be delivered to higher units or traded to other local units, it has considerable independence in organizing the economic activities within its sphere.

The local unit endeavors as much as possible to be economically autonomous. Production plans are adjusted to meet local consumption needs, and administrative boundaries are drawn to enhance the likelihood that this will be done. Boundaries of suburban communes, for example, are drawn to contain both farm and industrial areas. Small market towns are combined with the surrounding countryside to form a single commune, but larger market towns are divided into halves or thirds, each with its own commune. Each commune contains a small industrial area which serves the adjoining rural areas within the same commune. Factories in these commune industries produce goods mainly to meet the needs of the commune's urban and rural population, and the local farm produce is similarly oriented to the needs of all the population of the commune.

As much as possible, administrative boundaries are drawn to coincide with natural marketing areas, but when feasible, goods are distributed within an administrative unit even though the distribution conflicts with geographic convenience. Many communes, for example, have their own rice-husking and peanut-oil processing plants, simple spinning, weaving, and sewing shops, small furniture factories, and machine tool and handicraft shops. They also have construction crews for building housing. Brigades within the commune usually have repair shops for smaller machinery as well as sewing shops and other simple handicraft shops.

The county level has more specialized production facilities, requiring greater inputs of capital and skill, designed to meet the more specialized needs of the communes within the county. For even more specialized products, two or three counties may combine their efforts. Despite the chaos resulting from producing small steel furnaces with inadequate planning in 1958-59, by the early 1960s most counties were producing their own steel or were combining with one or two other counties to produce steel. These steel plants are primitive by modern Western standards, more comparable to late nineteenth-century European steel plants than to modern ones. A small county or a combination of two or three large communes commonly operates a small brick kiln to service local needs.

This pattern of local autonomy minimizes false reporting of figures to higher levels, reduces supply problems and bottlenecks due to red tape, makes minimal demands on the limited transport network, and permits frequent adjustments of production to meet local needs. Furthermore, the program of decentralized administration and intermediate technology plays a key role in absorbing labor. The Chinese feel that in the short run these advantages compensate for whatever they might lose from the decreased capacity to develop modern machinery and economies of scale.

Toward Equality and Security

The Chinese communist leaders came to power determined to provide at least a minimal level of security for everyone and to reduce inequalities between rich and poor. They have followed wage and price policies that make available, and in effect subsidize, a minimum of food, inexpensive cotton clothing, and limited housing at prices which everyone can afford. Economic plans are devised to produce this minimal consumer's package, and agricultural and industrial production are now adequate, leaving a moderate margin for reinvestment. Transport facilities have been expanded, ensuring that a minimum of food is available throughout the country, even in time of natural disasters.

At the same time, the government has vastly reduced waste due to unnecessary consumption by socializing private enterprise, by placing limits on top salaries, by setting high prices on nonessential consumption goods, and by waging incessant criticism campaigns against waste. Officially, some former businessmen whose enterprises were nationalized have been given some interest payments, but in fact the dangers of showing "bourgeois thought" and "bourgeois tendencies" are so great that few businessmen withdraw interest from the bank. For all practical purposes, private profits in enterprises of any size were eliminated. The impact has been to prevent excess consumption and to eliminate the extremes of wealth and poverty.

Nonetheless, substantial inequalities continue to exist even after the Cultural Revolution. In part this is because resources for remote areas are still highly limited and because the effort to develop modern industry for the nation's defense and transport facilities requires a concentration of resources in areas already richer than average. And in part it is because motivating those who are making greater contributions to the economy requires differential privileges. This is reflected in the salary system which was regularized after socialist transformation in 1955-56.

After socialist transformation, all employees of the state apparatus, whether employed by the Communist party, the administrative state bureaucracy, state educational institutions, or state mining, industrial, or commercial enterprises, were incorporated into a standardized salary system. Separate ranking systems comparable to civil service in the West were applied to employees in different specialities--to teachers, technical workers, industrial workers, cultural workers, and so forth. Because cost of living varied greatly from one part of the country to another, the actual salary a person of a given rank received was adjusted for local cost of living. For most workers (except for apprentices and a small number of subcadre level jobs), a salary in an area with an average cost of living would begin at about $35 to $50 jen min pi per month. A very high level technician and a top administrator might receive as much as $250 j.m.p. a month, and a top level official in Peking may officially receive about $360 a month.[1] During the revolutionary struggle those serving in the Chinese communist army or party and Chinese communists serving in the administrative bureaucracy had been supplied only with necessities and a small allowance. In the early 1950s the establishment of a salary scale system and the gradual transition from single men's dormitorylike living conditions to family life served to increase the differentiation between the several million people in the movement. For the nation as a whole, however, the effect of the new salary system was to standardize income and to reduce disparities by raising minimum standards and eliminating excessively high pay.

People who are not employed by the state do not have such regular incomes. Most are paid by handicraft cooperatives or by rural production teams (which are also, in effect, cooperatives). Co-op profits are distributed to members at intervals, largely on the basis of their contribution to the co-op. In fact, because the fixed prices at which co-ops must sell their goods leaves co-op members little margin for profit, the income of co-op members is below that of state employees. Private enterprise is permitted only at the bottom of the economic scale, for peddlers, small handicraft repairmen, traditional Chinese druggists, and so forth, so that the income of independent practitioners is generally below that of co-op members. Since the number of independent entrepreneurs is very small, in general one may distinguish two broad categories of workers: state employees and co-op (including agricultural production team) members. In order to see how the state tries to reduce inequalities it is necessary to consider several major kinds of inequalities: among state employees, between state employees and co-op members, between co-op members, and between regions.

Inequalities among State Employees. In the first several years after coming to power, communist leaders reduced the range of salary differentials; but since a state salary system became established in the mid-1950s there has been no major reduction in the range of salary inequalities. The ratio of highest to lowest paid workers in large enterprises or major government offices is still on the order of ten to one. In fact, by the late 1950s the bureaucratic structure had achieved considerable stability, and even the amount of mobility was limited.

In the early 1950s, up through 1956, the number of state employees had expanded rapidly. Many older businessmen and officials who worked under the Kuomintang were retired early, and many of the new employees were loyal communists and Youth League members in their twenties and early thirties. Many of these young people were quickly promoted to middle level and even higher level positions, and sizable numbers of still younger people were brought into the lower positions. With the economic contraction after 1960, the number of positions at the middle and higher levels could not expand significantly, and even lower level positions became fewer. Because a whole cohort of people in middle level positions were still only in their forties and fifties at the beginning of the 1970s, there were not the proportion of retirements found in a more mature or slow-growing bureaucratic structure. Only the political rectification campaigns which dismissed some officials and sent others down to lower levels opened up sizable numbers of new positions. Because the economy in the mid-1960s had not developed significantly above 1958 levels, the effect was to freeze the size of the hierarchy and to reduce opportunities for mobility.

During the cultural revolution, leaders announced their determination to reduce salary differentials between state employees. Although reductions have been achieved, recent information indicates that basic salary differentials have not been greatly altered. Apparently, better-paid employees are so accustomed to their standard of living that substantial reductions would affect their morale, and significant salary increases for lower-paid employees would divert more capital than the government deems wise.

Inequalities between State Employees and Co-op Members. Not only do state employees receive guaranteed salaries which are higher than those of co-op members, but they also receive welfare benefits not accorded to co-op members. State employees are covered by a state health system and receive guaranteed sick leave and retirement benefits. Women employees are granted seven weeks' leave when they give birth to children. The state simply does not have enough funds and facilities to provide welfare benefits to members of co-ops.

As a result, the state assigns handicraft cooperatives and rural production teams the responsibility of caring for their own sick and aged members and for bearing the medical expenses of members seen at clinics and hospitals. The extent to which co-ops do in fact provide welfare benefits varies greatly from one co-op to another. Suburban co-ops which grow and sell produce for the city markets earn considerable income and with good management the co-op may put aside a significant portion of its earnings to cover welfare benefits. Since they are close to the city, high quality medical care is available. On the other hand, co-ops which are far from urban areas and which are not well managed may have a marginal level of income and may not have enough foresight to put aside some of their profits to cover welfare benefits for their members.

In contrast to the standardized state wage scales, the variation between the millions of production teams and other co-ops is so great and the data available so limited that it is difficult to estimate average peasant income. Data available from a number of production teams make it clear that it is not uncommon for adult males to earn between $30 and $100 j.m.p. twice a year, after each of two harvests. The semiannual salary is thus within the range of the monthly salary of a young state employee. However, several qualifications are necessary. This rural income is calculated after grain has been distributed to each household, and so the peasants do not have to purchase grain. Rural families do not pay for vegetables which are grown on their private plots, and in some cases the excess produce from these plots may bring the family as much annual income as their share of team profits. Furthermore, rural families do not ordinarily pay rent. Given the limits of data, it is difficult to be more precise than to acknowledge that peasants have a much smaller variety of food and belongings and own far fewer factory-produced goods. They typically have adequate food, but except for suburban truck gardeners they do not have an income that allows them to buy much more than the minimal necessities of household furniture, cooking equipment, farm tools, and clothing.

The state could readjust prices to favor production teams and other co-ops. One reason such readjustments have been very limited is that state factories produce goods of higher priority, and the government does not want co-ops to become so profitable that they attract workers and other resources away from state industry. The major way of improving conditions in the countryside has been to send out more cadres and educated youth to help raise productivity. State public health workers organize vaccination and inoculation campaigns, train paramedical personnel, and provide guidance for more complicated public health problems. The barefoot doctor campaign is merely the most recent version of an ongoing effort to expand training for paramedical workers and upgrade rural health services. As for other welfare services, the state does not supply capital, but it encourages the production teams to provide basic necessities for the aged and infirm.

Inequalities between Co-op Members. Co-op members have considerable leeway in determining how they will divide the profits between members. Usually they rely on a complex system which takes into account varied skill levels, tasks performed, and politics (class background and cooperativeness). Commonly these contributions are tallied daily in the form of work points, but sometimes overall assessments are made when products are sold. In the case of rural production teams, points are totaled at the time the harvest is sold, and the profits are divided among members on the basis of these points. Although the profits are dispensed on the basis of individual members' contributions, they are distributed to the household as a unit. The chief inequalities within the production team are thus between the households that have more adults of working age and those that have a higher proportion of young and old dependents.

One of the basic contradictions within production teams concerns how much of team profits should be distributed to some families on the basis of need (those with a high proportion of aged, small children, or infirm) and how much should be distributed strictly on the basis of contributions to the team. When communes were initially formed in the fall of 1958, there was an effort to decrease rural inequalities by maximizing distribution on the basis of need rather than contribution. Within a year or two this had such a deleterious effect on production that it was abandoned. "We should not," said a major editorial, "drop into the utopian dream of skipping the socialist stage and jumping over to the communist stage." The initial communes also endeavored to reduce inequalities between local teams by greatly expanding the size of the basic accounting unit, (the commune), which sometimes included tens of thousands of people, but this also proved deleterious to production and was quickly abandoned. By 1962 the typical production team, the new basic accounting unit, was down to approximately fifteen to twenty-five households. Clearly, peasants had to see that their individual labor would appreciably affect their incomes, and this was not possible with such large-scale units. Co-ops are expected to supply a minimal level of food and housing to all members on the basis of need, and then to distribute most of their profits on the basis of the contribution of household members.

Inequalities between Geographical Areas. The east coast and especially the more industrialized areas of Manchuria and Shanghai have a much higher standard of living than the more remote inland areas. The variation between rural localities is reflected in a talk by Mao, who said, "There are poor and rich brigades, poor and rich villages. . . . It is mainly differences in resources, conditions, administration, and history which result in . . . divergences."[2] Not only are there salary differentials, but the whole range of educational and medical facilities in the remote mountainous and frontier areas is considerably below that of the more advanced urban areas. Because of transportation difficulties, for example, many people living in remote areas have no access to highly trained doctors. Even the level of technology and the variety of foods are inferior to those of farmers living in more fertile areas on the plains.

At the time of the First Five-Year Plan there were intentions to relocate major industry farther inland in order to have more balanced regional development. By the early 1960s, however, with the emergency effort to recover agricultural productivity, investments in irrigation, fertilizer, and pumping stations were in those areas which would get the quickest return on investments and make the most substantial difference rather than in the most remote and backward areas. Similarly, in advancing industry to the latter 1960s, more effort was made to concentrate and improve industrial facilities in Shanghai, Tientsin, and Manchuria rather than in the inland areas. After the clashes with the Soviets in 1969, with the desire to increase military capacity rapidly, investment again went not to the backward areas but to the advanced areas capable of producing the needed supplies with great speed.

Again, the major effort to build up backward localities is through the extension of transport and communication facilities, through administrative and technical personnel coming down from the cities, and through solid collective organization and mass mobilization. The examples of localities in which this combination of outside and local mass effort have led to dramatic improvement are widely publicized to inspire other areas.

73

Yet a country as poor as China, regardless of ideology and intention, cannot yet provide a thoroughgoing welfare program for all the people. There are not enough well-trained doctors, for example, to service all the Chinese hinterlands. The state treasury is inadequate to provide the social security benefits provided even by nonsocialist Western countries. What the Chinese have done is to throw the welfare responsibility on local cooperative units and to apply advice, encouragement, and pressure to the cooperatives to look after individual members. This has had a measure of success, but there are still vast differences in income, health care, and education between more industrialized urban areas and the hinterlands.

It is difficult to estimate whether the inequalities in the standard of living between people living in the more remote backward areas and those living in urban areas have increased or decreased over the last two decades. At a minimum it seems clear that the constant attention to rural co-ops and the mobilization of workers in the countryside has brought sufficient improvement in backward areas so that the gap has not appreciably increased. Furthermore, as opposed to the opportunities in a free enterprise economy for individuals to develop great concentrations of wealth, in a socialist economy these opportunities are limited to their rise in rank in the state hierarchy. Since there has been little rise in rank, opportunities for the rich to become richer are strictly limited. Furthermore, the rationing system has an equalizing effect, not only because food staples are equally distributed but because many of the nonrationed foods are priced higher so that the people with greater income have their income absorbed more rapidly as they purchase nonrationed foods.

One other factor which should be considered in estimating inequalities is the widespread availability of public facilities. Many places of recreation, at local cultural stations, are free to all. Museums, books, newspapers, magazines, movies, plays, and operas are available to wide groups without charge. Loudspeakers make radio programs accessible regardless of whether one owns a radio. Many items like bicycles are available to people through their jobs. Although some recreational facilities and banquets are more available to higher officials, a systematic effort is made to bring plays, operas, radio broadcasts, traveling movie projector teams, and so forth, to more remote areas. In short, the wide sector of public services available to all serves to further minimize the effective income differential.

Morale: Progress and Poverty

Americans who have visited China since the reopening of relations in 1971 have been impressed by the spirit of the Chinese people. They have noted their optimism about the future, their enthusiastic support of national effort, their willingness to accept discipline and engage in physical labor, and their high level of public morality. The absence of public display of grievances does not mean that there are no motivational problems. One who complains about conditions is likely to be criticized as a reactionary, and one who complains about his own circumstances is likely to be criticized even more severely for self-centered bourgeois individualism. But during the Cultural Revolution, when there was a more open airing of grievances, a number of problems did come to the fore. Among them were the following:

The Resentment of Peasants and Other Co-op Members against Privileged Members of the State Hierarchy. Those who had irregular jobs in the city, those who were hired for temporary construction projects, and those who worked in co-ops brought complaints against the more privileged members of society. Gradually those employed in regular positions in the state hierarchy were much more satisfied and less vocal in complaining about the system.

The Resentment of Those Rectified Politically, Especially Those Sent Down for Long Terms of Physical Labor. Those who have earlier been rectified must behave with unusual caution and must continually display their devotion to the regime. The more serious cases are still under controlled supervision and must report regularly to the local police station. Many feel they were criticized unfairly and harbor grudges against those who criticized them.

The Frustration of Those "Transferred Downward." Although many Chinese do go to the countryside and other lower level units with idealism and with the desire to build up the backward areas, many feel that they are being sent unfairly to more difficult living situations and try to resist the assignment or, failing this, to find some way to come back to the cities. In the early part of the cultural revolution, some of the first objects of attack were the local neighborhood police stations responsible for rounding up urban youth, and prominent among the attackers were those who had been rounded up and sent to the countryside. Many who were sent down complained that they had been promised they would be in the countryside only for a set term, a promise that was not kept.

The Frustration of Reduced Expectations. Many of those complaining during the cultural revolution had hoped to obtain the white-collar jobs for which they had been educated, but the contraction of opportunities for employment and promotion in the early 1960s led to serious disappointment and frustration. Although this argument was not voiced directly because the complainant would be accused of bourgeois individualism and careerism, the targets selected for attack, the press attacks on careerists, and the propaganda urging youth not to be so careerist make it clear that this problem was absolutely central. By the late 1960s many had scaled down their level of expectations, and with moderate but steady growth the sense of acute frustration was not as great as in the early 1960s.

By Western standards, the material conditions of many ordinary Chinese workers, to say nothing of the peasants in more remote areas, are at poverty levels. Except for the period of 1959-61, malnutrition has been essentially eliminated, but the amount and variety of food, the heat available in cold areas, and the limited clothing available in many parts of China would be considered substandard by most Westerners.

Although the communists have not yet raised the material levels of peasants in remote areas to the standards of the more advanced Asian countries, they have undoubtedly made an enormous impact on the "culture of poverty"--on the fatalism, resignation, and defeatism which plagued China before 1949 and which still plague many of the slums in Western cities.

There is no simple explanation for the high public morale observed by visitors to China. One reason is that a population which experienced such moral degradation and discouragement in the late 1940s is relatively satisfied to accept firm direction from the leadership. China's success is also related to widespread appreciation for the government's thoroughgoing program of eliminating banditry and organized vice, which in turn required popular support. Their success is also related to the plain style of officials and their low level of corruption, and to a determination by top leadership to criticize, demote, and fire cadres guilty of deviations. It is related to the penetrating organization at the grass-roots level and to the willingness of members of small groups to criticize fellow group members and to apply psychological pressure when necessary. It is related to the fact that the government has had a respectable growth rate which has brought a minimal level of consumer goods and security to all. It is related to the genuine conviction of most leaders that they are helping the people. It is related to the fact that most of the progress is brought about by small units like production teams, where people can see that the fruits of their labors and of collective organization have made an appreciable impact. It is related to the excitement of the early stages of the industrial revolution when the first electric facilities, the first irrigation pumps, the first telephones, radios, and movie screens were introduced. It is related to the effectiveness of the propaganda message which publicizes people's successes and blacks out complaints. It is related to the recent mood of government relaxation and willingness to make more concessions to consumers.

It is not that the government's success in intermediate modernization has eliminated frustration or, for the present, even poverty. The determined efforts to send people down from higher levels, to purge and demote a variety of people, and to get everyone to participate in manual labor have generated considerable dissatisfaction. It is, rather, that the level of progress and the very tight control over deviations has been sufficient to contain the criticism and to prevent it from being organized into an effective resistance movement.

Birth Control

In 1958, at the height of the optimism of the Great Leap Forward, Chinese leaders were convinced that the economy would expand rapidly. Just as Russia, which had a population excess in the early 1920s, perceived a population shortage with the expansion of industry by the 1930s, so the Chinese leaders in 1958 believed that China would soon be short of population to perform intensive labor tasks once the economy expanded. By 1961, however, with economic contraction, it was clear that action had to be taken to control births. Even at the height of the Great Leap Forward birth control devices were available, but by 1961 leaders began to introduce a concerted policy to keep population growth down.

Just as late age at marriage has been found to be the most significant factor responsible for the decline in the birthrate in Taiwan, so the Chinese on the mainland were aware of the importance of age at marriage, and they began a policy of encouraging later marriage. Articles began appearing giving reasons why men should not marry until their late twenties and women should wait until at least twenty-five. Although there was no rule that couples had to wait until such an age before marrying, some "overeager comrades" were in fact assigning to two different places younger men and women who had grown too serious about each other.

Once the government made a firm decision to encourage population limitation, it began to publicize the advantages of a small family for the individual and for the state. Through the well-developed organizational structure of study groups at work, in the neighborhood, and at school, people were given not only the rationale but the information necessary for birth control. Free abortion was readily and freely available, and the pill and the coil were widely distributed. In the countryside, there has been a renewed effort to extend medical services through the barefoot doctor campaign, and these doctors also bring information about birth control.

Again, implicit threats are used as incentives to make the program effective. In the city, couples with three children may not receive ration coupons for the next child, forcing the family to share less food. Parents with too many children in the country as well as the city may be strongly advised to undergo sterilization.

The availability of a welfare system is critical in developing positive motivation for birth control, for the traditional expectation has been that children will look after their elderly parents. Most families want to produce two or more boys to ensure that at least one will live and be able and willing to support them. The elderly still expect to live with their children, but those on a state salary can expect a lump-sum retirement payment that will ease the financial problem in their old age. In the countryside, the critical issue is whether the production team has achieved enough stability and sufficient reserve funds so that elderly people without prosperous sons can feel secure that they will be cared for by the production team. This requires a stable and successful production team and the expectation that no basic change will occur. It also requires a method of postharvest distribution that includes adequate support for dependents even if they have no family members earning points on the production team. After the turmoil of 1959-61, production teams have begun to achieve some stability, and higher level officials have continued to push them to support their needy members.

In the last several years, model urban areas have begun a more concerted effort to work through neighborhood organizations to get each family to commit itself to a plan for family size. The state supplies sufficient birth control information, pills, abortion facilities, and pressure to ensure that families come close to following their plans. Inner party directives ask local areas to reduce the net growth rate to 1% a year by 1975. Visitors are informed that this low rate has been achieved in many urban areas, although it is acknowledged that rural rates are still higher.

Growth, Employment, Equality, and Control

Unfortunately, foreigners have not been given enough information or permitted to observe Chinese programs in enough detail so they can evaluate differential effects of specific Chinese programs. What is clear, however, is that China has proved the viability of a conception which combines a rapid growth policy with a program for reducing unemployment and rapidly improving the living conditions of ordinary workers and peasants. By concentrating excessive manpower in the less modern sector, the Chinese have not slowed down their industrialization in order to achieve fuller employment. It is not clear when mass labor projects will reach the point of diminishing returns or when industry, transport, and bureaucratic efficiency will develop so that these projects are no longer an effective way of absorbing manpower and increasing growth. But at present they are an effective way of absorbing manpower while still contributing to growth.

Similarly, in the Chinese experience a more equitable distribution policy is seen as fully consistent with economic growth. The Chinese feel that eliminating the waste caused by conspicuous consumption by richer classes insures that more resources will be channeled into productive areas; yet egalitarianism has not gone so far as to deprive the leadership of needed administrative or technical talent. They feel that a moderate rise in the standard of living in the countryside adds more to peasant "activism" and therefore to production than it detracts from potential saving. In short, they do not see full employment and widespread distribution as tradeoffs to achieve long-term growth.

However, the Chinese effort to reduce unemployment through sending great numbers of people to more remote areas and organizing mass labor projects requires an impressive system of public control. Similarly, the effort to reduce inequalities by a far-reaching rationing system and sharp restraints on conspicuous consumption is not possible without political restraints. The Chinese model of growth combined with relatively full employment and fairly equitable distribution must thus be undergirded by a very effective control system.

The Limits of the Intermediate Model

In the early 1960s, when models of autonomous communes and counties were trumpeted, all counties were expected to follow suit by building their own fertilizer plants, their own small iron and steel furnaces, their own machinery plants, and other light industrial plants necessary for meeting most local needs. By the early 1970s, visitors to Peking were told by economic ministry officials that such plans were not rational for all geographic areas. The model had been tried to some degree in all localities, and its limits were more clearly recognized. Ministry officials acknowledged, for example, that sending coal and iron ore to every county so it could produce its own steel was far more expensive and put more strain on transport resources than sending finished industrial products. In places like Manchuria and the Shanghai area, which are more industrialized and have better transportation, economies of scale have been achieved that make some county plants unnecessary. The result is that the model of local autonomy is already being modified and is no longer proclaimed as it was in the early 1960s. Both in the most advanced industrial areas, where economies of scale are having their impact, and in certain remote areas, where natural resources are not available to supply small steel furnaces, the model of local autonomy is no longer pursued so vigorously. Yet for some decades to come, a combination of economic and bureaucratic reasons suggest that it will continue as the dominant model for most of China.

Notes

The most detailed account of local rural organization may be found in A. Doak Barnett (with a contribution by Ezra F. Vogel), Cadres, Bureaucracy, and Political Power in Communist China (New York: Columbia University Press, 1967). The fullest account of rural industry is contained in an unpublished manuscript by Jon Sigurdson, Rural Industrialization in China, (forthcoming, Cambridge: Harvard University Press). The most detailed work on the program of sending down rural labor is in the forthcoming work of Thomas Bernstein. The best explicit statement of the Chinese approach to development is the work by Mao contrasting his program with the Soviet approach to development, Miscellaney of Mao Tse-tung Thought (Joint Publications Research Service, 20 February 1974, #61269-2, pp. 247-313).

[1] This data is based on the detailed salary scales published in Zhongyang caizheng fagui huibian (Central Government Financial Regulations), 1956, pp. 224 ff. Although more recent regulations are not available in the West, prices in China have remained quite stable over the years, and examples given recent Western visitors of salaries in specific localities show little variation from the 1956 salary scales.

[2] Miscellaney of Mao Tse-tung Thought, p. 159. See also p. 270.

PART TWO

POLITICS AND ADMINISTRATION

Chapter 4.

THE RULING PARTY IN A MATURE SOCIETY

Richard Lowenthal

The Problem

This paper deals with the impact not of the total process of moderniz-ation, but of the achievement of a certain level of industrial maturity on the political system of communist-governed single-party states. In other words, it is concerned with what, in Western discussion, is now frequently called the "postmobilization phase" of such systems.[1] As I have argued elsewhere, in com-munist regimes this term denotes the approximate completion of two closely inter-woven but conceptually distinct processes. On the one hand, it means--just as it does in noncommunist "dictatorships of development"--that modernization has reached a point where the need for politically forced development fades away, because the process has begun to acquire a momentum of its own. On the other hand, it means that the specifically "totalitarian" communist attempt to trans-form social structure in the direction of the ideological goal of the "class-less society" by repeated "revolutions from above" has to be abandoned as well, because at the stage of development reached, the economic cost of such violent interruptions of the continuity of production becomes prohibitive. We are dealing with a stage in which politically forced development is replaced by the inherent dynamism of an industrial society, and planned revolution from above is replaced by spontaneous social evolution from below.[2]

For the ruling parties, reaching that stage means losing their accus-tomed function of forcing economic development combined with the revolutionary transformation of society. Their central problem is how to maintain their claim for a monopoly of political decision after abandoning their self-set task of using political power as an instrument for ideologically conceived social change. If they wish to hold onto their power in the more or less mature societies they have helped to create, they have to adjust to a new, postrevolutionary role, find-ing the appropriate new forms of organization, new methods of operation, and new ideological legitimation required by it. The various ways in which they have attempted and may yet attempt to do this, and their chances of long-term success, are the subject of this essay.

Although the long-term aspect of this problem is largely speculative, its theoretical discussion can by now be undertaken on the basis of a consider-able body of experience. The Soviet Union, which--because of the duration of communist rule, its model role for other regimes and, last but not least, its importance as a world power and as center of a bloc--remains the "classical" country for any study of this type, has been increasingly confronted with the problems of industrial maturity since the middle fifties. Its political system may be said to have definitely entered a "postrevolutionary" stage since the adoption, at the twenty-second congress of the CPSU in 1961, of a new party program[3] which described the further changes in the social structure needed for the achievement of communism, not as an operative task of the party but as an expected by-product of the steady increase in productivity, standard of living, leisure time, and educational level to be achieved under its leadership. The CPSU has thus been concerned for a full decade with the role change we are dis-cussing.

Among the other Communist parties that have come to power by an authentic, indigenous revolution in an underdeveloped country, only the League of the Communists of Yugoslavia has so far been faced with similar problems, and that for an even longer period. In fact, the role change (of which the party's change of name, adopted at its sixth congress in 1952, was an outward expression) was forced on the Yugoslav communists as a slightly delayed consequence of their conflict with Stalin, at a time when most of their country, could hardly yet have been described as industrially mature. Their exposed position in this conflict created an urgent need both for a broadening of domestic support and for improved economic relations with the West, and these proved incompatible with further attempts to inflict violent transformations on the social structure. Ever since the attempts to combine economic reform with the creation of organs of "socialist self-management" on one hand, and the decollectivization of spring 1953 on the other, the Yugoslav communists have been consciously experimenting with the development of new organizational forms, new methods, and new legitimating ideas for their party without ever abandoning its monopolistic position.

On the other hand, communist parties have also come to power, owing to the expansion of the Soviet Union's power sphere at the end of World War II, in two industrially developed countries of East Central Europe--Czechoslovakia and East Germany--as well as in such semideveloped countries as Poland and Hungary. In all these countries, they have imposed major social transformations on the Soviet model, notably nationalization of industry and radical land reform followed by varying degrees of collectivization. In the industrial countries, this was accomplished without regard to the level of economic development and at times at its expense, and in the semideveloped countries it was accompanied by efforts at accelerated, if at first extremely one-sided, industrialization. After Stalin's death, and particularly after the East European "de-Stalinization crisis" of 1956, the increased autonomy of the East European ruling parties and the awakening Soviet interest in a more rational division of labor led generally to greater efforts at balanced economic development. Moreover, as a result of the compromise that ended that crisis in Poland, forced collectivization there was stopped and largely reversed; consequently, the Polish communists, alone among the parties of the Soviet bloc, have been fully confronted with the problems of postrevolutionary rule since that time. In the other bloc countries, the effort of the ruling parties to impose social transformation based on the Soviet model continued for some time, if rather more slowly and cautiously. But soon after the CPSU program of 1961 announced the definitive end of such "revolutions from above" in the Soviet Union, the corresponding process stopped throughout its power sphere. Since that time, all the ruling parties of the European Soviet bloc have clearly entered the postrevolutionary phase, and those that have reached a more or less industrial level of modernization (which by now may be said to apply to Poland and Hungary as well as to Czechoslovakia and East Germany) have had to face broadly similar problems in adjusting to a change of function.

The available experience of the attempts by the Soviet Union, Yugoslavia, and the East European members of the Soviet bloc to cope with those problems, and the state of scholarly discussion about them, suggests that they can best be examined from three main angles. First, how far and on what conditions can a communist single-party regime meet the requirements of efficiency and rationality of a modern industrial society that has to compete with noncommunist industrial societies? Second, how far and on what conditions can it respond to the shifting interests of the various groups in an increasingly differentiated society, permit their articulation, and yet maintain a monopoly of their arbitration? Third, how far can it meet the conditions resulting from the first two sets of problems and at the same time develop a credible form of legitimation reconciling its ideological traditions with its new role? Finally, a question of necessarily speculative nature, but ultimately of decisive importance, arises: How far are the required adjustments of party structure, governing methods and legitimating ideology likely to produce in their turn unforeseen and unintended consequences which are liable to undermine in the long run the very system they were intended to stabilize?

Some Hypotheses and "Models"

In the present paper I shall attempt only a brief survey only of points that seem relevant to answering these questions. Before embarking on the attempt, however, it will be useful to recall a few of the principal hypotheses or models that have so far been put forward in scholarly discussions of our problem, both to test them against the available experience and to make our own tentative answers more precise by confrontation with them. I propose to describe them respectively as the hypothesis of monistic rational tutelage, the model of the stages of bureaucratic enlightenment, the hypothesis of the diversity of possible degrees of pluralism under authoritarian control, the model of nonideological legitimacy arising from postrevolutionary consensus, and the hypothesis of the irreplaceable role of democracy.

The possible stability of monistic rational tutelage is the hypothesis put forward in George Fischer's book The Soviet System and Modern Society[4] as an alternative of the view that the high degree of functional differentiation of modern industrial society must necessarily lead, through the granting of increasing social autonomy, to its constituent groups to toleration of the organized pursuit of their interests, ending in a pluralistic political system. Fischer concedes that the complexities of an industrial society will make increasing administrative autonomy of subsystems,notably decentralizing reforms of economic planning,inevitable in advanced countries under communist rule, and that this situation will also set up pressures for social autonomy. But he suggests that these pressures may be successfully contained, short of permitting pluralistic institutions, by a party conceiving its "monistic" monopoly of decision as a "tutelage" over society and its various groups.

One condition for the stability of this modified "monist model" is, in Fischer's view, that the leading positions in party and government should increasingly be filled by "dual executives" enabled by their training and career to combine the skills of political leadership with the expert knowledge required for decisions in their special fields, primarily in economic policy; the bulk of the book is devoted to detailed evidence designed to show that the share of such "dual executives" among the Soviet communist leaders is indeed increasing. Other conditions, not explicitly stated as such, are implied in Fischer's acknowledgment that his "monist model" is derived from one of the three alternative paths for Soviet development outlined as early as 1954 by Barrington Moore, Jr.--the path of "technical rationality" under continued party control.[5] Moore assumed that a ruling party which decided to make economic growth an "end in itself" could succeed in holding down conflicts of interest in the name of the "rational" values of its secular materialism, implying that those values should both be sufficiently concrete to permit "rational" decisions in every conflict over economic, social, and cultural priorities and generally enough accepted to legitimate the party's right to monopolize decisions in their name. Since Fischer does not attempt to justify these implications, his argument turns out to be addressed chiefly to the problems of efficiency and rationality and only marginally to those of interest arbitration and party legitimation.

The model of successive stages of bureaucratic enlightenment has been put forward, with slight variations, by Alfred G. Meyer and Peter C. Ludz, on the basis of a typology of bureaucratic organization developed by the industrial sociologist Rensis Likert. It proceeds from Meyer's thesis that the Soviet Union can best be understood as a giant, all-embracing bureaucracy, comparable to a modern corporation extended over the entire society, and that therefore the evolutionary pattern of the bureaucratic structure of big corporations may offer a clue to the evolutionary tendencies of the Soviet political system.[6] For the former, Likert has developed a scale ranging from "exploitative author-

itative" through "benevolent authoritative" to "consultative" and finally to "par-
ticipative" forms of organization, in descending order of the role of coercion and
fear and ascending order of cooperation and trust, variety of interaction and
communication, and scope for the delegation of decisions; the participatory type
in particular is characterized by interaction of groups as well as individuals.[7]
According to Likert, the evidence of management studies shows that corporations
tend to evolve along that scale because it leads both to improved information at
the point of decision and to improved motivation for all employees at each successive stage, thus ensuring rising efficiency. Following him, Meyer first
suggested that the increasing complexity of bureaucracy--with its need for diminishing coercion and command and increasing decentralization, use of incentives
and participation--was producing in the Soviet Union a similar transition from
"exploitative" through "benevolent" to "consultative authoritarianism," tending
ultimately to a form of "participatory bureaucracy."

Ludz has generalized the argument for the evolution of communist regimes in industrial societies and used it to explain their transition from
"totalitarianism" in its Stalinist and destalinized forms (which he identifies
with Meyer's first two stages) to the "consultative authoritarianism" characterizing the GDR from 1963. He also has employed it as a basis for predicting evolution in a "participatory" direction under the pressure of rising demands for it
with the spread and improvement of higher education propelled by the needs of
technical progress.[8] Meyer sees the same expectation as a plausible basis for a
theory of (partial) convergence of the communist and Western democratic systems,
but makes it clear that he foresees universal bureaucratization rather than
democratization as the basic tendency of the modern world, though he does not
exclude the possibility that the Soviet Union could "become increasingly
pluralistic so that the party turns into a hidden multiparty system."[9] But neither
he nor Ludz develops this question of the possible political forms of the
"participatory" stage. Their model, too, is shaped by considerations of efficiency and rationality rather than by those of interest arbitration and party
legitimation.

By contrast, Gordon Skilling's analysis of the <u>diversity of degrees of
pluralism under authoritarian control</u> is entirely based on his pioneering studies
of the role of interest groups in various communist-controlled societies and the
response of the ruling parties to them.[10] In one sense, Skilling seems to offer
only a negative answer to our problem, since he rejects any belief in inevitable
or irreversible tendencies for the evolution of communist systems and specifically
denies that the choice between different solutions depends predominantly on
economic factors. Yet the value of his contribution for our discussion lies
in just his classification of the different solutions so far attempted for combining a measure of pluralistic interest articulation with the maintenance of
single-party rule. Skilling groups at one end of his scale "<u>quasi-totalitarian-
ism</u>" of the Stalinist type, in which group formation is illegitimate in theory
and severely limited in practice, and at the other end the "<u>anarchic
authoritarianism</u>" of the Chinese cultural revolution, in which a breakdown of the
party institution was accompanied by open and frequently violent group conflict
limited only by Mao's personal authority. He then distinguishes three other
categories of direct relevance to our subject.[11]

The first, for which he adopts Meyer's and Ludz's term of "<u>consultative
authoritarianism</u>," is characterized by the intact monopoly of decision by the
party leadership and strict refusal to tolerate spontaneous group activity,
although groups within the bureaucracy may be permitted to articulate both their
own interests and those of broader social strata before making a decision, and
both individual experts and professional groups may be consulted. This is the
system characteristic of the more sedate East European states during most of the
sixties and of the Soviet Union since the fall of Khrushchev. Skilling sees a
looser type of "<u>quasi-pluralistic authoritarianism</u>" in Hungary and Poland from
Stalin's death to the October crisis of 1956, in the Soviet Union under Khrushchev, and again in Czechoslovakia and Poland in the years preceding the "Prague

spring." Their common denominator is that nonbureaucratic, spontaneous, and in part critical groups are active, exerting influence on sections of the leadership and possibly encouraged by them, though they are not granted institutional legality and decisions are still made at the top. Such situations are likely to provoke a coercive backlash and are thus inherently unstable. Finally, Skilling analyzes a system of "democratizing and pluralistic authoritarianism," of which Yugoslavia since the early fifties and Czechoslovakia under the reform leadership offer two different variants. Here, independent groups are institutionalized and play a recognized role in the political process, though the regime remains essentially authoritarian in maintaining strict party control of the levers of power and in excluding political alternatives to its rule. The major difference between these two experiments in legalized pluralism is that in Yugoslavia, the initiative for granting autonomous rights to workers, managers, and nationalities came mainly from above and in slow stages and was not intended to include toleration of critical intellectual groups; whereas in Czechoslovakia in 1968, the planned changes enacted by the reform leadership converged with a spontaneous movement from below to legalize critical opinion groups and restore the autonomy of mass organizations and thus exposed the leadership to active pressures for quick changes as well as to conservative counterpressures. Nevertheless, up to the Soviet invasion the leadership had succeeded in holding the process within evolutionary bounds. On the basis of this analysis, Skilling neither predicts nor excludes a form of communist rule that would evolve, on Czechoslovak lines, even further toward democratization.

The most ambitious attempt so far to develop a comprehensive theory of "established one-party systems" is Samuel P. Huntington's model of nonideological legitimacy arising from postrevolutionary consensus.[12] It is based on the author's interpretation of the postrevolutionary experience of both communist and noncommunist one-party systems, among which he includes the case of Mexico, irrespective of the particular nature of the revolution and the ideology concerned. Huntington's model covers all three main aspects of our problem, but his argument centers on the issue of legitimation. Starting from the recognition that in a postrevolutionary period both the ideology and the dynamic, "charismatic" leader lose their usefulness for guiding the transformation of society and tend to give way to bureaucratic institutionalization under oligarchic leadership, he goes on to suggest that because of the broad, pragmatic consensus which follows the completion of a revolutionary process, ideology is no longer needed to legitimate the "established one-party system" either. On the contrary, now that both the new social structure and the political procedures of the system have become accepted by the bulk of the nonbelievers, ideology becomes a potentially harmful, divisive force-a source of superfluous disagreements. Hence, the familiar tendency toward an erosion of ideology in the postrevolutionary phase, far from endangering the stability of the one-party system, appears to Huntington to be in its interest--and he expects the leadership eventually to recognize this, despite the initial backward-looking resistance of the "middle-level apparachiki."

Once ideological obstacles are removed, the leaders will then be increasingly able to meet the needs of a mature society by "adaptive" reforms within the system. Thus they will gradually accept the economic changes advocated by "innovative managers" for the sake of technical rationality and economic efficiency, and grant an increasing functional autonomy to them and other (administrative, military, scientific) experts within "depoliticized" subsystems. They will be ready to institutionalize a plurality of interest groups while confining them to "corporate" forms so as to preserve the party's monopoly to arbitrate between them as sole interpreter of the general interest. They may even come to provide inner-party institutional channels both for policy disagreements and for electoral career competition between individuals, while continuing to prevent political group formation and effectively isolating the intellectual critics, who alone may continue to question the basis of the consensus in their ideological search for "meaning."

Finally, the opposite hypothesis--the irreplaceable role of pluralistic democracy for mediating consensus in modern conditions--has been advanced on the most general theoretical level by Talcott Parsons.[13] Parsons regards the "democratic association," defined in the Western sense and used as a principle of organization both for government and for society in general, as an "evolutionary universal" such that only systems that develop it can attain certain higher levels of adaptive capacity. Communist party rule, he predicts, cannot in the long run fully match democracy in political and integrative capacity; it will prove unstable and either make adjustments in the general directions of electoral democracy and a plural party system or regress into generally less advanced and less effective forms of organization, failing to advance as rapidly and as far as otherwise could be expected. His basis for this prediction is not simply the increasing complexity and differentiation of advanced societies, but the dependence of power on a consensual element, linking the power system to the higher-order consensus at the value level. "No institutional form basically different from the democratic association can ... mediate consensus in its exercise by particular persons and groups, and in the formation of particular binding policy decisions....Providing structural participation in the selection of leaders and formation of basic policy, as well as in opportunities to be heard and exert influence and to have a real choice among alternatives, is the crucial function of the association system from this point of view."[14]

Parsons' unhesitating assertion of the universal significance of Western forms of democracy is thus based on the argument that, first, in a complex society decisions must continually be made between different interests and values whose implementation requires the consensus of an enormous majority; and second, that these decisions cannot be legitimated, and hence the consensus cannot be assured, in the long run by other than democratic methods. As an additional point, Parsons refers to the spread of education in communist systems, because educated people will come to expect to be trusted with a share of political responsibility. "This can only mean that eventually the single monolithic party must relinquish its monopoly of such responsibility."[15] Parsons' argument, while taking for granted the effects of the need for efficiency, such as increasing social differentiation and improving education, thus rests primarily on the requirements of interest reconciliation and political legitimation.

Technical Rationality and Economic Efficiency

The pressures exerted on a communist party ruling an industrial society by the requirements of technical rationality and economic efficiency are of many kinds. We may tentatively list them as the need for liberation of scientific research from dogma; the need for a free flow of technical and economic information and practical criticism; the need for forms of planning, administration, and training that give scope for managerial initiative and technological innovation; the need for the selection, training, and consultation of competent elites; and the need for elite security under the rule of law.

Liberation of Research from Dogma. Science is today recognized in East and West as a "productive force" of vital importance for technical and economic progress. Freedom of research from political interference and dogmatic blinkers is thus a condition for the competitive development of any industrial society. The delay in Soviet computer development owing to the initial ideological prejudice against cybernetics, and the waste of capital incurred by communist-governed economies owing to the prolonged refusal to count interest as a part of production costs are only two of the most striking illustrations.

Experience shows, however, that attempts at dogmatic direction of research in the natural sciences have by now ceased in all advanced societies under communist rule; the final eclipse of Lysenko after the fall of Khrushchev was the last spectacular act of liberation. The integrity of the official dogma has been preserved and rendered harmless by confining its exponents to the philosophical interpretation of scientific results after the event. Political interference with research still occurs in the form of setting priority targets, but its risks and advantages do not seem qualitatively different from those stemming from the allocation of research funds in Western countries.

The social sciences, on the other hand, are still an ideological battleground throughout the Soviet bloc, though normally not in Yugoslavia. Recognition of the fact that the party was no longer shaping the social structure at will, but had to respond to unplanned social developments and therefore needed to know them, led to the revival of empirical social research in the Soviet Union and the bloc from 1962.[16] In Poland, its pursuit had been driven underground only during the climax of Stalinism. But because of the central place of the theory of social development in Marxist-Leninist doctrine, the Soviet license for empirical research in this field was linked from the start with the attempt to preserve a monopoly of theoretical generalization for the doctrinaire exponents of "historical materialism."[17] Since neither the doctrinaires nor the social scientists have been prepared to respect this artificial and unscientific line of demarcation, conflicts exhibiting a mixture of scholarly discussion, doctrinaire denunciation, and administrative interference recur in sociological institutes throughout the bloc[18] and at least occasionally damage the quality of empirical work and training. Efforts in the Soviet Union to develop a kind of political science distinct from the doctrine of "scientific communism" seem to have been confined to the theory of public administration and to have borne little visible fruit. On the other hand, scholarly institutes dealing with the political, economic, and social development of countries outside the bloc have come to enjoy a considerable freedom to put forward divergent interpretations of reality--in the terminology of the doctrine--that may serve to justify, and at times even stimulate, policies.

Economists in the Soviet Union and the bloc, while paying lip service to the Marxian theory of value, have long been able to make important contributions to realistic cost accounting and to sponsor alternative proposals for planning reform, based on theoretical views ranging from "market socialism" to mathematical simulation of demand. Although it remains a matter of political decision which subjects are open to discussion in the official periodicals at what time, the limits appear to be set more by concern for the ideological purity, and to affect application rather than research itself. The one major blow in recent years has been the decimation of Poland's economists, as well as less striking losses in other branches of the country's intellectual life, by the anti-Jewish measures of 1968/69. But this must be listed as an illustration of the risks of arbitrary rule rather than of dogmatism.

Broadly speaking, then, although the dogmatic handicap in the natural sciences has virtually disappeared, in the social sciences it has noticeably diminished under the impact of practical needs but is still present in the Soviet Union and the bloc countries as a risk impairing the continuity of their development. It will fully disappear only if Marxist-Leninist dogma loses its importance for the internal cohesion and external legitimation of the ruling parties.

Freedom of the Flow of Information. Loyal domestic critics of the Soviet system lay much stress on the need to improve the flow of information and criticism as a condition for overcoming the increasing technological gap between it and the West, above all the United States.[19] While freedom of information and criticism may of course be regarded as generally desirable on other grounds, only some particular aspects of it are directly relevant in this context.

The first is the freedom of exchanging scientific, technological, and economic information with noncommunist countries. This fully exists in Yugoslavia but is still limited in the Soviet Union and the bloc, though even there the improvement has been considerable, particularly on the "import" side. In principle, all Western scientific and technological information is now available to Soviet and bloc scholars; in practice, bureaucratic limitations on the import and distribution of scholarly publications often prevent it from reaching the most interested people promptly or at all. Limitations on direct correspondence and on the participation of Soviet and bloc scholars at international meetings have the same effect. Soviet technological achievements are now widely offered for international patents, but the tendency to preserve secrecy about actual production processes makes it difficult for the outsider to judge their value in application.[20] It seems, however, that these obstacles to the flow of information are mainly due to bureaucratic rigidities, some with specific roots in Russian culture, that may be hard to overcome but could in principle be remedied without major changes in the political system.

The same applies even more clearly to a second aspect: the sluggishness of the flow of information between research institutions and industry and between different industrial units. This appears to be due in part to the organizational separation of technological research from production in Russia and the bloc nations;[21] in part, again, to the tradition of bureaucratic secrecy; and in part to the absence of competition. The last factor will have to be discussed in the context of economic reform; the first two can clearly be overcome without substantial political change.

The third and last aspect of the information flow that has direct relevance to efficiency is the flow of practical criticism from the bottom to the top within each production unit or administrative or research institution, and from the units charged with applying rules or technical innovations to the units responsible for inventing them. The main obstacle here is a rigidly hierarchical and authoritarian climate that offers subordinate individuals or institutions no incentive for useful practical criticism but instead tends to make them feel that it would be unwise to provoke the disfavor of their superiors. This climate, deeply rooted in traditions of Russian bureaucracy and management and transferred to the bloc countries in the Stalinist period, has long been recognized as harmful by the political leadership and is being officially denounced. Actual improvements, however, seem to be slow and are more noticeable outside the Soviet Union than inside. A more effective change seems to depend on a combination of decentralizing planning reforms and changes in training and education with conscious efforts to develop more consultative or "participatory" patterns of management; this is clearly the type of problem envisaged by the Meyer-Ludz model.[22] Yet the question arises whether it is an accident that these management patterns have been evolved in countries where workers enjoy the protection of independent trade unions, civil servants have job security with a high probability of automatic promotion, and managerial personnel may change to competing firms in case of conflict with their superiors; or whether the difficulty of creating similar patterns in communist single-party states is due to the absence of such institutional props for individual independence in their system.

We may provisionally conclude that significant improvements of some economically relevant kinds in the flow of information are possible without substantial change of the Soviet type of one-party government, but that an improved flow of critical information from the bottom upward may require for the critic greater security against dismissal and career disadvantages for the critic than are at present offered by that system.

Scope for Managerial Initiative. At the level of achieved or approaching industrial maturity, where the physical creation of basic industrial plant and the attending infrastructure is no longer a task of the highest priority, the improvement of cost efficiency, the pace of technological innovation, the extension of the variety of consumer goods, and the raising of their quality become increasingly important standards for the effectiveness of the economic system. They clearly depend on the data available to the producing units for calculating their cost and anticipating demand, and on the manager's scope for responding to

both. Price reform to reflect costs and demand more accurately and planning reform to increase the manager's need to respond to these market indicators and to
free him from detailed bureaucratic directives are therefore at the core of all
programs for economic reform in systems originally characterized by central administrative planning for political priorities, from the various stages of
Yugoslav "market socialism" since 1952 to the most recent experiments in the
Soviet bloc.

A critical survey of all these reform programs is of course both beyond
the scope of this essay and beyond the competence of its author. Following, with
minor modifications, a suggestion of R. V. Burks,[23] I propose to distinguish between limited and radical types of reform, with regard to both their economic effectiveness and their impact on the political system.

The limited type of reform, as now attempted in the Soviet Union and approved by it in a number of variants within the bloc, rejects free price formation
on the market and retains a considerable amount of central planning for physical
quantities, thus continuing to limit the autonomy of the managers of production
units. It seeks, however, to correct the officially fixed prices so as to make
them better indicators of real cost, including interest and depreciation of fixed
capital; to delegate a number of planning decisions to subordinate branch authorities or "trusts"; and to reduce the total number of physical indicators prescribed to the manager of individual units while making "profits" (in the sense of
return over cost) an important monetary indicator for measuring and rewarding
their success. This type of reform will clearly improve both the data and the incentives for rational cost calculation, though the data may still lag behind
actual changes; for official prices will be corrected only at comparatively long
intervals, and the scope for reacting to the incentives will be restricted by
the remaining indicators, preventing, for instance, the automatic dropping of a
production line that has become unprofitable from lack of demand. Within the
same type, it should also be possible to reduce those obstacles to technical innovation which depend on specific planning regulations, such as the fear on the
part of both managers and workers of losing part of their income by interruption
of production runs, though under the system of physical quotas this may require
clumsy types of bureaucratic exceptions.[24] A lifting of the ban on dismissals
following the introduction of labor-saving inventions, although open to political
and ideological objections in a communist context, is in principle also conceivable within the framework of a limited type of economic reform.[25] On the other
hand, such hurdles to technological innovation as the lack of risk-taking by small
independent firms, or the absence of a market for producer goods, clearly cannot
be overcome within the limited reform program. Nor will it, failing as it does
to provide a competitive market for the consumer, be able remotely to match the
performance of capitalist industry in the quality and variety of consumer goods.

The radical type of reform--as instituted by Yugoslavia, planned by
the Czechoslovak reform leadership of 1968, and cautiously approached by Hungary
recently in different variants--accepts the principle of free price formation of
the market and of competitive independence for the managers of socialist enterprises. The central planning authorities seek to determine the level and directions of economic activity by monetary and credit policies, including direct investments where necessary; they do not attempt to prescribe to the managers what
goods to produce in what quantities, where to procure their materials or machinery
or how much labor to employ. The enterprise retains its profits after paying
interest and very substantial taxes, and bears the risk of loss, including the
risk of bankruptcy. A country under this system may, but need not, invite
foreign capital under certain precautions nor need it, while permitting its
enterprises to conclude import and export contracts with foreign firms, abandon
the control of foreign exchange to the extent that Yugoslavia has done at times:
there is no reason why a socialist market economy should be more extreme in its
liberalism than many capitalist countries. Clearly, a radical reform of this
kind will create the same incentives for rational cost calculation and for cost-
reducing technical innovation, including product innovation, as exist in capital-

ist market economies; it will also create similar incentives for improving the quality and variety of consumer goods. Its actual success in meeting these demands will, of course, also depend on a variety of other factors, from the size and skills of the population of the country concerned and the starting level of its capital stock and technology to the ability of its monetary authorities and the strength of the political factors producing inflationary pressures. But as far as the economic system goes, the radical type of reform appears in principle fully capable of meeting the requirements of technical rationality and economic efficiency of an industrial society on the basis of public ownership of the means of production,because it permits a high degree of autonomy to the "economic substystem."

Turning to the political consequences, there seems no reason to doubt that the limited type of reform is compatible with an essentially unchanged system of single-party rule; it has been specifically designed for that purpose. For the radical type of reform, both Soviet critics and Western sympathizers have argued that it must "logically" lead to the institutionalization of a pluralism of social and ultimately political groups, as the examples of Yugoslavia and of the Czechoslovak reform experiment of 1968 are said to have proved.[26] In fact, the experience of those two countries seems to show something rather different. Tito's creation of the "workers' councils" in 1950 <u>preceded</u> the first major economic reform of 1952 (though it gained practical importance only afterward), and the Czechoslovak reforms, adopted on paper before 1968, began to be implemented only after power had passed to a new leadership that was deliberately aiming at a "new political model" as well as an economic one.[27] The actual course of events, both in those two countries and in others where reforms have remained limited, suggests rather that radical planning reform hurts so many entrenched interests that it can be carried out only if other social forces are mobilized for an attack on the bureaucracy in the course of a major political transformation. For the groups that stand to lose in a radical reform include not only the huge staffs of the economic administration on all levels, but also those regional and local members of the party machine who used to be largely occupied in dealing with the recurrent deadlocks between different branches of that economic bureaucracy.[28]

The strength of their resistance not only accounts for the rejection of radical reform in the Soviet Union and most bloc countries to date, it also explains why even a consistently reform-minded leadership could not so far overcome it without appealing to other social groups and according them institutional rights. In particular, granting quasi-entrepreneurial powers to managers, including the power to reduce staff, could hardly have been pushed through without simultaneously granting increased rights to workers' councils or increased autonomy to the trade unions or both. In short, radical reform of the economic system as defined here appears to be one of the pivotal issues where the requirements of technical rationality and economic efficiency can be fully met only at the price of political changes that would create institutional forms for interest articulation and raise the problem of redefining the role of the party itself.

However, resistance by the economic bureaucracy and sections of the party bureaucracy may not be the only reasons for the paucity of communist attempts at radical planning reform, and for the slowness of even the limited progress that could be expected from more circumscribed reforms. There is evidence that in many cases, particularly in Russia, the managers themselves are far from happy at the prospect of even a limited increase in their autonomy and responsibility. Besides their sense of insecurity (discussed above in the context of obstacles to the flow of critical information), this seems to be due to a system of education that for a generation,and in Russia even longer,has stressed the virtues of conformity and unquestioning obedience far more than those of independent judgment and initiative; and also a type of professional training that has focused on technical competence and administrative discipline to the exclusion of economic thinking in terms of a choice between alternatives. Thus even well-conceived, limited reforms are unlikely to bear their full fruits without major changes in the principles and practice of education and professional training as

well as in the leadership style of management boards and administrative organs-
changes that appear most urgent and most difficult in the Soviet Union itself.

   Elite Selection and Expert Consultation. Communist party regimes govern
the countries under their rule by means of two interlocking types of hierarchies-
the various branches of the state administration and the party hierarchy itself.
The state administration is supposed to exercise essentially bureaucratic functions, that is, to carry out political decisions and to some extent to prepare
them by submitting the necessary information and the possible alternative courses
of action to the political organs. The party is supposed to retain a monopoly on
policy decisions at all levels as well as to stimulate and supervise their execu-
tion by the state administration. It also decides on all appointments of responsible state personnel. The hierarchies are interlocking because normally all key
positions in the state administration are filled by party members, many of whom
also belong to the corresponding party committees and may be switched over to
full-time positions in the party hierarchy at other stages of their career.

   The efficiency of such a regime in governing an industrial society in
general and managing the publicly owned economy in particular clearly must depend
on a high level of specialized competence in the various branches of the state
administration, and on adequate general education and broad technical and economic
understanding in the higher party organs that make the decisions and select the
administrative personnel. The question arises as to how far communist parties
ruling industrial societies are conscious of this need and are capable of training
and selecting elites who combine the required degree of competence with the
necessary political-ideological commitment to the party's goals, so as to fill
the key posts in party and state with cadres that are "red and expert," in the
Chinese terminology, or "dual executives," in George Fischer's term.[29]

   The answer appears to be that, with few exceptions, all the communist
parties concerned have become aware of this necessity, and that obstacles to com-
plying with it in practice have been due less to causes inherent in the system than
to the competing claims of deserving veterans of the party's struggle for power--a
factor that tends to diminish with the passage of time. In the Soviet Union, the
first major steps for replacing the elite of revolutionary veterans by an elite of
postrevolutionary technicians were taken by Stalin during the Great Purge and sub-
sequently were continued by changing the party statutes at the eighteenth congress
in 1939. Ever since then, the share of cadres with higher education in general and
technical training in particular has been high, both in the senior ranks of the
party and in management.[30] Fischer's figures suggest that Khrushchev's attempt to
reduce the privileges of the "new class" by his educational reform and his rotation
rules for party offices have made no major difference in this tendency; they show
a steady increase in the share of "dual executives" in the leading party organs for
the years up to 1961.[31] Even more important, both Fischer's study and an independent investigation for the same period by Frederic Fleron show a growing share in
those organs for people who have not only undergone technical training but have
been "co-opted" into the party leadership after a considerable period of responsible professional experience in industry or agriculture.[32] The one persistent
weakness in the qualification of Soviet managerial and administrative cadres appears to be the low importance attributed to properly economic (as distinct from
technical) training[33],a fact that relates to my previous remarks on obstacles to
effective economic reform.

   In Yugoslavia, the need to rely on spontaneous solidarity of party members in the conflict with Stalin has considerably slowed down the removal of undereducated veterans from key positions in industry and administration. But the defeat of the chief exponent of the veteran outlook, Aleksandar Rankovic, in the
party crisis of 1966 opened the way to a decisive advance of qualified cadres in
industry,[34]as well as to a drastic rejuvenation of the party leadership in all
republics and a corresponding increase in the better-educated element. The
renewed tightening of federal discipline following the recent events in Croatia is
unlikely to reverse this broader tendency. The Chinese communists alone, who

coined the "red and expert" formula but suffered from a particularly serious shortage of cadres corresponding to it, have twice forsaken it--in the course of the Great Leap Forward of 1958-60 and again in the Cultural Revolution of 1966-68.[35] Whether and when the needs of industrial development will enforce a return to it, along with other adjustments, remains to be seen.

Among communist regimes created as a result of the expansion of the Soviet power sphere in Eastern Europe, the claims of old party members have played a role in delaying the selection of well-trained cadres similar to that of the claims of revolutionary veterans in Yugoslavia. This role has been most marked, of course, where the communist parties were traditionally strong before they came to power, as in Bulgaria and--more important in our context--in Czechoslovakia, both countries in which the party membership is known to this day to be both overaged and undereducated to a striking degree. On this basis, Czechoslovakia became the one industrial country under communist rule in which the majority of senior managerial, technical, and administrative posts were held until the late sixties by people without adequate professional training--a factor which no doubt contributed to the specific inefficiency of the country's industry and through it to the wave of discontent that led to the overthrow of the Novotny leadership at the turn of 1967/68. Up to the end of 1961, East Germany suffered from a similar lack of qualified economic and technical cadres for an entirely different reason:the attraction of rival West Germany for its trained technicians. But after the building of the Berlin wall had stopped the main exit for would-be refugees, the adoption of a limited economic reform in early 1963 was combined with a deliberate policy of promoting higher-educated nonparty personnel in industry and giving communist members of the economic and technical intelligentsia responsible posts in the party,thus showing that the previous situation had not been a matter of ideological choice.

Openness for the promotion of qualified nonparty members of the intelligentsia to industrial and administrative positions appears to be characteristic of traditionally weak ruling communist parties as they approach the industrial level of development, as the otherwise very different policies of the Hungarian and Rumanian communists show. Whereas the Rumanians, like the East Germans, seek to recruit these technicians for the party and continue to reserve at least important administrative positions to party members, the Hungarian leadership under Kadar has gone further in loosening the interpenetration of party and state hierarchies by opening some responsible positions in the government bureaucracy to loyal nonparty men. The future of this latter experiment, which like some aspects of the Hungarian economic reform tends toward greater "subsystem autonomy" than is at present regarded as acceptable elsewhere in the bloc, may still be considered uncertain. But the ability of communist regimes to train and select increasingly qualified elites as they become increasingly confronted with the problems of industrial society must be accepted as confirmed by the overwhelming bulk of the evidence.

Even a well-educated communist leadership, however, can no more aspire to universal knowledge of the increasingly complicated problems it has to decide than any other political leadership; nor would it be wise to rely for specialized knowledge exclusively on its subordinates in the respective branches of the state administration. Apart from the need to hear the views of groups whose interests will be affected by impending decisions,an aspect to be discussed presently in the context of interest articulation,the leadership must also have access to the opinions of independent experts; that is, experts outside the particular bureaucratic hierarchy concerned, whether scientists or outstanding practitioners in the field. In a regime with a party-state monopoly of published opinion, such access must be specially organized by encouraging public discussions of as yet undecided issues, or by creating channels for the individual or collective consultation of experts by the leading party organs.

The Soviet Union itself has led the way in developing such methods of consultation. Licensed public discussion of difficult issues before their decision--allowed as an exception even in Stalin's time on the abortion law--has become fairly normal under his successors on a wide variety of issues ranging from economic reform, to the internal organization of collective farms, to problems of literary policy or even of military strategy. But there is always the understanding that once the party leadership has decided, the discussion must stop. In the Khrushchev era, a number of central committee meetings were used as forums for a kind of mass consultation of expert practitioners in the field on the agenda--ranging from industry and agriculture to literature and the arts--though the "show" character of these meetings gave rise to the question of how far the intention was genuinely consultative and how far they were meant to mobilize pressure on the constituted party organs in favor of decisions preferred by the first secretary. More certainly authentic were the less publicized consultations of individuals and small groups of experts by the party secretariat that are known to have been practiced during the same period and to have been continued by the post-Khrushchev collective leadership when the closed character of central committee meetings was restored as part of the return to stricter institutional rules.[36]

Altogether, there seems to be no reason why a postrevolutionary communist party regime, recognizing by definition that not all practical decisions raise questions of principle and that many depend on expert knowledge, should not encourage experts to give frank advice without fear before such technical decisions are taken. As with the capacity of such regimes to select technically qualified officeholders, the verdict on their capacity to consult qualified independent experts must thus on the whole be a favorable one--with the one reservation that the important qualification of thinking about economic problems in terms of a choice between alternatives tends to be poorly developed, for ideological reasons, by the kind of training available in those countries.

Elite Security under the Rule of Law. It is often asserted that an industrial society cannot develop maximum efficiency except under the protection of the rule of law. In fact, it may be open to dispute whether the legal security of every citizen is necessary for industrial efficiency. But it seems clear that maximum efficiency is incompatible with major interruptions of the continuity of production by massive terror directed against entire social strata or categories of citizens, and that such efficiency requires that responsible administrative and managerial elites feel personally secure in executing their duties. To that extent, the proclamation of "socialist legality" as a core principle of destalinization was addressed to two prime requirements of the industrial society: it proclaimed the end of mass terrorism as a means of planned transformation of the social structure, and it assured the elites that honest mistakes and failures would no longer be treated as culpable sabotage.

Nevertheless, even today no communist party regime can be said to practice the rule of law in the full sense of the term--not even in Yugoslavia. In all of them, the independence of the judiciary can in fact be suspended in cases which the party leadership views as politically important. The number of such cases has, of course, been greatly reduced; penal sanctions not covered by unambiguous, preexisting law are no longer used to achieve such political purposes as the "liquidation" of undesirable classes or supposedly disloyal national groups, but only to silence individuals or groups who are self-confessed critics of the regime. The point is that the limits of permitted criticism are liable to be suddenly changed by the political leadership in the light of changing political situations and imposed on the judiciary with retroactive effect as interpretations of vaguely formulated laws. A critical view published with the intention of keeping within the known limits of tolerated dissent may thus be punished as treasonable--or, in the Soviet Union today, lead to confinement in a psychiatric institution-following a change of policy. That this has been repeatedly confirmed in Yugoslavia as well shows that we are dealing not with a peculiarity of this or that country or stage of development, but with a basic characteristic of single-party regimes, communist or otherwise. A party determined to hold on to its monopoly of power evidently wants to be sole judge of the point at which danger to that monopoly begins, and therefore cannot grant the "legal subsystem" full independence.

This incompatibility of one-party rule with the rule of law need not, however, impair elite security in the sense relevant for efficient economic development,at least not in all circumstances. What matters for efficiency is not the freedom to criticize the political system itself, but the freedom of the administrative, managerial, and scientific elites to advise and act in their own sphere of competence without fear of penal sanctions if their advice is rejected or their action proves unsuccessful. This kind of security in the responsible exercise of one's specialized judgment did not exist under Stalin. It does exist today both in the Soviet Union and the bloc, and it has existed in Yugoslavia for a long time, even though, as was pointed out above, the career disadvantages of finding oneself on the wrong side of a technical argument may still be disproportionately large in the former countries.

Moreover, the borderline between "safe" disagreements within one's special field and "dangerous" ideological criticism of the regime is normally quite clear. Only if a general crisis of authority led to a state of serious disaffection among large sections of the elites,say, among scientists and technicians,could the lack of legal guarantees lead to actions harming the efficient development of the country. Short of such a crisis, we may conclude that despite the continued absence of true rule of law, elite security in the advanced countries under communist party regimes is sufficient for the needs of economic and technical progress.

Summary. Our discussion has so far shown that communist-party regimes, in the form developed in the postrevolutionary stage of the Soviet Union, are capable, without major further changes, of making considerable adjustments to the needs of a mature industrial society for technical rationality and economic efficiency. Notably, they can free research in the natural sciences from dogmatic shackles; substantially improve the flow of scientific, technical, and economic information both between their own institutions and in exchange with the noncommunist world; achieve limited but useful economic reforms by decentralizing planning techniques and increasing the scope for managerial initiative, particularly in combination with reforms in general education and professional training; systematically raise the educational level and specialized competence of political, administrative, and managerial elites and develop techniques for the consultation of independent experts, and assure a substantial level of elite security even without the full guarantees of the rule of law--all within the limits of a "consultative authoritarianism" still based on monopolistic and "monistic" party control.

On the other hand, a number of problems have appeared that cannot be solved without further changes in the system. In particular, unhampered progress of the social sciences seems to require a major change in the importance of Marxist-Leninist dogma for the cohesion and legitimation of the ruling party. A free flow of critical information from the bottom to the top requires a degree of job security for workers and career regularity for managers and officials that seems impossible to achieve without independent trade unions and a degree of autonomy in the "administrative subsystem." A radical economic reform, enabling the economic system, in principle, to match the efficiency of capitalist economies, requires a dismantling of entrenched bureaucracies and a degree of autonomy of the "economic subsystem" from party intervention, both of which have so far not been achieved in any communist-ruled country except as a result of a major political crisis and with the help of the granting of institutional rights to a plurality of interest groups. Appropriate training and appreciation of economic elites has so far proved possible only in the context of a "revisionist" approach to economic problems linked to this radical type of reform. Finally, transition to a rule of law in the full meaning of the term seems incompatible with any type of single-party rule.

Interest Articulation under One-Party Tutelage

No political system, however despotic, can do without some form of interest articulation. Even a totalitarian system determined to annihilate entire
social groups by organized revolutionary violence needs to know which particular
interests each of its measures is going to hurt, since it does not wish to an-
tagonize all the people all the time. What distinguishes a totalitarian system
is not that the social groups do not exist or that their interests are not
noticed, but that they have no recognized place in the political process and no
autonomous organizations. Even some of the sudden changes in policy and leadership composition that took place in the final years of Stalin's rule have always
been interpreted as the dictator's way of resolving conflicts among his subordinates which were at least in part expressions of wider group interests;[37]
thus the purge of Zhdanov's erstwhile supporters in the "Leningrad affair"
apparently reflected the defeat of an effort to restore the primacy of the party
apparatus over other power machines; the fall of Andreyev reflected the defeat of
the interest of agricultural productivity by the advocates of stricter party
control in the countryside; and the rejection of Khrushchev's plan for the
creation of "agrotowns" reflected the defeat of the zealots for yet another
major social transformation by the combined warnings of agricultural and industrial bureaucrats, who pointed to the cost of a new wave of peasant alienation on
one side and a massive rehousing effort on the other. But in Stalin's time,
these conflicts of interest could find expression only in a contest of his immediate subordinates for the ear of the Vozhd, and any attempt at political group
formation was considered illegitimate and correspondingly dangerous, as the fate
of Voznesensky showed.

The authoritarian one-party regime that has developed from the recognition that, at the level of the industrial society, the cost of further "revolutions from above" has generally become prohibitive, is distinct from the preceding
totalitarian stage in that it no longer claims the need to fight hostile classes
within its own society. It must therefore regard the interests of all existing
social groups as legitimate in principle. That these interests are viewed as
"nonantagonistic" means, in the official view, not that no conflict between them
is conceivable, but that such conflicts are sufficiently limited to be reconciled
by the higher wisdom of the party. The party's monopoly of decision thus becomes
in one important aspect a monopoly of interest arbitration, or to use the expression first conceived by Dr. Sun Yat-sen for his vision of a noncommunist one-party
regime,a kind of tutelage over the plurality of social groups.[38] The new relation
between the ruling party and the legitimate group interests within an industrial
society may, however, take very different institutional forms, have very different
effects on party organization, and show different degrees of stability according
to the cohesion and skill of the party leadership and the amount of active pressures arising from below.

Informal and Bureaucratic Interest Articulation. The method of regular-
izing interest articulation that requires the least visible change in the party's
organization and operation consists of encouraging the various sections of the
bureaucracy and the party-controlled mass organizations to speak up in the inner
councils of party and government on behalf of those sectors of society for which
they are held responsible--to act, within certain limits, as their representatives.
Thus the party secretary or Politburo member responsible for agriculture or heavy
industry or consumer goods will be expected to present the case of "his" interest
in the highest party organ, as will the party-selected trade-union leader who has
a seat there. The leaders of the armed forces will argue their claims on the budget and their views on strategy and the requirements of national security, as the
heads of the secret police will present theirs on internal security. A corresponding role will be played by the leaders of the official youth organization and,

in those East European states where formal remnants of noncommunist parties have been preserved within a "National Front," by some of their cryptocommunist controllers. All this is so much a necessity of day-to-day government that, as stated above, it must have taken place to some extent even in Stalin's time. The difference is that in the postrevolutionary phase, such quasi-representative consultation becomes part of an established routine and ceases to be risky. In particular, it is now also regarded as normal and legitimate that the top spokesmen of those various interests concert their views within a circle of their responsible collaborators or subordinates; the range of consultation is thus widened, and the sections of the higher bureaucracy as well as the leadership of controlled mass organizations are in fact permitted to act as informal groups.[39]

Some of the licensed public discussions I mentioned in the context of elite consultation may also be viewed as a type of encouraged informal group activity, including a measure of toleration for informal "opinion groups" within the profession, for example. Discussions among economists on planning reform; among agricultural administrators, experts, and practitioners on the Kolkhoz statute; among lawyers about court procedure; among writers and "culture functionaries" about cultural policy; and even among military leaders and experts on strategic problems[40] come to mind. From the party leadership's viewpoint, the value of such discussions is that they are not dependent exclusively on one official opinion from each sector; from the viewpoint of the people concerned, these discussions are often a chance not only to make their opinions heard but to test the support for them within their profession, and even to attempt for a time to concert their campaign with like-minded individuals without serious risk of reprisals, so long as they do not try to continue organized cooperation after an adverse decision.

The forms of informal and, as far as mass groups are concerned, exclusively indirect-articulation of interests and consultation of their representatives described so far may be said to constitute the minimum necessary for the functioning of a communist party regime in an industrial society. With Gordon Skilling, I would say that they define the group aspect of a system of "consultative authoritarianism."[41] Experience so far suggests that they are the only forms likely to be adopted by such a regime without the pressure of a major political crisis. For a number of years now, this "minimum form" of interest articulation has been clearly used by the post-Khrushchev leadership of the Soviet Union and has become a model for most countries of the Soviet bloc. But while it has, from the party's point of view, the advantage of drawing a reasonably sharp line against the risk of open political pluralism, its weakness is that interest articulation remains so selective, and above all so indirect, that the risk of major misjudgments of the political and social situation by the leadership cannot be excluded. The problem of the flow of information, discussed above from the angle of economic and technical efficiency, thus reappears here from the angle of effective political leadership. The failure of Gomulka to correctly judge the effect of the price increases that led to the Polish workers' riots of December 1970 may be taken as a classic example of too indirect "interest articulation" leading, through poor political feedback, to the crisis of a communist party regime.[42]

Institutionalized Interest Representation and Party Arbitration. More directly representative, and indeed democratic, forms of interest articulation, particularly for the working class, have repeatedly arisen spontaneously in the course of political crises and been tolerated or even explicitly legitimized by communist regimes for a time. This applied, for instance, to the Polish workers' councils created in the destalinization crisis of 1956, though they promptly lost all significance with the consolidation of Gomulka's leadership in the following years. Again, after the December crisis of 1970, the new workers' councils elected were accepted as "legal" by the new trade union leadership, and the unions themselves were called upon to act more autonomously in representing the workers' interests, but no definite institutional framework has yet been created that would permit the prediction that the change will be more permanent this time.

Most far-reaching,of course, was, the democratization of the Czechoslovak trade unions and the rise of a number of other autonomous groups representing various interests and political tendencies within the framework and with the active encouragement of the Czechoslovak reform regime of 1968; but this experiment was cut short by armed Soviet intervention before any attempt to reconcile a diversity of organized interests and opinions with the continuing single-party rule into a "new political model" could find a definite institutional form.

Thus the only form of institutionalized interest representation under communist one-party rule that has shown enough stability to be described as a systematic alternative to the minimum type of interest articulation discussed above remains that evolved by Yugoslavia. Launched during the national crisis caused by the conflict with Stalin with the creation of workers' councils on the initiative of the political leadership, and conceived as a deliberate effort to oppose an alternative model of "socialist self-management" to the Soviet type of "bureaucratic state capitalism," the Yugoslav system has over the years developed a whole network of institutions representing the interests of groups of producers, local communes, and nationalities. Of course, the Yugoslav communists soon became conscious of the dilemma that if party members in these organs of "self-management" were bound by central directives, the new organs would be as little representative as the Soviets and mass organizations in other countries under communist rule, but that if they were not so bound, the party would lose control over their actions. Yet, despite many ups and downs, the dominating tendency in the long run has been to solve the problem by major changes in the party rules, permitting the party members in the representative organs, and even those in the state administration, to vote and act according to their socialist conscience and confining centralistic discipline to a diminishing range of issues of vital importance to the country and the regime as a whole.[43] In the course of time, a point has been reached where not only workers' councils, communes, and trade unions genuinely seek to press the interests of their constituents, but where the electorate has normally a genuine choice between two (communist) candidates for parliament, and where the chambers of the national and federal parliaments occasionally defeat government proposals, with the press fully reflecting the conflicts of interest arising on various levels.

Obviously, this system permits a much fuller articulation of the interests of most sections of the population than the system of indirect representation by sections of the bureaucracy, where it still fails at times owing to pressure from the top or collusion of local functionaries. Strikes may break out that in the general political climate cannot be suppressed by force but have to be accepted as warning signals. Moreover, "self-management" has made it possible to win broad acceptance for the radical economic reforms (described as "market socialism") that permit a high degree of autonomy for the economic subsystem. At the same time, both self-management and market economy remain ultimately limited by what are in effect the reserved powers of the federal government and banking system to intervene if the top party leadership regards it as necessary, for example, to counteract the inflationary tendencies arising again and again from uncoordinated investment decisions and income increases, so that conflicts between the central authorities and the organs of economic self-management are a recurrent phenomenon.[44] Generally speaking, the major political decisions are not left to the outcome of conflicts and compromises between the autonomous interest groups, but are still in the hands of a party leadership that acts in full knowledge of their demands but is not ultimately bound by them. In that sense, Skilling's phrase "pluralistic authoritarianism" or Ludz's "participatory authoritarianism" may be said to apply to the Yugoslav system.

One weakness of this system in terms of economic efficiency is that the politicization of many economic decisions, particularly investment decisions, at the factory and commune level gives the combination of self-management and market an inflationary bias that can be corrected only by the central authorities' periodically interfering with the market in the opposite direction. Another weakness in terms of single-party control is its inherent tendency to democratize the party itself, as centralistic discipline is loosened while party members active in self-management organs tend to import their interest-bound outlook into inner-party debates and decisions. This problem has gained particular importance since the 1966 defeat of the centralistic rear guard led by Rankovic decisively increased the autonomy of the party organizations of the national republics, thus making possible a divergence of outlook among some of the rejuvenated national leaderships of the sort that produced the dramatic intervention of the federal party executive in 1971 in Croatia.[45] Ultimately, a pluralistic and participatory authoritarianism of the Yugoslav type exposes the authoritarian top leadership to the risk of a situation where it can control undesirable developments at the participatory basis only by the use of a few reserved levers of power--such as the army, the mass media, and the central banking system.

Finally, there is a potential weakness in the basically static character of a type of interest representation that accords fixed shares to given oc-
cupational and local groups. In fact, not only does the importance of such groups change with the evolution of the economic and social structure--this could be taken care of, though awkwardly, by periodic revisions of the electoral and constitution-
al laws--but individuals have many kinds of interests and are more concerned about one or another of them as the situation changes. A Slovene Catholic worker, for instance, may wish to react to one acute issue primarily as a worker, to another as a Slovene, and to a third as a Catholic. One fundamental advantage of a sys-
tem of party competition over a system of the "corporative" or standische type, even if the corporations or estates are assumed to be democratically organized, is that a system of party competition permits the individual to choose, at a given moment, according to which of his interests he wishes just then to cast his vote. Compared with this flexibility of interest aggregation by competing parties, the representation of a fixed list of interests has an inherent rigidity that may fail to reflect major changes in the outlook of the population, so that the leaders are not alerted to them in time.

Two Conditions for Stable One-Party Tutelage. Interest articulation, I
have tried to show, is possible in communist one-party systems in an indirect "minimum" form or in a far-reaching institutionalized form, requiring changes ranging from quiet adjustments in the style of party and government leadership to major alterations in the party's structure, discipline, and concept of its role. Interest aggregation, in the sense of the formation of coalitions of interests aiming at winning a majority in the leading party organs, is incompatible with stable one-party tutelage, for it constitutes "factionalism" or the germ of a hidden pluralism of parties behind the single-party facade.

That such coalitions are incompatible with a stable single-party system does not, of course, mean that they do not happen in communist regimes; it means that they are a sign of an unstable leadership structure and a potential cause of political crisis. A ruling party in which coalitions of interests fight for control is no longer the independent, authoritative arbiter between all groups of society but is the object of a quasi-democratic process.

The simplest reinsurance against such a development in a one-party re-
gime is, of course, the presence of an uncontested leader. Thus the presumed groupings among Stalin's subordinates mentioned above[46] were not coalitions of the kind discussed here, since they could not hope to win factional control by them-
selves but could only influence the ruler by their arguments. More important in our context, the uncontested authority of Tito was for many years a guarantee of the cohesion of the Yugoslav communist leadership and of the stability of the Yugoslav system of institutionalized representation of interests under party tutelage.

By the same token, the struggle for leadership succession after Stalin's death favored the formation of interest coalitions, if only of sections of the bureaucracy speaking indirectly for sectors of Soviet society. Thus, Khrushchev is believed to have defeated Malenkov, who sought to appeal to the state administration and to the consumer interest in general, with the help of a coalition of the party machine and the "military-industrial complex" in 1954-55, and again to have outmaneuvered the "antiparty-group" and its supporters in the industrial bureaucracy in 1957 with a coalition of the party machine and the army leadership.[47] When the primacy of the party machine and Khrushchev himself as its head were no longer contested following the dismissal of Marshal Zhukov later that year, there was no further sign of "coalitions of interest" influencing major decisions. But as he successively alienated various sections in his final years-- the secret police by his zeal for continuing de-Stalinization, heavy industry by his promises to the consumers, the army by his tendency to one-sided reliance on rocketry and by the Cuban adventure, and his own party machine by his experiments with the party structure and his tendency to public appeals over the head of the leading party organs--Krushchev's leadership ceased to be uncontested, and the coalition formed for his overthrow was no longer as risky as it would have been in Stalinist conditions.[48] Yet the point to stress is that all these coalitions were short-lived; they were not part of the normal functioning of the system but were part of its disturbance during the transition from one stage of its development to another.

One basic reason for Khrushchev's fall was his apparent failure to understand fully the needs of the new stage which he had done so much to bring into being. A single-party system that acts as tutelary arbiter over the interest groups of an industrial society which develops largely on its own momentum is clearly less in need of dynamic personal leadership and more in need of institutionalized bureaucratic routine than a totalitarian revolutionary system that seeks to propel society by main force in a preconceived direction.[49] In creating that bureaucratic routine, Khrushchev's successors have also shown that at the stage of tutelary rule over a mature society, leadership cohesion may be assured not only by an uncontested leader but also by a stable collective--not in the sense of doing without an outstanding spokesman in the person of the General Secretary, but rather of tying him and all others to the collective discipline of the Politburo by strict ground rules. Indeed, contrary to expectations that were widespread in the West, the post-Khrushchevian leadership of the Soviet Union has not repeated the succession struggles that followed both Lenin's and Stalin's deaths. Its composition has undergone remarkably few changes in the course of ten years and two party congresses; its internal differences, which are bound to exist in any group responsible for the policy of a great country, have to be guessed at from indications that are scantier than ever, because its members have made it a rule not to speak out publicly on controversial issues before they have been decided. Clearly, they seem to have grasped that a preservation of the party leadership's function as an arbiter above the conflict of partial interests requires that no member of the inner circle of that leadership should appear to be identified with any one of those interests, nor with any coalition of them.[50]

But there is a further condition for the stability of the tutelary one-party system that does not depend on leadership cohesion alone: the permitted articulation of interests must never be allowed, under that system, to take the form of an attempt to mobilize the masses on behalf of them. In Russia, the case for a controversial proposal may at times be argued--with the permission of the leadership, though without participation of its members--in the press, particularly in specialized periodicals with limited circulation, but occasionally even on a discussion page of the official dailies. In Yugoslavia, it may be voiced in the resolutions of autonomous organizations and in the chambers of parliament as well. But in either country it must be argued in restrained and responsible tones, intended to convince the leaders and the responsible representatives of other views-- not in emotional tones calculated to mobilize the masses and thus increase the weight of the particular group involved and to put pressure on the leadership. It may be properly objected that this is too aseptic a view of politics to be followed in a conflict of interests or opinions in any country, however authoritarian its system of government. But it has been stated here in this bald form to offer a standard for judging just where the public articulation of interests becomes dangerous for the tutelary role of the single party.

To put it in different words: what the party leadership expects by permitting the articulation of interests, in either form, is to be made aware of their existence and their arguments, in order to judge between them with full knowledge of the situation. What it does not want, and indeed cannot tolerate if it is to retain final control, is the kind of fight for the public mind that produces a clear majority for one side or the other, thus tending to put the leadership itself under pressure and take the decision out of its hands. Thus, when the Soviets and their Warsaw Pact allies accused the Czechoslovak reform regime of "abandoning the leading role of the party," they may have been motivated not merely by the fact that the Prague leaders had permitted the growth of autonomous interest and opinion groups which could express their views in the press and the mass media; above all by the impression that, owing to the origin of this new freedom in a political crisis, the outcome of the clash of opinions and the direction the movement was taking no longer depended on the will of the reform leadership itself. Again, the most serious reproach belatedly raised by Tito and the executive bureau of the Yugoslav Communist League against its erstwhile leaders in Croatia during the recent crisis was not that these leaders had demanded an absurdly exaggerated sort of autonomy for their republic during debates in the constituted organs of party and state, but that they had tolerated and encouraged the development of a nonparty cultural mass organization and mass circulation press which mobilized popular pressure for these demands--thus creating a movement they themselves could no longer control. 51

Summary. The preservation of a monopoly of decision by a communist single-party regime functioning as an arbiter between the varied conflicting interests of an industrial society it recognizes as equally legitimate in principle clearly raises more fundamental dilemmas than did the mere task of ensuring the rational and efficient progress of the economic system. If the ruling party clings cautiously to the minimum type of consultative authoritarianism, permitting only an indirect and strictly limited form of interest articulation, it will remain the prisoner of its own bureaucracy to an extent that limits the scope of possible economic reform, slowing down technological progress and economic growth below what might otherwise be possible. But it will also run the risk of sooner or later seriously misjudging the needs of society, a misjudgment which could provoke a crisis of the regime--be it by an explosive movement from below or by a breach of leadership solidarity, with some faction linking up with important discontented groups in a bid for power.

If, on the other hand, the party chooses a bolder form of pluralistic or participatory authoritarianism, it will be able to develop a more progressive economy and receive better "feedback" from the various sectors of society. But it will find itself perpetually trying to balance the contradictory elements of a highly heterogeneous and therefore potentially unstable political system, combining the institutionalization of quasi-democratic elements with the authoritarian nature of ultimate power. Though the conditions of stability for such a systemstrict leadership solidarity "above the battle," and prevention of mass mobilization by any group may be clearly defined, they are difficult to preserve in the long run in the political climate created by pluralistic and participatory institutions. For the changing needs and moods of a dynamic society breed ever-new temptations for both party leaders and group exponents to offend against them, and once that happens, a political crisis confronting the authoritarian and the "democratizing" elements of the regime is at hand.

Legitimation and Ideology

The change in the function of a communist party governing a postrevolutionary, mature society, and the consequent adjustments in its methods of government, as well as in the structure of the party itself, inevitably raise in a new form questions about the legitimation of the regime and the ideology of the party. From this point of view, they present the communist leaders both with new opportunities and with new immediate and long-term problems.

The new opportunities are inherent in the end of the "revolution from above" and the risk of recurrent waves of mass terror it implied for the subjects of the regime. The party now has a chance, and a need, to make peace with society:to create, in the words of Khrushchev's new party program of 1961, a "state of the whole people," or to acquire, in the language of sociology, an authority based on a consensus of values.[52] The new immediate problems arise from the difficulty of finding an ideological definition for the party's new role that is convincing for its own members and particularly for its core, the apparatus--a substitute for the class struggle that is compatible both with reality and with the Marxist-Leninist tradition. The new long-term problem consists in justifying to "the whole people", that is, to the various groups of the increasingly mature society, why just this party, in this composition and with this ideology, should be the ultimate arbiter of all its conflicts--why, even given a broad consensus of values, it is entitled to a specific role above society and to a permanent monopoly of ultimate power.

Value Consensus as a Basis for Authority. It is a common historical experience that most regimes created by revolutionary violence acquire effective legitimacy, both for their own subjects and for the outside world, simply through passage of time; people grow up with them and come to regard them as normal. One condition for this gradual acceptance, however, is that the revolutionary violence has come to an end: a regime that conducts recurrent war against important social groups cannot expect to benefit from it. Though Stalin's constitution made a first attempt to proclaim the successful elimination of all hostile classes in the Soviet Union and to achieve a new, socialist legitimacy for the regime as early as 1936, a mass terror against supposed "enemies of the people" was stepped up at the same time and remained a potential--and at times actual--weapon of the regime throughout the Stalin era. Only Khrushchev's de-Stalinization prepared the way for the achievement of internal peace, and only his party program of 1961 ambiguously drew the conclusion that the state had ceased to be a "dictatorship of the proletariat" because the domestic class struggle was at an end.

This change in the official legitimation of the regime was based not only on recognition that continued revolutions from above were not practical at the stage of industrial maturity reached, but also on a realization that they were no longer needed to preserve the fundamental socialist achievements. The Soviet leaders could afford to renounce the actively transforming role of the state because, in contrast to Mao Tse-tung, they no longer feared that the spontaneous development of their society would lead to the rebirth of serious capitalist tendencies. In fact, neither the competition among collective farms, nor the residual role of private plots and private livestock, nor the existence of a kind of market relations between country and town, nor the more recent efforts at a reform of economic planning have posed any substantial threat to the public ownership and control of the means of production. This reality of economic development within a secure framework of public ownership and control forms the solid foundation for the practically universal acceptance of "socialism" by the Soviet population, including most of the bitter political critics of the regime.[53]

Its acceptance appears almost equally universal in the bloc countries of Eastern Europe and in Yugoslavia. There, the exception granted for small private artisan, repair, and service shops appears in no way to have undermined, but rather to have strengthened, approval of the general principle of public ownership and control. Nor is acceptance of public ownership in industry confined to countries where a large part of the existing factories have been built by the state, so that state industry has become a symbol of national economic progress. Even in Czechoslovakia, where industry was largely founded by private enterprise and has deteriorated under state management, the period of free expression of opinion in 1968 brought no significant demands for a return to capitalism. More surprisingly, the agricultural collectives, whose origin in Russia goes back to the worst horrors of the Stalin period and from which the Yugoslav, Polish, and Hungarian peasants escaped en masse in the fifties as soon as they got a chance (with the Hungarians driven back into them after their uprising was defeated) no longer appear to be seriously controversial where they have continued to exist--though the true opinions of the peasantry are always particularly difficult to know.

If the peoples of Russia and Eastern Europe have largely accepted forms of public ownership that distinguish a "socialist" from a capitalist industrial society, they appear to have no less universally adopted the values which both modern systems have in common as opposed to traditional societies: belief in the central importance of material progress, measured in technical productivity and standard of living, for the good life; in advancement according to merit and reward according to performance; in the development of the sciences; and in rational choice of means for given ends. Of course, conflicts occur, just as in the West, between some of these values and remaining traditional religious values, and also between the officially proclaimed and accepted values on one side and social reality on the other; for example, between the socialist ideal of increasing equality and the extent of elite privileges, or between the ideal of economic progress and the actual performance of state-managed industry. But the grievances caused by such "contradictions" do not diminish the importance of the statement that a great deal of value consensus by now exists between the ruling parties and the peoples of Russia and Eastern Europe.

No less important, however, are the exceptions to this consensus. The most general though perhaps the least serious among them is that nowhere do people appear to have accepted the belief in communism's ultimate goal of the classless society. The massive boredom and cynicism that greeted Khrushchev's attempt to popularize the vision of the communist future in the Soviet Union may be taken as typical for other nations as well. The importance of this disbelief is greatly diminished by the fact that the utopian goal by now is no longer relevant to the actions of ruling parties (and to the thinking of large numbers of their members). Still, it means that communism has no foreseeable chance of being accepted in its original meaning as a secular religion by the peoples of Russia and Eastern Europe.

Of much greater potential political virulence, but over a rather more limited area, is the continued belief of sections of the people under communist rule in liberal individualist values which the ruling parties either openly reject or at best acknowledge in an insincere and half-hearted way. While these values—of individual human rights, of freedom of opinion and association, of the disinterested pursuit of truth, of the rule of law--are perfectly compatible with socialist values of public control of the economy and with general modern values of efficiency and rationality, they are in basic conflict with the needs of self preservation of an authoritarian single party regime. The explosive nature of this conflict was last demonstrated in the 1968 crisis in Czechoslovakia, the communist-controlled country where the traditional hold of these "Western" values is strongest. Such values may be presumed to be of substantial, though less universal importance in several other East European countries and among some of the national minorities of the Soviet Union, though in Russia proper they have a live tradition mainly among sections of the intelligentsia and are the source of its dissent.

Both of potential benefit and danger to the stability of communist party regimes are finally the values of nationalism. The identification of the CPSU leadership with the greatness of Russia, as well as with a supranational "Soviet patriotism," has become traditional since Stalin's time, and its integrating value among the Great Russians is deliberately exploited--not without striking concessions to Great Russian chauvinism.[55] Among the non-Russian peoples, the effect has been more mixed. The recurrent troubles between the all-Union authorities and the intelligentsia, and sometimes sections of the party elite, of various nationalities indicate that the official formula, and above all the official practice, of brotherly unity has after half a century still failed to satisfy important sections of those nations that have substantial prerevolutionary cultural traditions. With a number of others, and even with the less developed sections of the former, the policy of integration through the expansion of literacy and the widening of career prospects may have been rather more successful though the satisfied sections are naturally those about whom least is heard.[56] On balance, I feel uncertain whether nationalism may still be more an integrating than a disintegrating factor for the Soviet regime, and more a source of authority based on consensus than of conflict between rulers and peoples.

In Soviet-dominated Eastern Europe, on the other hand, nationalism was at first the most explosive single source of broad popular rejection of most of the new regimes, with the exception of Bulgaria and initially also Czechoslovakia. But here the changes have been substantial since the middle fifties. The increased domestic autonomy granted to the East European governments by Khrushchev, in part voluntarily, in part under the shock of the Polish and Hungarian events of October 1956, enabled them not only to broaden their domestic support by material reforms but to act and appear as spokesmen of national interests even in relation to the Soviet Union. This growing national identification of the communist leaderships obtained further room for maneuver with the chance to exploit the Sino-Soviet conflict from its first signs in 1958-59 until the final open break in 1963. On this basis, but also on that of the external limits of autonomy as demonstrated by the Soviet intervention in Hungary, a measure of consensus on national interests has been established between rulers and ruled in most East European countries--with more stress on "independence" in Rumania and more stress on "realistic caution" in Hungary and Poland.[57] Even the East German leadership, faced with the special problem of legitimating a state artificially dividing a nation, has gradually succeeded in winning increasing state loyalty on the basis of improving autonomy, growing economic performance, and increasing weight in the bloc. Only Czechoslovakia, where the reform leadership achieved immense nationwide popularity but turned out to have overstepped the limits of Soviet toleration, suffered a new intervention resulting in a newly imposed regime without visible chances of winning consensus on national or other values. Yet in some of the other countries, notably in Poland, the limits of autonomy and the ideological weight that should be given to national values have remained a subject of dispute within the leadership itself, making the future of this issue as a factor of regime legitimacy uncertain and precarious.[58]

Finally, in Yugoslavia, national independence and national unity--in the special sense of ending fratricidal conflict among the Southern Slav nationalities by a federal solution--have been among the basic values proclaimed in the communist struggle for power, and reaffirmed in the subsequent conflict with Stalin. Yet the value consensus on these issues, one of the strongest assets of the regime, was slowly eroded by differences between the party organizations and governments of the national republics regarding the extent to which the wealthier parts should help to finance the development of the more backward ones; and more recently seriously damaged, following a decisive increase in the autonomy of the republican parties and a generation change in their leadership since 1966, by the open conflict between the Croatian and the federal leadership that ended in a political purge of the former and the arrest of large numbers of spokesmen for a movement it had encouraged.[59] While both the party leadership and the great majority of the people of Yugoslavia no doubt continue to stand for national unity and independence, confidence in the leadership's ability to act wisely in defense of these values is thus seriously shaken, at least for the moment.

In sum, the communist parties governing more or less mature societies can by now rely on a considerable measure of value consensus to legitimate their postrevolutionary regimes. If they have nowhere succeeded in inculcating popular belief in the final utopian goals they have in practice abandoned themselves, they are also nowhere faced with serious opposition, either to socialist forms of ownership or to the effort at economic development. Even the issue of nationalism, while continuing to involve them in difficult conflicts, has in most countries ceased to be a basic obstacle to popular recognition of the legitimacy of the

regime, and in some it is effectively used as a major asset. A fundamental conflict of basic values between people and rulers continues, indeed, to the extent
that a tradition of liberal individualism or humanism has deep roots among the
people. But this conflict normally remains latent and comes to the surface only
when serious failures of regime performance raise the question of legitimacy in an
acute form.

For the authority of a regime not only requires a value consensus between rulers and subjects, but also rests on the conviction of those subjects that
the ruling institutions are appropriate to the pursuit of the common values; and
that conviction, in turn, while depending in part on performance, also depends on
the plausibility of the reasons the rulers offer for the necessity of their
particular political system.

The Ruling Party's Problem of Self-Legitimation. Why should a state
that no longer describes itself as a "dictatorship of the proletariat" but now
calls itself a "state of all the people" continue to be a single-party state?
Why should a party that no longer sees its task in transforming society by the
annihilation of hostile classes continue to claim a monopoly of political decision? Recent Western discussion of the legitimacy of postrevolutionary communist
regimes in industrial societies has paid far more attention to the problem of
value consensus between rulers and ruled than to this problem of justifying the
continuation of one-party rule in conditions of industrial maturity. Yet while
the new conditions, as I have shown, make the achievement of value consensus
considerably easier than before, the justification of the ruling party's monopoly
becomes more difficult.

The problem arises immediately not in the relations between the ruling
party and society--the broad social groups are hardly in a position to raise such
fundamental questions, except in an open crisis--but inside the communist party
itself: the party members, and above all the party officials, who insist on a
new definition of the party's "leading role." That is the ideological synonym they
use for what outsiders describe as the party's control of the levers of power and
its monopoly of policy decision; officially, the party does not "rule," it only
"leads" the organs of power by means of its scientific insight--not only in
Yugoslavia, where party and state offices have for that reason been strictly
separated, but also in the Soviet Union. Even so, where is the need and the
justification of a "leading" party in a socialist society that allegedly tends
to develop in the right direction, toward the higher stage of communism, on its
own momentum?

In the Soviet Union, where the problem has been dimly perceived since
the adoption of the new party program in October 1961, a first attempt at an
answer was offered within a year by Khrushchev's reorganization of the party into
separate industrial and agricultural sectors; the principal task of the party
henceforth was to raise production and productivity, because economic growth and
technological progress were the necessary and sufficient conditions for rapidly
approaching the higher stage of communism without further revolutionary upheavals.
But Khrushchev's solution exposed the party officials to many inconveniences in
practice and was not convincing in theory. In practice, the apparachiki were held
more directly responsible for current economic results in their area than they
liked-after all, not all of them were "dual executives" in the sense of being experienced in industrial or agricultural problems--and they became involved in awk-
ward conflicts of competence with the regular economic administration, while those
who had specialized in the interpretation and spread of ideology now felt reduced
to a marginal role. In theory, no good reason could be given why industry and
agriculture should develop more effectively if the bureaucracy of a single party,
however Marxist-Leninist, was superimposed on the specialized economic administration of the state. In fact, cancellation of the party's reorganization into
separate sectors according to production was one of the very first decisions of the
Central Committee after Khrushchev's fall; his answer to the problem of the party's
new role had clearly failed to convince those to whom it had been addressed in the

first place.[60]

The first reaction to the failure of the Khrushchevian approach was a great stress on the party's role of ideological guidance, expressed in the creation of new ideological commissions on all levels. But in the absence of a true operative function of ideology and serious popular interest in the final goal of communism, this by itself offered no satisfactory self-legitimation to the party either. Yet as the problem became increasingly pressing with time, it also became sufficiently clear to admit of only one answer: the alternative to the party's monopoly is to permit free play of pluralistic social forces, and the true justification of the former is that the latter constitutes an intolerable danger to the socialist foundations. In short, the new role of the party is to guarantee the unity of a complex socialist society in the face of the unceasing subversive efforts of the enemy.

In the absence of hostile classes at home, the enemy consists of the capitalist forces in the outside world. Even in periods of peaceful coexistence and international detente, they are assumed to work unceasingly to destroy the socialist societies by ideological subversion. In so doing, they do not merely rely on individual "revisionists" and critics of the regime but seek to exploit and exacerbate the genuine differences of outlook and interest that may arise between the countries of the bloc. The party monopoly is needed to foil these efforts, not only by vigilance against enemy agents but by ensuring that the inevitable domestic and intrabloc conflicts remain nonantagonistic.[61]

The fundamental Leninist belief in the danger of leaving society to itself has thus reappeared in a new form, because the continued monopoly of the party can be justified in no other way. Once the danger of the spontaneous rebirth of capitalist tendencies justified the need for the party's power to impose ever new violent revolutionary transformations on society. Now the danger that routine conflicts of interest between productive classes could take a destructive turn justifies the need for the party's power of tutelage. Only one thing remains inconceivable: that a mature society could find ways to solve its problems without a guardian.

The irreplaceable value of this type of self-legitimation of the ruling party at the new stage is confirmed by the fact that all communist leaderships, including that of pluralistic Yugoslavia, fall back on it when their authority is challenged. The enemy against whose subversion the unity of the Volksgemein-schaft has to be protected by the guardian-party may vary according to time and country--in Yugoslavia and even in Rumania the danger of Soviet intrigue has at times taken the place of Western machinations. Again, the party-assured solidarity of all classes may sometimes be presented offensively as a precondition for national achievement rather than defensively as a safeguard against decay, as in the more nationalist phases in Rumania and Poland and also at times in the Soviet Union. But the structure of the legitimating ideology remains the same in all cases.

One effect of this need for an ideology of tutelage is a tendency to preserve the dogmatic framework of "Marxism-Leninism," as codified by Stalin, in its essentials; a more flexible and open form of Marxism will not supply the arguments for retaining the party's authoritarian role. We can now see that the resistance of the ruling parties in the Soviet Union and the bloc to any liberation of the social sciences from Marxist-Leninist dogma is due not just to the traditionalism of their professional ideologists but to a well-grounded fear of having the party's authority undermined by a new enlightenment.[62] It is true that the Yugoslav communists have chosen a different solution: in their doctrinaire statements, they stress almost exclusively the self-managing aspect of their system and prefer to keep silent about the reserved powers of the party. Accordingly, they have been able to adopt an undogmatic, "revisionist" type of Marxism that is compatible with a free development of the social sciences while largely dispensing with "Leninist" accretions. This solution is certainly more progressive in the sense of facilitating the development of a modern society, but it has the disadvantage that any use of the reserved powers by the central leadership is contrary to the image of socialist self-management presented by the official doctrine and therefore has to be justified ad hoc in terms of acute danger to the unity of the country; this tends to dramatize any intervention of the central organs to a point that is bound to strain their credibility in the long run.

Further, although the ideology of tutelage and its Marxist-Leninist superstructure fulfill their primary purpose of giving confidence and cohesion to the party elite, they are clearly unattractive to the intellectual elite of any modern country. The result, reported uniformly from the countries under consideration, is that though the party is successful in recruiting gifted technicians eager to find scope for constructive work, usually after they have completed professional training and gained some practical experience, it is now chiefly opportunists without conviction who choose the classical political career route from activity in the communist youth organization into the party machine; the intellectual elites either keep strenuously away from political life or turn to open and systematic criticism of the regime.

Finally, the tutelary role offers little scope for useful activity to the rank and file members and basic organizational units of the party. After all, the ruling parties had been developed for the needs of the "mobilization stage"--for an active struggle to transform the social structure and the consciousness of the masses, to win cooperation and achieve a change of values and behavior by a mixture of coercion and propaganda. In the postrevolutionary, authoritarian regime administering a mature society, the ordinary party member may still have a role to play in his unit of a mass organization or in local government--even if only the role of popularizing the latest slogans and preventing things from getting seriously out of line; but just what is he to do in the party unit of an enterprise or an administrative institution? In Yugoslavia, as we saw, the problem has been solved by permitting party members to act normally on their own, as responsible socialist citizens, reserving their disciplinary obligations for big issues and times of crisis. But in Russia and the bloc, the leadership continues to waver between relying on the administrative and managerial hierarchies--which leads to atrophy and discouragement of the basic party units--and reactivating these units as organs for "stimulating" the bureaucrats and managers and reporting on them, which may easily disorganize management and administration.[63] In general, one feels that in a mature society the ruling party needs its "basis" only in terms of crisis. Hence the Soviet solution leaves the party with too much dead weight organization in ordinary times, while with the Yugoslav solution it may have difficulty in mobilizing a following when it needs it.

In either case, it is not easy for the ordinary party member to preserve a belief in his own function, or for the party organization to recruit members who genuinely believe in the cause. From Russia to Hungary, from Poland to Yugoslavia the complaints are repeated about party members who join in the hope of career advantages but believe in nothing more. The party's self-legitimation by an ideology of tutelage is convincing enough for the apparachiki, but it does not seem to convince anybody else. It does not attract the intellectual elites, and it does not inspire the party's own rank and file. Wherever the "movement regime" has become "extinct,"[64] the moral fiber of the ruling party's membership appears to be in decline.

The Precariousness of Institutional Legitimacy. Value consensus, we suggested is a necessary but not sufficient condition for the legitimacy of a form of government. It is not enough that the people who rise to the top under that system profess a belief in the kind of values their subjects care for; there must also be a widespread conviction that they will normally feel obliged and be qualified to make decisions that promote those values effectively.

In the short run, the most effective way of assuring that conviction is the performance of the regime; in fact, a new and unfamiliar regime can only begin to acquire legitimacy by success. In the context of communist parties ruling mature societies, that means that progress in achieving prosperity and increasing national power, or widening the scope for national independence, is the beginning of all legitimacy. But even in the best instance, it can only be a beginning, quite apart from the factors we have discussed that may prevent such a success in many cases and that for a much more general reason.

That general reason is that no political system whatsoever can guarantee continuously successful performance. Hereditary absolute monarchy may bring a nitwit to the throne; liberal democracy may produce a succession of mediocre heads of government. In either case, popular discontent may rise and force an abdication of the one or a resignation of the other. But if the system is regarded as legitimate, better performance will be sought by a change of responsible persons within it. Thus the legitimacy of a system of government is based not on confidence in its uniformly good performance, but on confidence that the institutional procedures by which rulers are selected and decisions are made offer a reasonable chance of such performance.

What we are asserting is that for maintaining authority in modern conditions and in the long run--and we are discussing the long-run prospects of communist one-party rule--there is no alternative to legitimacy based on institutional procedures. Of the famous alternatives formulated by Max Weber, traditional legitimation does not apply to modern societies, and charismatic legitimacy can survive the death of the charismatic leader and the onset of routinization only if its character becomes increasingly procedural. True, procedures based on pluralist democracy under the rule of law are not a priori the only conceivable ones, even under conditions of an industrial society.[65] The point is merely that under those conditions, any other solution that is to last also has to be justified in procedural terms.

With regard to communist one-party rule, this means the party must make plausible that its monopoly will normally tend to bring well-qualified people to the top and lead to decisions about political, economic, and social priorities that correspond to the broad interests of the community and strike a fair balance between its various groups. What is in question here is not the probable competence of the communist leaders as economic experts or administrative technicians but their fitness as a true political elite--as guardians of the national interest and arbiters between group interests. Yet, for reasons discussed in the preceding section, the probability that the postrevolutionary single-party regime will produce such a political elite either in fact or in the eyes of its subjects tends to decline as time goes on. As we saw, the ruling parties have no apparent difficulties in recruiting efficient administrators and managers, but they are faced with a deterioration in the character and talents of those who go in for a truly political career. The aging leadership, hardened in the period of revolutionary transformation, are themselves distrustful of their ambitious would-be successors, inclining to doubt their dedication to the cause and their ability to preserve unity in dealing with controversial issues, which the older leaders recognize as a condition for the regime's survival. At the same time, the lack of ideological conviction and moral sincerity notable among a growing number of party members tends to lower the party's prestige among the population at large.

At present, the undermining of the authority of the party regimes by such developments is no more than a long-run tendency. In the East European bloc countries that, because of the foreign-imposed character of communist rule, were most liable to dramatic crisis situations, it could even be argued that legitimacy has increased rather than declined. Although the uprisings in East Germany in June 1953 and in Hungary in October 1956 challenged the principle of communist party rule, the Czechoslovak reform movement of 1968 remained to the end an attempt to improve rather than abolish that rule, and the Polish workers in December 1970 were merely concerned to remedy grievances and improve their rights within the system, achieving a change of leadership into the bargain. But this relative increase of legitimacy from a near-zero level is clearly due to the special situation of that group of countries--to the previously discussed increased identification of the ruling parties with national interests and to the popular realization that, because of their situation within the Soviet power sphere, improvements can be achieved only through these parties.

On the other hand, in Russia and Yugoslavia--whose home-grown party regimes have suffered no similar dramatic crisis--some indications of a long-run decline in legitimacy may be noticed. In both countries, the fiction that the party knows best is openly challenged by an intellectual elite:in Yugoslavia by legal publications that are tolerated most of the time, in the Soviet Union through underground documents increasingly signed by their authors in an effort to secure the right to be heard.[66] The challengers depict the party not as the enlightened vanguard of the nation, but as a bureaucratic incubus justifying its claim to power by antiquated doctrines (in Russia) or by hypocritical pretenses that society is already governing itself (in Yugoslavia). The numbers of these dissenters are small, and they do not constitute an organized political force. But they do pose a growing problem to the leadership, causing division over how to handle them and tempting some of the members to protect them as potential allies on specific issues.[67] Their critique, by gradually filtering into the minds of larger strata, particularly among the young, may prepare the ground for more powerful challenges if specific failures of the regime should one day lead to a crisis situation.

Summary. Among the three aspects of the problem of legitimacy we have examined, the development of a value consensus between rulers and ruled has appeared relatively favorable to the postrevolutionary communist regimes. This goes for the extremely widespread acceptance both of socialist values, such as public ownership, social justice, and solidarity, and of the values of modern industrial materialism; for example, rationality, productivity, and meritocracy. Even on national values the measure of consensus has greatly increased in the bloc countries of Eastern Europe, and the balance between their integrating and disintegrating effects in the Soviet Union may not be as unfavorable to the regime as is sometimes assumed. The one critical issue in this field remains the persistence of the values of liberal individualism in Czechoslovakia and to varying lesser extents in other communist countries, including parts of the Russian intellectual elite.

By comparison, the ruling party's problem of defining the postrevolutionary role for its own cadres has appeared rather more difficult. The solution finally adopted by the Russian and Soviet bloc parties--the role of protecting the unity of an increasingly complex socialist society against the subversive efforts of the capitalist enemy--satisfies the apparachiki's need for justification at the price of a hardening of dogma, a persistent need for some degree of tension in relation to the noncommunist world, with a corresponding limitation of contacts, and increasing friction with the intellectual elite. The Yugoslav alternative of pretending that the party exercises guidance without power avoids the freezing of Leninist dogma and the artificial tensions and barriers towards the West, but causes comparable troubles with the intelligentsia because of its evident insincerity. Both versions fail to give a satisfactory role to the party rank and file and hence to maintain its conviction and dedication. Both fail to attract people of first-rate character and talent into a political career.

On this basis, the third and decisive aspect--the legitimation of the party's tutelary role before the people at large through the plausibility of the one-party regime's institutional procedures--appears to have deteriorating prospects in the long run. With the party professionals increasingly recruited from among ambitious opportunists, the ideology increasingly marked by either antiquated dogmatism or patent insincerity, and the rank and file increasingly becoming cynical and corrupt, the aptitude of the one-party regime to produce a true political elite and a successful policy in the national interest is bound to become less rather than more plausible, and the legitimacy of its monopoly of power to be increasingly challenged, first by the intellectual elite and later by wider strata.

Concluding Remarks

Our examination of the role of a postrevolutionary ruling communist party in a mature or near-mature industrial society suggests that the problems of assuring technical rationality and economic efficiency in such a society are not by themselves as decisive as is frequently assumed. Although many of those problems can be solved by a communist party regime with comparatively minor adjustments, some of the more difficult ones can be overcome only by a drastic reduction in the power of both the economic and the party bureaucracy, and thus requires greater autonomy for pluralistic social forces as a counterweight, or liberation from "Marxist-Leninist" dogma to an extent which is bound to raise doubts about the legitimacy of the party's power.

The development of at least an informal and indirect, if not an institutionalized, pluralism of more or less autonomous interest groups under the ruling party's tutelage thus appears to be a condition for the survival of communist party rule in advanced and complex societies. But at the same time, any step toward the practical, ideological, or institutional admission of a plurality of social forces is bound to raise serious dilemmas both for the cohesion of the party's leadership in practice and for the doctrinaire interpretation and legitimation of its new role to its own cadres.

Thus, all the problems Communist one-party regimes face in determining the possible forms and limits of their adjustment to the needs of industrial societies ultimately converge into the question of the ability of such regimes to acquire a long-term legitimacy that is based not only on (1) a value consensus between rulers and ruled and (2) a doctrinaire self-legitimation of the party which satisfies its own cadres, but also on (3) the plausibility of their claim that their procedures of leadership selection and policy decision are likely to meet the needs of a modern society. But we had to conclude that this plausibility, and with it the institutional legitimacy of the party regime, are bound to decline in the long run. For the limits and conditions within such a regime can solve the problems of efficient development and pluralistic representation in a modern industrial society are beset with too many dilemmas and therefore ultimately too cramping--both for the society and for the ruling party itself.

There is, of course, nothing particularly original in this conclusion. If the foregoing essay has anything new to offer, it is rather in the route by which the conclusion was arrived at--the effort not to confine the analysis to the problems of economic efficiency or group conflict or legitimacy, but to look at each of them in turn, focusing on their interaction. For that reason, I propose to end this presentation by confronting my views with the various hypotheses and models to which I referred at the beginning.

To start with George Fischer's hypothesis of monistic rational tutelage,[68] his observation of the growing role of "dual executives" seems perfectly convincing for the Soviet Union and highly plausible for other communist-ruled modern countries. But the underlying concept--borrowed from Barrington Moore, Jr.--that the requirements of technical rationality are sufficient to define the "correct" path of social and economic development for any competent leader, is by no means equally convincing; it ignores the persistent conflict of group interests over priorities at which the real problem begins hence the need of new qualifications for the ruling elite in terms of their _political_ ability as distinct from their expert knowledge.

Moreover, although Fischer starts with the intention of proving the viability of a "monist" political system in modern conditions, his last-minute introduction of the concept of "tutelage"[69] (taken over, according to his own statement, from Edward Shils's analysis of certain noncommunist regimes in underdeveloped countries) appears to involve him in a logical contradiction. For Shils uses the term in the original meaning given to it by Dr. Sun Yat-sen, who combined the long-term aim of a Western-type pluralistic democracy with the conviction that the conditions in his country required an "educational" period of one-party rule before it would be "ripe" for democracy; the tutelary function thus became the justification, from a democratic point of view, for a one-party dictatorship admitted to be undemocratic but held to be necessary for a time. It is regimes of monopolistic or predominant single-party rule which see their own function in this provisional light that Shils has classified as "tutelary democracies." By contrast, the ruling communist parties describe their monopoly as the truest possible form of democracy and wish to make it permanent, and the point of Fischer's hypothesis is precisely that they may succeed in this. Of course, Fischer is entitled to use the term in a different sense from Shils, as I have done myself in the foregoing pages. But at the very least, the idea of a tutelary regime seems to me to imply the attempt to preserve authoritarian control over a recognized plurality of autonomous social forces. To that extent, "monistic tutelage" is a contradiction in terms, as strict monism can only be preserved so long as the need for tutelage is not admitted.

I conclude that Fischer, by concentrating on the problems of technical rationality and economic efficiency while ignoring their links with the problems of arbitrating conflicts of interest and their consequences for the nature of the regime, has stopped short of the decisive issues determining the future of communist single-party regimes governing mature societies.

A similarly one-sided preoccupation with "rationality" is the basis of the model of successive stages of bureaucratic enlightenment developed by Alfred G. Meyer and Peter C. Ludz.[70] This is made explicit in Meyer's somewhat naive analogy between the Soviet Union and a giant corporation. "Rationality" is an unambiguous concept only if it refers to the adequacy of a particular choice of means to given ends; in a corporation, where the end is clearly given, the rational solution to any particular problem may therefore be defined precisely, at least in principle. But politics, even in a communist regime, is always concerned with the choice of priorities between different ends—and here one solution is not demonstrably more rational than another, at least as a rule. Specifically, Rensis Likert's analysis of the management patterns of modern capitalist corporations, describing the evolution toward consultative and finally participatory forms because of their greater rationality,[71] in fact excludes from its scope the major conflicts of interest between management and labor as groups. It can do so because in a modern capitalist democracy these conflicts—say, on wages and employment security—are largely settled outside the particular corporation between the organizations of employers and the trade unions, or by political action of a legislative or executive character. Moreover, as we have seen, the advantages of consultation as described by Likert already presuppose the degree of job security for workers and of competitive alternatives for managerial personnel that are assured by strong trade unions and a competitive structure of industry under modern Western conditions.[72] To transfer Likert's analysis to a state-managed economy under communist one-party rule—where neither the protection of the workers by independent trade unions nor the free mobility of managers to competing firms can be taken for granted, and where the problems facing "USSR Inc." include the major policy decisions about the balance between nationwide interest groups as well as the patterns of administrative and managerial organization—is _prima facie_ an unconvincing analogy.

This is not to say that the concepts of "consultative authoritarianism" and "participatory authoritarianism" formed by Meyer and Ludz on the basis of that analogy could not be useful for describing certain modern forms of communist party rule, provided they are separated from the assumption of automatically valid analogy to the evolutionary patterns of Western corporation management and hence to a "rational" tendency of political evolution based on that analogy. As we have seen, Gordon Skilling has taken over both concepts in this politically descriptive sense, and I have followed him here.[73] But they can be useful only if applied to the real process of political decision-making in communist-governed countries on the basis of an examination of relations between the political leadership and the various informal or institutionalized interest groups, without a priori assumptions about the compatibility or incompatibility of particular forms of consultation and participation with the reservation of the core of the authoritarian structure--the party's monopoly of power. In particular, Meyer's afterthought about the possible evolution of a hidden multi-party system,"[74] like Fischer's afterthought about "tutelage," concludes his argument with a bare hint at the point where the real problem begins.

From what has been said, it is obvious that I am much indebted to Gordon Skilling's insistence on the importance of interest groups and interest conflicts in communist-governed societies in general, and to his analysis of the diversity of possible degrees of pluralism under authoritarian control in particular.[75] Where I have tried to go further is in distinguishing between forms of pluralism that are by their nature incompatible with the stability of the one-party system, arising only in transitional periods of conflict within the top leadership or at times of general crisis of the system's authority, and forms that have proved capable of developing a minimum of institutional stability. On the basis of such conditions of stability, I have concluded that only two of Skilling's five variants seriously qualify as possible systematic solutions to the problem of interest arbitration under communist tutelage--the solution at present practiced in the Soviet Union and most of the bloc, and that of the Yugoslav system--and I have gone on to discuss the specific advantages and weaknesses of either for the preservation of communist rule in modern conditions.[76]

Where I part company with Skilling, however, is in his austere refusal to regard any theoretical statement about the prospects of the system in modern conditions as possible. I tend to agree with his rejection of a one-sided economic determinism, and in particular with his statement that the actual history of communist-ruled countries shows no tendency toward evolution in a straight line from stages of lower to stages of higher consultation and participation. Indeed, factors of national culture, of succession crises in leadership, of the character of particular leaders and of interbloc relations have often determined the direction and timing of turning points in particular countries. Yet, as I have tried to show, there is a real connection between the problem of pluralism and the problem of economic efficiency in the sense that the attempt to stop at the minimum stage of consultation keeps the leadership dependent on a degree of bureaucratic centralization that prevents the degree of autonomy for the economic subsystem required for maximum efficiency.[77] On the other hand, there is also a connection between the growing problem presented to the ruling party by the need to arbitrate between the interests of a complex modern society and the growing difficulty of legitimating the party's monopoly of decision in the eyes of that society.[78] What the evidence from apparently random succession of more or less pluralistic forms of authoritarianism presented by Skilling really seems to suggest is the existence of an unsolved dilemma between the requirements of the one-party system's full adaptation to the pluralistic needs of a mature industrial society and the requirements of legitimating its continued monopoly.

This statement is in sharp contrast to the views of Samuel Huntington, the one author who treats the issue of legitimation as central in his thesis of a growth of nonideological legitimacy arising from postrevolutionary consensus.[79] Our objection to that thesis does not concern the existence of such a value consensus itself, which we have found largely confirmed in communist regimes ruling mature societies, but rather concerns the assumption that it will eventually enable such regimes to dispense with the remnants of their ideological doctrine and thus overcome the tension between that doctrine and the procedural aspects of legitimacy. As this has not, in fact, happened in any communist-ruled country so far, Huntington's thesis is largely based on an analogy between communist and noncommunist one-party regimes that have reached the "institutionalized" stage in general, and on the case of Mexico in particular.

Mexico's ruling "Party of Revolutionary Institutions" (PRI) has indeed developed an apparently stable monopoly of arbitration between interest groups organized in corporate form, while allowing the role of ideology to be reduced to that of symbolic reassurance offered by ritualized repetition of certain standard phrases. Yet Mexico's ruling party was created not to conquer power by revolution, but to regularize the procedures of a victorious revolutionary coalition both for deciding presidential succession and the nomination of officeholders in general and for arbitrating between interest groups. It has never established a formal single-party state, always tolerating the existence of minor outside "parties," and above all has never outlawed the competition of organized groups inside the party. Its ideology of national independence, enlightenment, and social progress has never embraced utopian and universal goals, confining itself to objectives that were vaguely defined but clearly limited in space and time. Its leaders have from an early date normally risen by their skill in balancing pluralistic organized interests and arbitrating between them, and they have never had to justify pragmatic actions in terms of a utopian doctrine. Hence the Mexican PRI has never had to face the problem of self-legitimation following a postrevolutionary role change which communist parties ruling mature societies face, and it has been geared from its foundation to the development of the postrevolutionary, procedural legitimacy that is proving so troublesome to the communists. Even so, a regime of the Mexican type is apt to produce its own dilemma at a different point, that is, the "contradiction" between the more or less democratic character of such recognized groups as trade unions and peasant organizations, which keeps them alive and attractive for responsible and independent-minded citizens, their consequent tendency to form varying coalitions within the corporate system, and the effort to preserve for the president and party leaders an authoritarian power of arbitration between them; in a crisis this could well lead to conflicts endangering the stability of the system.[80]

It is thus hardly accidental that even the communist regime that has gone furthest in institutionalizing a pluralism of organized interests, that of Yugoslavia, has tended to fall back on ideology whenever that pluralism seemed to endanger its monopoly on final decision each time with corresponding damage to its capacity for adaptive reform. This suggests that while Communist regimes ruling mature societies could conceivably evolve further toward an acceptance of ideological erosion, such an evolution also would lead away from the monopoly of the party--a halfway house on the road to democracy.

With that statement, let us turn to the argument presented in the last major hypothesis mentioned in the introduction--that of Talcott Parsons. Although or perhaps because, he is not specialized in the study of communist one-party systems and has not, in the essay I quoted,[81] discussed their special features in any detail, his approach to the problem appears to be the only one that fully takes into account the interaction between all three aspects discussed here--rationality and efficiency, tutelage over interest groups and arbitration of their conflicts, and legitimacy of the regime. At the end of the present attempt at a more detailed examination, I find myself with the same broad result that Parsons arrived at from considerations of general theory, and in agreement particularly with his formulation of the central point which I have here described as the dependence of long-term legitimacy under modern conditions on institutional procedures. To quote him once again: "No institutional form basically different from the democratic association can....mediate consensus in its exercise by particular persons and groups and in the formation of particular binding policy decisions. At high levels of structural differentiation in the society itself and in its governmental system, generalized legitimation cannot fill this gap adequately."

To state my agreement with Parsons's general line of thought does not, however, mean that I have come to believe in the "inevitability of democracy," or in the inevitable convergence of communist-ruled and Western democratic systems on the political basis of the latter. It merely means that I share his conviction that modern societies which cannot adopt the basic institutions of pluralistic democracy but persist under the control of an authoritarian single-party monopoly will be likely both to fall below the potential of economic achievement which they could otherwise reach, and which their advanced democratic rivals do reach, and to fall victim to recurrent political crisis owing to a long-term decline in legitimacy. Such crises may end in brutal oppression and reaction or in an overthrow of communist-party rule by another form of authoritarian rule, or in limited or far-reaching democratic reforms; nothing that has been stated here enables us to predict a particular outcome to particular crises, or to believe in a "logical" process of democratic reform by stages. Societies at any stage of development may fail to solve the problems of transition to the next stage or even fall back. Whether they will do so may depend on a whole complex of contingent factors (above all historical and cultural) specific to their individual situations. All we can assert on the basis of our examination of modern communist-ruled societies in general is that those which do not evolve in the direction of pluralistic democracy will in fact fail to solve some of the crucial problems facing them and will have to pay the cost of such failure in one form or another.

Notes

[1] Following David Apter, The Politics of Modernization (Chicago: University of Chicago Press, 1965), the concept of "mobilization system" has been introduced to the study of communist-party regimes by Chalmers Johnson, "Comparing Communist Nations," in Change in Communist Systems, ed. C. Johnson (Stanford: Stanford University Press 1970), and used in various other essays in that volume. See also Alexander Dallin and George W. Breslauer, Political Terror in Communist Systems (Stanford: Stanford University Press 1970).

[2] For this interpretation of the phase of "posttotalitarian" maturity in Communist systems, see R. Lowenthal, "Development vs. Utopia in Communist Policy," in Johnson, Change in Communist Systems, pp. 108-116.

[3] Text in Pravda, 2 Nov. 1961.

[4] George Fischer, The Soviet System and Modern Society (New York: Atherton Press, 1968).

[5] Barrington Moore, Jr., Terror and Progress-USSR (Cambridge: Harvard University Press, 1954).

[6] Alfred G. Meyer, The Soviet Political System (New York: Random House, 1965), pp. 243, 262-67, 472.

[7] Rensis Likert, New Patterns of Management (New York: McGraw-Hill, 1961) pp. 222-236.

[8] Peter C. Ludz, The Changing Party Elite in East Germany (Cambridge, Mass: 1972), pp. 40-43.

[9] Alfred G. Meyer, "Theories of Convergence," in Johnson, Change in Communist Systems, pp. 326-27.

[10] For the analysis discussed here, see H. Gordon Skilling, "Group Conflict and

Political Change," in Johnson, Change in Communist Systems, for the underlying concepts and studies, see H. Gordon Skilling and Franklyn Griffith, Interest Groups in Soviet Politics (Princeton, N. J.: Princeton University Press, 1971).

[11]Skilling, "Group Conflict and Political Change," pp. 222-29.

[12]Samuel P. Huntington and Clement H. Moore, eds., Authoritarian Politics in Modern Society: The Dynamics of Established Party Systems (New York: Basic Books, 1970), particularly chap. 1, "Social and Institutional Dynamics of One-Party Systems," by Samuel P. Huntington, and chap. 17, "Conclusion: Authoritarianism, Democracy and One-Party Politics" by Samuel P. Huntington and Clement H. Moore.

[13]Talcott Parsons, "Evolutionary Universals in Society," American Sociological Review 3 (June 1964), pp. 338-57. (I am referring to this broad theoretical statement rather than to Parsons's essay "Communism and the West: The Sociology of the Conflict," in Social Change, (New York: Basic Books, 1964), ed. Amitai and Eva Etzioni, where the argument is somewhat colored by political hopes of convergence and rapprochement.)

[14]Parsons, "Evolutionary Universals," pp. 355-56.

[15]Ibid., p. 356.

[16]For an analysis of this development, see Rene Ahlberg, Entwicklungsprobleme der empirischen Sozialforschung in der UdSSR (Wiesbaden, 1968). For selections of recent Soviet research, see G. V. Osipov, ed., Studies in Soviet Society, vols. 1 and 2 (London: Tavistock Publications, 1966 and 1969), and Rene Ahlberg, ed., Soziologie in der Sowjetunion, Freiburg: Rombach, 1969.

[17]Ahlberg, Entwicklungsprobleme.

[18]See, for instance, Kurt Marko, Dogmatismus and Emanzipation in der Sowjetunion (Stuttgart, 1971), pp. 176-84, on the Levada affair, or the fate of Hegedus in Hungary.

[19]See particularly the letter addressed to the Central Committee of the CPSU and the Council of Ministers of the USSR by A. D. Sakharov, V. F. Turchin and R. A. Medvedev on March 19, 1970, now published as "Manifesto II" in Sakharov Speaks, (New York, 1974), pp. 116-34.

[20]Cf. R. V. Burks, "Technology and Political Change in Eastern Europe", in Johnson, Change in Communist Systems, for this and other aspects of the problem.

[21]Ibid., pp. 281-82. Also Arnold Buchholz, "Wissenschaftlich-Technische Revolution and Wettbewerb der Systeme," Berichte des Bundesinstituts fur ostwissenschaftliche und internationale Studien (Koln) no. 52 (1971), pp. 74-76.

[22]Cf. pp. 83-84 and notes 6-9 above.

[23]"Technology and Political Change", pp. 289-91, where the radical type of reform is labeled "type A" and the limited one "type B."

[24]On the need for changes in the planning mechanism, see L. I. Brezhnev's official report to the 24th congress of the CPSU, Pravda, 31 March 1971; also Buchholz, "Wissenschaftlich-Technische Revolution," pp. 71-72.

[25]In Poland, massive dismissals were carried out under a limited reform program during 1970 and contributed to the accumulation of working class discontent that led to the riots in December of that year. Georg W. Strobel, "Die Dezemberkrise 1970 in Polen" in Berichte des Bundesinstituts, no. 9 (1972), pp. 8-9.

[26]Burks, "Technology and Political Change", pp. 293-94.

[27]Zdenek Mlynar, who headed the reform leadership's "Commission on the New Political Model," had publicly, if cautiously, raised the issue already in his article "Problems of Political Leadership and the Economic System," World Marxist Review, Dec. 1965.

[28]Burks, "Technology and Political Change," pp. 296-97.

[29]Cf. pp. 82-83 and note 4 above.

[30]For details see Lowenthal, "Development vs. Utopia," pp. 57-59.

[31]Fischer, The Soviet System and Modern Society.

[32]Frederic Fleron, "Representation of Career Types in Soviet Political Leadership," in Political Leadership in Eastern Europe and the Soviet Union, ed. Barry R. Farrell (Chicago: Aldine, 1970), pp. 108-40. See also Frederic Fleron, "Co-optation as a Mechanism of Adaption to Change," Polity, Journal of the Northeastern Political Science Association (1969), 176-201.

[33]See M. Lavigne, "La formation des cadres supérieurs de l'économie en URSS," in Annuaire de l'URSS 1969, pp. 445-60, on the comparatively low share of trained economists among Soviet managerial personnel.

[34]See Lowenthal, "Development vs. Utopia," pp. 70-73, and particularly Joseph T. Bombelles, Economic Development of Communist Yugoslavia (Stanford: Stanford University Press 1968), pp. 68-69 on the belated elite change in Yugoslavia.

[35]See Lowenthal, "Development vs. Utopia," pp. 63-66, and particularly Franz Schurmann, Ideology and Organization in Communist China (Berkeley: University of California Press, 1966), pp. 293-96, and the contributions by Tang Tsou and Franz Schurmann, in China in Crisis, ed. Ping-ti Ho and Tang Tsou, (Chicago: University of Chicago Press, 1968).

[36]For a specialized study, see Tatjana Kirstein, Die Konsultation von "Aussenstehenden" durch den Partei - and Staatsapparat sowie den Obersten Sowjet der UdSSR (Berlin, 1972).

[37]See in particular Robert Conquest, Power and Policy in the USSR (New York: St. Martin Press, 1961), and John A. Armstrong, The Politics of Totalitarianism (New York: Random House, 1961).

[38]The concept of "educational dictatorship" or "tutelary government" is developed in Sun Yat-sen's Fundamentals of National Reconstruction, English ed. (Chungking: China Cultural Service, 1945), and in his Memoirs of a Chinese Revolutionary, English ed. (Taipei: China Cultural Service, 1953). It was his reaction to the failure of the attempt to introduce Western democratic institutions into China during the Republic of 1911. The concept of "tutelary democracy" in Edward Shils, Political Development in the New States (The Hague: Mouton, 1962), is an analytical tool based on the experience of the Kuomintang

regime, on similar ideas and developments in Kemalist Turkey, and on later comparable regimes in the ex-colonial states of Asia and Africa.

[39]For many examples see Skilling and Griffith, Interest Groups in Soviet Politics.

[40]Ibid.

[41]Skilling, "Group Conflict and Political Change."

[42]This view has been developed by the Polish economist W. Brus in the article "Contradictions and Ways to Resolve Them", in The Economics and Policies of Socialism, ed. W. Brus (London, 1973), p. 106.

[43]See Lowenthal, "Development vs. Utopia," pp. 68-73, for some of the zigzags of this development.

[44]Ibid.

[45]For an analysis of the Croatian crisis and its aftermath, see Zdenko Antic, "Yugoslavia's Dramatic Year," in Radio Free Europe Research, Comm. Area no. 1299, 26 Feb. 1972; and Paul Lendvai, "Letter from Zagreb," Encounter, Aug. 1972.

[46]P. 95 above.

[47]See, for example, Wolfgang Leonhard, Kreml ohne Stalin (Koln: Verlag fur Politik und Wirtschaft,1959).

[48]See Michel Tatu, Le pouvoir en URSS (Paris: B. Grasset, 1967); and Carl A. Linden, Khrushchev and the Soviet Leadership (Baltimore: Johns Hopkins Press, 1966).

[49]See R. Lowenthal, "The Revolution Withers Away," Problems of Communism, vol.14, 1 (1965), pp. 10-17.

[50]Cf. R. Lowenthal, "The Soviet Union in the Post-Revolutionary Era: An Overview," in Soviet Politics since Khrushchev, eds. Alexander Dallin and Thomas B. Larson (Englewood Cliffs, N.J.: Prentice-Hall, 1968).

[51]See note 45 above.

[52]On postrevolutionary value consensus, see Chalmers Johnson, Revolutionary Change (Boston: Little, Brown, 1966), and the same author's introductory essay "Comparing Communist Nations" in Johnson, Change in Communist Systems. Also see Zvi Gitelman, "Power and Authority in Eastern Europe," in Johnson, Change in Communist Systems.

[53]On the support of "socialism" by Soviet dissenters, see, for example, Zev Katz, Soviet Dissenters and Social Structure in the USSR, (Cambridge: Center for International Studies, MIT, 1971) and the documents quoted there.

[54]Ibid.

[55]The leadership of Komsomol and the political development of the Soviet Army may have particularly favored that tendency. Cf. Roy Medvedev, On Socialist

Democracy, (New York, 1975), pp. 88-90.

[56]Ibid., pp. 82-87.

[57]Before the invasion of Czechoslovakia, there was a large measure of agreement among Western students about the development of a consensus on national interest between rulers and ruled in most East European countries, based on "destalinization" combined with the acceptance of the inevitability of Soviet hegemony. See, for example, Gordon Skilling, The Government of Communist East Europe (New York: Crowell, 1966); Ghita Ionescu, The Politics of the European Communist States (New York: Praeger, 1967); Kurt London, ed., Eastern Europe in Transition (Baltimore: Johns Hopkins Press, 1966). The events of August 1968 seem to have made no decisive difference to this trend except in Czechoslovakia and for a time in Poland.

[58]The role of the "partisan faction," led by the former security minister Moczar, in opposing first Gomulka and then Gierek is an indication of the potential for ideological and political conflict of the "national issue" in Poland.

[59]See note 45 above.

[60]Cf. note 48 above.

[61]The crucial importance of the struggle against "ideological subversion" for justifying the party's monopoly was first clearly developed in L. I. Brezhnev's report to the plenary session of the CC, CPSU in April 1968, under the impression of developments in Czechoslovakia and their beginning repercussions elsewhere in the bloc. Pravda, April 11, 1968. (See also his speech to the nineteenth conference of the Moscow city organization immediately preceding the CC plenum Pravda, March 30, 1968.)

[62]Cf. above, p. 87 and note 18.

[63]In the Soviet Union, the tendency to reactivate the basic party units in all government institutions has been strongly pushed by Brezhnev since the CC plenum of December 1969, and has been endorsed in the resolution on his report to the twenty-fourth congress of the CPSU, Pravda, 6 April 1971.

[64]In the sense of Robert C. Tucker, "On Revolutionary Mass Movement Regimes," in The Soviet Political Minds, ed. Robert C. Tucker (New York: Praeger, 1963).

[65]Rational or legal legitimacy in Weber's sense is not necessarily democratic, but is necessarily procedural.

[66]For surveys of "Samizdat" documents, see, for example, Abraham Brumberg, In Quest of Justice (New York: Praeger, 1970), and Katz, Soviet Dissenters and Social Structure in the USSR.

[67]The "Political Diary" (Politichesky Dnevnik), in particular, which first became known in the West in August 1971 after enjoying a restricted but clearly tolerated circulation among critical party intellectuals for more than six years, contains internal evidence of links with "liberalizing" elements of the leadership; see Kurt Marko, "Einige Uberlegungen zur Dissidentenbewegung in der Sowjetunion," in Berichte des Bundesinstituts no. 57 (1971), pp. 8-11, 17-20. Cf. also Roy Medvedev, op. cit., pp. 56-58 on the "party democrats."

[68]Fischer, The Soviet System and Modern Society.

[69]Ibid., pp. 146-48

[70]Cf. pp. 83-84 above; Meyer, The Soviet Political System; Likert, New Patterns of Management; Ludz, Parteielite im Wandel; and Meyer, "Theories of Convergence."

[71]Likert, New Patterns of Management.

[72]Cf. pp. 88-89 above.

[73]For Skilling's views see pp. 84-85 above; Skilling, "Group Conflict and Political Change"; and Skilling and Griffith, Interest Groups in Soviet Politics. For my use of his models, cf. pp. 96-97 above.

[74]In Meyer, "Theories of Convergence."

[75]Pp. 84-85 above; Skilling, "Group Conflict and Political Change" and Skilling and Griffith, Interest Groups in Soviet Politics.

[76]Pp. 95-100 above.

[77]p. 90 above.

[78]Pp. 107-108 above.

[79]Pp. 85-86 and note 12 above.

[80]See also the chapter "Is Mexico the Future of East Europe: Institutional Adaptability and Political Change in Comparative Perspective" by Melvin Croan in Huntington and Moore, Authoritarian Politics in Modern Society.

[81]P. 85-86 and note 13 above.

[82]Parsons, "Evolutionary Universals," pp. 355-56.

PART THREE

DIFFERENTIATION AND EDUCATION

Chapter 5.

EDUCATIONAL GROWTH AND THE SOCIAL STRUCTURE IN THE USSR[1]

Mervyn Matthews

Explanations of Soviet Educational Expansion

A massive improvement in the availability of education is a well-rec-ognized part of the modernization process. In this paper we shall be concerned with the growth of educational facilities in the USSR since the mid-fifties, and with their impact on Soviet social structure. Few of the social problems which have emerged as a result are unique to the Soviet Union, but they have been generated there in a particular manner and mix. Although analysis is hindered by a scarcity of information, particularly on negative trends, the basic patterns can be discerned.

The spread of education in the USSR is usually justified by Soviet officialdom in ideological terms.[2] Soviet theorists insist on regarding it as one of the ways of banishing the distinction between mental and physical labor, this being a major prerequisite for the creation of a classless society. The individual should be trained so that he can move more easily from one job to another and should be encouraged to adopt a new, communist attitude toward labor. He should be taught to love his work--any work--because it benefits society. The gap between the educational levels of workers of mental and physical labor must thus be narrowed and eventually closed. Educating the masses also fits Leninist-Stalinist doctrine regarding the development of a new, socialist intel-ligentsia. This group comes into being while socialism and communism are being constructed; with the advent of full communism it will lose its identity, but that is still a problem for the future. The indications are, however, that rising educational levels in the USSR have not in themselves brought the achievement of these aims nearer. On the contrary, social differentiation is still considerable, and many problems familiar to bourgeois societies are very much in evidence.

Soviet educational expansion can be explained more satisfactorily in terms of practical necessity. The Soviet economy, like others, needs people with knowledge and special skills to develop it. A complex industrialized society de-mands a more elaborate school system to promote the socialization of its young. Soviet polity or, in Soviet terms, the socialist society requires that the tenets of Marxist ideology and the official Weltanschauung be inculcated into every citizen. And finally, the propaganda value of a vigorous education policy is not to be ignored. Measured from this angle, the success of the drive to educate Soviet citizens is much more apparent.

Some Quantitative Changes in Soviet Education, 1964-72

By international standards the Soviet achievement in educational cover-age is quite impressive. In 1970 the eight-year school was said to be taking just under 90 percent of the children in the relevant age groups, and a full ten years of general (or "middle") schooling was being obtained, in various ways, by about 67 percent of young people.[3] The leaving age for the full general school was seventeen, though the minimum age for employment in industry was still only fif-teen. Soviet society has therefore become one of mass educational opportunity, though it still lags significantly behind the United States. According to 1970 figures, 90 percent of American youth were enrolled in high school at sixteen or seventeen years of age.[4] The Soviet advance has, however, been much more rapid than the American one, and as far as ten-year general school graduations are concerned, the main impact has been felt only since the early fifties. By 1970 nearly 16 percent of the employed population was said to have had ten years of general schooling, and another 10.5 percent the equivalent, with some specialization.[5] Thirty-four percent of the American population aged over twenty-five years had then completed high school, but this age grouping obviously understated the American achievement vis-à-vis the Soviet one. An analysis of roughly comparable attainment levels for the two societies is shown in Table 1.

The other major index of educational expansion which concerns us here is the availability of higher education. In 1970, the USSR was second only to the USA in the size of enrolment in full- and part-time higher educational establishments (vuzy). Comparative figures for the number of graduations per 100 of the population (in our view a more reliable measure) showed that in 1964 the USSR was running seventh (with 1.57) to the USA (3.24), Japan, the Philippines, the Netherlands, Northern Ireland, and New Zealand.[6]

The coverage of higher education in terms of age groups is difficult to estimate for the USSR, owing to the popularity of part-time study and the broad spread of age involved. To judge from the general proportions, however, it is possible that by 1970 some 15 percent of the people in the main student age groups were engaged in full- and part-time courses, taken together. As far as we are aware, no official figure has been issued for this. According to the United States Department of Health, Education, and Welfare in 1970, 40 percent of American eighteen to twenty-one-year-olds and 30 percent of the twenty-one to twenty-four-year age group were attending universities. The proportion of part-time students was much smaller than in the USSR.

The extent to which Soviet society lags behind American society in these dimensions is thus fairly clear. Given continued American progress in the field of higher education and current Soviet plans, it seems unlikely that parity of level will be achieved for many years. On the other hand, it could be argued that if Soviet per capita income is a third or a quarter of the American figure, as many suppose, then Soviet society is much better educated relative to its means.

The chronological changes in the availability of general and higher education in the USSR are shown in Figures 1, 2, and 3. To make the picture a little fuller we have given indices for the number of seventeen-year-olds in the country and intakes into the middle special educational institutions. Our ignorance about the size of the age groups in the classrooms makes these exercises very approximate, but the main trends are nevertheless evident.

The more significant ones may be summarized as follows. First, between 1954 and 1970 there was a marked increase in the proportion of the relevant age groups attending the ten-year schools. Second, there was a stabilization, in the last three years, of the rate of graduation from these schools; this was in fact accompanied by a modest increase in enrollments to those low-grade trade schools (proftekhuchilischa) which provide a leaving certificate. Third, there was a rapid, though uneven, growth of middle special educational institutions, which was explicable in terms of the increase in the general educational facilities, current need for skills of this level, and the comparatively restrictive vuz intake policy. Finally, there was a slow rate of increase of overall intakes into the vuzy, with a tendency, dating from the fall of Khrushchev in 1964, for the weight of full-time higher courses to increase. The main disruptive factors reflected in figure 1 should also be noted. The number of seventeen-year-olds and school leavers fell by over half between 1956 and 1961--an echo of the wartime fall in the birth rate. The strange peak in graduations from the ten-year school in 1966 was due to the abandonment of Khrushchev's attempt to switch from ten to eleven years

Table 1

EDUCATIONAL ATTAINMENT LEVELS

USSR--Percentage of Persons 16 Years Old and Over[1]			United States--Percentage of Persons 14 Years Old and Over[2]	
School Levels	1959	1970	School Levels	1970
Higher (14-16 yrs)	2.6	4.5	Four-year college or University	9.1
Incomplete higher	1.2	2.0	Junior college	11.2
Middle special (10-12 yrs)	5.4	8.0	Junior and senior	
Full middle general (10 yrs)	6.8	9.4	High school 9-12 years	53.7
Incomplete middle (7-9.9 yrs)	23.1	28.8	Elementary (8 yrs)	13.1
Primary (0-6.9 yrs)[3]	60.9	47.2	Elementary (0-7 yrs)	12.8
Median number of years of education	5.9	7.3	Median number of years of education	12.1

Note: This table is intended to show the educational achievements of the USSR and United States in roughly comparable terms. The U.S. attainment is slightly understated vis-a-vis the Soviet as a result of the wider spread of age groups.

[1]From A. S. Goodman and M. Feshbach, Estimates and Projections of Educational Attainment in the USSR, 1950-85 (Washington, 1967), tables 1 and 2.
[2]From Statistical Abstract of the U.S. 1971, table 165.
[3]Two columns combined.

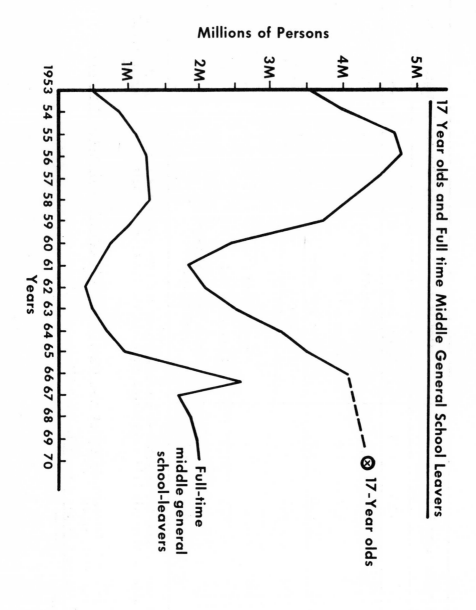

Figure 1

17 Year olds and Full time Middle General School Leavers

Millions of Persons

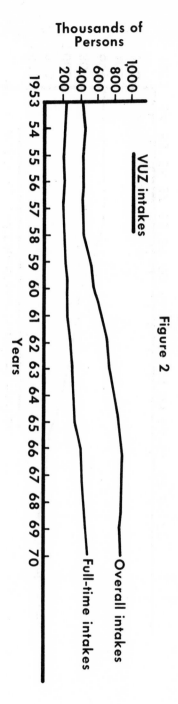

Thousands of
Persons

VUZ intakes

Figure 2

Overall intakes

Full-time intakes

Years

126

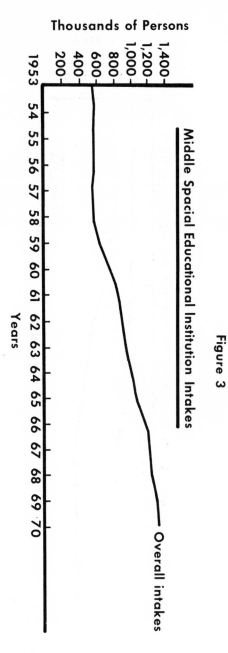

Thousands of Persons

Middle Spacial Educational Institution Intakes

Figure 3

Overall intakes

Years

Sources: Figure 1. seventeen-year-olds-estimates from J. W. Brackett,
New Directions in the Soviet Economy (Washington, D.C.: U.S.
Government Printing Office, 1966). The 1970 figure is my
own rough estimate from the 1970 census returns. Middle
general school leavers-1953-58 S. L. Senyavski, Rost rabochego klassa (Moscow, 1966), p. 60; 1959, 1960: N. DeWitt,
Education and Professional Employment in the USSR (Washington, D.C., 1961). p. 592; 1961-64, 1968-70, Ezhegodnik
bolshoi sovetskoi entsiklopedii section entitled "Narodnoe
obrazovanie i kulturno-prosvetitelnye uchrezhdenia," relevant
years; 1965, Pravda, July 26 1965; 1966, Ekonomicheskaya
gazeta, July 1966; 1967, Izvestia, July 16 1967.

Figures 2 and 3. Narodnoe khozyaistvo SSSR, relevant years.

of general schooling, with the result that two classes graduated together. Except for this, school leavers would presumably have been more evenly distributed between 1965 and 1966.

The educational aims of the Soviet government for the period up to 1975 have been outlined in the Ninth Five-Year Plan and a number of secondary documents. According to one authoritative interpretation, about 93 percent of the nation's young people were to obtain ten years of schooling.[7] The proportions of young people destined to complete various types of institutions below vuz level were evidently planned as follows:

Full-time general school (ten years)	63.1%
Full-time middle special educational institution	12.8%
Full-time trade school, with school-leaving certificate	8.2%
Part-time general school	8.5%
No middle education (residue)	7.4%

These figures are not without interest. They imply that the USSR should reach a very high point of saturation of general education (as a ten-year system) by the middle of the decade. Second, they indicate a reasonable retreat from the long-standing official aim of providing a full ten-year education, or its equivalent, for everyone. Possibly the counsel of certain level-headed ministers has prevailed. Third, the planners may have tacitly recognized that in Soviet society, as in every other, a certain proportion of the population is incapable of benefiting from full-time schooling up to the age of seventeen. They seem to have proposed two figures for this group, one of a provisional character (8.5 percent) and one residual (7.4 percent), making just under 16 percent in all. There would be no reason otherwise why planned, part-time school enrollments should not be extended to cover the residue. Last, as far as the general school proper is concerned, the data seem to confirm the leveling out of graduations reflected in Figure 1. It does not appear that much progress is expected in extending the coverage of the general school, either regionally or by social group, in the near future.

According to the same five-year plan, the intakes into full-time vuz courses are to increase by some 20 percent. Given the growth in student numbers of about 3 percent a year. It seems clear, therefore, that in numbers of people enjoying general and higher education, the Soviet Union has reached a sort of educational plateau which slopes only gently upward.

The Social Character of the Soviet School

It is usual, in large complex societies, for different sectors of the school system or types of school to be associated (I use a loose term deliberately) with specific social groups. The school structure to some extent depends on the social structure, but it may be consciously used to change it.

The history of the school in Soviet Russia is, from this point of view, most interesting. Here we have a society in which the prerevolutionary upper classes, the most active users of the limited educational facilities, were mostly swept aside. The postrevolutionary leadership prided itself (frequently without reason) on its understanding of, and closeness to, the uneducated masses. The Bolsheviks' educational program included the elimination of illiteracy, schooling for all workers and peasants, and the creation of a new "intelligentsia." It was a program which demanded the strictest administrative control of all formal education.

I contend that the Soviet general school, which is the hub of the system, has become an internally differentiated organization, despite its outward appearance of standardization for the equal benefit of all. Different sectors of it seem to have become associated with different social groups. The other types of educational institutions in the USSR have also developed their characteristic "social complexion" partly as a consequence of steady social pressures and partly as a result of deliberate, if veiled, government policy.

From the early 1930s until the mid 1950s, the keynote of the general school at all levels was uniformity. There was a standard curriculum, a standard school uniform, a ban on "tracking," and so forth. This pattern, especially in the senior classes, was most suited to the children of the intelligentsia, who, it was presumed, would all go on to vuzy afterward. There were, in addition, special ten-year schools for children gifted in languages, music, and the arts. The function of social selection in these decades was not performed by different types of school or tracking but was largely "arithmetical" and resulted from the relatively small number of places in the eighth through tenth classes. The Khrushchev "polytechnization" policies, implemented from about 1955, at a time of rapidly increasing availability of places, may be regarded as an attempt to make the curriculum more practical and useful for the masses. By the end of the sixties, general education had become so widespread as to rob general school senior classes of much of their old selectivity. The school still served, of course, as a selective agency in that the children from more favored homes did better in the classroom, tended to stay on longer, and were more anxious to proceed to an institution of higher learning when they left.[8]

There is evidence that since the virtual abandonment of Khrushchev's polytechnization schemes in the mid-sixties, the authorities have permitted, and even encouraged, increasing differentiation in the Soviet school system, so as to continue to satisfy the requirements of various social groups. At least five types of differentiation can be distinguished:

1. Schools for gifted children continue to exist. In the mid-sixties there were more than 3,500 of them, nearly all in the republican capitals. The schools for the linguistically and artistically gifted were supplemented in 1962 by schools for young mathematicians attached to vuzy.[9] (The "boarding schools" which Khrushchev favored were, incidentally, not elitist, but were designed primarily for deprived children.) A high proportion of the pupils at the special schools evidently come from the upper classes. Indicative are some figures on the special musical schools in White Russia in the late sixties.[10] Of 2,580 pupils at the music schools in five oblasts and the Minsk choreographic uchilishche, 30 percent were workers or the children of workers, 4 percent were of peasant origin and 66 percent came from employee families. (The social composition of the republic in 1959 was workers 35 percent, peasants 49 percent, and employees (i.e., nonmanual workers) 16 percent).[11] The pressure to get into special schools is very great, and such schools usually skim off the "best" children. They have in fact been criticized for fostering elitist attitudes among their pupils.[12]

2. The law of November 1966 envisaged the introduction of optional courses in the upper classes of the general school, with, in some cases, special advanced theoretical courses. By 1971 "up to 40 percent of the pupils in the seventh to tenth classes" were studying subjects over and above the school program.[13] By the beginning of 1970-71 there were 1,200 schools containing

393,000 pupils, with special advanced courses:[14] the number of them, it was stated, had not increased in the preceding years, though they could not be considered "harmful." The extra hours became, in some cases, "boring extra lessons cramming would-be vuz candidates or backward pupils."[15] Thus there was evidently a tendency for them to turn into preparatory courses for vuz entrance. Some schools, indeed, have special links with vuzy and get teaching help from them. There are occasional reports of unofficial tracking by ability, and to some extent social origin.

3. Clear distinctions can be made between the several schools in any given town or district. Sometimes such distinctions depend on individual teachers or directors and are rather ephemeral. Yet it is probable that a more permanent interrelationship exists between a school and its catchment area. One would expect the best schools to be found in the centers of large towns, where there are more amenities (and where the more influential families live). Objective study of this is not possible, but hints that this pattern holds are made from time to time by Soviet writers.[16]

4. Many well-documented distinctions still exist between the quality of education in rural and urban schools. Apart from considerations of size, the latter schools have less well trained and more mobile teachers, worse facilities and a higher dropout rate. The lag in achievement of their pupils is recognized by vuz admission commissions.[17]

5. The school system is supplemented by a small but apparently important system of private tutors, whose services are by no means cheap and are thus restricted to wealthier families. In recent years this practice has been the subject of a great deal of unfavorable comment in the press, though there have been voices in favor of it.[18] M. N. Rutkevich implied (in Izvestia, 16 March 1971) that it was not important, but other observers have claimed that a sizable proportion of vuz students make use of private tutors. Significantly, a demand for some sort of state control of this activity was made in the spring of 1972.[19]

6. The low-grade and short-term trade schools, which in 1972 took just under two million pupils, are mostly the preserve of poorer working-class and peasant children. Some of these schools are being converted to provide a proper school-leaving certificate, like the general schools. In 1971, there were 156,000 pupils in this improved type of institution. According to K. P. Buslov, the middle-special educational institutions which offer two- to four-year courses also seem to attract children from the lower classes.[20] Of 2,092 students in these institutions in White Russia in 1969-70, for example, 70.7 percent were said to be of worker origin and 12.2 percent of peasant origin.

7. Finally, there is the problem of the 10 percent of the country's youth who do not complete even eight-year school, and the large residue of ninth and tenth class dropouts who go straight to work in a factory or on a farm. The majority of these new Soviet workers are trained, if they are trained at all, in very short courses of a few months' duration at their places of work. In 1970, for instance, the figure was 4.5 million. It is strange that these young people should receive so little attention from Soviet or foreign observers; in the USSR they are usually mentioned only in debates about the effectiveness or desirability of formal versus informal manual training. In any case, it would be fairly safe to presume that these workers are from the poorest and least privileged groups in Soviet society.

From a Western viewpoint this kind of differentiation can be regarded as perfectly normal. In America, for example, the Coleman report and other reports have revealed, on the basis of a score of indices, considerable variations in the quality of public schools and the social composition of their pupils.[21] This is quite apart from the private—and on the whole privileged—schools which cater to a tenth of United States pupils. One might hope that Soviet sociologists will eventually pay proper attention to this aspect of the Soviet school system.

The Impact of General Education on Soviet Society

The expansion of general education does not usually have dramatic, clear-cut effects, but its effects are nonetheless important. C. A. Anderson, for instance, has listed no less than thirteen ways in which the school system can affect society.[22] As far as the Soviet Union is concerned, the observable social consequences of educational expansion may be grouped under a few related headings.

A Rise in General Educational Standards. The increase in the proportion of the population with general schooling results, of course, in an all-round improvement in the educational picture. I have already referred the reader to Table 1 for purposes of USSR-United States comparison. Soviet figures for 1959, with an estimated median number of years of education, are also provided there. There is no doubt that the educational level of the population rose very commendably in the eleven-year period--between the censuses, a fact which requires no further comment.

School Leavers' Aspirations. Many Soviet social surveys bear witness to the fact that the overwhelming majority of general school leavers wish to go on to a full-time vuz, although only about one in five can do so. The others are obliged either to take a job straightaway or to enter a middle- or low-grade technical training school. This variety of educational "inflation" has become a subject of widespread debate.[23]

It can be explained in several ways. As noted, the general school was long regarded as a stepping-stone to the vuz, and this attitude proved very tenacious. The intakes into the vuzy did not keep up with the output of this school. The principal explanation for the widespread desire for higher education probably lies, however, in the unsatisfactory nature of the jobs awaiting school leavers (which I will discuss below). The social problems that resulted were significant youth unemployment and, presumably, disenchantment. The main actions taken to ease the situation included the Khrushchev polytechnization drive, the establishment of vocational guidance and youth employment services, more general improvements in labor market machinery, and the organization of mass social surveys throughout the country to try to map the problem.[24] One may conclude that many young people were eventually forced to modify their attitudes under the pressure of circumstances.

The Discrepancy between the Occupational and Educational Structures. A major dysfunction has arisen between the Soviet educational system and the occupational structure. The latter is not yet attuned to take the numbers of well-educated, or for that matter, well-trained workers the schools can provide. There is a high proportion of unskilled, unmechanized, badly situated, relatively badly paid, and generally unattractive jobs in the economy.

References to shortages of skilled workers are common, but such shortages are usually a consequence of local conditions, while unemployment of skilled or unskilled workers is not admitted in official pronouncements.

A proper analysis of this problem lies beyond the scope of this paper and, in view of the state of Soviet labor statistics, would be a difficult exercise anyway. But the following facts provide some impression of the situation.

The labor census of 1962 reputedly showed that only 15 percent of all Soviet workers were unskilled and 24 percent were semiskilled, though these data have been criticized. Forty-four percent of the jobs in industry were said to be manual.[25] More recent references suggest that such figures gave too favorable an impression. In December 1972 a writer in Pravda claimed that "at present about 60 percent of the workers in industry and construction work manually." A figure of 50 percent was given elsewhere for construction workers alone, accompanied by the claim that the proportions of mechanized and manual labor in the industry had not changed over the preceding ten to fifteen years.[26] The overwhelming majority of persons employed in agriculture (who then composed some 27 percent of the labor force) do unskilled and unmechanized work. The level of mechanization in trade also is low.

Most of these manual jobs can be done adequately by young people with much less than ten years of general schooling. It was recently stated that most young people starting work in Moscow in fact needed no more than five or six years of general schooling to do their jobs adequately. According to one observer, by 1970 about 60 percent of the jobs in Soviet industry required less than eight years of general education from the workers. The figure, he thought, might fall to 50 percent by 1980.[27]

The discrepancy between the location of the population and the location of natural resources has long been discussed, but no easy solution is in sight.[28] Young people do not, on the whole, like leaving large towns. As far as pay is concerned, there is much evidence that the earnings of a third or more of the less-skilled Soviet labor force are not sufficient to ensure a standard of living for their families above the officially recognized minimum.[29] More education seems to sharpen young people's distaste for "dirty" jobs. An individual's view of the prestige hierarchy of occupations varies, of course, with his own experience, but it seems that in general Soviet school leavers develop much the same scale as exists in the United States and other industrialized societies.[30]

Attitudes toward Labor and Working Relations. A number of studies have shown that more education changes people's attitudes toward work. Better-educated workers demand higher levels of satisfaction and are more likely to be discontented if their jobs are not interesting enough. The relationship is by no means simple, but there seems to be some correlation.[31]

The Soviet version of the theory that a better general education enables a young person to learn a job and move to more demanding work more quickly was first put forward by the economist S. Strumilin in the twenties, and it has since been often regurgitated.[32] However, as some writers have pointed out, the ability to learn quickly is of little use if a better job is not available, which must often be the case.

Rapid changes in levels of educational attainment tends to create attitudinal "generation gaps." The influx of relatively large numbers of young people with ten years of schooling behind them into less-educated working kollektivs causes social frictions which have on occasion found their way into the press. There seems to be something of an inversion of skill-level and seniority in the Soviet industrial labor force, the average age of unskilled workers being higher than that of skilled workers.[33] A particular kind of resentment has been caused by young people who take "dirty" jobs for a short time to increase their eligibility for vuz entry under existing regulations. In general labor mobility seems to be higher among younger, better-educated workers, though the young are usually the most unstable part of labor forces everywhere.

Difficulties in the Countryside. Special reference should be made to the consequences of educational progress among rural dwellers, and the peasantry (or collective farmers) in particular. The latter, in 1970, made up about 44 percent of the rural population.

Educational levels are still significantly lower in the villages. In 1967 nearly 60 percent of the workers in industry were said to have had over seven years of education, but the corresponding figure for collective farm workers was only 35 percent.[34] Less than a quarter as many specialists work in the villages per thousand of the employed population. Despite the geographic and economic difficulties involved, the authorities have made considerable progress in educating the younger generation of village folk. In 1971, with an urban-rural population ratio of 1:0.75, the equivalent ratio of pupils in the upper classes of urban and rural schools was 1:0.71.

The rather specific problems of educational growth in the countryside may be summarized as follows:

a. The social changes involved have been more sudden, owing to the lower initial levels of education. According to the 1959 census, while in the towns the proportion of young people aged twenty to twenty-four with more than seven years of schooling, but less than higher education, was four times greater than that of sixty to sixty-four year-olds, the corresponding factor for the village was about sixteen.[35] The social strains and stresses may thus be expected to be greater.

b. The problem of dissatisfaction with work arising from "too much education, together with the desire to obtain more education, or better cultural amenities," is an important reason for the drift of young people away from the villages.[36] As in the towns, the chances of solving this problem will be slim for years to come.[37] The effect of opening general schools in rural areas is more complex than appears at first sight. Higher educational and cultural levels are found in the larger villages, which sometimes attract population from the smaller ones merely by virtue of having better schools.[38] It seems, however, that the presence of a general school in a small community can also lower educational levels, because young people develop higher aspirations after attending it and go off more readily.[39] More educational facilities promote drift, but better cultural amenities appear to slow it down.

c. Many young people from the villages gain several years more schooling after moving to towns. According to one small study conducted in 1967, about a third of the migrants went on to achieve a marked improvement in their educational levels in urban conditions.[40] The majority of migrants are teenagers and young people in their twenties, boys and girls with several years of general schooling, who, it seems, initially moved into less attractive jobs in construction and the service industries. One of T. I. Zaslavaskaya's studies showed, incidentally, that up to two-thirds of the would-be town dwellers who came to Novosibirsk in 1960 and 1965 could not get the necessary residence permits from the militia; about half of them went back home.[41]

d. The government's social policy for the rural population is quite straightforward. It consists of creating a rural intelligentsia, transforming the passportless, unqualified peasant, and creating a rural proletariat skilled in handling agricultural machinery-in other words, a class of "mechanizers." The mechanizers, predominantly young males with some general education and low-grade technical training, make up perhaps 12 percent of the collective farm labor force. They earn significantly more than the body of unskilled workers and are socially rather distinct. Official policy has been to ensure them good rates of pay and as much social prestige as possible. Until 1958, of course, the mechanizers were attached to Machine Tractor Stations or state farms, and were not collective farm members at all. The difficulty now, however, is that their skills make them very migration prone. Despite a big training program, the number of them on the job has been almost static; the ratio of mechanizers to tractors (which should be at least two men per machine) actually fell from 1.0 to 0.9 between 1965 and 1969.[42]

e. Greater educational opportunity seems to be at least partly destructive of the traditional way of life in the countryside. Sociological writers sometimes hint that an unpleasant hiatus occurs between the disappearance of old farms and the establishment of the new, more urbanized ones.[43] The USSR is, of course, by no means alone in this respect; unique, perhaps, is the extent to which the phenomenon is concealed.

Comparative Considerations. The USSR and, for that matter, other countries of the communist bloc are unique only in a relative sense. Economic and educational progress seem to be rather difficult to align anywhere.[44] Outstanding discrepancies, especially too much education of one kind or another, have been observed in Japan, Ghana, Latin America, and other countries. It seems that the United Kingdom may be touching the upper limit of graduate production within the old conceptual framework of what jobs a graduate should do. Inevitably, that framework will have to be changed. The phenomenon is interesting in a Soviet context partly because it reveals inadequacies of Soviet-type socioeducational planning, which is supposed to be comprehensive.

American experience in this matter has, of course, its own peculiarities. A paper devoted essentially to Soviet problems is not the place for a detailed account of these, but the following parameters may be mentioned. The proportion of young Americans who go to four-year colleges is much higher, and may be as much as 40 percent (college dropouts, by definition, have lowered their horizons). Second, the American occupational structure is vastly more favorable to better-educated workers, providing better rewards, fewer "bad" jobs and very few rural jobs. Third, the growth rate of United States educational facilities has been different, allowing better integration; and, finally, the reactions of the parties concerned have been dissimilar. Americans are used to a high youth unemployment rate; the least satisfied young people can, if they wish, start their own business or go abroad; and there is plenty of scope for protest, some rather violent, against the world in general. The "aspiration gap" observable particularly among American rural and colored youth, is thus less striking than in the USSR.

The Expansion of Higher Education and the Intelligentsia

We take the term "intelligentsia" to mean only graduates of Soviet universities and institutes, though Soviet sociologists usually employ it much more loosely to cover also middle-grade specialists and "praktiki" (persons who hold higher- or middle-grade jobs without formal training). We shall address ourselves specifically to the social background of those general school leavers who get a vuz place.

The growth of mass higher education began in the late twenties, with the First Five-Year Plan, and the censuses for 1939, 1959, and 1970 gave the number of degree holders per thousand of the population as 8, 23, and 42 respectively. The actual total for 1970 was 8.3 million (backed by 2.6 million persons with incomplete higher education). This was an impressive achievement, though some 13.4 million Americans had four years or more of college education at that time.[45]

Soviet higher education has always been strongly technical in character: In the 1969-70 academic year, about 54 percent of the vuz graduates were trained in the sciences: the corresponding figure for the United States was about 25 percent.[46] Strict control of education may have its illiberal aspects, but it certainly has enabled the USSR (and other countries of the Soviet bloc) to avoid the less productive, arts-orientated, trends characteristic of many developing lands. It has been argued that even when higher education is promoted for sound economic reasons in the early stages of industrial development the social demand for a degree eventually becomes the most important factor in educational growth. Higher education may thus develop a momentum of its own and divorce itself from occupational needs.[47] The Soviet leadership seems to be aware of this danger. In scope and technical bias Soviet vuz education is supposed to accord, very broadly, with the officially defined requirements of the economy.

Today, in most "open" societies, the trend is to provide as many college places as is economically possible, without (as Martin Trow suggests) too much regard for graduate employment afterward. But since there is rarely enough room in college for everyone, it is believed that students should be selected by their "ability." The difficulty lies, of course, in defining and measuring this elusive quality. In conditions of relative shortage, and without state intervention, any system of higher education tends to be monopolized by the middle and upper classes, who can do more to develop their children's aptitudes.

The underlying Soviet assumption in this matter is that the vuz contingent should be drawn from the main social groups-workers, peasants, and employees-in proportion to the size of these groups, because there are no "inherent" differences of ability between them. The same goes for candidates from town and country, or different geographical areas. The Soviet intelligentsia is held to be truly a people's intelligentsia because it is open to all.

On a more practical plane, the Soviet leaders recognize the need to produce unsophisticated graduates who will take unattractive jobs in harsh surroundings. (The knowledge that their own children could be safely provided for has no doubt helped them preserve this egalitarian stance.) This "egalitarianism" has been facilitated by important factors of a more general nature. First, the rapid aggrandizement of the intelligentsia for at least three decades made inevitable the heavy induction into the vuzy of people of lower social origin. Second, the authorities have, since the early fifties, detected signs of exclusive attitudes developing among the existing intelligentsia and have thought it necessary to take measures to counter them. These included:

1. Khrushchev's post-1955 amendments to the vuz entry rules and juvenile labor legislation so as to favor candidates who had done a period of work in factory, shop, or farm.

2. The encouragement of part-time higher education, which was thought to be more accessible to the poor; in 1970 this type embraced 52 percent of all students.

3. The establishment (in September 1959) of a system whereby enterprises and institutions could recommend conscientious workers and peasants for admission to vuzy, paying them maintenance grants while they studied on the understanding that they would return to their former place of work after graduation.

4. The establishment (in August 1969) of preparatory, departments in vuzy for workers, peasants, and demobilized servicemen (veterans) who wanted places in them.

5. A lowering of entry standards for workers and peasants. In recent years admission commissions have evidently been authorized to upgrade weak candidates from these social groups.

6. The establishment of high quotas for peasants in pedagogical and agricultural vuzy: It is noteworthy that in 1970 these institutions contained nearly 40 percent of all students.

7. More active Komsomol participation in primary selection procedures.

Unfortunately for the ideologues, the clash between official theory and social reality has not been resolved in favor of the former. The children of the Soviet intelligentsia still get far more places than they would be entitled to as a social group if strictly "proportional" criteria were applied. "vuz suitability" seems to be as unequally distributed among social groups in the USSR as it is in bourgeois societies, and attempts to shift the balance toward the less favored have not been very successful. Let us look at the facts available.

Public discussion of the problem has had a very strange history in the USSR. A set of figures for the social composition of the student body was issued in 1939. The next open reference to it apparently dates from September 1958, when Khrushchev specifically deplored the tiny representation of workers and peasants in Moscow vuzy. With the rebirth of Soviet sociology in the 1960s many other figures became available, but they were nearly all too local to be of much value.

A reasonably useful set was, however, published by the economist L. Manevich for 1964 (table 2). It is interesting to compare these (and the figures for the corresponding social groups) with the breakdown for 1938 (table 3). In the prewar years, part-time study was relatively unimportant and was not shown separately in the data. Table 4, which is derived from tables 2 and 3, illustrates (by means of a simple arithmetical ratio) the relationship between the social composition of the student bodies and the size of the corresponding social groups for the same years. Some interesting features emerge. As late as 1938, long after collectivization had been effected, the few remaining independent peasants and skilled craftsmen were still providing three times as many students as their tiny social groups warranted numerically. The advantage enjoyed by students of "employee" origin is clear and long-standing. Noteworthy also is the fact that in 1964 the correspondence courses, designed primarily for workers and peasants, were two-thirds composed of students with employee backgrounds.

In November 1972, V. Elyutin, the Soviet minister for higher and middle special education, provided foreign newspaper correspondents with a few more all-union figures on students' social status (table 5). All of these sets, taken together, allow us to draw a few extremely tentative conclusions about trends over time. In the immediate prewar years the intelligentsia provided a disproportionately large number of students, and the collectivized peasants correspondingly fewer. The workers, in numerical terms, received about their just share. By the mid-sixties, despite adverse pressures listed above, the intelligentsia had actually increased its hold on the vuz places; the workers' opportunities of getting a vuz place had in relative terms shrunk (although the total number of vuz places was, of course, greater), and the peasants had improved their ratio by half. Elyutin's figures suggest that under Brezhnev official policies have at last been biting; the opportunities for the children of employees seem to have been marginally restricted, whereas the peasants have gained considerably.

We must, however, emphasize the probability that these meager data understate the dominance of the children of the Soviet intelligentsia in the vuzy for the reasons summarized below:

1. Given the long-standing government policies for favoring workers and peasants in vuzy entry procedures, it is likely, as we point out in a footnote, that candidates tend to play down or conceal employee status when filling out application forms.[48] On the other hand, there is certainly a category of young people who are prevented from attending a vuz by "material difficulties," or as we would say, poverty. O. I. Shkaratan has stated that 21.4 percent of the Leningrad schoolchildren who went to work in 1963 gave this as a reason for not continuing their studies, though he asserted that the figure had fallen to 7.3 percent by 1967.[49]

2. The statistical category of "employee" comprises both the intelligentsia (in the Soviet sense) and workers of low-grade mental labor, though the latter really form a different social group. It seems that a disproportionately large part of the "employee" students come from the intelligentsia alone. A more differentiated categorization of the "workers" and "peasant" classes might show that the children of the better-paid toilers

Table 2. Social Groups and the Vuz Student Body, circa 1964

Social Groups[1]	Percentage of Total Population	Percentage of Vuz Student Body[2]			
		Full-time Courses	Evening Courses	Correspondence Courses	Overall
Employees	21.0	41.0	47.1	67.3	53.5
Workers	54.1	39.4	50.6	25.7	34.9
Peasants	24.8	19.6	2.3	7.0	11.6

[1]From Narodnoe khozyaistvo SSSR v 1964, p. 33. The figure "employees" is an approximation for all workers of predominantly mental labor. Private peasants and craftsmen then made up only 0.1 percent of the population.

[2]From E. L. Manevich, Problemy obshchestvennogo truda v SSSR (Moscow, 1966), p. 63.

Table 3. Social Groups and the <u>Vuz</u> Student Body, circa 1938

Social Groups	Percentage of Total Population[1]	Students' Social Origins	Percentage of Total Student Body in <u>Vuzy</u>[2]
Employees	17.7	Employees	42.2
Workers	32.5	Workers	33.9
Peasants (collectivized)	47.2	Peasants (collectivized)	16.1
Peasants (uncollectivized) and craftsmen	2.6	Peasants (uncollectivized)	5.6
Others	---	Craftsmen and others	2.2

[1] Figures for 1939 from <u>Itogi</u> <u>vsesoyuznoi</u> <u>perepisi</u> <u>naselenia</u> <u>1959</u> (Moscow, 1962), p. 92; "employees" in the sense of all workers at predominantly mental labor.

[2] Figures include part-time students, who were not listed separately; E. N. Medynski, <u>Narodnoe</u> <u>obrazovanie</u> <u>v</u> <u>SSSR</u> (Moscow, 1947), p. 168.

Table 4. Vuz Access Ratios by Social Group

(A "socially equal" ratio, in the sense that each social
group provides a part of the student body proportionate
to the size of that group, would be 1:1.)

Social Origin of Students	1939 All Students	1964			
		All Courses	Full-time	Evening	Correspondence
Employee	2.38	2.55	1.95	2.24	3.20
Worker	1.04	0.65	0.73	0.94	0.75
Peasant	0.34	0.47	0.79	0.09	0.28
Other[1]	3.00	-	-	-	-

Sources: As for tables 1 and 2. Also Narodnoe obrazovanie, nauka i kultura v
SSSR (Moscow, 1971), p. 152.

[1]Uncollectivized peasants and craftsmen.

Table 5. <u>Social Groups and the Vuz Student Body</u>

<u>Circa 1971</u>

Social Groups	Percentage of Total Population[1]	Percentage of Vuz Student Body[2]	Vuz Access Ratio[3]
Employees	25	53.1	2.12
Workers	55	36.2	0.66
Peasants	20	10.7	0.54

Sources: 1 <u>Narodnoe khozyaistvo SSSR v 1970</u>, p. 22
2 V. Elyutin, quoted in the <u>Times</u> (London), November 23, 1972.
3 As in table 3.

were more favored, too. S. P. Pavlov stated specifically in March 1962 that only a third of the students claiming "peasant" status were really peasants, the remainder coming from the rural intelligentsia.[50]

3. The Soviet system of higher education consists of some 500 vuzy, which contain several times that number of faculties. All these entities vary in quality, the kind of employment they offer their graduates, and general attractiveness. There is reason to believe that students from the more favored families congregate in the better vuzy and faculties. A comparison of the students in six Latvian vuzy, for example, shows an expected variation in social origin.[51] There are frequent indications of this pattern in Soviet sources.

4. One would expect that the attrition from vuzy, which is quite considerable over a five-year course, would affect, in the first instance, the weaker students.[52] There is some evidence that these students tend to come from less favored backgrounds in the USSR. N. M. Morozov has suggested, on the basis of a small study conducted in a vuz near Moscow, that the dropouts were mostly poor students who suffered from bad living conditions, or rich students who were not concerned about their future.[53] The Polish experience points in the same direction. It is, of course, a phenomenon which has been well documented at the general school level. The social composition of graduates may therefore be less equitable than that of the first-year students.

The expansion of higher education in the USSR evidently affects the social mobility pattern in a manner common to other industrialized societies; namely, the top layers of the social structure derive the first benefits, and tend to retain this advantage over long periods.[54] The further expansion of facilities gradually helps the less fortunate. In this respect--to revert for a moment to ideology--the provision of higher education militates against social homogeneity for a long period of time. The uniqueness of Soviet experience may be traced to the gap between official ideas and existing social problems, and to the manner in which the Soviet authorities have attempted to influence the social patterns. It is an ongoing struggle.

Notes

[1]I am grateful to the trustees of the Leverhulme Foundation for assistance in gathering material for this paper.

[2]Concepts taken from A. K. Kurylev, Preodolenie sushchestvennykh razlichii mezhdu umstvennym i fizicheskim trudom-problema stroitelstva kommunizma (M.G.U., 1963). This work bears, not surprisingly, the imprint of certain Khrushchev policies. I have taken these points as being generally representative of this genre, without attempting to evaluate them or trace their development.

[3]Narodnoe obrazovanie, no. 6 (1972), p. 5. For slightly higher estimates see Uchitelskaya gazeta, 27 February 1971, and Narodnoe obrazovanie, no. 7 (1971), p. 2.

[4]Statistical Abstract of the U. S., 1971, tables 155 and 165.

[5]Itogi vsesoyuznoi perepisi naseleniya 1970 goda 3:408

[6]Compendium of Social Statistics, ser. K, no. 3 (New York, 1968), table 37. The other figures were 25.8, 19.5, and 18.2 per thousand respectively.

[7]Sovetskaya pedagogika, no. 5 (1971), p. 20.

[8]This phenomenon has been much commented upon both inside the Soviet Union and abroad. Two key articles on it are by V. N. Shubkin, in Voprosy filosofii, no. 5 (1965), p. 57, and I. M. Musatov, in Izvestia sibirskogo otdelenia akademii nauk, no. 9, seria obshchestvennykh nauk, 3 (1965): 58.

[9]The establishment of schools with some instruction conducted in a foreign language was provided for by a law of 4 September 1947. For background notes on music schools see Nicholas De Witt, Education and Professional Employment in the USSR (Washington, D.C.: National Science Foundation, 1961), p. 216.

[10]K. P. Buslov et al Struktura sovetskoi intelligentsia (po materialam BSSR) (Minsk, 1970), p. 110.

[11]It is expedient to mention at this point that the Soviet categorization of social groups into worker, peasant, and employee (terms which I shall use frequently below) is very unsatisfactory. The "employee" category in particular is open to criticism since it embraces both the favored intelligentsia and low-grade nonmanual workers who earn little and are at the bottom of the prestige scale. Furthermore, it seems that the average Soviet form-filler can put down virtually what he pleases in the "social status" column. I personally have never heard of any verification. It may well be that, given the "proletarian" nature of the regime, the proportion of "employees" is often understated, to the benefit of "workers" and peasants. But if anything at all is to be written on social selection, there is no alternative but to use the data at hand.

[12]Pravda, 18 June 1971.

[13]Narodnoe obrazovanie, no. 12 (1971), p. 17.

[14]Narodnoe obrazovanie, no. 7 (1971).

[15]Uchitelskaya gazeta, 19 August 1971.

[16]See, for example, N. V. Okonskaya, in "Materialy treitoi zonalnoi nauchnoi konferentsii po filosofskim naukam, (apr. 1965)," Perm, 1966, p. 195.

[17]Uchitelskaya gazeta, 30 June 1970, p. 2.

[18]See Literaturnaya gazeta, 22 December 1971; Uchitelskaya gazeta, 7 August 1971; 30 November 1971; 15 December 1971.

[19]Literaturnaya gazeta, 8 March 1972; Sovetskaya Rossia 30 December 1970. See also my comments in "Survival of the Private Sector," Times Educational Supplement, 23 July 1971.

[20]Buslov, Struktura Sovetskoi intelligentsia. See also M. N. Rutkevich and F. P. Filippov, Sotsialnye peremeshchenia (Moscow, 1970), p. 157.

[21]J. S. Coleman et al. Equality of Educational Opportunity (Washington, D.C.: U. S. Dept. of Health, Education and Welfare, 1966).

[22]See his essay in Myron Weiner, Modernization: the Dynamics of Growth (Washington, D.C.: U.S. Information Agency "Voice of America" Broadcast, 1967).

[23]Detailed expositions are to be found in O. I. Shkaratan, _Problemy sotsialnoi struktury rabochego klassa SSSR_ (Moscow, 1970), p. 337; V. N. Shubkin, _Sotsiologicheskie opyty_ (Moscow, 1970), p. 204; Rutkevich and Filippov, _Sotsialnye peremeshchenia_, p. 240; V. S. Nemchenko, et al., _Professionalnaya adaptatsia molodezhi_ (Moscow, 1969); and V. A. Yadov and V. I. Dobrynin, _Molodezhi i trud_ (Moscow, 1970), pp. 72 ff.

[24]For summaries of the sociological aspects, see "Education and Social Mobility in the USSR" by H. H., in _Soviet Studies_, 18 (1966-67), p. 57; J. Azrael, "Bringing up Soviet Man: Dilemmas and Progress," _Problems of Communism_, May-June 1968, p. 23. Youth employment problems are reviewed in my book _Class and Society in Soviet Russia_, (New York: Walker and Co., 1973).

[25]F. V. Konstantinov et al., _Stroitelstvo kommunizma i razvitie obshchestvennykh otnoshenii_ (Moscow, 1966) p. 69; A. I. Notkin, _Struktura narodnogo khozyaistva, SSSR_ (Moscow, 1967), p. 210. It is not, of course, easy to define these terms. For an interesting criticism of the figures, see Shkaratan, _Problemy sotsialnoi,_ pp. 330 ff. No comparable figures from the 1965 and 1969 census have come to my notice at this time.

[26]_Pravda_, 6 December 1971; _Stroitelnaya gazeta_, 20 August 1971.

[27]V. V. Krevnevich, _Vliyanie nauchno-tekhnicheskego progressa na izmenenie struktury rabochego klassa SSSR_ (Moscow, 1971), p. 387.

[28]For a brief outline see R. H. Reed, _Estimates and Projections of the Labor Force and Civilian Employment in the USSR, 1950-75_ (Washington, D.C.: 1967), p. 9.

[29]"Income Distribution under Communism and Capitalism, Part 2," by P. J. D. Wiles and Stefan Markowski, _Soviet Studies_ 22: 487; also _Radio Liberty Research Bulletin_ no. CRD 74/71 (Munich) by Mr. Keith Bush.

[30]Interesting Soviet prestige hierarchies are given in V. N. Shubkin, M. N. Rutkevich and F. R. Filippov, _Sotsialnye peremeshenia_, footnote 23 above; (Chap. by V. V. Vodzinskaya); G. V. Osipov and J. Szczepanski, _Sotsialnye problemy truda i proizvodstva_ (Moscow,1969). For data on Poland see Kazimierz Slomczynski, _Zroznicowanie Spoleczno-Zawodowe i jego Korelaty_ (Warsaw, 1972), p. 162.

[31]It was competently explored in the well-known book _Chelovek i ego rabota_ by A. G. Zdravomyslov, V. P. Rozhin, and V. A. Yadov (Moscow, 1967).

[32]See V. N. Yagodkin's totally unoriginal _Ekonomicheskie problemy podgotovki kvalifitsirovannykh rabochikh kadrov v sovremennykh usloviyakh_ (Moscow, 1967), p. 61; also V. A. Yadov and V. I. Dobrynin, _Molodezh i trud_, p. 151; Shkaratan, _Problemy Sotsialnoi_, p. 348.

[33]Shkaratan, _Problemy Sotsialnoi_, p. 394. Data from an extensive survey.

[34]_Narodnoe khozyaistvo SSSR v 1968_, p. 34.

[35]_Itogi Vsesoyuznoi perepisi naselenia 1959_, SSSR (Moscow, 1962), pp. 77, 79. See also Yu. V. Arutynyan, _Sotsialnaya struktura selskogo naselenia_ (Moscow, 1971), p. 163. Figures from the 1970 census are unfortunately not comparable owing to different age groupings.

144

[36]Arutyunyan, Solsialnaya struktura, pp. 235, 264; T. I. Zaslavskaya, Migratsia selskogo naselenia (Moscow, 1970), pp. 252, 131.

[37]Arutyunyan, Solsialnaya struktura, p. 239.

[38]Zaslavskaya, Migratsia, p. 245.

[39]Arutyunyan, Solsialnaya struktura, p. 153.

[40]A considerable amount of work has been done by Soviet sociologists on migration patterns, Zaslavskaya, Migratsia, p. 271. See also T. I. Zaslavskaya, Sotsialnye problemy trudovykh resursov sela (Novosibirsk, 1968), p. 65.

[41]Zaslavskaya, Migratsia, p. 266.

[42]T. I. Nedorezova, Sblizhenie urovnya zhizni selskogo i gorodskogo naselenia (Moscow, 1971 [brochure], p. 20.

[43]Ibid, p. 158

[44]Phillip H. Coombs, The World Educational Crisis (Oxford: At the University Press, 1968).

[45]Statistical Abstract of the U. S., 1971, table 165.

[46]Narodnoe khozyaistvo SSSR v 1970, p. 646. Statistical Abstract of the U. S., 1971, p. 130. Proportions estimated by the author.

[47]Martin Trow, "Education and the American occupation structure" (paper read at the University of California at Berkeley, April 1963), and R. J. Havighurst, quoted in J. K. Folger and C. B. Nam, The Education of the American Population (Washington, D.C., 1967), p. 166.

[48]For a rare reference to this see Sovetskoe zdravookhranenie, no. 10 (1971), pp. 41-45.

[49]Shkaratan, Problemy Sotsialnoi, p. 441.

[50]Komsomolskaya Pravda, 6 March 1962.

[51]M. E. Ashmane in Uchenye zapiski Latviiskogo G. U., vol. 158, Sotsialnye aspekty obrazovania (Riga, 1971), p. 72.

[52]Official data on full-time graduations in 1965 and 1970 suggest an attrition rate of about 12 percent over the original acceptances. This is certainly an underestimate, facilitated by the practice of transferring part-time students to full-time courses as vacancies occur. Rates varying between an improbable 5 percent and 43 percent (1958-64) are given by V. Komarov in an article in Sotsialno-ekonomicheskie problemy narodnogo obrazovania, ed. V. A. Zhamin and S. L. Kostanyan, (Moscow, 1969) p. 196.

[53]N. M. Morozov article in Uchenye zapiski Moskovskogo oblastnogo pedagogicheskogo instituta 1968, vol. 210, nauchny kommunizm, no. 1, p. 107. See also the article by T. A. Lependina and others in Uchenye zapiski Gorkovskogo gos. universiteta, no. 91, seria sotsiologicheskaya (Gorki, 1969), p. 41.

[54]See for comparative purposes, R. J. Havighurst, "Education and Social Mobility in Four Societies," in <u>Education, Economy and Society</u>, 1961-66, ed. A. H. Halsey, (London, 1966).

PART FOUR

URBANIZATION

Chapter 6.

NONCOMPARATIVE COMMUNISM: CHINESE AND SOVIET URBANIZATION

B. Michael Frolic

I don't think we can conceive of modernization taking place without ur-
banization--an urbanization that is rapid and almost convulsive, focused around a
heavy concentration of industrial technology, and producing a set of values, attitudes and beliefs--an "urbanism"--which we claim characterizes modern man.[1] To
be modern is to be urban, and vice versa. "Industrial," postindustrial,"
"Western," "urban," and "modern" man tend ultimately to be the same person en
route from rural idiocy toward modern life and values--from a narrow, impover-
ished, status-ridden countryside to fast-paced, achievement-oriented, leisure-
conscious cities.

But do all modernizing regimes follow this exact road, or can some find
a different path? More specifically, do communist[2] nations also urbanize in the
ways we automatically assume that modernizing nations must urbanize? And if they
do not, where is the difference? Is their urbanization qualitatively or quan-
titatively different? Can their urbanism be considered unique, and if so, does
the new communist man differ markedly from modern (industrial, postindustrial,
urban, Western) man? Certainly the stated goal of both Chinese and Soviet
planners has been to fashion such a person--one who is socially conscious rather
than selfishly individualistic; cooperative instead of competitive; integrated
into, rather than alienated from, his environment. This was the sort of person
that Marx expected would live in his postrevolutionary society, although he and
Engels understandably were vague about the specific details of individual transformation and the nature of the new environment.[3]

This lofty Marxist goal seems to have dissolved in the harsher realities of the modern Soviet urban setting, and the ideal of a new type of man may
have become a victim of rapid urbanization. Several generations of policies
ostensibly designed to make Soviet cities and their inhabitants different and
better than whatever existed elsewhere may have instead produced Muscovites who
are only grayer and poorer versions of their London and New York cousins.
Current Soviet social surveys point to the increasing homogenization of Soviet
and Western man in a common crucible of urbanization, and these studies admit
there may be some irreconcilable contradiction between socialist policies and
urban culture, with the latter emerging as the dominant factor.[4] Thus, in the
words of one Moscow town planner, "An apartment, a telephone, a car, individualism, isolation--it is almost impossible to ignore these factors or to plan around
them."[5]

Perhaps Soviet planners and officials have been unable to manage urbanization as they had hoped because they tried to transform values in the midst
of rapid industrialization and urbanization, rather than at an earlier developmental stage. The Chinese are apparently avoiding this peril by skirting the

My thanks to York University, Toronto, and to the Russian and East Asian
Centers, Harvard University, for their assistance, and to the Centre for Continuing Education, University of British Columbia, for providing an opportunity
to revisit China. For an earlier version of some of the ideas expressed in
this study, see my "Noncomparative Communism: Soviet and Chinese Cities,"
Journal of Comparative Administration 4, (November 1972): 279-309. My thanks to
to William Hanna, Jerry Hough, Ezra Vogel, and Zev Katz for their useful advice
and assistance.

issue--that is, by trying to transform values without (or before) urbanizing. Officially, they depict the city as an unfavorable, indeed dangerous, environment for the nurturing of the new Chinese man. Although cities are tolerated, they must neither be encouraged to grow nor venerated as the Soviet Union has done. The new Chinese man is a peasant, "covered with mud and honest sweat of toil, tempering his heart red in the process," whereas his urban brothers and sisters can at best "talk but not work."[6] Industrial development is not yet the all-consuming end that it became for the Soviets, so Chinese cities do not exert the kind of economic "pull" on the hinterland that occurred in the Soviet Union in the 1930s, when hordes of peasants entered the cities, almost doubling the country's urban population in one decade. Moreover, China has developed a "reverse push" policy of systematically expelling large numbers of urban dwellers, mainly high-school graduates, from cities to the countryside for permanent resettlement. By significantly reversing what we assume to be the "normal" population flow between town and country during modernization, the Chinese today have staked a legitimate claim to uniqueness.

It is in this context, of unique Soviet and Chinese approaches (and responses) to the urbanization question, that this study was conceived. The first premise was that the Soviet Union and China have produced distinctive urban strategies and policies for transforming the urban environment, the values of individuals living in that setting, and even the role of the city itself. These policies and strategies were not always the primary goal of communist planners, and sometimes they were perfunctorily followed rather than explicitly applied. Nor are the two communist urban "models" similar in nature and design, even if we take into account the Chinese "developmental lag," that is, substituting the Soviet Union of 1930 for the China of 1958 or 1973. What the two models have in common is their desire to produce a new environment in which new values can be created, and their insistence that their urbanization and urbanism is different from, and superior to, the Western brand. My second premise was that Chinese and Soviet urban strategies differ substantially from each other. The Soviet urban model appears with each passing day to move closer to the West, whereas the Chinese stubbornly persist along their original journey away from the mainstream of modernization. Thus, while the two models are "communist" in name and in basic assumptions about the nature of man, they are dissimilar in current practice. I shall examine these premises in the following sections of this study, first through a loose comparative framework using four categories (national urban policies, socialist urban policies, community organization, and problems of urban development), and then by a discussion and analysis of current trends in Soviet and Chinese urban development.

National Urban Policies

Urban objectives are subordinate to national objectives--the most important of the common features shared by the Chinese and Soviet models. Priorities are centrally determined, and urban development takes place within a national population grid in which growth is restricted in some sectors and encouraged in others, and where the movement of people from country to town (and vice versa) is officially managed. These policies are developed on party instructions in centralized planning institutes (for example, the USSR Town Planning Institute) and then put into practice through party and state resolutions and directives.[7] The head of the demographic sector of the USSR Town Planning Institute notes, "Deliberate limitation of the population of cities containing more than 500,000 inhabitants has been a long-standing Soviet policy. We limit the excessive growth of cities for three reasons. First, cities become uneconomical if they are too big. Second, it is harder to manage and administer large agglomerations of people. Third, we want to prevent the overconcentration of people in the more industrialized western part of the USSR--we need to fill in some of the vast spaces in the Soviet east." Chinese urban officials express similar views, and the head of a Shanghai housing project observes, "Since the middle 1950s we have followed a policy of rationally redistributing China's population throughout the country, to lessen China's economic and strategic dependence on the eastern coastal areas. We have limited the population of our biggest cities and have encouraged people to go inland and build up our Western areas."[8]

Both the USSR and China restrict industrial expansion in large cities. Promyslov, the current mayor of Moscow, notes that the city's growth rate has been reduced owing to policies "which prohibit the construction of new factories in Moscow, based upon priorities restricting industrial development in large Soviet cities."[9] This policy is also advocated in China; in the late 1960s factories and research institutes were moved out of Peking and relocated beyond commuting range.[10] New industrial projects are funneled into smaller cities and towns to deconcentrate major cities and to stimulate economic growth in less developed areas. New towns have been created to exploit natural resources (oil at Taching, hydroelectric power at Bratsk) and to encourage population movement into Chinese and Soviet frontier regions. In keeping with Chairman Mao's policy of zi li geng sheng (self-reliance), an increasing number of small factories are located in China's rural areas to "decentralize" a part of the economy and slow down the growth of cities, while also contributing, in time, to the transformation of rural values.[11] Traveling through eastern China, one is occasionally startled to see such factories awkwardly sandwiched between thatched village houses or in the midst of fields--factories that would never have been put there if China did not have a national policy promoting urban deconcentration and industrial dispersion.

China and the Soviet Union both want to narrow the urban-rural gap during modernization, to "eliminate the differences between town and country," though they approach this Marxist goal from opposing perspectives. Soviet urban planners and officials assume that the differences between town and country will vanish when the country resembles the city. Cities are the modern sector, and it is in that urban image that the USSR has been modernizing, from the time Stalin decided to industrialize and urbanize, utilizing the labor of millions of peasants driven off the land during collectivization. Today the Soviet countryside lags behind the urban sector and remains a depressed area from which each new generation can hardly wait to escape. China, on the other hand, has formulated an urban policy which favors countryside over town. During the Cultural Revolution, purifying and revolutionizing values of rural life were re-emphasized as campaigns of hsia-fang and shang-shan hsia-hsiang--sending millions of urban cadres and youth "down" for short-term or permanent stays in the countryside--were accelerated. Cadres who had allegedly succumbed to the temptations of urban corruption, laziness, bureaucratism, and conservatism, are "taking a bath" while working among the peasants or in special rural schools (May 7 Cadre Schools), and high-school graduates are being asked to leave their homes and families to settle permanently in the countryside. Other policies designed to help uplift the countryside include increasing investment in village housing and in other amenities; upgrading local cultural and educational facilities, and giving first priority to rural youths in the new admissions policies of urban universities; inflating the value of rural produce to raise incomes; generating a measure of economic self-sufficiency through a network of small-scale factories utilizing local resources.

Being part of a system in which national priorities prevail over local demands, Soviet and Chinese municipalities find that what they perceive to be urgent "special needs" are not invariably viewed as being in the national interest by policy makers in Peking or Moscow. Nor do cities have much control over budgets, industrial location, production, and the staffing of major urban posts. Municipal revenues are allocated through a centralized financial apparatus which permits practically no local independence. In the Soviet Union, less than 10 percent of municipal revenue comes from taxes on local sales and properties leveled by municipal governments, whereas New York City raises almost two-thirds of its operating revenues in this manner. Soviet and Chinese city governments have almost no effective control over industries located on their territories; most factories are accountable to higher-level ministries and committees, paying scant attention to city governments. Top urban posts in both countries are staffed by higher party and stage organs, and all municipal "decisions" are subject to approval by these organs--following the fundamental principles of dual subordination and democratic centralism--so that every city party organization is held accountable for its actions to a higher party body.[12] This obviously restricts local autonomy compared with North American municipalities, though Soviet and Chinese urban officials would argue that urban autonomy is a phony issue raised by bourgeois critics. One Leningrad offical replied, "Look at New York City. Where is its so-called autonomy? A freedom to shrivel up and die? What powers does that city have that we do not have in Leningrad?"

Socialist Urban Policies

Not only is communist urban policy "national," it is also "socialist," and this socialist urban policy has four elements: planning; public ownership and use of land and other resources; standardization/equalization; and public services and facilities. Urban development must first of all be planned, from the center down to the smallest municipality; spontaneous urban development is by socialist definition an impossibility. Promyslov notes that Moscow has just approved its most recent city plan. "Compared with other major cities such as Tokyo and New York," he said, "Moscow is fortunate. We have the capacity to plan for the future. For example, we anticipated the private car era by building wide streets and establishing a first-class public transportation system." Although planning is equally valued in China, there are far fewer detailed urban master plans there, reflecting the lower priority the Chinese place on investment in urban infrastructure and spatial design. According to one Nanking official, this may be changing: "It gets more complicated all the time. Where do you build a sewer? What size? How do you relate it to the other parts of a city? That is why we will need more detailed urban planning, and this is possible only in a socialist country which emphasizes planning and which has the means to enforce its planning laws."

Public ownership of land and economic resources makes urban planning feasible, facilitating urban redevelopment, slum clearance, and the construction of new urban areas by stressing social need rather than the economics of location and supply and demand. What North American town planner wouldn't be envious of a situation where planning decisions can be made instantly, in the public interest, without the agonies and delays of zoning, land speculation, and expropriation? When Moscow redeveloped her central core in the 1920s and 1930s, planners were able to move any person and any building at any time to a new location--only technology (or its lack) could limit the nature and extent of the city's redevelopment, and the same can be said of the regeneration of central Peking in the 1950s. This control over land use and the economic resources of the urban region has not always worked out in practice, particularly in those Soviet and Chinese "company towns" where one or two giant industries under another jurisdiction manage to thwart integrated urban redevelopment.[13]

Standardization/equalization establishes that all citizens have an equal right to cheap urban facilities, regardless of where they live or who they are. The price of a square meter of housing space, a two-kilometer bus ride, a good meal, a pair of shoes, an hour in the public bathhouse, the tenth row at a concert--these ought to be reasonably similar within cities and among cities, so that those residing in Harbin or in Minsk will not have advantages over those living in Irkutsk or Lanchow. Of course it is impossible to standardize or

equalize so precisely, given regional and local differences, individual preferences, and wage differentials. Still, when two hundred grams of hamburger (<u>kot-
lety</u>) eaten in Irkutsk costs the same as an identical amount of hamburger eaten
in a Leningrad restaurant thousands of miles away, at least part of that goal is
being realized.

The fourth element in socialist urban policy, provision of public
facilities and services, may be the most ideologically inspired and innovative,
since it assumes that if public facilities existed people would use them collectively, and in so doing their selfish, individualistic attitudes and values
would be transformed. The planners favor state-built apartments and public
transportation systems over private houses and individually owned automobiles;
and communal dining halls, public parks, and day-care centers over private kitch-
ens, private gardens, and stay-at-home housewives. Some of these facilities are
valued by most citizens, for example, day-care centers, public parks, and public
transportation, but others, especially communal eating facilities, have not caught
on or are too expensive to build and administer. Thus a considerable range of
private alternatives still exists in Chinese and Soviet cities. The average
Muscovite is not able to own a house in town, but he can decide to eat in his
apartment or go to a cheaper public mess hall; he can choose whether to save up
for five years to buy a car or ride the subway and use his money for something
else; his wife can choose whether to stay at home and take care of little
Anya or deposit her in a day-care center on her way to work. This dualism will
continue indefinitely, perhaps forever, as an uneasy balance has been struck
among ideological imperatives, economic realities, and persisting values.

Community Organization

The new communist man is to take an active part in apartment house,
residents', and lane committees, public militia brigades, and similar organizations. This participation is seen as a creative process: residents acquire
group consciousness, a sense of belonging personally to a concrete part of an
abstract urban agglomeration. Additionally, a strong sense of community organization will make residents more receptive to, and aware of, the wishes and
policies of higher-level leaders,[14] and it fosters habits of self-government and
"the administration of things" which ideally should characterize the transition
from socialism to communism.

To meet these goals, policy-makers have experimented with various types
of urban subcommunities--the USSR with the neighborhood unit and the Chinese with
the urban commune. The neighborhood unit (<u>mikrorayon</u>), developed in the 1950s
integrated residential and service facilities in units of 4,000 to 18,000 inhabitants living in high-rise apartment buildings. The physical structure of these
units was of great importance--population densities kept low, plenty of green
space surrounding the buildings, three tiers of services, all within easy transportation range. Planners provided the necessary commercial, cultural, and
recreational facilities, so that residents would need to leave the neighborhood
only to go to work. Community consciousness would develop logically, from the
nature of the neighborhood's physical structure and functions, and from mass
participation in neighborhood-oriented tasks such as tree-planting, maintenance
of buildings, and volunteer militia work. Also in the late 1950s, the Chinese
developed the urban commune (<u>cheng shih kung she</u>), superficially similar to the
<u>mikrorayon</u> though differing in certain fundamental concepts, principally in the
inclusion of production as a community function and in its size (some urban
communes eventually included more than 60,000 persons).[15] Further, the Chinese
tended to carve communes out of existing urban areas, whereas the neighborhood
unit was formed in freshly constructed new suburban areas. Although the Chinese
were interested in developing community consciousness through participation, it

appeared that their primary goal was mass mobilization for production and political support rather than participation for sociopsychological change.

Although neither the urban commune nor the neighborhood units has endured as conceived, progress has been made in some aspects of community organization. First, it is almost impossible for citizens not to get involved; they may feel alienated, but not because they are ignored. A large corps of activists ensures that everyone is drawn into community affairs, into the large network of mass organizations. In a typical Chinese neighborhood, walls are thin and everyone knows your business; if your cousin from the countryside arrives for an unannounced visit, the public security official, acting on a neighbor's tip, will be there the next day. Second, as cities continue to grow in size and complexity, neighborhoods and suburban organizations acquire increased administrative importance, particularly in the area of housing allocation and maintenance. Higher level authorities can increasingly rely upon these subcommunities for administrative assistance at the lowest levels.

Problems of Urban Development

Frequent use of the hortative (should, ought) and of the future tense (shall, will) points up the precariousness of policies designed to reshape man and his urban environment. In the light of present reality, as I have already indicated, there are many failures, at least in the short run. Thus, while both countries have a national urban policy, some cities are favored over others, and many municipalities are generally not supportive of national restrictions on their autonomy. Municipal leaders chafe at limitations placed upon them by the center, and they dislike being told what to do by officials in Peking or in Moscow. Centralized planning, while egalitarian and comprehensive, is also inelastic, allowing little scope for local conditions or contributions. Planning also brings bureaucratization and ossification instead of innovation and flexibility. Planners make mistakes, and their omniscience is viewed with some suspicion in both countries. "Planners don't always know what is right," remarked a Soviet official, "especially those who insist on applying what works in Moscow to all cities, big and small." Town planners may also not be getting the job done. In the Soviet Union some urban master plans are still incomplete or lacking, and many cities do not have a chief architect, a situation which is far worse in China.

Important policies have proved either unworkable or only partially successful--for example, that limiting the population of large cities and dispersing population more evenly throughout each country. Although armed with the resources of a totalist state, planners simply have been unable to limit the population of their largest cities, or to effectively control population movement. Internal passports, control over residence requirements, and job opportunities in cities--none of these measures has worked well. Industrial expansion goes on within the largest cities, and small towns continue to stagnate economically. The demands of the economic planners for increased productivity per capita override the policies of the town planners when there is a conflict between them, and there are many such conflicts, especially in "company towns." Despite socialization of the means of production and public ownership of land, various ministries compete for scarce and desirable city space. A Moscow planner admitted, "Land has a value here, just as in New York. When two ministries want the same plot of land for a factory or for housing their workers, the 'price' of that land goes up and a concession is made to someone. Something, not necessarily money, is exchanged for the right to build on that land."

Urban infrastructure (housing, transportation, facilities, and services) remains poorly developed, mainly because of low urban investment priorities. Despite the past fifteen years of massive housing construction, Soviet cities have not made up for years of urban neglect, and per capita housing space still is only about 60 square feet (a room 6' x 10'). In Shanghai it is probably 20 square feet (a room 4' x 5'). All other elements in urban infrastructure are similarly retarded, though the situation is finally improving in Soviet cities. Socialist urban policies suffer because of a chronic lack of economic resources; public facilities remain unbuilt, and private alternatives are tolerated to ameliorate urban scarcities (cooperative and private housing represent a large proportion of the Soviet housing sector; private entrepreneurs continue to provide much-needed goods and services in Chinese cities). The neighborhood unit has been modified almost out of existence because of economic restrictions; densities were raised, the amount of green space reduced, and services skimped on or forgotten altogether. Although there has been significant progress toward standardization/ equalization of services and facilities, these are not distributed equally either among citizens of a particular city or among cities, owing mainly to shortages of these facilities and services in societies which have differential wages. Those that can afford them or who occupy a special status have first claim on these scarce goods.

Soviet urbanologists admit that there are contradictions between what should be and what is, although many argue that these are short-run problems, easily surmountable when adequate resources become available. This avoids the question of systemic incapacities to deal with fundamental problems of urban development--incapacities inherent in the nature of centralized planning and control, in the paramount importance attached to increased productivity per capita, and in the relationship between urbanization and socialist values. The Chinese appear to have made a pragmatic decision to postpone solutions to these problems or answers to these questions by focusing heavily upon the countryside, in effect paying lip service to the city. "We just don't have the resources to develop both town and country simultaneously," said one Chinese official, "so we have limited urban development. When you lack resources you cannot do everything that you wish." Is "lack of resources" a euphemism socialist urban planners use to brush aside fundamental incapacities to solve urban problems, or might the phrase only suggest that these policies were prematurely applied by those too eager to grasp at the future?

Current Developments

From less than 15 percent in 1920, the Soviet urban population has now reached beyond 60 percent. Moscow, which was supposed to stabilize at 5 million, has 8 million; cities with more than 100,000 inhabitants contain over half the urban population, and the highest rate of population growth occurs in cities with more than 500,000 inhabitants. Some Soviet urbanologists, therefore, are questioning the policy of size limitation, arguing that it is unenforceable. The leading proponent of this viewpoint says large cities are more economically productive, that urbanization and population concentration are inevitable and unstoppable, and that people will go out of their way to gain the benefits of urban bigness.[16] "Many commute daily to Moscow, spending up to two hours en route, from as far away as Serpukhov and Mozhaisk, from Kashira and Kolomna, sixty or more miles away," he states, concluding that "the present Soviet policy of regulating the growth of cities is not based upon a precise knowledge of these objective laws, nor of the relative advantages and disadvantages of cities of various sizes."[17] If these views become official policy, then the future direction of Soviet development will be away from equalization and more along the path taken by cities in the West during industrialization (i.e., unrestricted concentration of population in large units; stagnation of small towns and cities). In China size limitation poses a problem, but the circumstances and solutions are different. China is less than 20 percent urbanized, and while population concentration has occurred, the scale of the increase is smaller and more manageable. It is manageable because of China's policies of shipping surplus urban dwellers to permanent residence in the countryside and of minimizing industrial expansion in major cities to keep prospective new residents out. These policies are certainly unique, though the question is, "For how long?" If or when China industrializes more rapidly, will this policy give way to a more traditional Western (and Soviet) pattern?

As in modernizing Western cities, bureaucratization--the concrete expression of rationality, specialization of function, and routinization in the administration of urban affairs--is developing quickly in Soviet cities. Patterns of increased specialization, longer tenure, and higher educational attainments are most noticeable in the large cities, the Soviet modern sector. Professionalization of administration seems to be a logical trend, following the Western urbanization pattern, though its routinization, division of labor, and reliance upon technical expertise to solve problems of administration pose ideological problems for the transition to the stage of "administration of things." The Chinese, again, pursue a different policy, attacking the danger of bureaucratization in cities by sending millions of urban cadres on short-term stays in the countryside to "rediscover life." The Chinese insist that bureaucratization (professionalization) is neither inevitable nor desirable during development and have persistently attacked urban bureaucrats and rational/ technical criteria. "Redness" is what counts officially, though one Chinese official admits, "We are a pragmatic people, and it may be possible to reeducate our bureaucrats so that we can gain the benefits of their expertise. This way they can be of use to the society." Perhaps this will be the case, though it would be best to suspend judgment on the efficacy of the Chinese solution, at least until the country has committed more resources to urban development, thus increasing the tasks of municipal governments and making urban administration more complex. Then we shall see if the Chinese have indeed been able to develop a successful working style which rewards redness while rejecting routinization and specialization of function.

Decentralization, a process in which power is distributed to relatively more persons directly involved in urban life and administration, is an important element in Soviet urban growth. Urban governments have acquired more rights and duties in the past dozen years, particularly in the allocation and administration of housing. The daily administrative and coordinating functions of municipalities have multiplied, and increased decentralization permits more effective control over an ever-widening range of tasks. Soviet urbanologists recently proposed that "cities must have the economic and legal means for carrying out decisions effectively. This means we have to give them a significant degree of autonomy."[18] Planners want more attention paid to individual cities and their regions (conurbations) as a planning unit, and the mayor of Moscow emphasizes, "We plan for the entire region, not just the city of Moscow, recognizing the existence of a regional planning entity." Another facet of decentralization has been the enlistment of more citizens into low-level administration, though so far these duties are essentially participatory and pose no challenge to the decision-making authority of higher party and state organs.

Chairman Mao advocates self-reliance and economic decentralization as a solution to the problems of China's development. This concept goes beyond the Soviet idea of administrative (planning) decentralization. Mao is talking about fundamental economic decentralization within the system, the self-sufficiency of thousands of small units throughout China. "The localities should consider ways of setting up independent industrial systems. First of all coordinated regions and later, conditions permitting, a number of provinces should set up relatively independent, even though dissimilar, industrial systems."[19] Below the provincial level, every commune is exhorted to develop self-sufficiency. In the current period the Chinese stress the theme of self-reliance; officials talk of increased rights and duties for all localities over productive units and advocate further construction of small factories in the countryside. So far the degree of this decentralization is much less than is officially stated: important productive units are still directed from above, and small-scale factory production is developing slowly.[20] Possibly the Chinese fear the danger of too much decentralism, just as the Soviets do, or are modifying this policy for economic reasons--that is, the greater efficiency and productivity of larger industrial units in cities.

Urbanism--a set of values, attitudes, and beliefs of people living in large industrial cities--currently concerns Soviet urbanologists. They see urbanism as a positive phenomenon, and recent Soviet writings note the distinctiveness (autonomy) of the urban pattern of life (gorodskoy obraz zhizni) and its superiority. "The city is not just one of the forms present in existing society. It is the model for this society and will predominate in the contemporary period." "Urbanism is a type of culture, a social psychology intimately tied to conditions of life in modern urban agglomerations." This urban way of life is "a universal world process, although proceeding somewhat differently in various countries, depending upon their technological and economic growth, the character of their sociopolitical relations, and their respective cultures."[21] A Moscow official speaks of a "common metropolitan culture." "Go ahead, stand on any street corner in Moscow, New York, or London. It's all the same--masses of people, cars, noise, buildings, concrete, and so on."

Soviet planners are attempting to come to grips with these universal features of urban life and are now willing to borrow from Western experience to understand the urban phenomenon, to explain why certain socialist policies are not working, and to find solutions to problems of urban development. Does this mean full acceptance of the Western model of urbanization and rejection of such policies as size limitation, the neighborhood unit, and equalization/standardization? No, but it does imply that these policies will have to be substantially modified if Soviet urban growth is to be managed more effectively. Urbanologists now recognize a conflict between the values they would like to see developed in socialist society and the values that tend to emerge during urbanization, regardless of what was planned. Thus the neighborhood unit has not been successful, in part for economic reasons, but also because of "the values and technology of urbanization"--many people living in large industrial cities prefer anonymity and want to be mobile; they don't care to be cooped up in far-out neighborhoods; access to cars and telephones makes them establish friendships in other parts of town; the five-day work week and diversification of leisure opportunities encourages people to get away from home and neighborhood commitments.[22] The dilemma for Soviet planners and officials is how to come to terms with such "modern, urban" values, while creating a new communist man whose values differ substantially. Can he become socially conscious, cooperative, and integrated into the community in a setting which generates precisely the opposite values, and which Soviet planners now admit is part of a "universal" process?

The Chinese position is different, since they do not accept the concept of urbanism as a universal world process, or plan on looking to the West (or to the Soviet Union) for solutions to their urban problems. One Shihchiachuang official, echoing the rhetoric of the Cultural Revolution, said, "We reject bourgeois concepts of urbanism. We reject the assumption that urban life styles are superior to nonurban life styles. We reject the assumption that there inevitably must be a universal urban culture." On this particular point, the definition of urbanism, the Chinese and the Soviets disagree, and this disagreement over the present and future nature of the socialist city is reflected in the urban policies currently being formulated in each country.

Urbanization and Modernization

After comparing the two models and looking at current developments in each country, it is clear that they are dissimilar in many areas and that at present two communist models of urban development exist--the Chinese and the Soviet. The Chinese essentially have an antiurban strategy which avoids the central issue now being confronted by the Soviets--whether industrial, urban society imposes the same consequences on all modernizing societies. Why are these two models so different, given their common goal--the remaking of man in a socialist image? To a considerable extent the differences are historical and cultural. The Chinese have not traditionally been a nation of city-dwellers, and the Chinese city has not been idealized as the most desirable place in which to live. The Russians, however, by opening St. Petersburg (Leningrad) to the West in the early eighteenth century, made a real commitment to the city as the desired setting in which to live. Both Russia and China were peasant societies at the time of their respective revolutions, but Russia was more modern (in terms of level of technology, degree of social differentiation, and receptivity to new values and ideas). The Russians were more open to foreign ideas and to the concept of cosmopolitan culture; the Chinese, in contrast, appear on the stage of history as a tradition-bound peasant society, highly suspicious of foreigners and their ideas and of the urban setting in which those ideas are commonly expressed. This "developmental gap" between China and the Soviet Union has not appreciably narrowed, and China remains essentially a peasant society, whereas the Soviet Union has become a modern (in our sense) industrial nation.

Personality also has played a role in the evolution of distinctive Soviet and Chinese urban policies. Chairman Mao committed himself early in his career to the countryside, apparently in opposition to Soviet instructions. After twenty years in the wilderness he returned to pluck China's cities from the failing hands of the Kuomintang. Did Chairman Mao, in those twenty years outside the cities, acquire an antiurban "bias" which now determines the party's view of Chinese politics and of the urban sector during China's development? Does he hope to recreate in China the small peasant image of revolutionary simplicity allegedly remembered from Yenan? In contrast, can we ascribe the Soviet Union's decision to industrialize and urbanize rapidly to Stalin's influence? It was Stalin, according to all reports, who personally made the momentous decision to collectivize the peasantry, to crush them by force if necessary. From that watershed the Soviet leaders resolved in their minds any ambiguities about what Marx really meant concerning the elimination of differences between town and country.

I mention these factors to show just how complex any Sino-Soviet comparison can be and to acknowledge that the surface has been barely scratched in this study. There is so much we do not know. How, for instance, do we talk about "cities" in societies which do not properly define them? In the USSR a city can range in size from 4,000 upward, and in China from 2,000. But what percentage of that population is really "urban"? Even in Moscow not everyone is an "urban" dweller; the population includes recently arrived peasants, and also peasants actually farming within the city boundaries. Shihchiachuang has 700,000 inhabitants and, according to its officials, over 200,000 of them are peasants on communes situated inside the city; they are administratively defined as urban, but are rural in all other ways. When the Chinese transfer educated youth and cadres down to the countryside, what does "countryside" mean? A Shanghai cadre might be sent to a Sinkiang state farm thousands of kilometers away or to a commune within Shanghai, only a short bicycle ride away from the main part of the city. Another problem is that "cities" can be quite different from each other in size, function, and historical significance. As one Soviet official observed, "How do we deal with the problem of regional variations among cities? Cities may be basically similar when they have reached a certain level of economic development, size, and social differentiation, but in a country the size of the USSR, there are important regional differences to take into account. This makes it difficult to generalize about all Soviet cities." Beyond these difficulties is our lack of information about urban problems and policies in both countries. While this has improved somewhat in recent years for the Soviet Union,[23] there are still no published Soviet studies of the municipal decision-making process; no details of the financial and budgeting process; no studies of the relationship between politics and administration within a municipality and with higher territorial-administrative levels; no adequate published surveys of social conditions and structures within cities. The data problem for China is even greater, and no Chinese studies of their own urban development have recently been published, nor are any anticipated. Urban matters are rarely discussed in the national media; social science research on urbanization and urbanism appears almost nonexistent; hardly any town planners or urban architects are being trained; simple statistical information may be lacking, as China has not had a national census since 1957. In Nanking it took three days of repeated requests to obtain a rough approximation of that city's population. "You see," said an apologetic official, "We aren't really sure how many people live here."

While this inhibits detailed comparison of Chinese and Soviet urban policies, it need not deter us from stating what we can know. First, by using "cities," "urbanization," and "urbanism" as variables, we collect much needed information on how more than 300,000,000 persons live, from simple per capita housing space statistics to time budget studies and public opinion polls (in the Soviet Union). We identify specific urban policies--population size limitation, standardization/equalization, public transportation, to name just a few--and analyze their effectiveness in responding to (or guiding) the modernization process in each country. And we also acquire a better understanding of the nature of that modernization process.

Second, the policies of two "communist" systems can be quite different, as is shown by the dissimilarities of the two urban "models." Even though both have as their goal the creation of the new communist man, they have evolved contrasting strategies for attaining that goal; their respective views of the attractiveness of urban life differ sharply; the physical condition and quality of urban facilities and services contrast markedly in Soviet and Chinese cities. In comparing urban development in both countries, one is struck by just how differently two "communist" regimes approach a common problem--the growth of cities during industrialization.

Third, the Soviet urban model is moving in a direction similar to the Western one, and this means that value transformation in Soviet cities is becoming more "modern" and "urban" rather than "socialist," at least as their commitment to modern industrial society becomes ever more irrevocable. "Socialist" policies such as population size limitation and neighborhood units get swallowed up by urbanization processes which Soviet planners and leaders no longer pretend to control. Will the new communist man be a casualty of the inexorable homogenization of Soviet and Western man in an industrial urban setting? Whether the Soviets will still be able to forge a special urbanism in which at least a dualism of socialist and modern urban values prevails remains to be seen.

Fourth, China continues to pursue a unique urban policy though, until she industrializes more rapidly, it is too early to say whether she has found a permanent solution to problems of urbanization and modernization. Right now the policies of deliberately downgrading the urban setting, sending people to the countryside, and building up the rural areas seem to be working in the context of a development strategy that emphasizes agricultural production over industrial growth. If in the future this emphasis were to change, or if internal resistance to "antiurban" policies increases (i.e., if young urban intellectuals absolutely refuse to go to the countryside, no matter what, and peasants refuse to stay "down" forever), then perhaps the Chinese urban model will lose its uniqueness and will enter the mainstream of modernization, along with its Soviet communist brother.

Notes

[1] For a major study of the characteristics of modern man, see the many recent writings by Professor Alex Inkeles and his associates, e.g., "Making Men Modern" On the Causes and Consequences of Individual Change in Six Developing Countries," American Journal of Sociology 75 (September 1969): 208-25, and Alex Inkeles and David H. Smith, Becoming Modern (Cambridge: Harvard University Press, 1974).

[2] "Communist" and "socialist" are used interchangeably in this paper, except as note in the text.

[3] While both Marx and Engels accepted the necessity of urban society, they hoped that their postrevolutionary society would contain many "rural" values which were worth keeping--e.g., simplicity, interchangeability of roles, and smallness. This is part of the ambiguity of their position on the city, and also contributes to the vagueness of their concept of postrevolutionary man.

[4] Cf. Institut konkretnykh sotsialnykh issledovanii AN SSSR, Sotsiologicheskiye issledovaniya goroda (Moscow, 1969).

[5] Unless otherwise noted, interviews with Soviet and Chinese officials cited in this study were obtained on my visits to the USSR and China in 1969 and 1971 respectively.

[6] Nanking radio, 5 January 1969; and Lanchow radio, 16 January 1969.

[7] In a recent report on Canadian urban problems, the principal researcher concludes that Canada needs "nothing less than a national urban policy," an "agreed upon set of objectives," and a "federal urban policy" which relates "urban objectives" to "national objectives." See H. Lithwick, Urban Canada: Problems and Prospects: A Report Prepared for the Hon. R. K. Andras, Minister Responsible for Housing, Government of Canada (Ottawa: Central Mortgage and Housing Corporation, 1971), pp. 37-38, 64.

[8] John W. Lewis notes, "After 1956 a great deal of attention was given to the development of both coastal and inland cities, the creation of new towns and the upgrading of such west China cities as Urumchi, Lanchow, and Paotow" The City in Communist China (Stanford: Stanford University Press, 1971), p. 17.

[9] From transcripts of interviews with Promyslov conducted in 1971 by Dan Dimancescu and Crocker Snow, Jr.

[10] From interviews with former residents of Peking now living in Hong Kong.

[11] One Chinese official remarked, "There are so many of these new factories and towns that often we cadres can't find a new town or factory because they aren't on our maps." Another reason for the decentralization may be strategic. In his view, "The more decentralized China is, the harder it will be for anyone to destroy us."
Locating factories in the countryside "narrows the gap between work and peasants . . . training a new type of working people for the countryside" (NCNA, Peking,

20 January 1969).

[12]See Kao Ying-mao, "The Urban Bureaucratic Elite in Communist China: A Case Study of Wuhan, 1949-1965," in Chinese Communist Politics in Action (Seattle: University of Washington, 1969), pp. 216-67, and my Soviet Cities in Transition (Cambridge: MIT Press, forthcoming, 1975), chap. 6.

[13]For a recent analysis of the company town phenomenon, see W. Taubman, Governing Soviet Cities: Bureaucratic Politics and Urban Development in the USSR (New York: Praeger, 1973), especially chap. 7.

[14]This differs from current Western conceptions of community organization, where communities organize to demand rather than to receive.

[15]For descriptions of urban communes, see J. Salaff, "The Urban Communes and Anti-City Experiment in Communist China," China Quarterly 29 (Jan.-Mar., 1967): 82-110; Shi Ch'eng-chih, Urban Commune Experiments in Communist China (Hong Kong: Union Research Institute, 1962); F. Schurmann, Ideology and Organization in Communist China (Berkeley: University of California Press, 1966), pp. 360-99. For the mikrorayon see R. J. Osborn, Soviet Social Policies, Welfare, Equality and Community (Homewood, Ill.: Dorsey Press, 1970), chap. 7.

[16]"The productivity of labor in cities with a population of over 1,000,000 is 38% higher than in cities with a population of from 100,000 to 200,000 and the return on assets is almost twice as high. . . . In the unanimous opinion of urbanists, the formation and development of conurbations constitutes the most characteristic feature of twentieth-century urban growth patterns," (V. Perevedentsev, Literaturnaya gazeta February 9, 1969).

[17]Ibid.

[18]Sotsiologicheskiye issledovaniya goroda, pp. 9-10, and L. Kogan, A. Akhiezer, and O. Yanitsky, "Urbanizatsiya, obshchestvo i nauchno-teknicheskaya revolyutsiya," [Urbanization, Society, and the Scientific-Technical Revolution], Voprosy filosofii 2 (February 1969): 50-53.

[19]Jen min jih pao, 14 October 1969.

[20]For a recent discussion, see J. Sigurdson, "Rural Industry and the Internal Transfer of Technology," in Authority, Participation and Cultural Change in China, ed. S. Schram, pp. 199-232. (Cambridge: At the University Press 1973).

[21]Sotsiologicheskiye issledovaniya goroda, pp. 1, 5, 19.

[22] For more details see my "Soviet Urban Sociology", International Journal of Comparative Sociology, December, 1971, pp. 234-251.

[23]For sources and a discussion of recent developments in this area, see my "Soviet Study of Soviet Cities," Journal of Politics 32 (August 1970): 675-95.

Chapter 7.

SOCIAL CONFLICTS OF UNDERURBANIZATION: THE HUNGARIAN CASE

György Konrád and Iván Szelényi

Hungarian urbanization produces social tension not because of its excessive speed but rather because of its relatively slow rate. This proposition may
well produce numerous objections, since housing construction and communal development can barely keep up with the number of people moving to towns and those already living there. Those responsible for managing local government affairs in
towns tend, as well, to feel a certain hostility toward the masses of villagers
who settle in newly built dwellings and overcrowd public transport, schools,
shops, and hospitals. For that very reason, the inhabitants and officials of
country towns look on their own growth with mixed feelings. They would like to
keep ahead of the others, but they nevertheless consider that the flood of newcomers, the "Johnny-come-latelys," dilutes their true substance and is a social
danger.

The growth rate of the urban population, while not booming (as we
shall see later), is in fact too fast compared with that of the urban infrastructure, so that Hungary shows the symptoms of "overurbanization" common in
the developing countries--lines for beds; men living in cellars and lofts, in
woodsheds and sties, in old buses, circus wagons, and caves; whole settlements
of lean-tos built on the fringes of towns (not as extensive, perhaps, as the
favella in Rio but hardly offering higher standards); and the price of sublet
rooms rising faster than that of any other goods or services. Overcrowdedness,
however, can result not only from overurbanization but also from underurbanization. Similar symptoms are often produced by differing and even by opposing
forces. In American cities, for instance, centers turn into slums through speculation made possible by a controlled real estate market; in a large number of
cities in Eastern Europe a similar slumming effect is produced by the total
absence of a real estate market that might prompt the landlords--the municipal
authorities--to make more effective use of this land.

Overurbanization in developing countries means that the growth in urban
population takes place at a faster rate than industrialization. The infrastructure is overburdened there because of the absence of effective demand in the
economic sense, that is, demand able to pay for the services needed owing to
unemployment. This then makes the extension of these services impossible. In
Hungary, on the other hand, and as far as we know in the other Eastern European
countries as well, the rate of industrialization keeps well ahead of the growth
of infrastructure, jobs in towns increase at a much faster rate than housing, and
those filling them are therefore forced to choose between commuting, subtenancies,
hostels, and temporary shelters. Overurbanization in developing countries is produced by the low level of industrial investment and insufficiency of employment.
Underurbanization in Eastern Europe, on the other hand, is the result of excessive
industrialization at the expense of the infrastructure. Central planning could only assure a high rate of industrial investment by making the growth of the infrastructure a variable of an industrializing economic policy rather than the result
of effective demand, by withdrawing infrastructure products in short supply from
the market, giving their distribution the character of administrative rewards,
and by making their value independent of wages.

"The town of X was given a hospital, the village of Y a school," the
newspapers report--and we might well ask; By whom? Wage-policy has adhered to the
attitude that since housing and the products of the infrastructure were not considered commodities but something the state on principle provided for all those
living on wages and salaries as an additional allowance, wages and salaries could

be fixed at a much lower level than in countries at a similar stage of economic growth. The proportion of industrial investment was too high, and that in investment goods too low, so that relatively little housing was built out of state resources. Thus the overwhelming proportion of those finding new employment could not be allotted dwellings in an administrative way, and their income was too small to allow them to obtain their own housing on the limited market for dwellings that sprang up alongside housing administration by the authorities. Should people travel to work from their former dwellings or should they move into the vicinity of their new places of employment? An economic policy industrializing in a one-sided manner did not allow this question to be decided by individual consumer preferences.

Overurbanization and underurbanization may well produce the same surface symptoms, but they are essentially opposite processes; they must therefore also be dealt with in radically different ways. What is certainly true, however, is that limiting city-directed internal migration by administrative measures, that is, not letting villagers who move to towns obtain housing, and so forth, is not only unjust but has also proven ineffective, both in the developing countries and in Hungary. The proposition that the relatively slow rate or urbanization—produced tension in Hungary refers to this underurbanization (greater rate of industrialization than growth of infrastructure) which, in our view, unavoidably resulted from the economic and social policy of the past twenty-odd years.

In what follows, we attempt to describe the symptoms of underurbanization, the causes of this process and the structure of social conflicts grouped around it. We should also like to point out the ways in which underurbanization handicaps the intensive stage of economic development which is about to get off the ground in Hungary. Limits on urban development also limit democratic processes in society in a double sense: the existing system of unequal regional distribution of goods and privileges becomes solidified, and the burdens of forced industrialization are unequally distributed among various social groups. Members of highly developed urban societies have greater freedom on principle, naturally dependent on the social system, than those in more poorly urbanized societies--as members of the work force, as consumers and as participants in cultural and public life. Putting a brake on urban development therefore at the same time handicaps the growth of a varied and mobile system of social relations that ensures greater personal autonomy.

Problems of Economic and Urban Growth

The myth of fast urbanization soon dissolves if we merely glance at census figures showing the increase of the urban population and those in nonagricultural employment.

The proportion of the urban population grew relatively slowly, though fairly evenly, during the past hundred years--at the rate of roughly 2 percent every ten years. A curve showing development between 1869 and 1970 dips only around 1949, surely owing to war damage in towns and the consequent migration of the urban population. Whereas the proportion of the urban population seemed to grow at a relatively faster rate between 1949 and 1970, urban development in fact was no faster than earlier in this century and was even slower than in the concluding third of the nineteenth century. Between 1949 and 1970, the proportion of town and city dwellers increased by 6.7 percent, but this was largely due to the regeneration of losses suffered by the urban population during the war. A more appropriate starting point, therefore, would be 1941, since the period between the wars can also be interpreted as one of regeneration in urban development after the First World War.

164

In the last three decades of the nineteenth century, the proportion of the urban population increased by 7.3 percent; this figure was only 4.6 percent for the period between 1910 and 1941, and about 5 percent for that between 1941 and 1970. Certainly no sort of boom in urban growth has occurred in recent decades. This becomes even more obvious for the past twenty years or so if the growth per decade of the urban population is calculated on the basis of the urban population as given by the previous census. In other words, the population of towns grew at a faster rate at the end of the nineteenth century than in the past quarter-century.

The importance of the relative boom of the 1950s is somewhat lessened by the fact that between 1941 and 1960--that is, in twenty years--the urban population grew by a total of only 12 percent. These statistical data can be confirmed by anyone who cares to take a stroll around any of the towns in Hungary. He would observe that the structure of these towns and the most characteristic buildings were due to the wave of urban growth at the end of the last century. One could, of course, argue that population growth as such was greater in the last three decades of the nineteenth century than in the three most recent ones. But even bearing that in mind, one can still show that in the former period urban population grew by 76 percent, as against a growth of 37 percent in the population as a whole; in other words, the rate of growth of the urban population was 40 percent higher than that of the country as such. In the past 30 years, the population of the country grew by 10 percent, that of towns by 25 percent--the difference being a mere 15 percent.

The rate of urban population growth, therefore, did not speed up. On the contrary, its rate--by decades--is only half that at the end of the nineteenth century, and increased only by 25 percent in the past twenty years. National income, however, increased threefold in the same period, and the number of those employed in industry (including the building industry) increased 2.3 times, showing that the increase in national income was the result not so much of increased productivity as of an increase in the labor force. All this allows one to conclude that the rate of urban growth fell behind that of industrial growth to a significant and unjustified extent, and that numerous social problems derive from these opening "scissors."

The relative backwardness of Hungarian urbanization also becomes apparent if the rate of urban population growth is compared with the relevant figures for other countries. In Hungary, 41 percent of the population lives in towns with more than 20,000 inhabitants; the figure for the developed part of the world as a whole--including Hungary--is 51 percent; it is 57 percent in northwestern Europe, and 61 percent in North America.

Such comparative slowness in Hungarian urbanization without doubt results from the country's economic policy and the strategy employed in furthering urban development, that is, the delay in urbanization derives from insufficient investment in the infrastructure.

In capitalist countries, and even in Hungary during the Austro-Hungarian monarchy, industrialization took place parallel with the development of the infrastructure. Roughly 50 percent of accumulation at that time was devoted to the development of the infrastructure, for example, during the great age of railway construction. In the 1890s, an average of 10,000 dwellings a year were constructed in Budapest, though the total population at the time was only half a million; that is, 20 dwellings were built every year for every 1,000 inhabitants. In recent years, not quite a third of investments were devoted to the infrastructure--too little to allow construction of a modern urban network that would keep up with industrial growth. Housing construction in Budapest in the 1960s was no higher in absolute figures than in the 1890s: 5.8 dwellings per 1,000 inhabitants were built.

According to Ivan T. Berend's calculations, the fixed capital resources of material production increased 127 percent in twenty years, those of nonmaterial production 71 percent; and the figures are similar in developed capitalist countries. The share of national income devoted to the infrastructure was rather small in industrially undeveloped Hungary, a total of 10 percent in 1950. This proportion, if anything, somewhat declined in 1970. In industrially developed countries, however, the rate of growth in investments, in employment and performance is highest in the infrastructure. The share of housing and communal investments is considerably higher in developed capitalist countries. According to calculations, the standard of supply of housing and communal services in Hungary is roughly 30 percent below **that** which the general development of the country would justify. This tendency was underscored in the 1960s, when housing construction essentially stagnated, though national income grew at an average rate of 4 percent per annum.

Twenty to 32 percent of the part of national income accumulated is devoted to housing construction in developed capitalist countries. This figure is 17 percent in the Soviet Union, 15.5 percent in Hungary, 15.1 percent in Poland, 6.6 percent in Romania, and 2.9 percent in Bulgaria. The average per 1,000 inhabitants in Hungary is 6.5 percent, as against an average of 8-10 percent for developed capitalist countries--though this is higher than in any other European socialist countries except for the 9.5 of the Soviet Union. Housing construction in towns thus fell behind the rate of growth in industrial employment. Urban housing stock in Hungary grew by 23 percent between 1960 and 1970, while at the same time the number of those employed by industry, including the building industry, grew by 34 percent. The great majority of these found employment in towns; the largest part of new housing in towns, however, was built not for them but to satisfy needs that had arisen earlier. Most of these men and women, newly employed in industry, were therefore unable to obtain accommodation in towns and, as a result, were forced to commute.

All these facts clearly indicate that in Hungary underdevelopment of the infrastructure, in what are called "nonproductive investments" in urban development and in communal services, is significantly greater than justified by the position of industry and the economy; that the share of national income devoted to communal investments is much smaller than in the capitalist countries of Europe; and that a one-sided strategy of industrial development (which in the past twenty years allotted industry 40 percent of investments that on many occasions did not prove particularly productive) necessarily found itself in conflict with the objective demands of urban development. Those concerned about the development of settlements and that of the infrastructure must emphasize this fact, especially since the share of industrial investments is due to go up slightly, to 42 percent, in the course of the Fourth Five-Year Plan period.

The fast growth in industrial employment and the underdevelopment in the infrastructure, principally in housing, leads to pseudourbanization, to the paradox, as we have seen, of men living in villages and working in towns. The village as a type of settlement was justified in terms of integrating domicile and employment; peasants, in order to be able to work the land, had to do without the advantages which an urban network of communal facilities was able to provide. In this connection, one might refer to the late Ferenc Erdei's views on the Hungarian type of country towns, the Mezőváros, which combined a permanent dwelling in an urban type of settlement with a more or less temporary shelter, the tanya, on the property to be worked, allowing the peasants to live in towns and yet earn their living on the land. Apropos the present paradox of commuting villagers, Erdei once said, in the course of a conversation, that he could understand someone living in a town without working there, but living in a village and working in a town seemed an impossible contradiction to him--a man living in a village and working in a town got the worst of both ends.

This train of thought primarily prompted work on the problems discussed in this paper. In our view, those who are forced to keep their village domicle while no longer employed there because of problems of urban underdevelopment are, on principle, at a disadvantage.

It is only natural, and needs no special explanation, that the slope of the urbanization curve also can be indicated by the occupational composition of the population in various types of settlement.

1. Hungarian society as a whole can be called urbanized as regards the occupational distribution of both all those in gainful employment and the heads of families. Even in villages, the heads of 64 percent of the households have their principal employment outside agriculture. Urbanization can be taken as even more advanced if actual work done, not the sector of the economy in which someone is employed, is taken into account. Manual work in agriculture, peasant's work in plain words, is the principal employment of only 21 percent of those in gainful employment; only a fifth of households, or their members, now belong in this category.

Change in this respect was extremely fast in recent decades. Of those in gainful employment, the proportion doing manual work in agriculture dropped from 36 percent to 18 percent. The 30 percent working in agriculture include those doing administrative work in producers' cooperatives as well as those doing industrial work within agricultural enterprises. Bearing in mind that four-fifths of the population, and even 64 percent of those living in villages, do not do peasant work, and that 71 percent of the population--56 percent of those living in villages--are not involved in agriculture in any way in their principal employment, one might well ask, Why so many of them are tied to villages? Villages do have industries, industries of some significance, but well over half the young people in villages are employed by industry--including service industries--elsewhere than at their domicile.

The tension between the employment of a socially urbanized village population and their domicile could lead to a potential fast swelling of the urban population; but it could also--thanks to supplementary activities organized by producers' cooperatives, which have shown surprising initiative in exploiting opportunities the market offers--lead, as seems to be the case in Hungary, to a peculiar and unique middling structure, perhaps a new type of village that is industrial and therefore on the road to urbanization.

We know very little about this very recent social phenomenon: the occasional news one gets about printing offices, the manufacture of spare parts for automobiles or of devotional objects--all within the producers' cooperatives--appears to be somewhat exaggerated. The high earning opportunities and labor migration from state enterprises back to enterprises of this sort certainly indicate that village society is beginning to create an interesting and elastic answer to the difficulties created by migration to towns--that they are in fact making a virtue of necessity. The significant boom in housing construction in villages is well known: the proportion of dwellings with two or more rooms is 51 percent in Budapest and 55 percent in the villages. This new type of enterprise may thus provide an important impetus not only for the urbanization of the village but for urban development as such.

2. Available data also suggest that no particularly significant correlation any longer exists between the administrative status of the settlement of domicile and the proportion of those in industrial employment: 59 percent of the population of Budapest and 52 percent of that of the villages are engaged in industrial manual work. The correlation is much greater for employment in the service industries: 40 percent of heads of households are so employed in Budapest, and only 12 percent in the villages; 43 percent of those gainfully employed in Budapest are doing clerical or professional work, while only 14 percent of those employed in villages do such work. Unskilled workers make up only 13 percent of the workforce in Budapest but as much as 39 percent of that in the villages.

All this suggests that what is characteristic these days of the difference between the population of towns and villages can be indicated to a lesser and lesser extent by the industrial-agricultural dichotomy and more so by that between industrial and agricultural work on the one hand and service industry, clerical, and professional work on the other. This means that the categories of vertical or hierarchical social stratification will prove of most use in making clear the differences between village and urban society. Families of a lower social status live in villages, and those of a higher social status in towns; the bulk of those in villages work with their hands, while one-third of those in towns do clerical or professional work, including two-fifths of those in Budapest and the larger towns. A significant number of these are employed in the service industries.

As can be seen, the process which generally characterizes urbanization of developed areas in the second half of this century is making fast progress in Hungary also. White-collar workers are the most important sector in towns, particularly in large towns, and towns are distinguished even more by the high proportion of those working in service industries--particularly in scientific research, education, and the upper reaches of the administration--than by the presence of industry. This trend would be even more obvious if the development of services linked to the infrastructure were not relatively backward in Hungary, as is indicated by the increase of those working in service industries from 22 percent to only 23 percent in the forty years since 1930.

It also follows that the acquisition of an urban dwelling, particularly one in a large town, is a considerable advantage, even a privilege, in Hungarian society, and one which those in the higher social stratum have a much better chance of achieving. The slope of the urbanization curve in industrializing Hungarian society therefore corresponds to that of social stratification. More than half of the village population does industrial work; roughly half the people do not work where they are domiciled. Almost half of those doing manual work in industry live in villages, but only a quarter of those doing clerical or professional work live there. One could add that the stratification of the working class itself indicates that a larger proportion of better qualified and better paid workers live in towns, while those with lower qualifications and earning less live in villages. Once again, the industrial-agricultural dichotomy is not what characterizes the difference between town and village these days; it can be better interpreted in terms of the hierarchy of social stratification. In this way, inequalities deriving from social stratification also find expression as territorial and regional inequalities.

The Causes and Social Consequences of Delayed Urban Development

The facts described above show that Hungarian urban development has suffered delays and that the country is underurbanized. Bearing in mind these facts and the ideas raised, an attempt must also be made to provide a more systematic explanation of the factors which caused the underurbanization of Hungary, the extent to which economic policy can be held responsible for it, or regional planning looked on as part of it.

All that can be said about the causes and consequences of slowed-down urbanization must be put in the form of hypotheses. Work designed to employ the methodology of empirical sociology in a search for the answer to questions outlined above will take many years and is only at the initial stages. It nevertheless seems appropriate to systematize our ideas, based on the facts already at our disposal, in such a way as to permit generalization in the later stages of this research in order to give it Eastern European relevance. This would permit its application to the period of socialist production which is about to come to a close and allow an advance indication of certain aspects of the nature of economic growth and urban development in the next stage.

The Role of Economic Factors in the Retarded Rate of Hungarian Urban Development. As indicated earlier, in our view, at least, the relatively slow rate of urban development in Hungary is largely due to an economic policy that set extensive industrial development as its principal aim. The emphasis on economic determinants does not mean that underurbanization was the necessary result or that no other alternative to regional development existed than that chosen by planning twenty years ago. It is up to economists to show the extent to which extensive industrialization was the only possible road economic development could take. All we should like to say is that a retrospective justification of the "only possible road" seems to be doubtful on principle.

As sociologists we are aware that an economic-administrative-ideological organization is developed in order to realize any kind of given--or believed to be such--economic objective, and that such an organization becomes more or less independent of its chosen goal, in turn by its nature influencing the character of the goal and also tending to reproduce the subjective and the objective conditions of its existence. Even if one accepts extensive industrial development as necessary, the resulting brake on the growth of the infrastructure and towns in no small measure follows the inner laws on which direction and planning operate--in the given case, on the principles, methods, and organizational structure of regional and town planning. As will be argued shortly, the fact that underurbanization, which follows from extensive industrialization, slows down further industrialization derives in the long run from this relative independence of the system of planning and direction.

Expensive industrialization--that is, a growth in industrial production resulting from neither technological progress nor an increase in the productivity of labor but from quantitative growth of a relatively backward means of production and of the labor force--demanded huge industrial investments and a large pool of free or cheap labor. This demand for labor and capital on the part of extensively growing Hungarian industry basically determined economic policy and agricultural policy, and the policy related to the infrastructure in particular. Agricultural policy, beyond fixing agricultural prices in a manner that subsidized industrial production, was in part also designed to supply the labor needs of industry; that is, in addition to extending the employment of women, policy relating to the infrastructure also had to ensure that the necessary capital was at the disposal of industrial investment.

Wages policy was closely related for, as mentioned above, the costs of the infrastructure were withdrawn from wages, thus allowing central stage organs to dispose of these funds independent of consumer decisions. Wages were fixed at a relatively low level, below the value of labor, producing certain contradictions peculiar to the system outlined. Fixing the price of labor below its value turned labor into "an article in short supply," leading to excess demands both in agriculture and industry, and necessitating administrative interferences in order to ensure a relative equilibrium in the supply of labor. Early in the 1960s, measures had to be taken to limit loss of labor on the part of agriculture; at present industry is urging measures designed to secure a supply of labor. It is certainly true, however, that the shortage of labor--generally the case in the way the economy was run until recently--must be ascribed to the absorption power of industry.

It follows from this that basic objectives of economic policy limited the principles and practice of regional planning, that they necessarily prompted regional planning to retard urban development. Regional planning in this sense includes not only planners and research workers specifically concerned with it, but all those--largely central--political, planning, and administrative organs that are called on to determine or influence the location and distribution of the instruments of urban development (that is, investments in general and particularly the structure of industrial consumption) by virtue of the positions they hold, the proposals they make, or the decisions they are entitled to take.

Regional planning that retarded urban development cannot be considered in terms of hostility either to villages or towns. (Hostility to towns or villages was part of the ideological background of regional planning itself, and thus played a subordinate role only in determining objectives or the means to achieve them.) Planning was defined from the start in terms of hostility to the infrastructure as demonstrated by economic policy; the ideology peculiar to planning was able to modify planning strategy only on that basis. An unusual situation indeed result- ed: planning took place within a value system opposed to large cities, which did not do much for the progress and growth of community services in villages and hamlets, though it helped put a brake on urban development--a most effective force, particularly in Budapest.

Those who determined the planning directives paid insufficient attention to objective factors involved in the growth of the settlement network. They did not analyze certain basic processes but were more inclined to justify what they were doing with the help of ideological directives. What often becomes only too obvious in this "scientific and ideological superstructure" is the desire to cover up social problems produced by planning, either by calling on some general social interest or by cloaking planning decisions which affected social interests in the guise of inviolable "technical decisions."

Equality was a frequently mentioned general social interest. In a number of earlier papers we have tried to show how this equality worked in practice in housing policy. Equality as a frame of reference was also most im- portant in regional planning and related economic planning. Policy and planning decisions relating to the infrastructure were particularly important in this respect. As we saw, the aim of centralizing infrastructure investment decisions and withdrawing them from the sphere of consumer decisions was to ensure an in- crease of industrial investment at the expense of infrastructure investment. Planning ideology gave this the appearance of considering the infrastructure so important that its goods and services had to be made available on an equal basis. Demand could not be allowed to become effective in terms of differentiated incomes. The exclusion of certain costs of infrastructure development in wages and their inclusion in the budget was meant to ensure equality to everybody, and independ- ence from social stratification in the distribution of these goods and services.

The budget, however, is determined by the clash of various interests, and it was only natural that the stronger interest--that is, industry, and in the first place heavy industry responsible for production and defense goods-- should come out on top. Here the Marxian truth "they don't know, but they do" is relevant. It is important to emphasize once again that social capital which is concentrated at the center and redistributed by a decision-making structure based on authority results in the spokesmen of industry, of "productive invest- ments," securing more than those of the "nonproductive" infrastructure. At the time the new economic mechanism was introduced, its critics and those of the market forces--who liked to refer to the democratic principle of equality--fre- quently remembered illusions as if they were truth, identifying the declared social policy principles of the 1950s with the actual policy carried out.

Equality is a basic starting point in Hungarian regional planning. Regional planning must face up to the fact that spontaneous forces can produce a certain disproportion. No country, however small, has attained economic development which was evenly spread over its whole territory. Equal development is as impossible as an equal race, where the runners are not allowed either to forge ahead or to fall behind. There are always leading industries which forge ahead, spur development, and indicate the direction and rate of growth with the help of investment incentives deriving from temporary disequilibrium. This process comes to the fore under a market and administrative regulating system, and the location of leading industries becomes a focus of growth. A precondition for the forging ahead of such a focus of growth, that is, an agglomeration, is the existence of a group of enterprises or an industry which can carry the others with it, allowing the multiplier effect to assert itself in that particular region, thus leading to further growth.

It is also natural that labor should flow to the foci of growth from the stagnating areas. Labor is more productive there, hence per capita income is higher. The development of these foci of growth can, however, produce a depression in more distant territories if the multiplier effect does not reach them. The necessary disequilibrium of growth, then, undoubtedly increases the social inequality of individuals and local communities in various regions. Social morality, on the other hand, demands that these inequalities be limited.

It was therefore only natural that regional planning should expressly declare putting an end to inequalities between regions to be one of its fundamental objectives. One might well ask, however, how this could be assured. Regional planning considered the distribution of places of domicile within the settlement structure as more or less given, thus taking as its objectives to ensure a more equal distribution of employment opportunities and social advantages. The marks of this way of looking at things can still be discerned today.

Given that the aim is to fix the present population distribution throughout the country, then a decentralization of industrial location, a limitation of the growth of great industrial agglomerations, and the encouraged industrialization of small towns and of villages turning into small towns, as well as limits on changes of domicile, would be the aims in a double sense: administrative measures would have to be taken to put a stop to both migration from depressed areas and migration to metropolitan agglomerations. Given that situation, we would welcome any lessening in the difference of the index of industrialization between the capital and the provinces, between developed and depressed areas, and between towns and villages. Then there would be no need to worry about the productiveness of investments or to calculate the optimum distribution of resources.

The aim would be a sort of cartographical symmetry: a little of everything everywhere, or at least in every major area in the country. One would have to indicate in advance what one wishes to achieve, predicting it as a likely trend: that is, a slowing down of internal migration and a considerable resistance to mobility on the part of the population. The principle that "every settlement takes one step forward" would have to be given moral emphasis. And the principles of regional planning would have to be ceaselessly confronted by industrial planning efforts to use resources to the optimum. Political and administrative limits would have to be put on further industrial growth in the capital; the establishment of further industrial plants in the Budapest agglomeration would have to be prohibited; obstacles would have to be put in the way of reconstructing certain plants; and economic executives would have to be rewarded if they succeeded in transferring industrial plants to the provinces, whatever the cost. One must presume in that case that it costs less to establish an industrial workplace than a dwelling unit.

One would have to accept as axiomatic that overcrowding in big cities is a major social calamity and that the building industry should not be allowed to construct more dwellings per annum in Budapest than it did early this century. One would have to go on presuming that the establishment of new plants would continue to express the main tendency of industrialization, and that industrial plant and equipment would continue to absorb more than half of productive equipment. One would have to become reconciled to the fact that productive investment would lead to plants employing a low level of technology and demanding low standards of skill, knowing the generally low standards of skill and training that prevail in the depressed areas, or else that a relatively unskilled labor force would operate advanced technologies in an inefficient way.

A system of central distribution of fuel and power resources would have to be maintained, with the justification--generally accepted by industry in the 1950s--that the stronger must give to the weaker. In this way, further growth of developed areas would be handicapped without at the same time giving rise to an effective industry and towns of urban appearance, and providing urban facilities in the underdeveloped areas. One would have to adopt and emphasize as a principle the view that industrial concentration and metropolitan agglomerations are a distorted development and, what is more, a distortion characteristic of capitalism. And one would have to forget that concentration is a spontaneous tendency evidenced in socialist industry as well.

Living in a big city would have to be interpreted as a disadvantage in itself; more precisely, the advantages would have to be denied those who desired to move there. One would have to dramatically emphasize disorganized phenomena in big cities and harp on difficulties of adjustment. One would have to maintain, presuming some sort of mythic force, that the metropolitan environment in itself leads to a birth rate which in the long run will not allow the population to reproduce itself, and one would have to be confident that underdeveloped areas with a high birth rate would continue to maintain such a rate despite industrialization. One would have to refer to the latter situation in terms of a normative statement, making it a basic condition of socialist development, and argue that industrial development must be proportional in all regions of the country. One would have to consider it a political achievement if the leading force of socialist society, that is, the working class, were distributed in such a way throughout the country that they everywhere became a close neighbor of the cooperative peasantry, and one would have to presume that this would lead to a strengthening of the socialist social system.

To sum up: Hungarian regional planning has been operating on the principle of maintaining a fairly even distribution of the population--a condition that is presupposed by the subsistence economy of feudal times, the low productivity and consequent need for a large labor force of agricultural societies, and the primitive hygienic conditions and communal services of preindustrial towns and is still considered to be a desirable optimum in a period of high-level industrialization at least until the year 2000 and beyond.

This is a reductio ad absurdum of the consequences of a certain point of view and the ideology that underscores it. Such a strategy of regional development is wrong also because it is unrealizable or can only be maintained given certain authoritarian central decisions, the political preconditions of which are such that one would prefer to do without. It is true, of course, that such a strategy was never present in a simon-pure form, excluding all compromises and rational decisions that pay some respect to reality; it can certainly no longer be found these days. It is a fact, however, that the Hungarian strategy of regional development is not sufficiently clear in its principles even today--that it hesitates between opposed values. Its inner, structural insecurity also is made apparent by the fact that in this, twenty-second year of the planned economy, there is still insufficient effective harmony between industrial planning, regional planning, and planning on the countrywide and administrative level. It is obvious that this organizational spread, this separation between planners and decision-makers, does not derive purely from the impotence of those concerned and an absence of their readiness to cooperate, but springs in the first place from the fact that their efforts and chosen values differ on questions of principle.

It is in this way that the heterogeneous objectives of the strategy of regional development continue to be destroyed by the actual processes of regional development; that the tendency toward concentration in the long run got the upper hand over attempts to deconcentrate, though these have been successful in many places; the limitations on internal migration in many ways resulted in making it more painful. And this is how it happened that reports on regional development are full of complaints against spontaneous processes; that the chance to produce some sort of equality continues to be postponed further and further into the future; that various groups of planners continually accuse each other; and, finally, that the economists, aiming at optimum growth, make shameful concessions to mistaken goals of social policy while the spokesmen for principles of social policy--whose idealism is getting sad and sour--complain about the conflict between their demands and reality. This is how it happened, as well, that a way of seeing the problem that is not thought through, and that is embarrassed by ideological taboos, set up a false dilemma between optimum solutions and human ones both in judging and regulating the structure of society. Finally, and this is even more painful, this is how it happened that the problem of the direction that development was to take remained the "private concern" of the "planners' club."

A rational structure of decisions would have regulated concentration and deconcentration in actual fact and have made the right to move capital resources and men devolve on those most competent to deal with the process of urbanization (that is, on a great variety of organizations and every single member of society). Instead, rational and not so rational, scientific and not so scientific alternative strategies of regional development all remained within the closed circle of the directing principles of bureaucratic planning--as if all that were involved was to govern the world as a wise or an unreasonable god. True enough, it is only a modest first step, but in our view at least, the government regulations increasing the weight of local enterprise taxes have been more important in terms of regional development than a methodology of planning or planning directives in the hands of regional planners could possibly be, however soundly they may be based on research and surveys.

Let us, however, get back to planning itself. It must be emphasized that regional planning based on the maintenance of the present population distribution is inconsistent with the actual process of structuring settlements, and that such planning does not occur independently of the economic process that basically regulates regional development. From the point of view of industrial development that wishes to minimize investment in the infrastructure, it is certainly not desirable to move the population to any significant extent, since such a population transfer would demand considerable investment in the infrastructure. Large-scale daily or weekly commuting is less damaging to these interests, involving only certain investments in transport. Where the population is fairly immobile in relation to domicile, investment in the infrastructure can be minimized. Regional planning, besides attempting to limit inequalities between regions and, in the first place, as argued above, inequalities in population distribution, also endeavored to produce "optimum" growth in the structure of settlements, insisting especially on the idea of a town of optimum size.

The debate between town and village was adjudicated in favor of the town. Ideological conflicts these days are lined up along the axis of large town-small town dichotomy; that is why the question of the optimum size of towns continues to be central in discussions among planners. The discussion is not new. Plato and Aristotle had a few hard things to say about corrupt Athens with its 100,000 inhabitants, holding up rural Sparta as a moral example. The culture of Athens has survived and a city still stands where it stood, but nothing has survived of Sparta--not to mention that Spartans could hardly have been able to philosophize on the dangers of big-city life. Intellectuals, planners, and philosophers have often protested against big cities, and no doubt big cities concentrate all the critical problems of society in themselves. Ever since plans of cities and utopias have been constructed, the ideal size of cities has always troubled men's minds. The suggested numbers are naturally so arbitrary that they are amusing. Campanella and Fourier went in for complicated calculations, trying to work out how many men were needed so a community would be neither too large nor too small.

It is a common feature of all utopias that those who create them think up hierarchical organizations where uniform units of equal size are placed next to each other. Once they reach a defined number, these form a unit with a higher function. This process goes on in the heads of the authors until a previously determined magnitude is reached and then proceeds no further. Such a town plan is similar to a division in the army that breaks up into brigades, regiments, battalions, companies, platoons, and sections--a mechanical hierarchy where each part functions as the planner prescribed. Curiously enough, the spokesmen of a romantic anticapitalism--protesting against the coal-devouring city, dreaming of the caste system of small medieval towns with their ghettoes for guilds and minorities and their unshakable hierarchy, and glorying in the remembrance of all things gothic--reached much the same result as the utopian socialists. Left-wing movements also become soaked in this hostility to large towns. According to Engels, socialism and large towns are incompatible. Lenin, on the other hand, was most sarcastic about the hostility to big cities shown by the Narodniks, pointing out the liberating effect of a system of metropolitan institutions, particularly in allowing the peasantry to free itself from the village community.

Socialist town planning--in revolt against the nineteenth-century town and all its spontaneity and anarchy, its real estate speculation that created belts of tenements hostile to man and miserable slums for the working class--wanted to start from scratch, consciously regulating and planning everything, producing equilibrium, symmetry, and proportion in the material environment of society. We know that planning, and what is more, mechanical planning which wishes to determine every process in a direct way, is not particularly inventive. It is a voluntaristic way of thinking that wants to interpret and shape the structure of society and the economy--a structure even more complex than that of a biological organism--according to the principles governing construction of mechanical systems. We also know that this kind of interference in the operation of a complex system, which cannot simulate its actual and regular processes, as a rule produces extraordinary turmoil, a huge number of unpredicted accidents, and an even greater anarchy than that it set out to tidy up. Systems and structures of the type encompassing towns and cities do not have to be simplified, they have to be made more elastic so that they themselves will be able to cope with the tasks that devolve on them. These days we are able to observe the age of anti-city regional planning with a certain perspective.

Let us add that the program in the Soviet Union aimed to settle almost empty areas in Siberia, where only 30 million people live even now, to create urban centers in huge rural environments, to plan new exploiting and processing industrial centers at places where raw materials were found, and to create new metropolitan centers in addition to Moscow and Leningrad. This attempt to spread the sources of power in the country throughout its huge, rural, and largely under-populated area showed significant rationality. After all, the degree to which this or that larger Soviet city is attractive is greater than that of the whole of Hungary and one or two neighboring countries combined. But we must also be aware that the younger generation of Soviet economists, sociologists, philosophers and architects is most critical of the splitting up of the sources of urban growth. They speak of the multiplier effect of large cities, considering them the motors of the scientific and technological revolution and the location of high standard social communication. They look on as conservative those town planners who wish to place the additional 100,000,000 persons expected by the end of the century in agglomerations of 500,000 inhabitants each. They themselves plan a number of multimillion inhabitant agglomerations.

In contrast to such modern ideas, Ebenezer Howard's notion of "new towns" created around London has been taken over by Soviet planning and socialist planning in general, including that in Hungary. These "new towns" are a most attractive achievement of modern town planning. But it soon turned out that a predetermined population of 30,000 was too small to ensure a high standard of facilities for all inhabitants. Their actual population in every case was more than was planned; as a result the network of facilities, designed for a smaller number, soon proved too tight. A revision of what was considered an optimum population has started everywhere, east and west, wherever towns had been built in accordance with the prevailing notions of the first half of the century. First the number was 30,000, then 50,000, then 75,000, then--giving a preference to round figures--100,000, and later, in larger jumps, 200,000 and 300,000 that could live in such arbitrarily designed towns. At this stage, the situation began to become absurd, and an increasing number of planners is now beginning to realize that the idea of optimum size is a will-o'-the-wisp. There is no such thing as a town of optimum size. A town can have 30,000 inhabitants and still be too big, and it can have a million people and be too small, depending on the socioeconomic functions it is meant to carry out.

Towns surrounded by walls came to an end, and so, a few hundred years later, have those whose limits can be clearly established in a rural environment. Towns in developed countries melt into the urbanized landscape, extending as feelers, axes, or stars, forming complex networks that rise as slopes out of less urbanized areas. Because of conurbations, limits cannot be established for towns with 30,000 inhabitants or for those with 3 million. The notion of an ideal or optimum size must therefore be placed in the museum of ideas, even as a way of stating the problem. The notion of optimum size proved an effective instrument in slowing the growth rate of towns and in justifying a relatively low level of investment in the infrastructure. From that point of view, a town is of optimum size if it can be developed with minimum work on the infrastructure. The notion of optimum size in that sense accords with the interests of industrial development.

We should merely like to indicate at this stage that the strategies of regional and town planning are interlinked and that they form a system which serves and justifies a similar economic policy. We have on a number of occasions pointed out that under the present housing system, the upper and, in part, also the middle strata obtain housing built with state resources, largely subsidized and distributed by the authorities. The large majority of manual workers, however, have to build or buy a small house of their own, regardless of whether they consider the way of life associated with living in a small house to be desirable. Building such houses, on the other hand, is limited by a whole series of regulations. Credit facilities are relatively poor, building is prohibited in belts designed to serve other purposes or in the process of being replanned, inner and outer areas are rigidly delimited without any transition (building in outer areas or buying a plot of land with the intention of building a house of one's own is forbidden), not to mention all the problems of obtaining building materials which those building their own houses suffer. All this is scientifically justified by the belief that small houses make large demands on communal services. Since communal services are provided below cost by the budgetary authorities as a gift to the population, one must thus carefully consider each case before providing those who build their own houses with such a costly present.

The point, though, is that providing a plot with all possible facilities costs about a tenth as much as providing an apartment built by factory methods, which is also distributed as a present. Even adding the cost of the building itself, the total is still considerably less than that of a modern dwelling unit of roughly half the size of the house produced by the bureaucratic planning and construction apparatus. The true alternative is whether an apartment worth 350,000 forints or facilities costing a tenth of that should be given as a present. There is an escape from the horns of this dilemma: workers wishing to move into towns can and do build their houses in their villages, largely because of the administrative restrictions mentioned. This means there is no way for village workers employed by industries in towns to contribute to the development of the urban infrastructure out of their own income while at the same time participating in the advantages of urban life.

We are trying to show that, given certain conditions, all that Hungarian regional and settlement planning has been able to do is to contribute to slowing down the process of urbanization, though it subjectively aimed to produce a modern urban network that democratically distributed all the advantages of society, and tried to justify what it did by referring to a number of relevant and irrelevant facts that either followed from each other or contradicted each other. One cannot expect that regional or town planning should operate against the economic order, since the economic use of space is a subsystem of the economy and necessarily follows the laws of that larger system.

The bulk of planners, however, identified themselves with the apologetic ideology derived from extensive economic growth to such an extent that they neglected to point out the operating principles of the economic system and the consequences of that sort of development. That is, instead of drawing attention to economic and social conflicts and technical troubles which derived from "saving on" the urban infrastructure, which in the long run handicaps industrial development, they projected into the future proportions already distorted and accepted and backed a planning mechanism which, by monopolizing every decision, makes it utterly impossible to plan the processes involved.

While the growth of urban infrastructure was slower than justified, it was not compensated for by a faster growth of communal facilities in villages, that is, the urbanization of the village. Indeed, progress in communal facilities in villages is handicapped even more systematically by the need for capital for industrial investments. The line of division, therefore, runs not between town and country but between industry and infrastructure. Pseudourbanization weighs as heavily on towns as on villages. Nevertheless, the antimetropolitan elements of Hungarian regional planning pointed out earlier had an effect on urban population growth that is particularly evident in the slowing down of Budapests's growth and the swelling in population of the belt surrounding the city.

We cannot go beyond describing pseudourbanization, its causes and effects, and we cannot deal with the ways in which delayed urbanization influenced regional inequalities, lessening or perhaps increasing them. We must, however, establish that the growth of Budapest was slow compared with that of other towns, and that country towns enjoyed certain advantages compared with the capital. More severe restraints than average on the growth of Hungary's single large city can hardly be explained simply by the interests of extensive industrialization. The reasons must be looked for in the hostility to large towns shown by regional planning.

Social and Economic Consequences

A structure of social conflicts stems from this pseudourbanization, which in turn derives from the policy of extensive industrialization and regional planning connected with it. This will have to be investigated still further, but present knowledge already suffices to show certain significant tendencies as well as to permit formulation of certain hypotheses which will aid future research.

One of the peculiar consequences of delayed urbanization is an unequal distribution of the burden of industrialization on some sections and strata of society. It is characteristic of pseudourbanization that the growth in industrial employment exceeds the population absorption capacity of towns; that is, an increasing number are forced to live in villages even though they are employed in industry. But "saving" on infrastructure expenditures was done not only at the expense of the rural population working in towns; it also delayed the growth in the standard of living of the urban population. For instance, standards of public transport have actually declined in recent decades.

The bulk of those newly employed in industry would obviously have preferred to move to town. They were unable, however, to obtain a house or apartment, since the minimum requirement is five years' residency in the town. Those who were able, or who received a strong push from the village, found a way of building in the belt of settlements surrounding the major towns. The majority, not being allotted a dwelling free of charge and not being able to purchase one given rational and regulated credit conditions, were stuck outside the towns. They were able to bring their labor to town, but all they got at the most was a bunk in a dormitory or hostel. Not only in Hungary but in the other socialist countries as well, a dwelling in town took on the character of a privilege. In Warsaw, for example, those from outside town cannot be allotted a dwelling and cannot buy one, for even to be allowed to register one's domicile with the Warsaw police one must have certification from one's employer that it is absolutely essential the employee be accommodated locally.

Given that even the right to registration, or the right to live in lodgings as a subtenant, is contingent on bureaucratic permission, one can well imagine that those of a higher status in the organization find it easier to obtain approval. Thus in a particular factory the majority of executives, technicians, clerical staff, and skilled tradesmen live in town, whereas the bulk of the semiskilled and unskilled workers have to commute. One could well say that urban accommodation in that way becomes a feudal right and that categories of first- and second-class citizens are set up for the metropolitan and rural population respectively, the privileges of the first being rigidified into monopolies by the administration. Turning urban accommodation and, speaking more generally, the whole of the urban infrastructure and the whole retail trade and institutional network into a privilege becomes wholly unjustified, since the infrastructure is in principle the sort of allotment paid for out of everyone's income, though not everyone has an equal chance to make use of it.

The problem of one million daily or weekly commuters long ago aroused social interest. But, in a most peculiar fashion, commuting is generally discussed as a problem of popular culture. Papers report that workers purchased hard liquor from pot-distillers and that they spend their traveling time playing cards in an alcoholic haze rather than reading novels. A series of newspaper articles showed, for example, that the villages in the Nyirseg area did not have enough industrial employment. Undoubtedly, serious problems arise in the families of weekly commuters because of their long absences, not to mention the extra burden on the family budget to feed and house the commuting member apart from the household. It is also certainly true that a significant proportion of daily commuters spend even more time on crowded public transport than those who live in big cities. A particular problem also arises because public transportation timetables are not adjusted to working hours, so that commuters' lives are spent in merely reproducing their labor power.

Time-balance data for commuting workers, however, reflect the social conflicts involved only in a secondary fashion, and this also applies to the social underprivilege at the back of them. Workers commuting from villages do not merely lose part of their leisure, they are also partially deprived of the urban infrastructure, to which the surplus value of their work also contributes. They have no part of urban housing, or the privileges afforded by the network of urban communal services, retail trade, entertainment, and culture, and since their children cannot attend urban schools that provide higher standards of education, they are passing on the disadvantages of commuting to their heirs even while the latter are still at school. This means that delayed urbanization has placed a significant proportion of the burdens of extensive industrialization on the shoulders of commuting workers without letting them share proportionately in the advantages. Though only a tenth of the Hungarian population are commuters, the disadvantages are felt by approximately a quarter of the Hungarian population, because the contradiction between urban employment and rural domicile also affects members of their families.

Commuters are largely peasants restratified as workers for eight hours a day only. Mainly semiskilled and unskilled, they make up the "new" working class in the sense employed by Istvan Kemeny in his work on the Hungarian working class. What is involved, therefore, is a homogeneous social group that can be described by defined sociological characteristics. The dispersion tendencies of large cities have also produced professional and clerical men and skilled tradesmen in Hungary who work in towns and live in garden suburbs, but these are not included here. The key to distinguishing between the two groups is whether commuting is freely and voluntarily chosen or is forced and thus a reflection of distributive inequalities.

Another question is the extent to which those at a social disadvantage are conscious of it. A public opinion survey might well justify those descriptive sociologists who overvalue the esteem in which the village community and the biological advantages of a rural abode are held. It is likely that the majority of those questioned would declare their position to be satisfactory and would not dream of moving into town, near their place of employment. One can frequently note, though, in the course of carrying out surveys, that people at a social disadvantage realistically estimate the low likelihood of being able to change their situation; hence, they see it in a favorable light and show even less desire for change than their actual dissatisfaction would indicate. It is in fact those who are privileged, in particular professional people, who tend to express dissatisfaction with their actual situation. Yet they can be considered the most mobile within both the housing and the settlement system. The sociopsychological preconditions for criticizing reality are generally created by a real chance for change.

There is no doubt that the "new" working class was able to turn some of its disadvantages to advantage. We only have to step outside the limits of towns to observe villages, particularly in industrial areas, where houses are newer and roomier than those in towns. We know of villages where families of unskilled workers have built themselves houses with a floor area of 150 to 180 square meters--houses of the average size in contemporary North America. There are people who, looking at such houses, tend to question our view of the social disadvantages of the "new working class"--professional men and women whose apartments, though obtained as a state favor, have a floor area of no more than 50 square meters. But the position of workers from the village appears less enviable if we bear in mind that their low earnings from industry and the minimum use they are able to make of the infrastructure are accompanied by a doubling of their working hours. After eight hours work and long hours spent waiting and traveling, they are often met at the station by their wives, carrying two hoes, and they go off to another four or five hours of work on land allotted to them as sharecroppers by the cooperative or on their own household plots, which in the course of the years were turned into extremely intensively cultivated dwarf holdings.

Thus a peculiar social class has come into being which lives in two economic systems at the same time and which shows great sensitivity toward movements that establish equilibrium between the two. If there is a boom in industry, its labor power is transferred there; if in agriculture, then its industrial work is limited or temporarily suspended. They make up the bulk of migratory labor that is so often cursed by industry, not because of any lack of discipline but because the conflict between domicile and place of employment predestines them to this form of fight for higher wages. Though "new workers" may appear to be defenseless at first sight, they are certainly not powerless in the great struggle that goes on where goods are distributed. We can now see that the given system of economic growth is working for them in a paradoxical way, and that this extraordinarily mobile section of society, not tied to any town, may well turn out to profit from the shortage of labor which is becoming chronic at the end of the extensive industrialization period.

Executive of industrial enterprises located in agricultural areas complain that whereas in an earlier period people were lining up outside labor recruiting offices, at present all publicity is proving useless. Booming agricultural producers' cooperatives are attracting the best of the skilled labor away from the industrial enterprises, since they can pay an hourly rate of 16-17 forints in their repair workshops and supplementary enterprises, whereas industrial enterprises are limited to a rate of 12-13 forints. The means of industrial executives are pretty limited in this match; they have to provide better working conditions, cleaner showers, better lunches, and so on, and the foreman must adopt a more polite tone of voice. But all that cannot counterbalance the necessarily low wages. When executives then enter into complex agreements with cooperatives that have greater freedom in the market and can thus, by various bookkeeping tricks, pay their own workers better in the interests of carrying out their productive objectives, the executives can easily find themselves in conflict with contradictory economic-legal regulations or the authorities' various interpretations of them.

The growth in the economic power of the "new worker" is largely due to the fact that agriculture was also able to turn disadvantages to advantage. A shortage of labor owing to the attraction of industry was counterbalanced by more intensive agricultural techniques, which are already bearing fruit in higher agricultural incomes. It is possible that we are at the threshhold of an historical period where a stable agriculture, rather than industry, sets the pace. Extensive industrialization has created an industrial system whose superstructure, found in towns (in contrast to that of the low-level labor force, which is in villages), is at present able to melt away because it is bureaucratically too rigidly tied down. Industry is now being punished for the monopoly position which it earlier enjoyed because of administrative steps taken in its interest.

Industry took away the financial resources from the infrastructure and as a result slowed down urbanization, at the same time depriving itself of a town-based labor force tied to industrial employment and an urban way of life and a more mobile labor force able to respond to economic changes in the labor marketplace. A large-scale social conflict of interests was thus produced, which will confront the strategy of economic policy with new alternatives in the immediate future. The situation might be dealt with by administrative methods such as a higher taxation on agricultural incomes and administrative limits on the mobility of labor as well as further delay of investment in the infrastructure and hence of urban development. The other possible answer means using economic measures to further develop the regulative system, particularly in the field of wages and incomes policy, and to insist--particularly on the part of industrial executives--that infrastructural investments be paid for partly through local government rates and taxes and partly as a result of strategic distribution decisions. One can observe to an increasing extent that industrial executives and regional planners are beginning to realize that industrial development and housing construction are indivisible. In this way, industry could answer the challenge of agriculture within the framework of economic competition. This answer would also produce a dynamic equilibrium on the labor market.

However paradoxical this may sound, we expect a boom in urbanization and at least a partial solution to the social conflicts of delayed urban development precisely from further intensive growth in agriculture and from the village's ability to create jobs where people live. This accords with the logic of this paper's argument.

PART FIVE

MODERNIZATION AND DEVIANCE

Chapter 8.

DEVIANCE, STRESS, AND MODERNIZATION IN EASTERN EUROPE

Walter D. Connor

Modernization and Deviance: Some Preliminaries

Among the "conventional wisdoms" of Western sociology, the idea that modernization entails an increase in various forms of deviant behavior is very widespread. Typically, the process of modernization has been seen as stressful for the personalities of those undergoing it, invalidating old rules to which custom and tradition have acclimated people and substituting new and unfamiliar ones. These changes take place within a large context: the transformation of the landscape by urban construction and growth, industrial development, and large-scale transfers of population from "old" rural-agrarian settings to "new" urban-industrial ones. It is in these new settings that social pathology, in various form such as crime, delinquency, and alcoholism, is seen to flourish to a greater degree than it did previously.

The nature of the causal linkage generally remains vague and unspecified in most writings on modernization; the assertion of the linkage is almost automatic. This is not surprising, since most students of modernization per se have only marginal interest in nonpolitical forms of deviance, and most students of deviance have relatively little concern with the broader aspects of modernization. Further, it should be noted that this image of "modernization" is not the only one--another, directly relevant to our purposes here, will be discussed below.

It is no simple matter to specify, with any greater degree of clarity than hitherto achieved for other regions of the world, the linkage between "modernization" as experienced by the socialist countries of Eastern Europe and the types and degree of deviant behavior within them. We can assume, and do, that modernization has an impact on the forms and rates of deviance, and we tentatively assume that its impact is usually in the direction of increasing the total amount. From here on, however, few things are clear, and two aspects of the "socialist" modernizing experience need to be taken into account before we proceed further.

The "Base Point" of Modernization

"Modernization" describes a process that begins "somewhere"; it implies a point in past time when, in contrast to the present, things were relatively "unmodern" or traditional. (Of course, that past point may represent a more "modern" stage of societal development than what went before it, which is to say that "traditional" societies are by no means static.) "Unmodernity" is a matter of degree, and it is important to specify the degree of modernity characteristic of the societies we examine, within the temporal framework adopted here.

"Backward" as they might be, the East European countries were relatively modern, having, in C. E. Black's words, "developed institutions in the traditional era that were readily adaptable to modern functions."[1] There were, of course, fairly wide differences in the level of development of, let us say, Czechoslovakia and Albania; but, to employ Black's periodization, all these societies had, long before their "socialist revolutions," embarked on the first phases of modernization. Czechoslovakia and Hungary began the "consolidation of modernizing leadership" in 1848, Poland in 1863, and Bulgaria, Romania and Yugoslavia in 1878--all can be seen as completing this phase and entering on the beginnings of "social and economic transformation" in 1918. Albania began the first phase in 1912, completing it and entering the second phase in 1925.[2]

Socialist modernization, then, had as its base point not the relatively undifferentiated, tribalistic social and economic structure of many contemporary Afro-Asian modernizing states, but an already fairly high degree of institutional development. If Eastern Europe as a whole seemed "backward," it was in contrast not to the "world" in toto, but to Western Europe and North America. In this sense, Eastern Europe's modernization resembles that of the USSR: while it is correct to view the Bolsheviks as, inter alia, "modernizers," and the period after 1928 as one of intensive modernization, the period between 1885 and 1914 was itself one of rapid economic development as well as of more gradual development of modern institutions.

The "Soviet Model" of Modernization

The political circumstances of postwar Europe created a situation in which "socialist" modernization proceeded according to a "model" whose pace, specific institutional content and political-economic character were forged by the USSR's experience. To a degree, such a course was "natural--as Black observes, the "models adopted by modernizing leaders, except in the societies that were the first to modernize, are always derived in a considerable degree from outside their own society."[3] "Adoption" of the Soviet model was less a matter of choice than of the realities of power, whatever legitimacy has been achieved in the ensuing years by the institutional frameworks that developed. The model included "standard" components--industrialization and urbanization--but also much that was nonstandard: a thorough socialization of industry and trade, collectivization of agriculture (with the exception of Poland and Yugoslavia), the establishment of one-party systems and governmental-party bureaucracies on the Soviet blueprint, and drafting of new legal codes on Soviet models. Never, probably, has "modernization" proceeded in such close correspondence with a "model" as in Eastern Europe between 1948 and the middle 1950s--even in states already "modern" by most standards, as were Czechoslovakia and East Germany.

What has all of this to do with deviance? Two points should be made in answer: First, the nature of postwar modernization is such that one must anticipate difficulty in showing how it affected types and rates of deviant behavior. The student of Afro-Asian modernization has, it seems, clearer issues to explore-- the impact during a colonial period of the partial or full imposition of a European legal system, proscribing as heinous crimes many traditionally accepted practices (e.g., suttee, female infanticide, etc.) while leaving unpunished practices traditionally regarded as criminal; the "inheritance" and attempt to modify or adapt such codes to new conditions by postcolonial native elites; the impact of such changes on both incidence of certain offenses and the mode in which they are handled. In Eastern Europe, the problems are less clear. It is evident that socialism creates "socialist property" and hence a new type of property offense, a new type of polity, and some new political offenses. But the total impact of such "normative innovation" remains unclear.

Leaving it aside for the moment, what is the specific impact of industrialization and urbanization on deviance? This question, it may turn out, is to be answered in much the same way as in nonsocialist societies at similar levels of development. The "socialist" component, the "Soviet model," may be insignificant. This, however, remains to be seen, and the data available may not allow satisfactory answers. The two aspects of East European modernization noted here give our inquiry a rather specific set of problems, and at the same time impose limits on their solution. Finally, one rather obvious cautionary statement will bear some emphasis: statistical data on deviant behavior, from whatever nation, are probably among the most flawed sorts of data nations collect. In ascending order of inadequacy, statistics on offenses known, on deviants apprehended, and on convictions or other dispositions are all very imperfect measures of the behaviors which concern us here. East European criminologists show themselves increasingly aware of this,[4] and the reader should be warned as well. Although a modicum of such data is used here, my intention has been not to abuse it. "Hard figures" may be more persuasive than simple commentary, but figures which purport to express the incidence of behaviors which their perpetrators attempt to conceal might after all, be better called "soft."

Two Models of Modernization

The term "modernization" is used relatively little among Soviet or East European scholars. To a significant degree, however, its component concepts (basically industrialization and urbanization) concern them no less than they concern their Western colleagues. In this section we attempt a brief exploration of what may be called the "Western" view of modernization and its linkage to deviance and then move on to characterize its "Eastern" counterparts-- wherein, as we shall see, there are important differences between typical views in Soviet literature and those expressed in other European socialist states.

In summary, the Western view sees the processes of industrialization and urbanization as inducing stresses and dislocations which lead to higher rates of deviance. This is most clearly seen in the areas that represent the "cutting edge" of modernization--the new industrial cities. Here we may quote Wilbert Moore at length, since his treatment in many ways epitomizes this perspective:

It is in the industrial city that the problems of community organization appear most starkly. Cities tend to throw into juxtaposition persons of different tribal, regional, or even national origin. Given the importance of language and custom, the residential patterns of cities are likely to be mixtures determined not only by income differences but also by cultural groupings. The sense of community identity or even of interdependence may be thin and rare, particularly among newcomers. It is the rapidity of urbanization that especially strains the capacity of the urban community to "absorb" the migrant even in the bare sense of getting him attached to the network of services, to say nothing of capturing his commitment to collective concerns.

In these circumstances, the maintenance of primary social controls is difficult and occasionally impossible. In a "normal" social structure, social codes are internalized early and are constantly reinforced by rewards and punishments (approval and disapproval) from "significant others." Exclusive theoretical concern with early socialization neglects the possibility that new values may be internalized at any time in life; in the same way, it is misleading in its neglect of demoralization. Without the support of family and friends for maintaining moral conduct, and faced with all sorts of conflicting standards and many opportunities for anonymous transgression, the individual may well become a social deviant.

Frustration, value conflicts, and loss of emotional security from significant others are likely to lead to various symptoms of apathy or alienation. Thus alcoholism, drug addiction, and mental disorders have a higher proportional incidence in cities even after all due allowances have been made for statistical errors.

Crime and juvenile delinquency are also disproportionately urban. The very impersonality of urban life, together with a possible decline in primary social controls, may lead the individual to reject accepted standards of conduct. A cynical, instrumental view of social conduct is conducive to law obedience only when the perceived risks of being detected in transgression are high. Crimes against property are

especially marked in cities. Personal violence is, perhaps, no
more common than in rural areas, but in the city it is more likely
to be paradoxically "impersonal," as in incidental instrument of
robbery.[5]

The greater complexity and sheer scale of urban, as opposed to
village, life; the impersonal and segmented relations of the urbanite and
factory worker in contrast with the personal, tradition-prescribed and particularistic interpersonal linkages of peasants; the weakening of primary social
controls and the blurring of behavioral prescriptions in cities as against their
strength and clarity in rural communities: while these distinctions are not
necessarily meant to imply that rural-traditional life is "idyllic," they are
the distinctions of which the Western view of "modernization and deviance" is
composed. In summary, they are perhaps overgeneralized, but may possess considerable utility as a tool for understanding the origin of some unplanned and
unsought consequences of striving for modernity.[6]

A notable feature of many Western views of modernization is economic-
technological "determinism," which deemphasizes the relevance of differences
in modernizing ideologies to the political cast of modernizing regimes. Given
the fulfillment of modernization goals to some significant degree, whatever the
"politics" of the struggle, it seems fair to say that, in a common Western view,
unplanned consequences--among them the sorts of social pathology that concerns
us here--were expected to follow more or less automatically.

Nowhere is the rejection of this view more clear than in the statements
of Soviet writers, who have assailed the idea that industrialization and urbanization are essentially similar processes, whether achieved under "capitalist" or
"socialist" auspices. E. Mel'nikova draws the line in a fairly typical
manner.

Industrialization brings about changes in the lives of people,
but in socialist society it is a positive social factor. The possibility of planned regulation of the phenomena accompanying
industrialization, such as urbanization, and migration of population,
makes it possible to neutralize the effect on people's life of possible
negative factors, linked with urbanization and migration (changes in
the habitual life surroundings, displacement of large masses of the
population, over-population, etc.).
A different situation arises in capitalist society. In it, in
connection with the impossibility of planning production, etc. unfavorable changes in the social conditions of the life of the population are created. It is precisely this, and not at all economic
progress itself, that can create conditions, facilitating the growth
of crime among youth.[7]

In this and other criticisms of Western views of industrialization's impact,[8]
socialist industrialization is presented as a process, sui generis, fundamentally different from and purged of those elements in the progressive "eradication"
of the roots of crime.

Even in the USSR (which has, in common with most other nations, an
urban crime/delinquency rate much higher than that in its less progressive and
"modern" rural areas), however, these blanket assertions are giving way to
cautious recognition of the fact that rapid urbanization and industrialization in
a backward country pose real problems. In 1968, for example, M. M. Babaev
addressed the linked issues of heavy rural in-migration to developing Soviet
industrial cities and the higher offense rates there as compared with rural
"feeder" areas. He viewed the situation as a product of the fact that "in many
cases the scale of organization and upbringing work does not yet correspond to the
scale of the phenomenon itself--the tempo and scale of city construction in the
USSR. As a result, in the cities there exists a larger quantity of negative

factors, promoting the formation of antisocial views, habits...than in rural locales."[9] Babaev did not expand in great detail on the "negative factors." But it is clear he had in mind the large-scale introduction of young male workers, predominantly of rural background and either single or at a distance from their wives and children, into cities undergoing rapid industrial development, but much less rapid construction of housing and leisure facilities. In this frontier-town environment, a high incidence of violent behavior is perhaps to be expected--but such migrants, male, relatively young, of rural origin, make up much of the population increase in older Soviet cities as well. With appropriate modification of phraseology, Babaev's observations on the situation of much migrants might have come from a Western social scientist.

> Processes of migration may be and often are accompanied by some
> negative phenomena: with the move to the city, social control
> over the young man on the part of the family, the immediate
> everyday environment and the like, which is as a rule more ef-
> fective in the village than in the city, weakens or is completely
> lost; the young man, coming from the village, is not always able
> to understand correctly, and manage to distinguish the real,
> progressive urban culture and as a result sometimes accepts the
> worst and most harmful things for the model of urban culture and
> "city behavior."[10]

Such statements hardly represent an indictment of Soviet city life for its "criminogenic" characteristics. But this, and some other Soviet writers' admissions,[11] indicate increasing recognition that socialist cities have "urban" problems.

Here, in fact, Soviet researchers are following lines staked out some time ago by their East European colleagues, notably in Poland. Wartime devastation, large-volume migration into the "Western Territories" reclaimed from Germany, intensive industrialization, and the growth of new urban centers all have turned Polish criminologists' attention toward urban social problems. The origins of these problems have been dealt with in a rather undoctrinaire, "de-ideologized" manner. One example, from a research study by J. Jasinski, lays out a general view of population migration in Poland and its hypothesized linkage to delinquency (linkage Jasinski finds supported by his data):

> In general, growth of juvenile delinquency, in countries which
> are undergoing rapid economic development, is due to the migratory
> movements which accompany this process....
> After the last war, we could distinguish in Poland two types of
> migration which resulted from different processes:
> a) The first population movement manifested itself during the
> war as a consequence of the occupation and at the end of the war
> according to the modification of frontiers. This migration came
> to an end several years ago.
> b) The second population movement still persists. It is due to
> the social and economic transformations which have been brought
> about by the industrialization and urbanization of the country.
> It is due also to the directives of our plan of economic invest-
> ment, which aims at leveling out the differences in regional
> development and to emphasize the territories recently recovered
> by Poland in the western and northwestern parts of the country.[12]

More specifically, the Yugoslav criminologist A. Todorovic notes that "it has been demonstrated many times that criminality is conditioned by a movement of population drawn from rural areas toward urban areas. This phenomenon is particularly marked in underdeveloped countries. Massive immigration into the cities brings with it, then, crises of housing, insufficient (public) health, problems of education, of instruction and of leisure, a slackening of public morality, a new mode of life. One may imagine that such a conjuncture would be eminently propitious to phenomena of social pathology."[13]

Generally, Polish criminologists seem to agree with such a characterization. Although we will defer consideration of research findings to another section, it is worth noting that their studies of delinquency, focused on such areas of intensive modernization as the new industrial cities of Konin and Nowa Huta, show high rates of deviant behavior and much the same elements of "pathology" of which Todorovic writes.

Though other East European countries discuss the issue less, it is likely that more and more writers are coming to view socialist economic development as sharing some "growing pains" with nonsocialist forms. In Bulgaria, for example, the intensive industrialization that has tripled the population of the city of Razgrad in two decades was seen as giving rise to new problems, including "hooliganism" and drunkenness.[14]

Thus, it appears that the effects of socialist modernization are coming to be viewed, in Eastern Europe and in the USSR, as problematic in several senses. Along with undeniable benefits in living standards, education, and a generally enlarged scope of experience, the unwanted consequences which seem to follow in the train of industrialization and urbanization are being recognized. It is, no doubt, somewhat early to speak of massive "convergence" of the two views of modernization--yet this is, on the evidence, the direction of the future.

It is now time to turn from general discussions to somewhat more specific concerns with various forms of deviant behavior, warning the reader that, given the gaps and inaccuracies endemic in statistics on deviance from any society, he should view with caution the picture drawn in the following pages.

Aggression

An attempt to summarize the "pattern of criminality" in even a single country is fraught with difficulties. To try to give an overview of such patterns for five or six countries involves a geometric expansion of these difficulties. Thus, the pages which follow can only provide some general indications of trends, patterns, and "styles" of deviance without being in any way exhaustive for all (or even any one) of the relevant countries. The present section, on aggression, provides a thumbnail sketch, with some statistics, of common antiperson and property offenses. Sections follow on "escapism," which deals with alcohol abuse in Eastern Europe, and "aggrandizement" (dealing with the types of offenses against socialist property typically called "economic crimes").

East European statistics generally give the impression of a decline in "registered crimes." In Poland, for example, 1937 showed 733,258 registered crimes, or a rate of 2,134 per 100,000 population; the corresponding 1963 figures were 421,656 and 1,374.[15] Comparisons of prewar and "socialist" figures for Hungary, Czechoslovakia, and Bulgaria show similar trends.[16] Although "socialism" is generally given credit for these downward curves, the experience within the socialist period has not been one of uninterrupted decline. In the 1960s the data indicate rises in the incidence of some types of crime, stability in others, and declines in yet others. Some figures here may be of interest:

In Hungary, the total number of registered crimes rose from 109,260 in 1964 to 121,961 in 1965 (while delinquency in 1965 increased by 23 percent over the 1962-64 average), gradually declining to close to the 1964 level by 1969.[17] However, in late 1971 the Hungarian minister of justice noted that crime of violence were "up" in the "last few years," linking this with a rise in offenses involving alcohol.[18]

In Poland, although summary statistics show a more or less general down-turn in the offense rate, "crimes against life and health" tended to increase between 1954 and the early to mid 1960s. In 1954 these totaled 18,332, and by 1963 the figure had climbed to 49,498.[19] In 1954, 2,039 persons were convicted of inflicting serious and especially serious bodily injury--in 1961, the corresponding figure was 4,820.[20] In terms of the total number of convictions in Poland, crimes against life and health represented 9.7 percent in 1954, and 18.3 percent in 1962.[21]

In Yugoslavia (where the rate of violent crimes remains, apparently, relatively high), crimes against life and health rose from 12.7 percent of all convictions in 1947 to 26.2 percent in 1961.[22]

In Czechoslovakia, interestingly enough, rates have risen since 1968. Convictions fell to 83,941 in 1968 (from 109,765 in 1967), rose to 101,933 in 1969, and grew again, by almost 50 percent, to 149,981 in 1970.[23] Plausibly, this growth reflects both anomic responses to the rapid and continuing political changes and retrenchment which "normalization" has brought, and an increasingly "tough" policy toward deviants of every sort.

Overall, national "profiles" of criminality show property crimes as the largest single category. In Poland, statistical series for 1961-70 show property crimes making up almost 40 to 50 percent of reported offenses and court cases,[24] while figures for Bulgaria and the GDR fall roughly within this range.[25] In Czechoslovakia, property offenses varied from one-fifth to about one-third of the offense total between 1958 and 1967, rising somewhat above one-third in 1968-69 and falling to slightly less than 20 percent in 1970.[26] Yugoslavia also seems less "occupied" with property offenses, which constituted only about 20 percent of total convictions in 1960-65.[27]

Crimes against the person generally occupy a much smaller "share" of the total but are difficult to deal with because of vagueness in categorization and, sometimes, "overlap" between antiperson and public-order offenses. For example, "crimes against the person" made up 26.2 percent of the total in Bulgaria in 1963,[28] which may indicate a relatively high rate of assault and homicide, or only a large number of offenses of slander, defamation, and so forth. In Yugoslavia, however, the picture is somewhat clearer: on the average, between 1960 and 1965 crimes against "life and health" made up about one-quarter of the crime total (measured in convictions), while offenses against "honor and reputation" exceeded this at 27.9 percent.[29] A tradition of aggressiveness and violence, especially in the more backward areas, may account for Yugoslavia's "peculiarity" here.[30]

In Czechoslovakia, where changing law enforcement patterns probably affect statistics greatly, the last ten years show uneven "growth" in violent offenses against the person. Convictions fell from 11,317 in 1966 to a "low" of 7,566 in 1968, and rose to 13,027 in 1970.[31] Poland's homicide rate (including attempted homicide) has, on the other hand, remained relatively stable over the years 1965-70, at slightly over 1 percent of the total offenses "found in preparatory proceedings."[32]

What of the contribution of minors to the total of criminality? Typically, when convictions of juveniles are viewed as a percentage of all court convictions, their role seems minimal; however, with the numerous nonjudicial "tracks" available for disposing of juvenile cases, such figures, if viewed uncritically, may be misleading. The figures which follow, drawn from different sources, are fairly typical: In Hungary in the early 1960s, about 6.7 percent of all convicted persons were juveniles; in the GDR in 1963, 13.7 percent of all criminal offenses were juvenile offenses;[33] in Czechoslovakia, juvenile convictions in the mid to late 1960s made up about 4 to 5 percent of the total.[34]

In Poland in 1968, 232,466 adults and 34,760 juveniles were convicted in courts of general jurisdiction. Juveniles, then, made up approximately 13

percent of the total "business" of these courts in 1968. But juvenile courts in
Poland sentenced 77,215 offenders in 1969, and should have been similarly "busy"
in 1968. Publication of "juvenile court" statistics from other socialist states
would perhaps reveal a somewhat similar pattern.[35]

Juveniles "concentrate" on garden-variety property crimes, in Eastern
Europe as (generally) elsewhere. Data for 1965, 1967, and 1970 show property
offenses as the large majority of all juvenile offenses in Poland and Yugoslavia,
and as a large component in Czechoslovakia.[36]

Escapism

Less disruptive and "anti," but surely as "deviant" in societies whose
official rhetoric is still "mobilizational" are behaviors of an "escapist" type--
ways of "coping" which involve the individual's intermittent or relatively permanent psychological removal from problem situations. In Eastern Europe, the most
widespread form of escapist deviance seems to be alcohol abuse (with some indications of a growing drug abuse problem as well).

In this, the area bears a strong resemblance to the USSR--the source
of so many of its postwar institutional and organizational "models." Although it
would be too much to say that the countries of Eastern Europe have had "imposed"
on them the strong and persistent traditional Russian "drinking culture",[37] in many
respects the pictures are similar. Official hand-wringing in the press and other
mass media, dark warnings about the damage to labor and lives wrought by drink,
interspersed with decrees raising prices, setting together time-and-place regulations, calls from more nonalcoholic "youth cafés"--all these are present in both
milieus.

Though per capita consumption statistics are notoriously misleading,
those available tend to indicate that alcohol consumption (and with it, alcohol
pathology) has undergone a large increase. In Czechoslovakia, annual consumption per capita (in liters of pure alcohol) climbed from 3.4 in 1934 to 4.5 in
1955: the 1968 reported figure was 6.2, and reports indicate a current figure of
over 8.0[38] Pricing policies aimed at encouraging consumption of nonalcoholic
drinks have seemingly had little effect. In 1958, Rude Pravo announced a price
increase of 20 percent on distilled liquor--a move calculated to allow a 5 percent
reduction in the cost of milk.[39] Today, the drinking habits of the "statistical
Czech" show little of the desired effect: annual per capita milk consumption
dropped from 122 liters in 1955 to 95 in 1965; beer consumption rose from 79 to
125 liters over the same period.[40] By mid-1971, it was claimed that about 7
percent of the national income was being spent on alcohol,[41] with the number of
alcoholics estimated at "about 1.5 percent" of the total population.[42] Judicial
statistics reflect an association between alcohol and crime: in 1967 the
procurator-general attributed one-third of the homicides, and 80 percent of
"rowdyism" offenses, to drunkenness.[43]

Perhaps worst afflicted with alcohol-related problems is Poland
(though in consumption statistics it falls behind many other countries).[44] Here,
elements of "custom" and "tradition" enter into drinking in a way not dissimilar
to the USSR. Drinking on the job, payday drinking bouts, and weekend drunkenness leading to a high rate of Monday absenteeism are widespread.[45] The claim
that "excessive drinking is often linked with certain religious ceremonies" in
Poland is one that echoes the voices of many Soviet writers.[46]

The figures again tell a story of growing consumption and growing
problems. By 1964, according to a deputy minister of health, alcohol consumption
had more than doubled over the prewar period.[47] Between 1955 and 1969, per capita

consumption rose 43 percent.[48] The "statistical Pole" of 1966 consumed 23.2 liters
of beer, 4.7 of wine, and 2.5 liters of pure alcohol (in the form of distilled
spirits) per annum.[49] By 1969, he had increased his intake to 30.4, 5.6, and
3.4 liters, respectively,[50] and was spending a considerable sum to satisfy his
thirst. In 1969, 46,000,000 zloty were spent on alcohol--representing about
24 percent of the total domestic market expenditure on goods, and the second
largest (after meat) item in the average family budget.[51] Estimates of the size
of the alcoholic population vary, but a commonly cited figure is 2 million
"habitual drunkards," a figure equalling about 10.9 percent of the total population in the productive age brackets.[52]

Other countries show somewhat similar patterns. In 1958, alcoholism
was regarded as the "most difficult problem" facing the Budapest public prosecut-
or's office, and according to Ministry of Health figures Hungarian consumption
increased from 6.8 liters per capita of pure alcohol in 1965 to 8.6 liters in
1970.[54] Changes in per capita consumption in Bulgaria (measured by sales figures
from 1957 to 1968) indicate a moderate downturn for wine (from 5.5 to 5.04 liters)
but rises for beer (7.4 to 27.47) and hard liquor (1.83 to 2.39).[55]

Of course, not every liter is downed by an "escapist," and total
consumption figures for the socialist countries are not nearly as high as for
some countries in Western Europe and elsewhere.[56] The attributed "social
costs" are evident. Rude Pravo claims 115,000 man-days of work lost in one
year owing to alcohol,[58] and Warsaw's Polityka assigns a 1969 loss of 1,600,000,000
zloty to 32,000 industrial accidents caused by drinking.[59]

East European writers frequently link alcohol with crime as a direct or
indirect "cause" of criminal behavior. While "causality" may be problematic,
statistics reflect a degree of association which makes serious concern quite un-
derstandable. One source connects 18 percent of all 1966 criminal offenses in
Czechoslovakia with alcohol,[60] and estimates run as high as a 50 percent share of
all criminal acts in Poland linked with drinking.[61] Writing of a "distressing
affinity" between drink and delinquency, the district attorney of Brasov
district in Romania noted most of the local "hooligans" were between eighteen
and twenty-five, and that 80 percent of their offenses involved alcohol.[62]
"Intake" statistics from the "sobering-up stations" in Poland, Bulgaria, and
Hungary also indicate increasing pressures on these facilities--some measure of
the problem of public drunkenness.[63]

The problem of alcohol abuse, then, is clearly one that hampers the
"performance," both general and job-related, of large numbers of adult males in
Eastern Europe. Given official commitments to "rationalization," increased productivity, and to "designing out" problems of friction and unpredictability in
social management, one might ask what factors hamper the success of the anti-
alcohol campaigns they mount. Beyond the obvious difficulty of rooting out
"drinking cultures" legitimated by tradition and supported by the need for
escape mechanisms in a world where these are scarce, the reasons seem mainly
economic.

Short-run profits from the sale of alcoholic beverages are enormous.[64]
The state monopolies produce cheaply and sell dear. Although price rises are one
of the "weapons" in the struggle with drink, they have been notably unsuccessful
in depressing the level of demand--but they have increased the cash inflow.
Alcohol absorbs a good deal of purchasing power in societies where consumer dur-
ables are often scarce, and individual outlays for housing, education, and medical
care are low. In some cases, internal trade networks are "locked into" situations
requiring a high rate of alcohol sales. In Hungary, for example, the heavy
(80 percent) tax on cognac and hard liquor produces billions of forints to
subsidize the prices of various basic food items.[65]

Complaints abound about the economics of public catering which causes
restaurants to "push" alcohol. In Poland, the margin of profit on restaurant

food is low, sometimes nonexistent, whereas that on alcohol is high, and fulfilling an establishment's "plan" (and ensuring bonuses for waiters and other workers) involves high-volume alcohol sales.[66] Suggestions that alcohol profits not be counted in plan fulfillment have so far gone unheeded [67]--not surprisingly, since advocates of such moves are generally at a loss to say how lost revenues would be recouped. Raising the prices of subsidized items such as foods is laden with risks, as the Polish events of December 1970 showed.

The problem of alcohol abuse is interwoven with state policy in a complex mesh of economic and social prioriites. Given such circumstances, one Polish critic may indeed be touching the truth when he writes that "one cannot talk seriously about combatting alcoholism under circumstances where a growing number of people want to drink, to get drunk, in which there are ample ways to obtain alcohol and people employed in trade and catering are financially interested in boosting its sales."[68]

Aggrandizement

Socialization of the means of production--one of the most critical elements "peculiar" to socialist modernization--implies, at least, a change on another level: that of individual and social consciousness. Essential in a socialist economy is "socialist consciousness" (or perhaps, conscientiousness). As coproprietors of the national wealth and economy, citizens only harm themselves if they steal or otherwise violate economic regulations. Manipulation of an administrative or supervisory post for personal gain is similarly seen as not only "wrong," but in a sense illogical.

Yet experience shows that consciousness (as Marx himself would acknowledge) has lagged behind institutional changes in political and economic spheres. Thoroughgoing "socialist consciousness" is as yet only a distinct goal, whereas corruption is seemingly endemic, to varying degrees, in the socialist countries of Eastern Europe.

Under the heading of "economic crimes," those involving abuse of position for (frequently huge) private gains occupy a good deal of space in the mass media. Similarly condemned are conversion and misappropriation of goods, for use or resale, by managers and employees in retail trade networks. The volume of such activity and the sums involved, viewed in the aggregate, are large indeed. Summarizing is difficult, given the diversity of means offenders employ, but a few examples from Hungary, spanning a fifteen-year period, may serve to give a "feel" for the phenomenon.

The buyer of the Kaposfo collective bought large quantities of lumber between October 1956 and April 1957--and fails to remember from whom. But the sellers swear that they have sold him less than the amounts shown on the purchase slips. In addition, 16 names, appearing on these slips, cannot be traced for the simple reason that these people never existed. Investigation proved that, with the help of his associates, the buyer forged the sales and embezzled the money. Not only must he be brought to court, but the leaders of the collective must also be impeached for having been slack in the management of the farm's affairs and for not having noticed that the buyer earned 75,000 forint in the period from October 1956 to April 1957.[69]

The Danuvia machine-tool factory deals with the design and construction of various types of machine. The management of this factory rejected, or refused, a customer of some work on grounds of shortage of capacity. The chief constructor of the factory

offered to carry out this work privately in exchange for a
substantial bonus payment, and it was duly completed by
factory engineers during their normal working time. The
chief constructor received his bribe, and gave a percentage of
it to the general manager and chief engineer for their collab-
oration. The chief constructor and chief engineer made a profit of about 250,000 forint before their activities were exposed in August 1971.

The general manager of a building industry enterprise was
said to have "sold himself his own car." What he did in fact
was to buy a Polish Fiat for 98,000 forint and sell it to his
own enterprise for official use; he then assigned the car for
his personal use, so that he alone used the car while the
enterprise bought it and paid for fuel and repairs. This
gentleman was involved in a number of other dubious arrangements: his wife was theoretically "employed" by three
agricultural co-operatives as a purchasing agent (the cooperative being under some obligation to the enterprise) but
in practice worked in none of them. He was also concerned
in malpractices concerned with apartments, etc. The case came
to light in July of this year [1971].70

Available statistics are spotty, but they do show a persistent problem, with
some tendency toward increase. Reviewing criminal statistics from 1964
through 1969, Magyaroszag observed that although the single offense of
"corruption" made up only a small percentage of the total number of known
crimes in Hungary in those years, it had increased over the five years (in
registered instances) by 47.5 percent--a larger increase by far than that
reported for all varieties of crime taken together.71 Sharp rises in all
crimes against the economy were reported between 1964 and 1965; in 1965 as compared to 1967, the number of such crimes rose by 57.2 percent, and the number
of accused by 38.2 percent.72 In Poland, the total number of "economic
crimes" went down by 1 percent in 1969 as against 1968, but the cost of such
crimes increased in the same period by 2 percent--for a 1969 total of 398
million zloty.73

The offenses considered here generally require "legal" access to
large sums of money or goods for their perpetration, and raise the question of
quis custodiet ipsos custodes?74 Small-scale theft by workers and employees
from their factories and enterprises is also very much a part of daily life,
and the aggregate damage to the economy from such offenses must be large. Large
"rings" made up of responsible officials who siphon off huge sums from the enterprises under their direction, and petty thieves who remove tools, materials,
and other goods from their jobs are linked in a moral universe where "socialist
consciousness" is notable mainly by its absence. The operating ethic seems
closer to "what belongs to everyone belongs to no one"--and hence is "available."

In Poland, the usual motive for theft is the fact that something
is just lying about. It may be a bag of cement lying on the ground or
a piece of extra equipment--anything that seems ownerless and tempting
to someone without moral guidance. So, we face the small-time thief
and the sociologist who justifies and excuses him.

"Everybody steals" means, in fact, that everybody must steal, because wages are low and they must somehow make ends meet. This
only masks common theft with hypocrisy. I have never met a thief
or even heard of one, who would set a limit on his stealing--say
2,000 zloty a month to help supplement his low pay, and who would
give this extra money to his thrifty wife or save it up for a TV
set. This would be moral discipline of a higher order.

Thieves of public property are helped not only by many things being
left around for them but also by our complicated price system, the

shadowy line between private and social or state property, and
shortages that lead to goods being sold under the counter.
   Just imagine a man writing a novel the size of Jan Gerhard's
latest trilogy if typing paper were scarce. He is not a
member of the Writers' Union--he cannot be until his work is
published. Obviously he would be tempted to get paper in some
shady way. Or take the case of someone who can't get a spare
part for his radio at the state repair shop but can from a
private repairman. No doubt someone stole the part from a
factory and some fence bought it.[75]

A Czech proverb, apparently widespread, makes the point more succinctly: "he
who does not steal from the state, steals from his family." And indeed, that
the state, rather than private citizens, should be the main target is not surprising. Moral reservations about appropriating goods tend to weaken when the
victim is large and impersonal, and in any case, as one former Czech judge puts
it, with thoroughgoing expropriation of private property, the state "had become
the owner of more wealth than it could possible protect."[76]

   Persistent problems, especially in the service sector, create fertile
soil for "speculation" and more individualistic forms of deviant or semideviant
enterprise. A market exists for cars for those who are far down the waiting
list but have cash in hand, for television sets assembled from spare parts
"appropriated" by electrical workers when state stores' supplies are insufficient
to meet the demand--and there are vendors who step in to fill the gaps. What of
these vendors? One may suggest that many feel underrewarded, and need income.
"Needs," of course, are relative. Whether "need" and "poverty" have been eliminated under socialism is a difficult question to answer--and for present purposes
probably irrelevant. The attraction of increasing one's income in a second job
or "auxiliary" activity is a strong one, and the tempted respond--even when
second jobs are often of dubious legality. In so responding, they (in contrast
to the large-scale "economic criminals") meet demands otherwise unmet, and
produce and profit in a "private" economy from the use of skills that may, in
fact, be underutilized in the socialist sector.

   Bureaucratic corruption is a problem most modernizing regimes face, as
they attempt to impose the same rules of modern bureaucracy on functionaries
socialized in other molds and on new recruits from among inexperienced but
politically "loyal" strata. Yet corruption in Eastern Europe and in the USSR
is not of the same sort as that in African and Asian nations whose modernization
began from a much more "traditional" base.[77] It is less "familistic," less
particularistic, and closely linked in its procedures with the characteristics
of a tight-planned economy, but flexible enough to switch to new operational
modes under the thrust of economic reform. One might suggest that these developing economies, "socialized" after the Soviet model, have in many ways shaped the
style and nature of the corruption to which they are prey.

                    The "Deviant Population": Some Characteristics

   Who are the deviants? What characteristics, besides their deviance,
distinguish them from the "normal" populations? With few exceptions, the
evidence available is largely impressionistic. But taken as a whole it suggests
some relatively consistent patterns, both among East European nations and between
them and other countries.

   Crime, delinquency, and drunkenness remain a decisively male "preserve,"
as they do in virtually every country which reports statistics on deviant
behavior. Of 26,437 delinquents convicted by Polish courts of general jurisdiction

in 1970, only 1,898 were female. In the same year, of the 166,049 adults convicted under public indictments, only 17,644 were women. In Yugoslavia, the
picture is similar, with almost four adult males convicted to every female.[79]
There is no evidence of substantial deviation from this pattern in the other
socialist states. One aspect of "modernity," however, affects this relationship: research in Poland indicates that, with urban residence, female offense
rates (or official processing of female offenders), climbs relative to the males,
who thus enjoy a lesser "domination" of deviance in cities than in the countryside.[80] Indeed, criminal-population sex ratios for Eastern Europe are not so
lopsided as in many other societies; as the Polish scholar Batawia notes, the
rate of female criminality is "relatively" high in Poland, and similar in this
regard to that in Hungary and Yugoslavia. [81]

Evidence from various sources points to overrepresentation of the less
educated and less-skilled among the deviant population. Jasinski finds that
although delinquents as a group are increasing in education (in 1954-58, 61 to
65 percent of convicted delinquents were in school, whereas in 1960 the figure
was 81 percent), their educational performance fell below national norms. Over
the period 1951-62, an average of 20 to 25 percent of delinquents dropped out of
school before reaching the minimum leaving age of fourteen. During the same
years, while an average of 10 to 25 percent of all pupils failed and repeated a
grade, more than 50 percent of delinquents did.[82] Similarly, crimes in Bulgaria
are said to be committed by young people of "low cultural standards,"[83] and
criminality seems to go hand in hand with lack of education and training. Sliven
okrug in Bulgaria, where the crime rate was twice the national average, was described as a place where the predominant labor-intensive and low-paid food and
textile industries gave little incentive for people to increase their educational
level or job qualifications. A large proportion of the local criminals were
dropouts.[84]

Information on the social origins or peasant status of juvenile and
adult offenders is not plentiful, and difficulties in comparing it with nationwide
distributions necessitate caution. The available data suggest, at least, a concentration of criminality and delinquency among lower- and working-class urban
populations (paralleling a situation confirmed for the USSR by existing Soviet
data).[85] Jasinski found that 60 to 62 percent of Polish juvenile and young adult
offenders in 1953-60 were drawn from workers' households, 19 to 22 percent from
peasant families, and only 9 to 10 percent from families whose livelihood was
gained in the "tertiary sector."[86] Similarly, a survey of 559 persons convicted
of "public brawling" in Poland in 1957-59 showed that 80 percent were workers,
10 percent farmers, and only 3 percent "brain workers."[87]

Tentative as it is, a picture begins to emerge of a mainly urban, industrial "underclass," relatively disadvantaged in terms of education, job skills,
and general "culture," as the breeding ground for much of deviant behavior in
socialist society. It is not an unfamiliar picture, in the light of findings in
other modern societies. Its accuracy receives additional support in the researches
of Polish criminologists concerned with the impact of industrial development and
rural-urban migration.

The notion of "urbanism" deserves some comment here. It refers less to
the quality and style of life in cities, as opposed to rural areas, than to
particular types of human relationships and modes of organization, wherever they
occur. Impersonality, formality rather than informality in organizing human
activity, a heightened "tempo" of life, reliance on formal rather than informal
means of social control--all these may be seen as more characteristically "urban"
than rural, but they are not limited to cities.[88] Thus, in assessing the impact
of modernization's "urbanism" component, we need to take account not only of the
growth of cities but also of the extension of "urban-modern" characteristics to
areas still denominated as "rural." Polish data allow us to do this to a certain
degree; the question whether or to what degree they can be generalized to some of
the other European socialist countries admits of no precise answer (except insofar

as the experience of a higher urban than rural crime/delinquency rate is universal), but an educated guess, in my estimation, would predict some parallels.

   The urban "advantage" shows up clearly in Polish delinquency research.
Batawia, analyzing conviction statistics for 1960 in the seventeen to twenty
age group, found, for the country as a whole, 47.3 convictions per 1,000 males:
in cities, the figure rose to 55.6 (or 1 in 20), and in the rural areas it fell
to 40.7 (or 1 in 24). For females the rate was considerably lower, but the
urban-rural difference was much larger, reflecting, perhaps, the greater degree
of "traditional" control over girls in the countryside. The figures for females
were 10.6 per 1,000 urban, and 5.1 rural.[89]

   Police statistics, also from 1960, serve to point up the differences
with greater clarity. Of all apprehended delinquents, 44.2 percent were drawn
from cities of 50,000 persons or more--such cities contained only 24.5 percent of
the total population. From the five cities with populations of 400,000 or more,
which included only 10.6 percent of the national population, came 20 percent of the
delinquents. For juvenile recidivists in 1960, this trend was even more marked--
83 percent of the recidivists were from urban areas and 17 percent from rural,
while the country as a whole had a population 48 percent urban and 52 percent
rural.[90]

   More to the point, however, are studies which treat "urban" characteristics as continuous variables, measuring the extent to which increases in
"urbanism" correlate with increases in the delinquency rate. Maroszek's research,
using data for 1957-61 from the sixteen districts in Gdansk voivodship, does
this. Maroszek measured the relationship between the delinquency rates (offenders per 1,000 of the eligible age group) by district and four other characteristics: (1) the percentage of urban population (ranging from 100 in Gdansk,
Gdynia, and Sopot to 12.5 in Kartuzy); (2) the percentage of population working
other than in agriculture; (3) the number of persons working in industry per
1,000 inhabitants; and (4) the percentage of arable land in the socialist,
rather than private, sector. Positive correlations were obtained in each case,
with r equaling, respectively, 0.67, 0.61, 0.56, and 0.56.[91] Jasinski notes,
additionally, that when attention is focused on rural areas alone, positive if
modest correlations exist between the level of delinquency and the percentage of
the labor force employed outside agriculture.[92]

   Maroszek's four characteristics are all reflections of socialist modernization (the first three also "universal" aspects of the process). In this
sense, then, whatever its merits or demerits in an economic sense, the
socialization of agriculture, as well as the rest, can be seen as part of the
extension of urbanism or "modernity" in the countryside--a process which apparently has some implications for deviant behavior. Poland, with its large private
agricultural sector for "contrast," provides the clearest illustration of this.

   Notable also in the Polish data is the fact that the urban-rural rate
differences in delinquency, although significant enough, are not overly large
(in 1960, for males, 55.6 per 1,000 to 40.7 respectively).[93] The urban-rural
differences reported for the USSR, for example, are much greater.[94] One might
argue here that Soviet rural areas are in fact much more "rural" in their quality
and style of life than Polish rural areas (despite the extension of socialized
agriculture in the USSR, this might be seen as the only "modern" element
characterizing the Soviet countryside, and then only in the restricted sense employed here). Despite the strong persistence of private agriculture in Poland,
the relatively shorter distances, easier communications, and better linkages
between city and countryside there may make rural areas more modern and urban
in quality, including relatively high rates of crime and delinquency in comparison
with the cities.[95] The same may well hold true, mutatis mutandis, for the better
developed of the other socialist countries--notably Czechoslovakia and Hungary.[96]

   Thus our picture of the deviant in his milieu, tentative as it remains, grows a bit fuller. Working-class males, young to early middle-aged,[97] generally low to average in education and skills, who confront the "modernity" of urbaniza-tion-industrialization either through "hereditary" residence in cities or migra-tion to them, or through the encroachment of urban qualities into still-"rural" areas--by and large, this seems to be the "recruiting pool."

Overall, the urban-rural "confrontation" seems to be drawn most clearly in the case of migration--characteristic not only of Poland, where the high crime and delinquency rates of "new cities" like Konin and Nowa Huta have been so inten-sively studied, but of the other more industrialized socialist countries as well. What applies to Poland probably applies in the others also. In Nowa Huta in 1954, in the heyday of socialist industrialization, the conviction rate per 1,000 in the seventeen to twenty age group was more than twice that for the country as a whole.[98] Large influxes of young men from farm families whose holdings were small created a whole new category of unattached males, living mainly in workers' dormitories, where "entire evenings were passed in playing cards or drinking, (where) there were veritable debauches in the total absence of organized leisure."[99] Some found no work at all; to survive, they "had only one means--commit a crime."[100] Others found yet more unfamiliar problems. The eighteen to twenty-year-olds generally found jobs paying more than the countryside offered and, de-prived of the parental guidance and control they had left there, spent their money drinking. The younger ones (fifteen and sixteen) found work only at much lower pay, suffering "grave material difficulties," and took to crime in large numbers.[101] This phenomenon, which Zakrzewski labels "premature emancipation," could scarcely be avoided. In the villages, "definite moral norms presided over the conduct of individuals," but in Nowa Huta, where the young had cast loose their moorings, "the old moral norms played no such role and the sanction of public opinion worked no more."[102]

Such difficulties, it seems, are neither socialist nor capitalist: what-ever the more general merits of the notion of "convergence," the costs of rapid and intensive modernization, with reference to deviance, appear to be inherent in the process itself. Poland did not escape them, nor is there reason to think that the other socialist countries, for which we lack information, did.

Socialism, Deviance, and Modernity

Viewed broadly, the data presented here offer some support for the "con-ventional wisdom" that modernization leads to increases in deviant behavior. Certainly, this is the way many Polish criminologists have interpreted the findings of their research, and there is given evidence that the "optimistic" Soviet view of socialist modernization is undergoing some small modifications in this direc-tion. Throughout Eastern Europe since World War II, large populations have made the transition from rural-agrarian to urban-industrial environments, a transition that for some is full of stress and likely to evoke different forms of maladjust-ment and deviance. This transition is unquestionable. Although still not as "modern" in many ways as much of Western Europe, the underdeveloped states of Eastern Europe have come a long way, and a student viewing them through the con-ceptual apparatus of "Western" sociology might expect the rising curve of deviance to appear.

Yet how clear is the picture? Virtually every socialist country cites crime and conviction statistics showing decreases in the rates when compared with prewar capitalism, and also unstable and mixed trends within the socialist period. What are we to make of these figures? First, it must be remembered that they apply primarily not to deviant acts themselves but to investigatory/prosecutory/judicial activity, which responds to "cues" other than those provided by deviants themselves. Arrest and conviction rates can rise or fall depending

on the level and volume of activity demanded of social control agencies, can vary
with growth or contraction in the personnel and other resources at their disposal,
and with changes in patterns of offender disposition. The institution of "social
courts," whose handling of some petty offenses outside the system of criminal
courts depresses the official "conviction" rate, is an example.[103] Also, many
potential cases are probably "adjusted" informally by police officers (as they are
in the United States). All this has some effect on the figures, but, in the very
nature of the case, we cannot specify that effect with any precision.

One is then, finally, brought to a recognition that the data we possess,
in their various forms, are simply not adequate for anything approximating a
"rigorous" test of the modernization-deviance hypothesis. But it can be argued
that for no society, or set of societies, has this hypothesis been so tested. If
we have not advanced far, it is not clear that we have fallen back. What we can
do is attempt to make sense of the information at hand. And here one can say that
the attention devoted to alcoholism, crime, and delinquency in both professional
and mass media discussions in Eastern Europe is convincing evidence that these
are seen as serious problems. Whether they are the "results" of modernity or
not, they coexist with it in time and are thus parts of the reality with which the
socialist regimes must reckon.

The processes of urbanization and industrialization in Eastern Europe,
as elsewhere, have removed people from more informal, yet also more tightly
knit contexts of traditional life. The family unit, deprived of traditional production and educational functions, and increasingly only one among many agents
of socialization, no longer exercises the sort of control over the behavior of
its members that it could in the countryside. The growth of unofficial "youth
cultures," notably in Poland, Czechoslovakia, and Hungary, removes adolescents
further from parental control, and these cultures, in more delinquent variants,
"shade off" into the juvenile offender population. Marital strains, divorce and
desertion, and other types of family pathology seem as characteristically "urban"
in Eastern Europe as elsewhere and are, to some degree at least, attributable to
the rapid changes life in socialist countries has undergone in the past twenty-
five years.

The problems of the family are but a part of the larger complex of
factors connected with urban life in general. Eastern Europe is more urban than
it has ever been before and is becoming even more so. Despite large allocations
of resources, and increasing attention to housing shortages, serious problems of
space and services, and of increasing the supply of other urban "amenities,"
still persist. If many socialist cities are now relatively "mature" and have lost
some of the "boom town" character of a Nowa Huta, they find that maturity too has
its problems. The adjustment made to city life by the working classes, even those
members whose urban residence is inherited, is one that quite clearly has its
"pathological" aspects, in heavy drinking, property offenses, and a modicum of
crimes of violence. The life of the urban lower classes is beset by "high rates
of desertion, separation, promiscuity, drinking, brutality, and incompatibility,
and...ever-present overcrowding,"[104]in the socialist as well as the capitalist
countries.

The socialization which transformed the economies of Eastern Europe
set new developmental priorities, altered the relationship of capital and consumption sectors, and changed the economic status of millions of persons. Its human
impact was diverse, given the differences in industrial-agrarian balance and
general presocialist economic development among the countries. In those East
European countries which ranked among the "better-developed" before the war,
socialism entailed deprivations for the working classes in whose name it was being
built as well as for the former "exploiters." Living standards declined and
remained depressed for a long time, providing at least part of the "agenda" of the
outbreaks of discontent in Berlin, Poznan, and Budapest in the 1950s. If, for
some, socialization of the means of production seemed to promise greater equality
and a leveling up of their economic status (though it may in fact have brought a

lowering of their living standard), for others (middle-level and small entrepreneurs, tradesmen, and professionals) it may have signaled the end of their personal "stake" in the economic system. Changes of this sort may easily enough give rise to the feeling, evidently widespread, that socialist property belongs to him who "appropriates" it. Furthermore, the organizational "tightness" of most socialist economies left the enterprising person little legal room to find an unsatisfied demand for some good or service, and to individually set about to meet it for his own profit. The "reform" phase into which some of the economies are heading has demonstrated (most notably, perhaps, in Hungary's New Economic Mechanism) how many such "enterprisers" appear, once legal restrictions are lessened.

Living standards are improving, but not, for many, rapidly enough to satisfy increasing demands, as younger populations (to whom the grim postwar years are scarcely memories) find "Western" consumption levels the relevant standard of comparison. Also, as market forces come to play a larger role in the reform economies, wage differentiation and rewards tied to performance threaten the relatively egalitarian pattern that prevailed, for example, in Czechoslovakia and Hungary; the lot of some is improving at a vastly more rapid rate than the lot of others, with attendant strains which may manifest themselves in a decreasing willingness of the "disadvantaged" to conform to the rules. It may indeed be that the industrialization experience of Eastern Europe as a whole, concentrated so heavily in nonconsumer sectors and demanding, at least in its earlier phase, enormous outpourings of effort in the absence of any immediate positive incentives, has created, over a generation, substantial segments of the population extremely alienated and unable or unwilling to "conform." As Etzioni observed, "Actors in many roles and situations, in order to conform, require, in addition to the motivation to do so and knowledge of the 'proper' paths to follow, the appropriate means. If the societal distribution of assets fails to provide these means... to one or another societal grouping, this failure alone will tend to produce large-scale deviance."[105] Which means, which "assets" are essential to conformity? This will no doubt vary to some degree with individual, idiosyncratic factors, but it seems clear that for many in socialist as in capitalist countries, the supply of means and assets falls far short of the necessary level. In Etzioni's words, "The extent and intensity of deviance will be greater, the less the patterns of the distributive structure and the political organization parallel the patterns prescribed by the symbolic-normative system."[106] Eloquent testimony here is provided by the situation in the USSR and Eastern Europe where, while the symbolic-normative system prescribes high status for the "worker" and a critical role to the whole working class and--in the persona of the "new man"--attributes to it all sorts of elevated moral and intellectual qualities, the distributive structure is such that it is from the urban working classes that criminals, delinquents, and alcoholics seem to be disproportionately "recruited." Although the symbolic-normative system underwent great change with the transformation from capitalism to socialism, the same strata provide the major share of deviants under both systems.

Consideration of "means and assets," and the distinction of distributive and "symbolic-normative" systems, redirects our attention toward viewing socialist modernization from the perspective of normative innovation. At the most "general" normative level, socialism replaced a system where status was largely attached to avoiding manual labor and attaining a white collar with one in which the horny-handed, overall-clad worker, in his collective entirety, became the central figure, superior in some deep sense to even the "socialist intelligentsia." Private property became suspect, and the "vesting" of national wealth in the "toilers" as a whole became its replacement. Where individualist ethics had prevailed, collectivist ethics were installed.

But normative innovations are not necessarily followed by parallel changes in the concrete order, and life does not reflect the themes of the political poster art in which socialist regimes excel. The workers in their numbers may function as "veto groups" at certain junctures--the most recent example being the Polish events of December 1970--but the class which must riot to make its point can scarcely be considered the "leading class" in socialist society. The substantial social inequalities, reflected only dimly in published figures on wage distributions, are a reality against which collectivist and egalitarian rhetoric must be measured. If psychological feelings of inferiority and real material disadvantage are important roots of deviance, then substantial amounts of deviant behavior may be expected in the socialist nations until reality coincides with the normative order established by socialist "innovators" a generation ago. To assert this is not to assign to "socialism" per se any inferiority as a mode of organizing human effort and distributing the proceeds, vis-a-vis other possible modes, but only to state that, in <u>concrete</u> terms, socialist societies, like other societies, tend to "get the deviance they deserve."

Notes

[1]C. E. Black, <u>The Dynamics of Modernization</u> (New York: Harper and Row, 1966), p. 114.

[2]<u>Ibid.</u>, p. 91

[3]<u>Ibid.</u>, p. 50

[4]For a discussion of the difficulties in estimating the size of the delinquency problem in Poland, see J. Jasinski, "Rozmiary ujawnionej przestepczosci nieletnich w. Polsce w latach 1961-1965," <u>Panstwo i Prawo</u>, no. 11 (1966), pp. 726-40.

[5]Wilbert E. Moore, <u>The Impact of Industry</u> (Englewood Cliffs, N. J.: Prentice-Hall, 1965), pp. 90-91

[6]See also Marshall B. Clinard, <u>Sociology of Deviant Behavior</u>, 3rd ed. (New York: Holt, Rinehart and Winston, 1968), pp. 80-98.

[7]E. B. Mel'nikova, <u>Prestupnost' nesovershennoletnikh v kapitalisticheskikh stranakh</u> (Moscow: Iuridicheskaia literatura, 1967), p. 145.

[8]E.g., for a criticism of Western views, see Iu. A. Zamoshkin, "Teoriia 'edinogo industrial'nogo obshchestva na sluzhbe antikommunizma," in <u>Marksistskaia i burzhuaznaia sotsiologiia segodnia</u> (Moscow: Nauka, 1964), pp. 94-113.

[9]M. M. Babaev, "Kriminologicheskie aspekty migratsii naseleniia," <u>Sovetskoe gosudarstvo i pravo</u> (hereafter, <u>SGIP</u>), no. 9 (1968), p. 89.

[10]<u>Ibid.</u>, p. 90

[11]A notable example is B. S. Vorontsov, N. I. Gukovskaia, and E. B. Mel'nikova, "O prestupnosti nesovershennoletnikh v gorode i sel'skoi mestnosti," <u>SGIP</u>, no. 3 (1969), pp. 103-8.

[12]J. Jasinski, "La délinquance des mineurs et des jeunes adultes en Pologne, de 1951 a 1962," in <u>La délinquance juvénile en Europe</u> (Brussels: Editions de l' Institut de Sociologie, Université Libre de Bruxelles, 1968), p. 55. (This volume, a collection of papers from a conference on delinquency held in Warsaw in October 1964, will hereinafter be cited as <u>La délinquance</u>).

[13]A. Todorovic, "Croissance des villes et délinquance juvénile," in La délinquance, p. 95.

[14]Pogled, 13 July 1970, pp. 8-9.

[15]See M. A. Gel'fer, "Sostoianie prestupnosti i nekotorye voprosy ee izucheniia v pravovoi literature zarubezhnykh sotsialisticheskikh gosudarstv Evropy" in Problemy iskoreneniia prestupnosti (Moscow: Iuridicheskaia literatura, 1965), p. 233, citing Rocznik Statystyczny, 1964, p. 507.

[16]See Gel'fer, "Sostoianie," pp. 228-29 and 237, citing Rude Pravo, 13 December 1960. On Bulgaria, see Ibid., p. 237, and M. I. Angelov, "Sostoianie i dinamiki prestupnosti v Bolgarii i perspektivy ee likvidatsii," Voprosy bor'by s prestupnost 'iu 8 (1968): 113-20.

[17]See Nepszabadsag and Magyar Nemzet, 24, 25, 26 June 1966 (EE, August 1966, pp. 48-49), and Magyaroszag, 17 January 1971 (RFE Hungarian Situation Report, 30 November 1971).

[18]Nepszava, 23 December 1971, p. 11

[19]Gel'fer, "Sostoianie," p. 235.

[20]Ibid., p. 240 n., citing Rocznik Statystyczny, 1956, p. 389; and Ibid., 1962, p. 443.

[21]Ibid., p. 239

[22]Ibid., p. 240

[23]Statisticka Rocenka CSSR, 1968, p. 124; Ibid., 1971, p. 549 (hereafter, SR CSSR).

[24]See Kriminologiia (2d ed.) (Moscow: Iuridicheskaia literatura, 1968), p. 85; see also Rocznik Statystyczny, 1966, p. 547; and Ibid., 1971, pp. 624-25.

[25]See Angelov, "Sostoianie," pp. 115-16, and Gel'fer, "Sostoianie," p. 231.

[26]For 1958-70 series, see SR CSSR, 1968, p. 124, and SR CSSR, 1971, p. 549.

[27]Kriminologiia, p. 86. See also Statisticki Godisnjak Jugoslavije, 1970, pp. 310-11.

[28]Angelov, "Sostoianie," pp. 115-16.

[29]Kriminologiia, p. 86.

[30]See the discussion of the persistence of "blood feuds" in Montenegro, Macedonia, and the Kosmet region in Borba, 7 October 1970, p. 4.

[31]SR CSSR, 1968, p. 124; Ibid., 1971, p. 549.

[32]Rocznik Statystyczny, 1971, p. 624.

[33]G. M. Min'kovskii, "Aktual'nye problemy bor'by s prestupnost'iu

nesovershennoletnikh v sotsialisticheskom obshchestve," Voprosy preduprezhdeniia prestupnosti 2 (1965): 165, 1967

[34]See Gel'fer, "Sostoianie," p. 237, and SR CSSR, 1968, p. 124 and Ibid., 1971, p. 549.

[35]See Rocznik Statystyczny, 1971, pp. 624, 631-32, and 634-35.

[36]For Poland: Rocznik Statystyczny, 1971, p. 635. For Yugoslavia: Statisticki Godisnjak Jugoslavije, 1970, p. 312, and Ibid., 1971, p. 513. For Czechoslovakia: SR CSSR, 1968, p. 124; Ibid., 1971, p. 549.

[37]See Walter D. Connor, Deviance in Soviet Society: Crime, Delinquency, and Alcoholism, (New York and London: Columbia University Press, 1972) pp. 39-42, for a discussion of Russian "drinking culture."

[38]Svet Prace, 22 July 1970, and Zemedelske Noviny, 6 January 1972 (RFE Czechoslovakian Situation Report, 22 March 1972).

[39]Rude Pravo, 1 April 1958 (cited in East Europe (hereafter, EE) May 1958, p. 44).

[40]Narodni Vybory, 16 December 1971, p. 25.

[41]Rude Pravo, 18 August 1971 (RFE Czechoslovakian Situation Report, 22 March 1972).

[42]Narodni Vybory, 16 December 1971, p. 25.

[43]Rude Pravo and Mlada Fronta, 28 January 1967 (EE, March 1967, p. 44).

[44]On this, and other aspects of alcohol problems in contemporary Poland, see Wea Celt's "The Problem of Alcoholism in Poland," published as RFE Polish Background Report, 9 March 1972).

[45]See Ibid., pp. 20-21, and also Tadeusz Grzeszczyk," Społeczno-ekonomiczne aspekty alkoholismu: Próba badań w województwie Łodzkim" Przeglad Socjologiczny, 14 (1960): 110-17.

[46]Tygodnik Powszechny, 1 March 1970 (RFE Polish Background Report, 9 March 1972 p. 28).

[47]Polityka, 15 August 1964 (EE, October, 1964, p. 51).

[48]Trybuna Ludu, 27 July, 1970.

[49]Gazeta Handlowa, 18 February 1966 (RFE Polish Press Survey, 26 February 1966).

[50]Trybuna Ludu, 27 July 1970.

[51]See RFE Polish Background Report, 9 March 1972, p. 10.

[52]Ibid.

[53]Magyar Nemzet, 31 December 1958 (EE, February 1959, p. 52).

[54]See RFE Hungarian Situation Report, 21 September 1971.

[55]See RFE Bulgarian Situation Report, 17 July 1970.

[56]RFE Polish Background Report, 9 March 1972, p. 7

[57]See Connor, Deviance in Soviet Society, pp. 41-42.

[58]Rude Pravo, 29 November 1966 (EE, January 1967, p. 36).

[59]Polityka, 19 September 1970, p. 2

[60]Rude Pravo, 29 November 1966 (EE, January 1967, p. 36).

[61]Prawo i Życie, 11 July 1971 (RFE Polish Background Report, 9 March 1972, p. 16).

[62]Scinteia Tineretului, 17 August 1967 (RFE Romanian Press Survey, 3 November 1967).

[63]Słowo Powszechne, 20 June 1967 (RFE Polish Press Survey, 28 August 1967), and RFE Bulgarian Situation Report, 17 July 1970. For Hungary, see Delmagyarorszag, 16 July 1971 (RFE Hungarian Situation Report, 21 September 1971).

[64]For the situation in Poland, see RFE Polish Background Report, 9 March 1972.

[65]Eszak-Magyarorszag, 6 February 1972 (RFE Hungarian Situation Report, 21 March 1972).

[66]See RFE Polish Background Report, 9 March 1972, p. 18.

[67]For suggestions in the USSR, see Connor, Deviance in Soviet Society, pp. 76-79. For Bulgaria, see Rabotnichesko Delo, 23 June 1968.

[68]Prawo i Życie, 31 October 1971 (RFE Polish Background Report, 9 March 1972).

[69]Somogyi Neplap, 11 February 1958 (EE, January 1959, p. 17).

[70]RFE Hungarian Situation Report, 30 November 1971.

[71]Magyarorszag, 17 January 1971 (see Ibid.).

[72]See Nepszabadszag, and Magyar Nemzet, 24, 25, 26 June 1966 (EE, August 1966, pp. 48-49).

[73]Życie Gospodarcze, 15 March 1970, p. 12.

[74]See Helena Kolakowska-Przełomiec and Edward Syzdul, "Przestępstwa gospodarcze w Polsce w świetle danych statistiki milicyjnej za lata 1962-1965," Panstwo i Prawo, no. 9, 1966, pp. 336-49.

[75]Polityka, 2 February 1969 (EE, April 1969, p. 53).

[76] Otto Vie, The Judge in a Communist State (Athens, Ohio: Ohio University Press, 1972), p. 167.

[77] For some views on corruption in the USSR and its differences from corruption in Afro-Asian modernizing nations, see Steven J. Staats, "Corruption in the Soviet System," Problems of Communism (January-February 1972): 40-47.

[78] Rocznik Statystyczny, 1970, pp. 631, 635.

[79] Statisticki Godisnjak Jugoslavije, 1970, pp. 310-12.

[80] See S. Batawia, "La délinquance des mineurs et des jeunes adultes en Pologne d'après les recherches criminologiques," in La délinquance, p. 131.

[81] Ibid., p. 131 n.

[82] Jasinski, "La délinquance des mineurs," p. 51.

[83] Rabotnichesko Delo, 8 July 1970, p. 3.

[84] Pogled, 8 March 1971, p. 11.

[85] See Connor, Deviance in Soviet Society, pp. 82-92, 154-57.

[86] Jasinski, "La délinquance des mineurs," p. 50.

[87] Brunon Holyst, "Z problematyki kryminologicznej oraz kryminalistycznej przestepstw z art. 240 i 241 k.k.," Panstwo i Prawo, no. 1., 1961, pp. 77-87.

[88] This distinction parallesl, in some ways, the one Alex Inkeles draws between "modernity" as a quality of personality, and the social/technological setting in which people live, which may still appear "traditional." See his "The Modernization of Man," in Modernization, ed. Myron Weiner (New York: Basic Books, 1966), p. 143.

[89] Batawia, "La délinquance," p. 131.

[90] Walczak, "La délinquance juvenile et le développement economique," in La délinquance, p. 145, citing data from a study by Batawia (see p. 144, n. 10).

[91] B. Maroszek, "Développement economique, structures sociales et délinquance juvénile dans certaines regions de la Pologne," in La délinquance, pp. 20-21.

[92] Jasinski, "La délinquance des mineurs," pp. 61-62.

[93] However, within a voivodship, the rate of the center city may be "two or three times" higher than that of the rural outlying areas (Jasinski, "La délinquance des mineurs," p. 61).

[94] See Connor, Deviance in Soviet Society, p. 93.

[95] This argument is advanced very tentatively owing to the lack of sufficient comparable Soviet data.

[96]Czechoslovakia and Hungary, like Poland, manifest the interesting partern of "commuting" village dwellers, who work in urban industrial jobs but, owing to urban housing shortages and the desire to maintain a small farm or plot, reside in "suburban" villages. Needless to say, the villages in this case became focal points for the confrontation of the "urban" and "rural" worlds.

[97]See Statisticki Godisnjak Jugoslavije, 1970, pp. 311-12, and Rocznik Statystyczny, 1970, p. 626, for data on age-structures of offenders in Yugoslavia and Poland.

[98]P. Zakrzewski, "Recherches sur la délinquance juvénile à Nowa Huta," in La délinquance, p. 74.

[99]Ibid., p. 78.

[100]Ibid.

[101]Ibid., p. 79

[102]Ibid., p. 80.

[103]On "social courts," see Obshchestvennye sudy v Evropeiskikh sotsialisticheskikh stranakh (Moscow: Izdatel'stvo Moskovskogo universiteta, 1968).

[104]See Mark G. Field and David E. Anderson, "The Family and Social Problems," in Prospects for Soviet Society, ed. Allen Kassof, pp. 397-98 (New York: Praeger, 1968).

[105]Amitai Etzioni, The Active Society (New York: Free Press, 1968), p. 328.

[106]Ibid., p. 329.

PART SIX

SCIENCE, TECHNOLOGY, AND MEDICINE

Chapter 9.

TECHNOLOGICAL INNOVATION AND SOVIET INDUSTRIALIZATION

Peter H. Solomon, Jr.

By now it is common knowledge that except in military-related endeavors the Soviet economy of the 1960s failed to generate the technological innovation desired by Soviet leaders,[1] even though during that decade concerned Soviet leaders dramatically increased their investment in science and introduced reforms to stimulate innovation.[2] The failure of these reforms suggests that the innovation problem had deep roots; but for the most part, these roots have remained unexplored, in the West as well as in the USSR.[3] Western authors have subjected to some scrutiny the recent Soviet difficulties with technological innovation,[4] and one writer has imaginatively explored their political implications.[5] None of them, however, has attempted to systematically probe the historical sources of the Soviet technological innovation problem.

The shortcomings in technological innovation in the civilian sector date back to the earlier years of industrial research and development (R and D) in the USSR. Neither in the 1920s, when industrial research in Russia began, nor in the 1930s after the decisive expansion of industrial R and D had occurred did the economy generate much technological innovation. These formative years of industrial R and D coincided with two important stages of Soviet industrial development--the recovery and reconstruction of the war-shattered industry and the period of intensive growth, the forced-draft industrialization drive.

The aim of this essay is to explain how the pattern of industrial development during the 1920s and 1930s shaped Soviet R and D in its formative years and, in so doing, to lay bare the historical roots of the contemporary innovation problem.

I shall begin with a short review of the attempts to remedy the innovation problem in the 1960s, in order to identify the obstacles to technological innovation in the contemporary period. The second and third sections examine in more detail Soviet industrial R and D in the 1920s and 1930s; in these sections I shall analyze both the innovation difficulties of those years and the origins of the obstacles to technological innovation observed in the 1960s. The concluding section briefly considers some reasons why these obstacles to innovation persisted from the 1920s into the post-Stalin period and explores the implications of Soviet management of innovation for other industrializing states.

At the very outset, let me explain the concept "technological innovation." This term refers to the process through which scientific knowledge is translated into new products or processes which are then utilized in the productive process. Thus, innovation refers to more than either research or invention. Although both research and invention represent sources of new

I wish to acknowledge the support of the Centre for Russian and East European Studies of the University of Toronto, which made possible part of the research on which this essay is based. I would also like to thank Sanford Lakoff, Thomas Rawski, and the participants of the ACLS Symposium on the Social Consequences of Modernization in Socialist Countries (Salzburg, 1972) for their comments on an earlier version of this paper, and Susan Gross Solomon for her helpful criticism at all stages.

ideas, these ideas must then be translated into new products or processes; and this translation requires further "development" activities, such as the designing, construction, and testing of models and the preparation of experimental production runs. Moreover, in our lexicon "innovation" requires the production of genuinely new technologies; small modifications in existing technology, however profitable, will be termed "adaptations" rather than "innovations." The distinction is important, because, as we shall see, the skills and the conditions which enhance the adaptation of technology do not necessarily encourage innovation.[6]

To detail the necessary and sufficient conditions for technological innovation is a difficult matter; for innovation is a subtle process, the result of a complex of social and psychological factors. Western studies of innovation have yielded two general conclusions: that technological innovation requires creative performances not only from scientific-engineering personnel but also from industrial administrators, and that innovation requires the presence both of the capacity to innovate and of a demand for it.[7] As we shall see, the validity of these propositions is supported by Soviet experience.

1

Despite a variety of reforms, as of the early 1970s civilian R and D in the USSR failed to produce the technological innovation required by Soviet industry. The failure of the specific reforms introduced to stimulate innovation in the 1960s is striking, for in these years the financial, ideological, and political status of science rose so dramatically in the USSR that persons involved in civilian R and D could hardly underestimate the premium placed upon success in the utilization of science and technology.[8]

Western observers have suggested several explanations for Soviet failures in technological innovation. One factor sometimes cited is the priority given to the advancement of military technology. Without doubt the large Soviet investment in military R and D and the attraction of some of the best scientists and engineers into this work did hamper civilian industrial R and D in the past.[9] But the sizable increase in total R and D spending in the USSR since the middle 1950s was so distributed that a shortage of funds could no longer be blamed for the failure of civilian R and D in the middle 1960s.[10] Admittedly, in comparison with the United States, less "spillover" of benefits from the military to civilian sphere seemed to occur in the USSR: but this fact could only contribute to the innovation problem in the civilian sphere, not generate or maintain it.

In their attempts to explain Soviet shortcomings in technological innovation in the 1950s and 1960s, most Western analysts have emphasized certain structural obstacles for which the recent reforms might not have provided sufficient remedy. The shortage of laboratories, testing facilities, and experimental factories allegedly limited development work in the civilian sphere. The transfer of research results to the designers, and of drawings and prototypes to the enterprise, was said to be hampered by the administrative and geographic separation of these activities. The planning system did not encourage the researcher to press the continuation of his projects into later development stages; nor did it provide incentives for managers to introduce new products or processes into production.[11]

These structural obstacles to innovation undoubtedly did account in part for the continuation of shortcomings in this area. Significantly, in military R and D, where the failure of innovation had been less of a problem in the post-Stalin period, most of these obstacles to innovation did not obtain.[12] However, it is my contention that in addition to structural obstacles to innovation, in the 1960s there were also cultural obstacles which reinforced the effects of the structural ones and made it difficult to stimulate innovation through simple reforms. The way most researchers, designers, and managers perceived their responsibilities in R and D militated against successful innovation. We shall illustrate the effects of "noninnovative" definitions of the roles of R and D personnel as we examine the failure of recent reforms in Soviet R and D.

Throughout the 1960s the Soviet leaders introduced piecemeal reform measures, but the culmination of the R and D reform effort was the major policy statement in the fall of 1968, the party-state edict "On improving the effectiveness of science and its utilization in production." This edict serves as a useful focus for consideration of the reforms because, like many comprehensive policy statements, it both continued lines of attack already operative and introduced new, original measures. The measures included in the edict may be grouped into two categories--those affecting the organization and general functioning of R and D and those aimed at increasing incentives for innovative activity.[13]

The organizational reforms included providing funds for the construction of new experimental facilities and of new combined science-production centers, "research corporations," and research complexes[14] as well as authorizing ministries to retain up to 2 percent of their assigned budgets as a reserve for especially important scientific-technological problems which might arise during the plan year.[15] But ministerial personnel were extraordinarily sluggish in taking up this mandate. According to S. Tikhomirov, a deputy chairman of the State Committee on Science and Technology, as of 1971 the twenty-five ministries surveyed by his staff had during the past three-year period allocated only 0.4 percent of their entire capital investment to the construction of these new facilities, and for technical reasons even these amounts had not been fully spent.[16]

Although the edict sanctioned the development of a wide variety of organizational forms to help bridge the "science-production gap," industrial administrators scorned "deviations" from familiar administrative and financial arrangements. For example, consider the reception of one "intermediary research firm." A group of young researchers and engineers formed a private firm to perform research and design work for enterprises on a contract basis. The organizers hired leading specialists from nearby institutes to work after hours as consultants, while they themselves executed the time-consuming details of the jobs, also on their own time. Local enterprises readily commissioned the firm, especially when the research institutes had refused their requests; and with the research firm working on a cost accounting basis and having virtually no overhead, a sound profit was achieved. A journalist reporting on the case posed the question, "Why have these firms not flourished and spread everywhere? The trouble is that they have powerful opponents...the banking and financial agencies.... An important financial official said to me: 'Initiative! Constant violations of existing instructions, statutes, and rules--that's their initiative!'"[17]

Reforms to improve the incentives for innovative efforts on the part of scientists and managers included revisions in the contract arrangements between research institutes and industrial enterprises and adjustments in the pricing of the products which resulted from innovations.

In the early 1960s research contracts had been used to encourage scientists to do more work of direct benefit to industry;[18] now in 1968 the contract instrument was chosen as a means of providing incentives for researchers to pursue the application of their findings. The 1968 edict called for the institutes to receive 1.5 percent of the annual monetary gain their research provided to the economy (not to exceed 6 percent of the research costs);[19] and for individual researchers to receive special bonuses as well based upon the economic effect of their work.[20] As of 1971, however, these measures were pronounced a failure, because the new contracts were rarely used. Resistance to the scheme was based partly on inertia and partly on the awkwardness of the administrative arrangements and the calculations required.[21] Even without using the new provisions, many contracts took almost as long to negotiate as the research contracted took to perform.[22]

Providing sufficient incentives for innovation to factory managers also proved to be a difficult task. The Funds for the Assimilation of New Technology, introduced in the early 1960s, failed in this regard because they compensated only for the costs of experimental production and not for the expenses associated with prior development work at the plant or for the loss of income which the break in normal production usually caused. The 1965 economic reform only complicated the situation by making profitability a criterion for enterprise performance. With this change it turned out that introducing new products or processes into production was often unprofitable for the enterprises, because the new product could not be priced high enough to compensate for the extra costs either of introduction into production or of manufacture. Thus, the adoption of new innovations could very easily reduce factory profits and, along with them, the director's bonus.[23] The 1968 edict went part of the way toward correcting the situation when it authorized small increases in the prices of products based upon innovations.[24] However, it turned out that these price increases were not sufficient to cover the increased costs of production. And managers were loath to risk loss of profit in order to meet the new demand for innovation.[25]

Overall, the 1968 party-state edict made little impact during the first few years. According to the Central Statistics Administration, for the economy as a whole more than half of the plans for the development of new technology went unfulfilled, in 1970 just as in 1968 largely because of delays and shortcomings in the design and development stages.[26] Part of the explanation for the reforms' failure was that they did not adequately correct the structural deficiencies in the R and D system. The new contracts designed to encourage researchers to pursue their projects through the development stages were too cumbersome to implement, and the price changes designed to spur managers to introduce new technologies did not work in practice.

But there was also a cultural dimension to the reforms' failure. The implementation of the reforms was beset by sluggishness, and sometimes resistance, on the part of the actors affected by them. Researchers, designers, factory directors, and economic administrators (especially the latter two) resisted reforms, largely, I suggest, because the reforms were not sufficiently radical to break down these persons' long-standing ideas about what their jobs required. The definitions of the responsibilities of R and D actors, which were inherited from the late Stalin years, discouraged innovation more than they encouraged it.

Let us consider how the researcher's, designer's, and manager's roles were defined from the beginning of the post-Stalin period.[27] The scientist at an institute and the designer at a design bureau were responsible neither for the relevance of their work to production nor for the task of seeing their projects through to implementation. Lacking contact with individual factories, most researchers and designers produced generalized solutions for problems, solutions which would be applied to an abstract set of conditions but which did not answer the needs of an individual enterprise. The application of these solutions might require modifications of design and supplementary research while the models were built, tested, and tried in experimental production; but these activities took place mainly outside the institute and design bureau, and the researchers and designers in these locations had little contact with them.

The director of a factory and the industrial administrator in a central agency felt responsibility neither for the development work necessary to utilize research results and designs nor for the introduction of new processes and products into production. These innovative activities contributed little to the manager's primary task, the fulfillment of planned production quotas; and they could even lower the gross output of the plant. Consequently, managers were loath to disturb production either to test new products or to introduce them into production. They would take risks and display considerable dexterity, even "entrepreneurship," in order to meet the production quotas upon which their bonuses depended, but not to improve the quality of a product or process.[28]

These role definitions of researchers, designers, and managers in the middle 1950s clearly did discourage innovation. It would be wrong to suppose that the role definitions of R and D personnel were unrelated to the structural context in which these persons worked. Far from it. The researcher's perception of his part in R and D derived in large measure from the administrative and geographic separation of research from production, and the manager's low sense of responsibility for innovation stemmed from the effects of the planning system. But it would be equally wrong to assume that the noninnovative role definitions had no impact upon innovation performance independent of the structural factors. Within a given structural context, once the responsibilities associated with a role become set for a period of time, an inertia effect takes over. Persons occupying roles become comfortable with the long-standing definitions of their responsibilities, and they tend to resist changes in them. Thus, once a role definition in R and D has been noninnovative for a number of years, that role definition itself becomes an obstacle to innovation; and it becomes necessary for purposes of reform to change both the attitudes of the role occupants and the structural environment in which they work.

Generally speaking, the longer the definition of the responsibilities associated with a given role has been set in the same mold, the more difficult it is to change the way that role's occupants perceive their job. It is already apparent that the noninnovative role definitions of industrial R and D personnel was a legacy of the late Stalin period to the post-Stalin years. How much more formidable these noninnovative role definitions would be if it turned out that they had been formed during the early years of Stalin's rule! As we turn to industrial R and D in the 1920s and 1930s, we shall look for evidence of the formation of noninnovative role definitions among R and D personnel, as well as for the origins of the structural factors which affected R and D in the contemporary period.

2

From its earliest days Soviet industrial R and D had difficulty generating technological innovation. Few examples of innovation flowed from its efforts either in the 1920s, when the first industrial research institutes were established in the USSR, or in the 1930s, when the major expansion of Soviet industrial R and D took place. Moreover, by the middle 1930s most of the structural and cultural impediments to innovation which we observed in the 1960s had already appeared. The priorities in economic planning and the administrative framework for R and D were set; and noninnovative role definitions had emerged for the principal actors in R and D.

The underlying reason for these developments, I contend, was that the industrial R and D system was established at a time when there was little or no demand for technological innovation. Neither in the 1920s nor in the 1930s was technological innovation a primary function or goal in the Soviet economy. From 1918 to 1927 the restoration of an industry shattered by war had first priority; and from 1928 to 1936 all efforts were devoted to the rapid expansion of industrial production using already existing foreign technology. Compared with these economic goals, domestic technological innovation was a peripheral concern.

The absence of demand for technological innovation during the formative years of Soviet industrial R and D had a number of consequences. It was responsible first of all for a divergence and later a conflict of interests between scientists and industrial administrators. Second, it affected a series of economic management decisions that shaped the structural environment of industrial R and D in the USSR. Third, the lack of demand for innovation facilitated the formation of noninnovative role definitions for managers, designers, and researchers.

Even before the Bolshevik Revolution the interest of industry and science diverged with regard to technological innovation. The first major phase of Russian industrialization (1890-1914) was based upon borrowed foreign technology, just as the later phase would be. In Czarist times foreign investors, encouraged by the state, imported machines from abroad and supplied technicians to put the plants into operation.[29] Czarist industry made strides through this technology policy, but Russian scientists drew little encouragement. Domestic technological innovation was needed neither by the foreign entrepreneurs nor by the Czarist state, and consequently neither partner was willing to support industrial R and D. Those Russian scientists who were ready to set aside the traditional theoretical bent of Russian science and follow their German colleagues into applied research were frustrated.[30]

The revolution ended the dilemma of the Russian scientists. In 1918, with Lenin's personal encouragement the Scientific-Technical Section of VSNKh (The Supreme Council of the National Economy) was founded, and under its sponsorship more than twenty-five research institutes and centers were established in the next nine years.[31] By the end of 1927 these institutes together employed 1,549 scientists, more than the Academy of Sciences at that time.[32] The sponsorship of industrial research at a time when the country was rent by civil war was a dramatic manifestation of the esteem in which Lenin and the Bolsheviks held science and technology. For Lenin, science became a symbol of progress and modernization; the Electrification Plan is the best known example of Lenin's attitude toward science, but industrial research also benefited from it.[33]

Nevertheless, Lenin's encouragement of the new research institutes did not make these institutes relevant to the needs of industry. Soviet industry was unprepared to absorb the new products or processes its R and D might provide; for it was actively engaged in rebuilding war-shattered plants and in restoring industrial production to the prewar level. Moreover, what little technological renewal there was at this time came from abroad.[34] In this context R and D aimed at technological innovation was inappropriate and impractical. Industry might use the research institutes for technical servicing, but the institutes were staffed by scientists ready to conduct research in the forefront of their fields. The scientists were hardly willing to divert their energies from advanced research to industrial problem-solving.[35]

As a result, industry and industrial science grew up independently and were only weakly linked. Although the institutes would sometimes produce results with an innovative potential, they were "as a rule weakly utilized, and for this absorption into industrial production no one took responsibility. Industry displayed great inertia and conservatism and willingly disregarded the institutes." Not surprisingly, the scientists tended to emphasize those lines of work which were the most promising scientifically, regardless of whether they might "have little real significance for industry."[36]

The administrative position of the research institutes may have contributed to the weak relations between scientists and factory managers. From its inception the Scientific-Technical Department of VSNKh was a separate unit, independent of the industrial departments and the trusts.[37] The separation of research administration from production management was an effective way of nurturing science institutions at a time when industry was preoccupied with other matters; but the separation did not further the cause of technological innovation, which required the cooperation of research and production units. One politician active in industrial administration regarded this separate administration of science as a mistake. More than once during the 1920s, G. L. Piatakov reportedly suggested that the control and financing of the institutes be transferred to the industrial trusts. For their part the scientists of VSNKh strenuously objected to this measure, which threatened to undermine their capacity to choose their own scientific objectives. A leading chemist who served as an administrator in the Scientific-Technical Section in the mid-1920s articulated the scientists' viewpoint when he wrote: "Industrial and administrative workers seldom realize that technological progress depends upon continued, systematic, fundamental [sic] re-search. An independent organization devoted to pure research, such as the Scientific-Technical Administration [sic], can accomplish much more than a group of trust-controlled laboratories which must concern themselves too much with routine problems."[38]

   The First Five-Year Plan witnessed the transformation of industrial R and D in the USSR. From less than thirty research institutes the VSNKh system increased to more than two hundred, and the number of scientists employed there grew from 1,549 (in 1927) to more than 9,000 (in 1932).[39] But this dramatic growth of industrial science had not been prompted by new demands for technological innovation. During the years of the forced industrialization drive, most of Soviet civilian industry had no more need for innovations than it had during the period of restoration. The industrialization drive was meant to achieve increased production using borrowed foreign technology.[40] Under the circumstances, Soviet industry required assistance in the absorption and utilization of this technology, not technological innovations.

   Why did the Bolshevik leaders undertake to expand industrial research at the very time when intensive technological borrowing made innovation a peripheral task? To answer this question one must refer to the ambitions of the politicians who led the industrialization drive. Stalin and his colleagues set out to make Soviet industry the equivalent of the most advanced industry in the West. This goal seemed to them impossible without the achievement of technological independence.[41] Their immediate aim was to use Western technical knowledge and experience; but once Soviet industry began to catch up with the West, they assumed it would acquire the capacity to generate its own technical advances.[42]

   Even though the Soviet commitment to industrial preeminence supplies a plausible rationale for supporting science,[43] it does not satisfactorily explain the premature and rapid expansion of industrial research before it was really needed. The missing piece in the chain of reasoning was that many Soviet politicians thought that the future (when technological innovation would be needed) was close at hand. Clearly they failed to appreciate the scope of the task of transforming a partially industrialized country into an industrial nation, naively believing that sheer effort could accomplish miracles in a short time. During the first years of the five-year plan, they expected that technological dependence on the West would end in a matter of years.[44] In practice, the pace of change was not as rapid as expected. It took most of the decade before Soviet industry as a whole had successfully absorbed the Western technology it had borrowed and before the new and reconstructed plants were working up to capacity.[45] And that technology was the technology attained in Western industry in the late 1920s. In civilian industry at least, catching up with the West and moving ahead on one's own were not simultaneous processes. The rationale for the gigantic expansion of industrial science during the first five-year period proved ill-founded. Technological innovation did not become a major need in civilian industry until after World War II, and by then the R and D system created in the early 1930s was ill-fitted to meet this need.

   Although civilian industry had little need for innovation during the early and middle 1930s, it did have requirements which R and D could in part fulfill. The transfer of borrowed technology through the mechanism of copying required engineering and design work and some research. When foreign designs of products were reproduced, it was often necessary to make adjustments for the peculiarities of raw materials available or for the requirements of local climate or market;[47] in addition, in the USSR efforts were also made to simplify and to standardize the machines produced and the processes by which they were made--simplification, so that workers less well trained than their Western counterparts would be able to perform the tasks;[48] and standardization, so that the fullest benefits of mass production might be obtained.[49]

   These tasks associated with the copying of technology--adjustment, simplification, and standardization--required adaptation rather than innovation. Scientists, designers, and engineers were called upon to produce changes in detail rather than in concept. Moreover, most of the adaptations did not entail improving the product or process, but rather tailoring it to Soviet conditions. By contrast, in Japan after World War II much of the R and D stimulated by technological borrowing (via licensing) also focused upon adaptation, but here the small changes generally constituted improvements in product or process which would make the Japanese variant competitive on world markets.[50] The adaptations required by Soviet industry in the 1930s were of a less creative kind than those needed by Japanese industry in the 1950s and 1960s.

In short, rather than bringing together the diverging interests of science and industry, the industrialization drive of the First Five-Year Plan period widened the gap and helped force the interests of the two parties into conflict. As in the 1920s, industry still did not need the innovative results toward which most scientists directed their research; but now, in addition, industry did need the help of R and D personnel to perform noninnovative tasks relating to the adaptation of borrowed technology.

The lack of demand for technological innovation was reflected not only in the conflict of interest between science and industry but also in a number of decisions taken in the early 1930s regarding the structure of R and D institutions and economic policy: the centralization of most industrial research in Moscow and Leningrad, the limitation on resource expenditure for the construction of experimental production facilities, and the establishment of priorities in industrial planning. To be sure, in making these decisions, the political leaders' main consideration was how their choices would affect the industrialization effort, not the impact of the choices on technological innovation. Yet their decisions seriously affected the future capacity of the industrial economy to produce and absorb innovations.

The new industrial research institutes were generally placed near Moscow or Leningrad; this meant perforce that they were geographically separated from most of the new industry.[51] Such geographic separation of research from production does not invariably retard technological innovation, but the combination of geographic separation with separate administration usually does.[52] Unfortunately, in the USSR of the 1930s the geographic and the administrative separation of research and production coincided; for when the new institutes were established, science and industry were already administratively separate. VSNKh continued to use a Scientific-Technical Administration (later, Section) to administer the institutes (both old and new), while production administration remained the responsibility of the industrial glavki.[53]

The central location of the new industrial research institutes was chosen not to maximize technological innovation but rather to facilitate the management of industry at the time of the industrialization drive. The research institutes were only one, and not the most important, source of technological know-how which might be utilized in the industrial reconstruction. Most of the information about new processes and products was coming from abroad; and in order to streamline and effectively manage technology importation, decisions about which technologies would be purchased and which would be used in particular industries were made the responsibility of the central industrial administration. It followed that the research institutes also belonged in the center, where they could feed their results and recommendations (especially those relating to the adaptation of foreign technology) to the appropriate industrial administrators, who were responsible for their applications.[54]

A second reason for placing the research institutes in the center was the Soviet leaders' belief in the efficiency of geographic centralization. With the institutes in the center one could establish a single large institute to service each branch of industry and thus avoid the "wasteful competition" (characteristic of American industry) which would result if individual enterprises had their own research establishments.[55] According to this logic, "head" (<u>golovoi</u>) institutes were designated for each of the major fields of applied science, most of which were relevant to the work of more than one branch of industry; and "branch" (otraslevoi) institutes were established to serve the needs of the particular industries. Both the head and the branch institutes, usually located in Moscow or Leningrad, had associate research centers (<u>filialy</u>) in provincial cities. There were also factory laboratories at some industrial plants, but these were not treated as major research centers.[56]

Soviet policy toward the development side of R and D during the 1930s also reflected the secondary position of technological innovation in the hierarchy of political concerns. Applied research is only the first and least costly stage of the innovation chain; no innovation can be completed and introduced into production without a series of other activities--the translation of research results into designs for new products or processes, the construction and testing of prototypes, and "batch" or experimental production. Yet in the 1930s, the growth of applied research in the USSR was not accompanied by a comparable expansion of the facilities required for some of these stages of the innovation cycle. Most research institutes themselves did not have the facilities for testing or batch production--the "head" institutes often had small laboratories, but the branch institutes usually lacked even these. Experimental factories were found only at a few leading institutes, and these were often occupied with actual production responsibilities.[57]

Despite the frequent complaints from scientists and administrators that the shortage of development facilities hampered the utilization of research, the regime did not invest in the needed facilities in most areas of civilian industry.[58] Most likely, the main reason was that such investment constituted a diversion from the goal of expanding heavy industrial production. It is also possible that some politicians misunderstood what science by itself could do for industry. They may have believed that scientists could make greater contributions to industry simply by devoting more time to practical problems; and that if science became "practicalized" it would help industry well enough, without new testing facilities.[59]

The industrial planning system introduced by Soviet leaders in the early 1930s not only reflected the low demand for technological innovation but also institutionalized it, especially for the industrial manager. Since the main goal was the rapid expansion of industrial production, the reliance in the planning scheme upon gross output as the basis for assessing industrial performance was natural. Whether intended or not, however, the effect of relying mainly on quantitative indicators of enterprise performance was to discourage efforts to improve product quality. The more managers concentrated on raising the amount of production, the less they paid attention to product improvement and innovation. As is well known, the reliance upon gross output as a criterion of industrial performance became a central and ongoing feature in Soviet planning for civilian industry, and this fact had sorry consequences for the development of an innovative capacity. For as long as industrial managers were judged mainly according to their success in meeting quotas, they had little incentive to participate in innovation.[60]

To summarize, we have seen that the establishment of industrial research institutes at a time when industry did not require technological innovation led first to a conflict of interest between science and industry about what industrial research institutes should do and how industry should cooperate; and second to certain decisions adversely affecting technological innovation-- decisions about the geographic placement of institutes, about the provision of development facilities, and about the system of industrial planning. We will now consider how the pursuit of industrial R and D in the absence of demand for innovation and the emergence of a structural context unfavorable to innovation affected the work of the individual actors in R and D.

3

        The early 1930s was the decisive time in the formation of the role def-
initions of Soviet R and D personnel. These were the beginning years for the
overwhelming majority of research institutes and design organizations and for many
industrial enterprises as well. And for a large proportion of the scientists,
engineers, and administrators who worked in these settings, these years marked the
first work experience.

        Learning on the job about the job is always a part of the training of
new personnel; it often determines which of the skills individuals bring to the
job they will develop most fully and how they will come to perceive their responsibilities. For the R and D personnel in the USSR of the 1930s, on-the-job
socialization was especially important. Few of the scientific-technical cadres
who joined the work force for the first time during the great expansion of industrial research and of industry were adequately trained.[61] There had been a large
increase in the number of scientists and engineers graduated from the vuzy during
the First Five-Year Plan, but not enough to staff 170 new institutes; vydvyzhenniki
had to be included at the institutes.[62] Even the best of the new cadres were
inexperienced, having been pushed through a traditionally theoretical education
which brought them into contact neither with research nor with industrial
practice.[63]

        The job experience of the new cadres, scientific and managerial alike,
did not encourage innovative skills or inclinations, for these persons began their
careers at a time when there was little demand for innovation and when structural
arrangements made it difficult to complete innovation. The result was that
researchers, designers, and managers developed habits of behavior and perceptions
of their job requirements which discouraged innovation.

                              Researchers

        Scientists at the industrial research institutes felt especially keenly
the conflict between science and industry which we have described above. One may
recall that in the early 1930s industry required the scientists' help in adapting
and implanting foreign technology; and industrial officials solicited this "relevant research" through contracts with research institutes (which supplied a significant portion of the institutes' income).[64] However, the staff of the institutes was composed of scientists, trained to advance their particular specialties
within the applied science fields. As scientists they preferred more challenging
research work, which might contribute, directly or indirectly, to technological
innovations.

        As a result of these conflicting interests, most research institutes
under VSNKh (from 1932 under NKTP, the Commissariat of Heavy Industry) pursued
both kinds of research. They performed tasks relating to the adaptation of
foreign technology and to special problems created by its absorption. Such
efforts often included design work as well as research and occasionally involved
the manufacture of small devices and parts as well. And the institutes did
scientific research, aimed at advancing lines of investigation which seemed
promising from the standpoint of technological development. This research represented the continuation of the investigations begun by the VSNKh institutes in the
1920s.

        It is difficult to estimate the balance between the two types of work
performed by scientists at the industrial research institutes. The practical

contributions of the scientists were highlighted in the handbooks issued by the Scientific-Technical Section of NKTP,[65] but other sources, including commentaries from factory officials, alleged that the institutes did nothing at all for industry.[66] My guess is that the truth lies somewhere in the middle; about half of the NKTP institutes' work seemed to have been devoted to the assimilation of foreign technology, and about half to scientific research aimed at innovation.

The distribution of the two types of work surely varied also from institute to institute, but again it is difficult to discover a pattern. Robert Lewis has suggested that the institutes outside of the chemical and electrical industries, at that time the research-intensive industries in the West, must have worked mainly on the assimilation of foreign technology.[67] But the literature does not seem to support this suggestion. For example, the leading institute in metallurgy, the Central Institute of Metals, engaged in a long list of scientific projects which bore little apparent relationship to the adaptation of foreign technology.[68] Another plausible division of labor was between the "head" institutes and the "branch" ones. The head institutes, which were organized around a scientific discipline or subdiscipline, probably did less practical work than did the branch institutes, which were designed to serve particular industries.[69]

Not only did scientists have to resist the pressure of immediate demands in order to pursue scientific research, but they were constantly frustrated in their attempts to see their results utilized. Research results could not lead to innovations when development and production did not follow research. Often designs for new products or processes were produced, but these novelties were neither tested nor introduced into experimental production. This was due partly to the absence of facilities for testing and experimental production and partly to the failure of the managers of production enterprises to free time for this work.[70] Such failures in the development and production stages of the R and D cycle could affect even the adaptations of foreign technology.[71] But the ideas that called for major changes in process or product were those most likely to die at the research or design stage, after their authors either published the results or placed them "on the shelf" at the institute's archive.

Thus researchers faced a paradoxical situation. The more their work was "practical" and likely to be utilized, the less it would be innovative (as it would involve the simplification, standardization, or adjustment of existing technology); the more the research was potentially innovative, the less likely it was to be developed and utilized!

This paradox affected how these industrial scientists perceived their jobs in two ways. First, the scientists began to attach status distinctions to the two kinds of work which they performed. Scientific research became the high-prestige work, whereas practical tasks, involving direct contact with individual enterprises, became a low-prestige activity.[72] Accordingly, many institutes began to relegate this "practical work" to a particular section of the institute, a small and nonprestigious one, while the rest of the institute concentrated on "real scientific work." When scientists did visit factories, they sometimes betrayed their feelings about these chores. Their visits were described as "episodic," and their attitudes toward plant technicians "haughty." According to factory personnel, the scientists "came, gave instructions, and left."[73] Second, the scientists developed a limited sense of their own responsibilities in undertakings related to innovation. Since they could exert little impact upon the implementation of their ideas and results, which would take place, if at all, at a far-off enterprise, the boundaries of their job became narrowly construed. Researchers were obliged to produce useful scientific results for publication and for delivery to design organizations, to the technical staff of the commissariat and to the factories; and that was all.[74] They were not expected to follow their projects through the later stages of the innovation process. Naturally, the plans of the research institutes reflected this reality; scientists successfully fulfilled their assignments when they delivered the research results to the central authorities. In drafting their research plans, the institute directors did not assign themselves tasks which they could not fulfill; nor did the officials who reviewed the institute's plans in the Scientific-Technical Section of NKTP and in the planning agencies require otherwise.[75]

Neither a disdain for the practical nor a limited conception of their responsibility would help industrial scientists contribute to technological innovation. Yet these became central features of the role definitions of researchers in applied science in the USSR during the early and middle 1930s.

Designers

The job of designer in technological innovation centers on translating research results and ideas into drawings of new products or processes, from which prototypes can be constructed and tested. Designers may also help arrange the first batch of production utilizing the new process or product. Their work requires a special talent for finding solutions to new engineering problems which arise in the development of innovations. After a short and theoretical education, most Soviet design engineers in the 1930s would have had to learn the required skills in the course of their job experience. Yet most of their work did not familiarize them with the tasks associated with innovation, but rather with other kinds of design problems.

Much of Soviet design work in the 1930s related directly to the transfer of technology and to its implantation in Soviet industry. Designers played an important part in the process of technological borrowing. They helped select the foreign products or processes to be copied, and they did much of the adapting of the foreign models to Soviet needs.[76] For example, during the first half of 1932, the design section of the scientific-technical committee for machine-building reviewed thirty-five to forty designs from foreign firms, using teams of eight to twelve persons which included designers, engineers, and representatives of the factories that would produce the machines. First, the teams considered the benefits of the various models and chose the most suitable one; then they simplified the design of the model chosen, sometimes adding design features from other models, and prepared a standard version for use throughout the USSR.[77] According to a Western observer, the Soviet designers usually selected the best foreign models available, but their eclectic approach to combining features from different models sometimes caused difficulties in practice.[78]

The skills the Soviet designers developed were those relating to the copying and manipulation of existing designs. Indeed, copying, simplifying, combining, and adapting became the hallmark of Soviet design engineers. "Free from the restraints, traditions, and competition of the capitalist system, [Soviet designers] develop their own methods of combining, learning how to extract the most advantageous features from the best existing models and systems."[79] However, this aptitude for "extracting....from existing models," did not encourage Soviet designers to devise new design concepts or features; instead, the designers displayed "signs of technological conservatism," according to one contemporary observer.[80] Through copying and adapting, Soviet designers facilitated the absorption of foreign technology, but their experience as adapters did not adequately prepare them for the more challenging design problems associated with innovation.

Since much of the design work was related to the transfer of technology, it must at least to some extent have been incorporated in industry; yet designers complained that many of their drawings were never used because of the shortage of development facilities.[81] Moreover, working on tasks helpful to industry did not bring designers into regular contact with production. With the exception of those few designers who worked directly at new plants, designers worked mainly in project institutes, designing new factories and planning the reconstruction of old ones, or in special design organizations; and these designers had only infrequent contact with the enterprises which might eventually use the new or modified products or processes which they had drawn.[82] Some designers not only worked apart from industry but also worked apart from each other, so that repetition of the same jobs at different design offices in the same city became a rather frequent occurrence.[83] Working separately, cut off from industry, most designers developed a limited sense of their responsibilities; their part in R and D was to design models of new processes or products, but usually not to follow those models through construction and testing.

The experience of the designer in civilian R and D in the first half of the 1930s introduced two elements into his role definition which discouraged innovation--an emphasis in problem-solving on adapting old methods rather than seeking new approaches; and a sense of responsibility which extended only to the initial design of adapted products or processes.

                                    Managers

Throughout the world the managers of industrial firms play an essential part in innovation; without their encouragement there can be no absorption or utilization of new processes or products. In the USSR of the 1930s, the managers' potential role in innovation was even greater because, in the absence of sufficient facilities for testing and experimental production, the completion of development work also depended upon their cooperation.

In the West industrial managers have frequently displayed a conservative attitude toward innovation; the risk in attempting innovations and the destabilizing effect they can have upon regular operations have made entrepreneurs wary of them. Before a firm will develop or utilize an innovation, its executives must be sufficiently persuaded of its benefits to counteract their natural tendencies to resist it.[84] In the USSR of the 1930s, however, managers could discern few benefits associated with innovation, and they were thoroughly discouraged from taking part in the innovation process.

The primary source of their discouragement, which has already been discussed, was the limited demand for technological innovation. Although factory directors were engaged in expanding production through borrowed technology, they had little reason to take part in the innovative process. In addition, the industrial managers were further deterred from innovative efforts by the circumstances under which they had to work to meet the new production levels. With the rushed tempo of forced industrialization, factory directors struggled to get results from factories which were partially constructed, with machines which were inoperable or required modifications, and with a labor force which was inadequately trained.[85] The directors sought the help of scientists and engineers--not to supply them with sources of innovation, but to solve pressing technical problems, such as training workers to operate new machines, adapting machines to the workers' capabilities, or maintaining quality control. Once the managers succeeded in overcoming these initial difficulties and getting their plants to operate with reasonable efficiency, they were not anxious to undergo the unsettling effects of interrupting production to test or introduce new processes or products. Nor were they encouraged to do so by the planners or the politicians. For the rest of the decade, the managers were expected to reap the benefits of the technological investment just completed by fulfilling and overfulfilling the high production quotas.

Not surprisingly, most managers in Soviet industry in the early and middle 1930s failed to take part in R and D, and some of them displayed considerable hostility toward innovation. The testimony of contemporary observers was unanimous. Researchers complained that the "well-known sluggishness of the managers" was responsible for the noncompletion of projects which the researchers had begun.[86] As a science administrator, N. I. Bukharin agreed with this explanation; he detected among the managers "a narrow and shortsighted 'practicism,' which considers research to be....like a large growth on the healthy body of real work."[87] The staff of the factory laboratories were especially sensitive to the managers' attitudes toward research. Throughout the early and middle parts of the decade, the laboratories struggled to extend their work from routine control tasks to scientific research, but in most factories they were unsuccessful because of the managers' disdain for research.[88] Engineers from one factory laboratory diagnosed the problem as follows: "Many managers do not see the connections between the mastery of technology and research work. There are even managers who understand the mastery of technology to mean only learning how to operate a machine imported from abroad!....Not for naught have some managers been scolded for their dependent attitude toward imports....In the factories many think that research work--that's something done somewhere over there, in the institutes, and that for the factory such work is a luxury."[89]

The industrial administrators in the glavki and the trusts seemed no more interested in innovation than were the directors of factories. According to one commentator, "the glavki are completely disinterested in the work of our institutes, especially the glavki in machine-building and their chief engineers."[90] Innovation failures in the peat industry were said to have stemmed from the "inertness" of the peat trust, Soiuztorf.[91] Economic planners in Leningrad oblast displayed a similar disdain for R and D.[92]

As it emerged in the early 1930s, the role definition of the manager--factory director and industrial administrator alike--included little attention to R and D. The managers regarded participation in technological innovation as a luxury, a task far secondary in importance to production itself. And they regarded scientific researchers as remote figures, offering little help in solving their everyday management problems.

4

We have explained how the technological innovation problem and its immediate causes, structural and cultural, developed in the USSR in the 1920s and the first half of the 1930s. The question remains how and why this problem persisted for another two decades before it was publicly recognized and challenged in the mid-1950s.[93] Because of the paucity of published material on Soviet R and D between 1935 and 1954, we shall be limited to suggesting some plausible answers to this question.

It is reasonable to suppose that the technological innovation problem could not have been solved without a substantial change either in economic policy, in administrative arrangements, or in both.[94] Already in the early 1930s scientific administrators had tried to improve relations between researchers and managers through simpler means. To overcome the distance and hostility between the parties, the administrators arranged joint conferences and encouraged the scientists to take the initiative in establishing regular consultations with factory personnel.[95] The Scientific-Technical Section also convinced NKTP to prescribe the obligations of the various parties in the innovation chain.

Institutes are obliged, quickly after testing their completed work in laboratory or semi-factory conditions....to communicate the corresponding technical report to the economic organ, trust, or independent factory, and in addition to inform the corresponding glavki and the Scientific-Technical section, indicating a suggested plan for reali-

zation and appointing its own brigade to help arrange the required work;
   The economic organ (trust, or independent factory) is obliged
within a month of receipt to review the suggestions of the institute and to guarantee either that it be put into practice
with the help of the brigade from the institute, or within that
time period to give a fully explained refusal, communicating
its conclusions in either case to the Scientific-Technical
section;
   The glavki (and personally the chiefs of their production
sections) bear responsibility for the prompt absorption of
completed scientific work into production.[96]

This list of obligations, which was issued in 1933, had little effect upon the behavior of R and D actors. They were already familiar with the rhetoric--they had
heard similar exhortations at meetings with science administrators, and a previous official list of obligations (from 1928) defined their responsibilities in
much the same way.[97] In the absence of demand for innovation and of structures
reflecting that demand, the researchers and the managers either could not or
would not observe the prescribed norms and did not accept them as definitions of
their responsibilities.

   By the middle 1930s the futility of trying to improve science-industry
relations through exhortation and prescription must have been apparent.
Recognizing the need for fundamental reform, a leading science administrator,
A. A. Armand, proposed in 1936 that the factory laboratories be expanded at the
expense of the research institutes, resulting in the transfer of much industrial
research to the factories. Armand contended that such a move would overcome the
separation of research from production and lead both to more relevant research
and to the completion of development and testing work at the plants.[98]

   There is no evidence that Armand's proposal was seriously considered.
Nor was there much time for such consideration, for within months the USSR was
shaken by the onset of the Great Terror. As a result, science policy debate in
the public forum ceased, and institutional reforms became improbable. At the
same time, the threat of impending war further reduced the chances of improvements in civilian R and D. Most investment in testing and experimental production
had to be used for weapons research, not to enhance innovation in NKTP.

   During the war itself there could be little consideration of nonmilitary
technological innovation; the war effort took priority over all normal domestic
concerns. But in the immediate postwar years (1945 to early 1947) a mild
liberalization in Soviet politics allowed the revival of public airing of criticism and reform proposals.[99] In this mood a leading engineer, I. P. Bardin,
described the lot of the factory laboratories. Many factory directors, he
reported, had failed to repair war-damaged laboratories, and there were cases
where laboratory buildings had been confiscated for production use. In addition,
Bardin hinted that there has been a general deterioration of conditions in
civilian industrial R and D.[100] What effect, if any, Bardin's complaints may have
had, we do not know.

   From 1947 to 1954 the published sources in the USSR tell little about
R and D policy; but it is clear from the condition of industrial R and D in 1955
that no major reforms were introduced.[101] The absence of an effort to enhance
innovation at this time requires explanation, for in the late 1940s and early
1950s civilian industry in the USSR needed technological renewal; the technology
borrowed at the end of the 1920s no longer was advanced by world standards. One
can suggest two factors which may have restrained Soviet leaders from taking
action to encourage innovation in civilian industry. First, under the shadow
of the Cold War, military R and D, and especially the development of nuclear
weapons had first priority among Soviet R and D projects; much of the investment
which might have been directed toward civilian technology was probably consumed by

these military programs. Second, Soviet relations with its new client states in
Eastern Europe seemed to preclude changes in the Soviet model of economic and
political development. At a time when Stalin and his Politburo were pressing
their "brothers" in the new socialist nations to follow the Soviet model it was
not propitious to modify that model even in detail, let alone in a major way.

We have seen that during the First Five-Year Plan Soviet leaders pursued an unusual policy in relation to civilian technological innovation. They
created the basis for an innovative capacity, an extensive R and D system,
before there was a demand for innovation. Such a fast pace of industrial growth
was anticipated that most leaders assumed that a demand for domestic sources of
technology would quickly emerge; but that demand did not appear soon enough.
After the period of intensive technological borrowing, politicians preferred to
reap the benefits of the technology just implanted; and the intervention of
Terror, War, and Cold War further delayed the creation of an effective demand for
domestic technological innovation.

The irony was that with the prolonged absence of demand for innovation,
the capacity to generate it also failed to develop as the leaders had intended.
The structure of R and D institutions and the economic planning system reflected
the actual low priority of innovation, and both of these in turn discouraged the
production of innovation by the R and D system. As a result of the lack of demand
and of the structural context reflecting it, R and D personnel came to perceive
their responsibilities in ways which militated against the completion and
utilization of innovations.

It is natural that a country which attempts to industrialize rapidly,
relying as it must upon technological borrowing, will have a low demand for
technological innovation. Yet that country probably will begin some R and D, if
only to expedite the transfer of technology.[102] Soviet experience suggests that
the time of intensive industrial growth based on borrowed technology is usually
the wrong moment for a country to establish a large amount of industrial R and
D, for an extensive R and D system can flourish only where there is some demand
for technological innovation. Without this demand, researchers, designers, and
managers do not develop the attitudes or the skills required for the pursuit of
innovation; and the absence of these attitudes and skills may cripple that
country's capacity to innovate for some time to come. Optimally, politicians and
administrators should ensure that a demand for innovation is created at the time
when the first industry R and D begins. But if generating such a demand is not
possible, then a small industrial research system should be created, to be expanded later when that demand finally does appear.

In further evaluating Soviet experience with technological innovation,
it is instructive to consider the experience of another rapidly industrialized
country, Japan. Like the USSR, Japan relied upon massive technological borrowing
during the decisive stage in its industrial development, the years 1945-65. During
the first postwar decade, Japanese businessmen paid little attention to the condition of industrial science they did not need; but when in the 1950s they decided
to adapt and improve the products and processes obtained by license, the entrepreneurs began to support R and D lavishly. The new Japanese industrial researchers became highly skilled at adapting Western products that could be sold
competitively in foreign markets--but not, as Japanese and Western science
administrators of the mid-1950s pointed out--at innovation.

As long as it was possible to purchase and adapt new American technologies, Japanese R and C continued to stress adaptation. But in the late 1960s
the purchase of technology licenses became more difficult for Japan, and for the
first time domestic sources of new technology seemed to be required.[103] No longer
could industrial research function merely "as the method of transmitting the
technology of Western products, or as a service to the established production
units";[104] R and D had to be regeared to produce innovations. The Japanese government's Science and Technology Agency took the initiative in calling for R and D

reform in its 1970 white paper, "New Demands for Technological Innovation."[105]

In its first decade and a half Japanese industrial R and D did not generate a strong capacity for technological innovation. As in the USSR, the low demand for innovation and the importation of Western technology led Japanese scientists and engineers to stress technology adaptation. Yet the Japanese innovation problem does not seem as serious as the Soviet one. There were some differences in the history of industrial R and D in the two countries which suggested slight advantages on the Japanese side. In Japan the best scientists worked in the civilian sector, for there was little military R and D to skim off some of the talent, as there was in the USSR. The Japanese mechanism of technology transfer, licensing, seemed to require more creative forms of adaptation than did the Soviet mechanism, copying. In Japan the growth of industrial R and D proceeded in a slower and more orderly way than in the USSR. However, the main source of advantage in the Japanese case was the presence of management skills evidenced by the extraordinary economic successes already achieved. Indeed, some Western observers found it difficult to imagine that the managers and politicians responsible for Japan's "economic miracle" could now lack the flexibility to shift priorities in the face of the new demand for innovation.[106]

Flexibility in matters of economic policy affecting industrial R and D was not shown by the Soviet leadership in the 1940s, 1950s, and 1960s. For the reasons we have discussed, Soviet leaders were unwilling to invest sufficiently in development facilities, to modify substantially the structure of R and D, and most important to revamp the planning system to provide incentives for innovation. Soviet experience with technological innovation suggests that whatever arrangements are made for R and D during the period of intensive technological borrowing, politicians should anticipate the likelihood that changes in administrative arrangements and economic policies will later be required. Those industrial and scientific institutions and policies appropriate for technological borrowing and adaptation will probably not be those best suited to the development and utilization of technological innovation.

Notes

[1]See L. I. Brezhnev, Otchetnyi doklad TsK KPSS XXIV sezdu KPSS (30 March 1970) (Moscow, 1971), pp. 98-102. In the 1960s the politicians of other industrial nations also complained that their countries lacked sufficient capacity for technological innovation. See Robert Gilpin, France in the Age of the Scientific State (Princeton, N.J.: Princeton University Press, 1968); "Japan seeks a new approach to technological innovation," Science Policy 1 (1972): 3-1

[2]Between 1957 and 1967 the science budget in the USSR doubled twice and by 1971 reached the figure of 13 billion rubles, an order similar to the United States science investment (16 billion dollars). V. G. Afanasev, "Upravlenie nauchno-tekhnicheskim progressom," Nauchnoe upravlenie obshchestvom 5 (1971): 76.

[3]Robert Lewis has initiated the historical study of Soviet R and D in the West with a solid description of industrial science institutions in their early years. See his article, "Some Aspects of the Research and Development Effort in the Soviet Union, 1924-1935," Science Studies 2 (1972): 153-79. A recent Soviet monograph also sketches the institutional development of industrial R and D in the late 1920s and early 1930s. See V. D. Esakov, Sovetskaia nauka v gody pervoi piatiletki. Osnovnye napravleniia gosudarstvennogo rukovodstva nauki (Moscow, 1971).

[4]R. Amann, M. J. Berry, and R. W. Davies, "Science and Industry in the USSR," OECD Report Science Policy in the USSR (Paris: OECD, 1970), pp. 381-558;

Gertrude Schroeder, "Soviet Technology: System vs. Progress," Problems of Communism 19 (September-October 1970): 19-30; Robert Campbell, "Problems of Technological Progress in the USSR," paper presented to the symposium on "Recent Reforms in Western Europe," held at the University of Missouri-Kansas City (16-17 July 1970); Ronald Amann, "The Soviet Research and Development System," Minerva 8 (April 1970): 217-41.

[5] R. V. Burks, "Technology and Political Change in Eastern Europe," Change in Communist Systems, ed. Chalmers Johnson (Stanford: Stanford University Press, 1970).

[6] OECD Reviews of National Science Policy: Japan (Paris, n.d. [1967]), p. 142; Author J. Cordell, "The Multinational Firm, Foreign Direct Investment, and Canadian Science Policy," Science Council of Canada, Special Study no. 22 (December 1971), pp. 46-48.

[7] Keith Pavitt in "Science, Enterprise and Innovation," Minerva 11 (April 1973): 273-77, summarizes the results of various studies of the conditions stimulating technological innovation. See also his The Conditions for Success in Technological Innovation, (Paris: OECD, 1971), and J. Langrish, et al., Wealth from Knowledge: Studies of Innovation in Industry (New York: Halstead Press, 1972).

[8] An indication of the rise in science's ideological status was its treatment by philosophers. Whereas at the beginning of the 1960s science was pronounced to be "in the process of becoming a productive force" in the USSR, by the end of the decade philosophers referred to science as "the most important productive force." Some philosophers and historians even posited that the eventual victory of socialism over capitalism would issue from socialism's superior capacity to utilize science and technology. See E. Arab-Ogly, "O sotsialnykh posledstviiakh nauchno-teknicheskoi revoliutsii," in Nauchno-tekhnicheskaia revoliutsiia i obshchestvennyi progress (Moscow, 1969), p. 8; P. A. Rachkov, Rol nauki v stroitelstve kommunisma (Moscow, 1969); N. V. Markov, Nauchno-tekhnicheskaia revoliutsiia: Analiz, perspektivy, posledstviia (Moscow, 1971); Sovremenaia nauchno-tekhnicheskaia revoliutsiia: Istoricheskoe issledovanie (Moscow, 1967) and in an expanded edition (Moscow, 1970).

As science became more important politically in the 1960s, science policy revived as a major field of policy-making in the USSR, and the fields of science studies--the economics, sociology, history, and philosophy of science, even law and science--developed rapidly. For a general statement about Soviet science policy, see D. Gvishiani, "Sotsialnaia rol' nauki i politika gosudarstva v oblasti nauki," Upravlenie, planirovanie i organizatsiia nauchnykh i tekhnicheskikh issledovanii 1 (Moscow, 1970): 22.

A useful review of Soviet science studies is E. M. Mirskii, "Naukovedenie v SSSR," Voprosy istorii estestvoznaiia i tekhniki, nos. 3-4 (1971), pp. 86-97, translated into English as "Science Studies in the USSR," in Science Studies 2 (1972): 281-94.

[9] Campbell, "Problems of Technological Progress." Also, Michael Boretsky, "The Technological Base of Soviet Military Power," Economic Performance and the Military Burden in the Soviet Union; papers submitted to the Subcommittee on Foreign Economic Policy of the Joint Economic Committee, Congress of the United States (Washington, D.C., 1970).

[10] The expanding science budget throughout the 1960s may well have included the costs of military R and D, but it is probable that the increases noted mainly affected the civilian sphere. Beginning in 1970, when the official defense budget of the USSR leveled off, the science budget started to increase at an even faster rate than before (approximately double), suggesting first that the increased costs

of military research were transferred as of 1970 to the "science budget" and second that the previous increments in the science budget had not included a sizable proportion of the increases in military R and D. The data upon which this analysis is based are found in Mose Harvey, et al. Science and Technology as an Instrument of Soviet Policy (Miami: Center for the Advancement of International Studies, 1972), p. 67.

[11] Amann, Berry, and Davies, "Science and Industry in the USSR"; Schroeder, "Soviet Technology"; Burks, "Technology and Political Change."

[12] Campbell, "Problems of Technological Progress."

[13] "O meropriiatiiakh po povysheniiu effektivnosti raboty nauchnykh organizatsii i uskoreneniiu ispolzovaniia v narodnom khoziaistve dostizhenii nauki i tekhniki," Postanovlenie TsK KPSS i Soveta Ministrov SSSR ot 24 sentiabria 1968 g., no. 760, Biulleten Ministerstva Vysshego i Srednogo Spetsialnogo Obrazovaniia SSSR (January 1969), pp. 2-18.

[14] Ibid., article 18 and article 23 (hereafter only the article numbers will be cited.)

[15] Article 6.

[16] Tikhomirov's remarks were recorded in O. Gribanova, "Ekonomicheskie problemy razvitiia nauki," Voprosy ekonomiki no. 10 (1971), p. 149.

[17] A. A. Trofimuk, "Razgovor prekrashchat rano," Literaturnaia gazeta, 9 June 1971, p. 1; P. Volin, "'Khikmet'--eto znachit mudrost (O sudbe firm-posrednikov)," Literaturnaia gazeta 9 June 1971, p. 10.

[18] The revival of contracts between industrial research institutes and enterprises (these contracts had been used widely in the 1930s but had fallen into disuse in the intervening decades) was designed to force researchers to choose topics useful to industry and to encourage industry to utilize the results. In practice, the system worked so well that factory directors succeeded in shifting contract R and D from innovation to adaptations whose principal virtue for the directors was that they left production undisturbed. See Amann, Berry, and Davies, "Science and Industry in the USSR," p. 232.

[19] Article 29.

[20] Article 31.
    There was also a more radical scheme introduced at the Karpov Physics and Chemistry Institute (with no relation to the 1968 edict). There the base pay of scientists was reduced by 25 percent at all levels and supplements of up to 100 percent made available on the basis of the accomplishments of each individual scientist. These accomplishments were to take into account the economic effect of each man's work. See Ia. Kolotyrkin, "Mera tvorchestva: Experiment v nauchno-issledovatelskom institute," Izvestiia, 5 February 1971, p. 3.

[21] B. Prakhov, "Dogovor v sisteme ekonomicheskikh sviazei nauki s proizvodstvom," Planovoe khoziaistvo no. 2 (1972), pp. 99-102.

[22] Gribanova, "Ekonomicheskie problemy."

[23] Amann, Berry, and Davies, "Science and Industry in the USSR," pp. 478-479; Schroeder, "Soviet Technology."

[24]The pricing scheme focused around the concept of "limit price," which specified the range within which new prices could be set. The allowable increase in the price of a product would be fixed somewhere between a minimum limit, below which the producer would find it unprofitable to manufacture the new product, and a maximum limit, above which the purchaser would be indifferent. The assumption was that a happy medium could be found, while retaining the existing system of prices used in the economy as a whole. See Article 38, and Schroeder, "Soviet Technology," p. 27.

[25]"Kak uskorit' tekhnicheskii progress. Beseda za stolom delovykh vstrech 'Pravdy,'" Nauchnoe upravlenie obshchestvom 5 (Moscow, 1971): 318-56; A Levin, "Kak rozhdaetsa sistema (marshruty teknicheskogo progressa)," Pravda, (30 July 1971); V. Bitunov and Iu. Tishunov, "Chtob i zavodu bylo vygodno (problemy i suzhdeniia)," Pravda, (18 August 1971). In addition to the limit price scheme introduced in industry as a whole, the 1968 edict also sanctioned an experiment suggested by the Ministry of Electrical Equipment. By special arrangement new products which resulted from R and D in that ministry would carry for two years a special surcharge above the permanent price. That charge would be calculated on the basis of the presumed economic effect which the improvements would provide for the purchaser. For those first two years, however, the research institute, the design bureau, and the factory would share the economic gain by splitting the income the surcharge supplied. This scheme was meant both to provide incentives for researchers and to make the introduction of new technology more profitable for enterprises. Unfortunately, the surcharge did not provide enough extra return to compensate factories for the loss of income the reduced production levels caused; and enterprises' directors were well aware that their contribution to profits would only be temporary. See Article 24; A. Borodachev, "Zvenia edinoi tsepi (nauka i rychagi progressa),"Izvestiia, (7 September 1971), p. 3; S. Tikhomirov, "Stimuly tekhnicheskogo progressa," Pravda (2 March 1971), p. 2.

[26]"Kak uskorit' tekhnicheskii progress," p. 354.

[27]The depiction of the "role definitions" of R and D personnel is based in part upon material provided by Amann, Berry, and Davies, "Science and Industry in the USSR" and in part upon my reading of Soviet sources.

[28]In The European Executive (Garden City, N.Y.: Doubleday, 1962), David Granick rated the Soviet administrator high on entrepreneurship compared with his European counterparts.

[29]Alexander Gerschenkron, "Problems and Patterns of Russian Economic Development," The Transformation of Russian Society:Aspects of Social Change since 1861 (Cambridge: Harvard University Press, 1960), pp. 42-71; John P. McKay, Pioneers for Profit: Foreign Entrepreneurship and Russian Industrialization 1885-1913 (Chicago: University of Chicago Press, 1970).

[30]Russian scientists had raised the question of industrial research institutes before World War I, and during the war they submitted more than twenty projects for industrial laboratories and institutes to KEPS, the organization for the study of Russian productive forces, which the Czarist government had established to help the war effort. M. S. Bastrakova, "Organizatsionnye tendentsii russkoi nauki v nachale XX veka," in Organizatsiia nauchnoi deiatelnosti (Moscow, 1968), pp. 176-77. For detailed examination of Czarist science policy and the struggles of Russian scientists to modify it, see M. S. Bastrakova, Stanovlenie sovetskoi sistemy organizatsii nauki (1917-1922) (Moscow, 1973). pp. 19-61.

[31]V. D. Esakov, Sovetskaia nauka, p. 83. On the Scientific-Technical Section and its research institutes, see also the collections of documents Organizatsiia

nauki v pervye gody Sovetskoi vlasti (1917-1925) Sbornik dokumentov. (Leningrad, 1968), pp. 232-238, and Organizatsiia sovetskoi nauki v 1926-1932 gg. Sbornik dokumentov (Leningrad, 1974), pp. 264-305. For details on the establishment and first five years of the Scientific-Technical Section, see Bastrakova, Stanovlenie sovetskoi sistemy, pp. 160-86.

[32]L. V. Zhigalova, "K istorii sozdaniia institutov nauchno-tekhnicheskogo otdela VSNKh," Organizatsiia nauchnoi deiatelnosti (Moscow, 1968), pp. 187-90.

[33]On Lenin's attitude toward science, see Esakov, Sovetskaia nauka, pp. 7-20; on the Electrification Plan, see Loren Graham, The Soviet Academy of Sciences and the Communist Party 1927-1932 (Princeton: Princeton University Press, 1967), pp. 70-71.

[34]See Anthony Sutton, Western Technology and Soviet Economic Development, 1917 to 1930 (Stanford: Stanford University Press, 1968).

[35]On the scientists' attitudes, see Vladimir Ipatieff, The Life of a Chemist (Stanford: Stanford University Press, 1946), pp. 361-62; and Esakov, Sovetskaia nauka, pp. 86-90.

[36]Esakov, Sovetskaia nauka, p. 86. Esakov's source on the conservatism of the managers, the weak utilization of research, and the scientists' reaction was a special study carried out by the Workers and Peasants Inspectorate (RKI) in 1927.

[37]"Dekret SNK ob uchrezhdenii Nauchno-tekhnicheskogo otdela pri VSNKh," (16 August 1918), in Organizatsiia nauki v pervye gody Sovetskoi vlasti (1917-1925) (Leningrad, 1968), pp. 78-82.

[38]Ipatieff, The Life of a Chemist.

[39]Esakov, Sovetskaia nauka, pp. 113-20. See also Lewis, "Some Aspects of the Research and Development Effort in the Soviet Union," for interesting and detailed compilations of manpower and budgetary trends during this period. According to Lewis, by the middle 1930s the Soviet Union was spending 0.6 percent (about) of its national income on R and D; compared with the United States which in the same period spent 0.35 percent.

[40]Western economists have realized for some time that Soviet industrialization in this period was based upon Western technology. But Anthony Sutton's industry-by-industry study makes the size of this borrowing effort clear for the first time. According to Sutton, Soviets used derivative technologies in every civilian industry, generally selecting the best available at the time. As of 1941, Soviet technological self-sufficiency was observed only in military industry. Anthony Sutton, Western Technology and Soviet Economic Development 1930-1945 (Stanford, 1971), pp. 3, 248, 292, 329, 340-48.

[41]As Lewis pointed out, the major Soviet leaders--Stalin, Trotskii, and Bukharin--agreed on the critical importance of science and technology for the Soviet economy. Lewis, "Some Aspects of the Research and Development Effort in the Soviet Union," p. 153. Note that Stalin's frequently quoted slogan during 1931 was "technology decides everything" (tekhnika reshaet vse).

[42]It is possible that some Soviet leaders regarded the current investment in applied science as relevant to the immediate need for technological innovation in the military sphere.

[43] Technological innovations have little connection with research-front science, but they do often draw upon the store of past scientific knowledge. It has also been argued that scientific training provides technologists with skill at problem-solving and the capacity to use existing knowledge. See Pavitt, "Science, Enterprise and Innovation"; Derek de Solla Price, "Is Technology Historically Independent of Science: A Study in Statistical Historiography," Technology and Culture, 6 (Fall 1965): 553-68. Also, Richard Nelson et al., Technology, Economic Growth and Public Policy (Washington, D.C.: Brookings Institution, 1967) p. and Harvey Brooks, "The Interaction of Science and Technology--Another View," in The Impact of Science on Technology, ed. Aaron Warner et al. (New York: Columbia University Press, 1965), p. 38.

[44] To bolster this conviction, the Soviet press in 1932 loudly acclaimed each instance of the reproduction of Western machines by Soviet industry as the beginning of "technological self-reliance!" Za industrializatsiiu (1932), passim.

[45] Alec Nove, An Economic History of the USSR (London: Penguin, 1969), pp. 228-31.

[46] David Granick has argued that it was inevitable that the USSR would fall behind the West in technology after its initial spurt based upon technological borrowing. See Granick, Soviet Metal-Fabricating and Economic Development Practice versus Policy (Madison: University of Wisconsin Press, 1967).

[47] Cordell, "The Multinational Firm," p. 53.

[48] An engineer from the lathe construction industry wrote in 1932, "Our young inexperienced cadres cannot handle the installation. This is why after the first series of lathes was issued that our workers came to the unanimous conclusion about the need to introduce a series of changes in their construction, without which the assimilation of these lathes in our conditions would be senseless." Simple copying of European and American technology in this field, the author pointed out, would not ensure the high tempos required; to achieve such tempos simplification of designs was necessary. E. Alperovich, "My poidem eshche bystree, chem shli do sikh por," Za industrializatsiiu, 29 October 1932, p. 3.

[49] There is a thorough analysis of the costs and benefits of standardization in Granick, Soviet Metal-Fabrication, pp. 44-47. Note that during the early 1930s there was a special journal devoted to standardization, Vestnik standardizatsii.

[50] OECD Reviews of National Science Policy: Japan.

[51] This deduction is easily reached by scanning the handbook Nauchno-isseldovatel-skie instituty tiazheloi promyshlennosti, ed. A. A. Armand, (Moscow and Leningrad, 1935).

[52] More recently, Bell laboratories in the United States discovered that either administrative or geographic separation of research from production was tolerable, even desirable, but that the combination of the two was inefficient. See Jack Morton, "From Research to Technology," in the R and D Game, ed. David Allison, (Cambridge, Mass., M.I.T. Press, 1969), pp. 225-26.

[53] The continuation of the separate administration of research institutes during the First Five-Year Plan period made considerable sense. The Scientific-Technical Administration had experienced science administrators, who were better prepared than others to manage the expansion of industrial institutes. Moreover, during the industrialization drive the administrators in the production glavki were busy enough without bothering with research institutes, whose work they regarded as peripheral to the main tasks at hand.

[54]From 1929 to 1931 the "planning technical-economic administration" (PTEU) of VSNKh had primary responsibility for technology in industry. Appropriately, during these years the "scientific-technical administration," which was responsible for the research institutes, was subordinated to PTEU. Esakov, Sovetskaia nauka, pp. 109-14.

[55]For this rationale, see V. V. Kuibyshev, Nauke-Sotsialisticheskii plan (Moscow and Leningrad, 1931), p. 14, cited in Lewis, "Some Aspects of the Research and Development Effort in the Soviet Union," pp. 166-67.

[56]E. P. Frolov, "Osnovnye zadachi zavodskikh laboratorii," Zavodskaia laboratoriia, no. 8-9 (1932), p. 5.

[57]V. Titov, "Pervaia vsesoiuznaia konferentsiia nauchno-issledovatelskikh institutov mashinostroeniia i rezultaty ee rabot," Vestnik machinostroeniia, no. 6, (1932), pp. 3-4; Nauchno-issledovatelskie instituty tiazhelnoi promyshlennosti, passim. Examples of institutes' manufacturing work are found in A. Khokhriakov, "Leningradskii institut metalov na fronte industrializatsii," Na fronte industrializatsii, no. 21-22, (1932), p. 48; and Lewis, "Some Aspects of the Research and Development Effort in the Soviet Union," p. 175. The exception to the rule of underequipped R and D institutions in civilian industry was the aircraft research, where institutes and design organizations were well supplied. In the opinion of Bukharin the aircraft industry possessed a model R and D. N. I. Bukharin, "Tekhnicheskaiia rekonstruktsiia i tekushchie problemy nauchno-issledovatelskoi raboty," Sotsialisticheskaia revoliutsiia i nauka, no. 1, (1933), pp. 28-29.

[58]Bukharin, "Tekhnicheskaia rekonstruktsiia i tekushchie problemy", p. 21; V. K. Vaksov, "Avtomobilstroeniiu neobkhodima experimentalnaia baza," Za industrializatsiiu, 17 January 1932, p. 3; Frolov, "Osnovnye zadachi zavodskikh laboratorii,", p. 10; N. F. Charnovskii, "Razvitie otraslei machinostroeniia na osnovakh nauchno-issledovatelskoi raboty," Vestnik metallopromyshelnnosti, no. 6, (1930), p. 10.

[59]On the practicalization of science, see Graham, Soviet Academy of Sciences, pp. 154-210.

[60]How the bias against innovation in the planning system affected the behavior and attitudes of industrial managers in the 1930s will be discussed below.

[61]On the training of the new scientific-technical cadres, see Kendall Bailes, "Stalin and the Revolution from Above: The Formation of the Soviet Technical Intelligentsia, 1928-1934," Ph.D. diss., Columbia University, 1971, especially pp. 216-404.

[62]Esakov, "Sovetskaia nauka," p. 117. Vydvyzhenniki were workers promoted into positions of managerial or technical authority without the requisite educational attainment. For a discussion of the vydvyzhenniki movement, see Robert Feldmesser, "Aspects of Social Mobility in the Soviet Union," Ph.D. diss., Harvard University, 1955.

[63]Some of these young scientists failed to meet even the low standard of the time. In 1933, some 10 percent of them were dropped from the institutes, and a number of institutes "chiefly the dwarf and frail ones, which did not possess qualified cadres" were also eliminated. N. I. Bukharin, "Nauchno-tekhnicheskoe obsluzhivanie tiazheloi promyshlennosti," Sotsialisticheskaia revoliutsiia i nauka, no. 3, (1934), pp. 4-5; reprinted in Nauchno-tekhnicheskoe obsluzhivanie tiazheloi promyshlennosti. Sbornik NISA i Tekhpropa NKTP k XVII sezdu VKP (b)

230

(Moscow and Leningrad, 1934), pp. 9-11. See also Lewis, "Some Aspects of the Research and Development Effort in the Soviet Union," p. 162. Complaints about the inexperienced young cadres were still heard in 1935. See "Soveshchanie nauchno-issledovatelskikh institutov zavodskikh laboratorii," Zavodskaia laboratoriia, no. 4, (1935), p. 127.

[64]Bukharin, "Nauchno-tekhnicheskoe obsluzhivanie," p. 3 (11).

[65]Nauchno-issledovatelskie instituty tiazheloi promyshlennosti; Nauchno-tekhnicheskoe obsluzhivanie tiazheloi promyshlennosti.

[66]"Pervaia vsesoiuznaia konferentsiia nauchno-issledovatelskikh institutov mashinostroeniia," pp. 4-6.
N. Iushkevich, "Pora razrushit 'monastyrskie' steny nauki," Za industrializatsiiu, 4 February 1932, p. 3; R. L. Veller, "Pokonchit' s otryvom nauchno-issledova-telskikh institutov ot zavodskikh laboratorii," Zavodskaia laboratoriia, no. 5, (1934), pp. 387-88.

[67]Lewis, "Some Aspects of the Research and Development Effort in the Soviet Union," pp. 171-72.

[68]See "Piatiletnyi plan rabot i razvitie vsesoiuznogo instituta metallov," Vestnik metallopromyshlennosti, no. 2, (1929), pp. 81-92; N. A. Ilin and B. P. Selivanov, "Tsentralnyi institut metallov," in Nauchno-tekhnicheskoe obsluzhivanie tiazhelnoi promyshlennosti (Moscow and Leningrad, 1934), pp. 100-104; "Tsentralnyi institut metallov," Nauchno-issledovatelskie instituty tiazheloi promyshlennosti, pp. 412-26.

[69]On the work of the 'head institutes," see Nauchno-issledovatelskie instituty tiazheloi promyshlennosti;and for reports in English on the work of some of them, J. G. Crowther, Soviet Science (London: K. Paul, Trench, Trubner, and Co., 1936). Examples of the practical activities of the "branch institutes"are found in the following sources: "Issledovatelskaia rabota po torfu," Sotsialisticheskaia revoliutsiia i nauka, no. 1, (1931), pp. 151-56; Zvenigorodskii, "Zavod im. Shmidta sozdaet novoe proizvodstvo--Institut neftannogo oborudovaniia na pomoshch zavodu," Za industrializatsiiu, 17 January 1932, p. 3; V. V. Titov, "Nauchno-issledovatelskie instituty mashinostroeniia i metalloobrabotki i osnovnye zadachi, stoiashchie pered nimi v 1931 g.," Vestnik mashinostroeniia no. 5, (1931); V. Sorokin, "Nauchno-issledovatelskii institut rezinovoi promyshlennosti," in Nauchno-tekhnicheskoe obshluzhivanie tiazheloi promyshlennosti (Moscow and Leningrad, 1934), pp. 187-93. Each of these institutes servicing the peat, oil, automobile, lathe, and rubber industries devoted a considerable portion of its efforts to the adaptation and modification of foreign technology and to other practical tasks.

[70]Frolov, "Osnovnye zadachi zavodskikh laboratorii"; Charnovskii, "Razvitie otraslei machinostroeniia"; Bukharin, "Tekhnicheskaia rekonstruktsiia."

[71]Vaksov, "Avtomobilstroeniiu neobkhodima."

[72]As an excuse for avoiding practical tasks which would require contact with local industry, certain Leningrad scientists emphasized that their first priority was work of "All-Union significance," the results of which they would report to Moscow. According to one critical observer, "the full estrangement on their (the Leningrad scientists') part from Leningrad will, undoubtedly, testify to the fact that they theorize in a vacuum, that they have no concrete image of an industrial enterprise, a kolkhoz, or a hydro-electric station, which they are obliged to serve." V. Shtein, "O planirovanii nauchno-issledovatelskoi raboty

v Leningradskoi oblasti," <u>Na fronte industrializatsii</u>, no. 24, (1930), pp. 5-10.

[73]See the speeches by R. L. Veller and A. A. Armand in "Soveshchanie nauchno-issledovatelskikh institutov."

[74]Getting research published and delivered was not always simple. According to A. A. Chernyshev, "Ob organizatsii planirovaniia nauchno-issledovatelskoi raboty v oblasti elektrotekhniki," <u>Sotsialisticheskaia revoliutsiia i nauka</u>, no. 6, (1933), p. 122, much of the research in electronics was "stashed on the shelves, remaining completely unknown not only to other institutions, but frequently even within the walls of the institution where it was performed."

[75]NKTP did prescribe a list of obligations of research institutes and factory directors in regard to R and D, but it did not stipulate that these obligations be reflected in the plans of institute or enterprise. See "O vazhneishikh zakonchennykh rabotakh nauchno-issledovatelskikh institutov NKTP, podlezhashchikh vnedreniiu v promyshlennost," Postanovlenie Kollegii Narodonogo Komissariata Tiazheloi promyshlennosti no. 87, Moskva, 8 fevralia 1933 g," <u>Sotsialisticheskaia revoliutsiia i nauka</u>, no. 2, (1933), pp. 228-29.

[76]V. V. Titov, "Soveshchanie glavnykh konstruktorov obedinenii, zavodov, i proiektnykh biuro Glavmashproma i Glavenergoproma," (ot 20-23 iuliia 1932 g.), <u>Vestnik metallopromyshlennosti</u>, no. 10 (1932), pp. 8-16.

[77]M. Ia. Shiperovich, "O peresmotre konstruktsii mashin (iz rabot konstruktorskoi sektsii Nauchno-teknicheskogo komiteta mashinostroeniia, fevral-iiul 1931 g.)," <u>Vestnik metallopromyshlennosti</u>, no. 10, (1932), pp. 15-20.

[78]Sutton, <u>Western Technology and Soviet Economic Development 1930-1945</u>, pp. 292,321.

[79]E. Perelman, "Tvorcheskie sily-sovetskoi tekhnike mashinostroeniia," <u>Za industrializatsiiu</u>, 2 January 1933, p. 3.

[80]Titov, "Soveshchanie," p. 8.

[81]Vaksov, "Avtomobilstroeniiu neobkhodima"; Titov, "Soveshchanie"; "Perestroit' rabotu proektiruiushchikh organizatsii," <u>Za industrializatsiiu</u>, 6 January 1933, p. 1.

[82]Shiperovich, "O peresmotre Konstruktsii mashin"; B. Usilevich et al., "Osvobodim kontrolnoizmeritelnoe khoziaistvo SSSR ot inostrannoi zavisimosti," <u>Za industrializatsiiu</u>, 18 February 1932, p. 3; "Na fronte 'gonat i peregnat'," <u>Na fronte industrializatsii</u>, no. 21-22, (1931), pp. 16-40.

[83]Titov, "Soveshchanie"; "Perestroit' rabotu."

[84]See Donald Schon, "The Fear of Innovation," in <u>The R and D Game</u>, ed. David Allison (Cambridge, Mass., 1969), pp. 119-34.

[85]See Nove, <u>Economic History of the USSR</u>, pp. 181-95

[86]D. A. Gerasimov, "Nauka i ee primeneniia v torfianoi promyshlennosti," <u>Sotsialisticheskaia revoliutsiia i nauka</u>, no. 2, (1934), p. 80.

[87]Bukharin, "Tekhnicheskaia rekonstruktsiia," p. 28.

[88]See the regular discussions of these problems in Zavodskaia laboratoriia, 1931-35.

[89]"O reorganizatsii nauchno-issledovatelskoi raboty na zavodakh," Zavodskaia laboratoriia, (1932), no. 3, pp. 8-9.

[90]Academician Britske, in "Soveshchanie nauchno-issledovatelskikh institutov," p. 117.

[91]Gerasimov, "Nauka i ee primeneniia v torfianoi promyshlennosti," p. 89.

[92]A lack of interest in R and D was also found among the economic planners in Leningrad oblast. See V. Shtein, "O planirovanii nauchno-issledovatelskoi raboty v Leningradskoi oblasti."

[93]In 1955 politicians with industrial and scientific administrators met to discuss the problem of technological "conservatism and stagnation"; excerpts from the speeches were carried in Pravda and Izvestiia and an edict urging the correction of the shortcomings followed soon after. "From Soviet Publications: The Industrial Conference," Soviet Studies 7 (1955): 201-213. The edict is mentioned in Amann, Berry, and Davies, "Science and Industry in the USSR," p. 394.

[94]It is problematic the extent to which one can change role definitions without modifying the structures in which those roles are embedded. However, although structural change must usually come first, the changes in attitudes and behavior may follow easily; conversely, the role definitions themselves may impede the very structural changes which were meant to affect them. To modify a long-standing role definition, one might suggest, structural change is a necessary, but not always sufficient, condition.

[95]For example, "Konferentsiia nauchno-issledovatelskikh institutov mashino-stroeniia v metalloobrabotki," Vestnik metallopromyshlennosti, no. 9 (1932), pp. 2-5; "Soveshchanie nauchno-issledovatelskikh institutov"; N. Bukharin, "Ko vsem nauchno-issledovatelskim institutam," Vestnik metallopromyshlennosti, no. 8, (1932), pp. 79-80.

[96]"O vazhneishikh zakonchennykh rabotakh."

[97]See "Ob organizatsii nauchno-issledovatelskoi raboty dlia nuzhd promyshlennosti," Postanovlenie soveta narodnykh komissarov SSSR, 7 avgusta 1928 g., Resheniia partii i pravitelstva po khoziaistvennym voprosam, Tom 1, 1917-1928 (Moscow, 1967), pp. 750-55.

[98]A. A. Armand, "Zavodskie laboratorii tiazheloi promyshlennosti," Zavodskaia laboratoriia, no. 5, (1936), pp. 518-23.

[99]For the effects of this liberalization upon policy debates in criminal law, see Peter H. Solomon, Jr., "Specialists in Soviet Policymaking: Criminologists and Criminal Policy in the 1960's," Ph.D. diss., Columbia University, 1973, pp. 64-66.

[100]I. P. Bardin, "Zavodskie laboratorii," Zavodskaia laboratoriia, no. 1 (1947), pp. 5-8.

[101]"From Soviet Publications: The Industrial Conference."

[102]On the requirement for some R and D to accomplish technology transfers, see Geogry Skorov, "Technology and Development: The Case of Developing Countries," in International Aspects of Technological Innovation (Paris: UNESCO, 1970).

[103]OECD: Reviews of National Science Policy: Japan, pp. 138-40; Hideomi Tuge, Historical Development of Science and Technology in Japan (Tokyo: Kokusai Bunka Shinkokai, 1961), pp. 155 ff.

[104]OECD: Review: Japan, p. 142.

[105]Science and Technology Agency of Japan, White Paper on Science and Technology (1970) "New Demands for Technological Innovation," cited in Science Policy, (1971): 3-1.

[106]Herman Kahn, The Emerging Japanese Superstate: Challenge and Response (Englewood Cliffs, N.J.: Prentice-Hall, 1970), p. 108; Maurice Glicksman, "R & D in Japan--A future That Will Challenge the U.S.," Research Management 14 (January 1971): 28-37.

Chapter 10.

HEALTH AS A "PUBLIC UTILITY" OR THE "MAINTENANCE OF CAPACITY" IN

SOVIET SOCIETY

Mark G. Field

An examination of the total amount of research done on the socialist countries, and on the Soviet Union in particular, reveals a discouraging lack of concern with one of the more fundamental resources of these nations--the health of their populations--and with the specific mechanisms devised for protecting and maintaining that resource. As one who has toiled in the vineyards of Soviet medicine and medical organization, I can attest both to the enjoyment of a kind of monopoly and to a sense of extreme isolation and loneliness. Indeed, the number of writers who have systematically turned their attention to this question can be counted on the fingers of one hand; one needs only the other hand to in- clude those who have dabbled in it.[1] It is almost as if this were of no sociological interest, worthy of no time and effort--certainly much less meaning- ful than steel production, the evolution of the gross national product, science, education, or the intricacies of party organization. It is known that people everywhere become sick or injured, and that they eventually die, so what else is new? It is also true that when people need medical care they usually try to see a physician, and that sick people are often put into hospitals where medical personnel (doctors, nurses, etc.) take care of them, in the Soviet Union and everywhere else in the world. Everybody knows that the Soviet Union has social- ized medicine, and that most doctors are women. What more is there to discuss?

As a sociologist, I argue that there is a great deal more to discuss. Medical services are provided within an institutional framework and thus are a legitimate area of concern for the sociologist. At the same time--and this will be the central focus of my presentation--the health system (which I shall define below) contributes to the existence and the functioning of the social system. Thus I would like to approach the significance of the Soviet Union's health system from a macrosociological, structural-functional perspective.

Maintenance Mechanisms: The Shaping and Preservation of Capacity

Any society or human group is in a constant state of metabolism as its members age, retire, and die, and as others are born. One can, as demographers do, develop and utilize quantitative metrics to chart the rate of that metabolism. One can follow, for example, the degree to which a society reproduces itself or fails to do so, the changing mix in the sex and age ratios of the population, and so on. Later I shall present some such data for the Soviet Union and the United

This paper is part of my general research on "Comparative Health Systems: Differentiation and Convergence," supported in part by Grant HS-00272 from the National Center for Health Services Research, H.R.A., the Public Health Service, U.S. Department of Health, Education, and Welfare. I also want to express my gratitude to the following persons who assisted me in this work at its various stages: Ms. Luisa Polosjuk, Ms. Sandra A. Peterson, Ms. Francine Miller, and Ms. Sharon A. Lefevre.

States. But one can also argue that the physical reproduction of life, by itself, is never sufficient to ensure the preservation and continuation of human social structures, since an important and irreducible component of these structures is their culture or "ethos." Since a culture is not genetically inherited, it must be taught or otherwise imparted to the younger generations.

The process of cultural transmission is often called "socialization." Essentially it consists of transforming the child, who has his own inherent potential, into a full member of society, capable of acting in that society. This process begins almost at birth, with the mother as the single most important agent of socialization, but it soon broadens to include other members of the family and primary groups; later it is mediated through socialization agencies such as the peer group, the school system, and work groups. Language skills and the ability to communicate are probably the first cultural items transmitted to the child, soon followed by other aspects of the culture: traits, values, habits, skills, behavioral patterns, and the ability to read, write, conceptualize, and so on. From the perspective of society as a social system, the major function of the socialization process is the "shaping of capacity." By "capacity" I mean the individual's ability to interact with other members of the society and to perform in the variety of roles he or she is expected to assume in the course of daily existence and throughout a lifetime. The capacity to act within social contexts must then be seen as a strategic component of social structure.[2] But equally fundamental, given the psychological and physiological nature of all human actors, is the "maintenance of the capacity" to act when that capacity is threatened by ill-health (psychological and physiological), trauma, and death (particularly premature mortality).

Thus, in addition to the intensely personal aspects of illness and disability and their emotional meaning to the individual in terms of suffering, anxiety, and dependency, incapacity owing to disease (and the ultimate incapacity of death or severe mental regression or retardation--a kind of social death) poses a functional problem to all societies as it affects capacity for role performance. Every society and culture has devised responses to that threat in terms of its ultimate meaning and of remedial actions to be taken. Occupational roles centrally concerned with health and illness have emerged in almost every society. Given the emotional significance of illness, incapacity, and death, religion, concerned as it is with meaning, and medicine, concerned with remedial action, have in the past often been coterminous. But with the increase of scientific knowledge and its application to illness, one can discern the rise of a fully differentiated medical and allied professional corps quite distinct from religious specialists.

If the major focus of the process of socialization is shaping the capacity to act, then the central task for medicine (or the health system) is "maintaining capacity" and prolonging life. In essence, socialization (particularly education) and medicine are "maintenance" mechanisms of society and contain many common elements; they are, for example, labor intensive and are important enough to usually be regarded as exempt from the market mechanisms of caveat emptor and ability to pay. Finally, in modern society, they tend to be performed within a professional context.

Historical Background

The development of medicine and the organization of the medical profession in prerevolutionary Russia was not distinctly different from that of other European countries. The medical profession, organized into associations granted a fair amount of autonomy, generally belonged to the liberal segment of the Russian intelligentsia. It often took positions with strong political overtones, primarily because it realized that improvements in medicine and medical care would be of little avail in bettering the life conditions of the population unless matched by parallel reforms in the polity and the economy. With the first revolution of 1917, the medical profession began to formulate plans for substantial health reforms which it expected to direct. But the response of the Bolshevik regime was disappointing, for it looked upon the medical profession (or any other prerevolutionary professional body) as a bastion of bourgeois ideology, dedicated to preserving the status quo and incompatible as a corporate organization with the new society to emerge in the wake of the October Revolution.[3]

At the time the Bolsheviks seized power in the fall of 1917, Russia was in the third year of a ruinous war; her economy was in a state of collapse; soldiers were deserting the front; and the government's administrative apparatus was paralyzed. In addition, the society was threatened by major epidemics and pandemics which caused many deaths among the already weakened population. The new regime, ruling most precariously from Petrograd, could only look with alarm at the people's deteriorating health as still another major threat to its stability and indeed to its very existence.

Typhus was the greatest problem, and of those who had it about 10 percent died-- a high proportion. There were also epidemics of cholera, relapsing fever, typhoid fever, plague, smallpox, dysentery, scarlet fever, measles, and malaria.[4] According to conservative estimates, the morbidity from typhus alone was 20 to 30 million persons, with a corresponding mortality of 3 million. By 1924 the total number of deaths from epidemics since 1916 was put at 8 to 10 million.[5] "Typhus," Lenin declared shortly after the Revolution, "among a population already weakened by hunger without bread, soap, fuel, may become such a scourge as not to give us an opportunity to undertake socialist construction. This must be the first step in our struggle for culture and for our existence."[6] In 1919 he faced the Seventh Congress of the Soviets with the simple choice: "Either the lice defeat socialism or socialism defeats the lice."[7] The historical record reveals that very early, almost immediately after the seizure of power, the Soviet regime took steps to establish its own public health and medical service, operating in line with the functional imperatives of the moment and within the ideological constraints derived from Marxism-Leninism. I have described at some length elsewhere[8] the early phases of the formation of the Soviet health service. I would like to recapitulate here only the more salient aspects of that process.

The first measures adopted by the regime were aimed at checking the epidemics rather than at establishing a health service concerned primarily with clinical medicine and personal medical care, although this later became a part of its program. Second, the Bolsheviks held that protecting the health of the population was a social problem and the responsibility of the society as a whole, to be resolved by the "people" themselves and by the agencies appointed by the people; that is, essentially it must become a responsibility of the regime and could not be left to the efforts of the medical profession, voluntary groups, or charitable institutions. Indeed, it may not be too far-fetched to state that from that point on health in the USSR became a public utility or, as Newsholme and Kingsbury put it, health became "socialized."[9]

Third, medicine and the protection of health (zdravookhranenie) must be viewed, like everything else, through an ideological prism. In any society the ruling class benefits most from the health system, and physicians work as the hirelings of that class. The new society arising from the 1917 revolution could not consider medicine nonpolitical or above politics or class, but had to see it as something which must serve the new ruling class, that is, the workers, peasants, and soldiers, or, to put it another way, the new ruling class must now have priority in receiving health services. The new regime dismissed protests by the medical profession that this violated the ethical universalism of medicine (which treats a sick person regardless of class and status) as pure sham, since doctors, as servants of the ruling class, had always favored that class. Fourth, in line with the change in the social structure, physicians as an occupational group must lose their special and castelike professional character, their superiority and privileges, and must, according to the egalitarian tone of the times, become "medical workers" on a par with or sometimes below (as part of retributive justice) the more "proletarian" members of the health occupations such as feldshers, nurses, and orderlies. And directly related to this, the prerevolutionary professional associations of physicians, as corporate groups, must either recognize the legitimacy of regime dictation on health matters or be dissolved as "bourgeois" or "counterrevolutionary." Thus, quite early in the regime's history medical associations of the prerevolutionary type were ruled out of existence and replaced by a Union of Medical Workers (Medsantrud). The elimination (or neutralization) of the medical profession as an autonomous force was described by a Soviet medical historian in these terms:

> Soviet public health historically was built and grew
> in the struggle against reactionary bourgeois medicine,
> among whose ranks were the reactionary ideologists from
> the "Pirogovist" camp....The ideologists of bourgeois
> medicine, emanating chiefly from the reactionary part of
> the Pirogovists, were hostile to the Soviet regime and
> not only rejected the term "Soviet medicine," but also
> rejected the very possibility of its existence.

> The Pirogovists rejected the class character of
> medicine, endowing it with above-class [nadklassnii]
> elements. Standing on the idea of the solidity of the
> bourgeois order in society, not recognizing the dictator-
> ship of the proletariat as a new world historical type of
> proletarian democracy, Pirogovists opposed the idea that
> public health should be a state matter under a Soviet type
> of regime and said that it must be turned in its entirety
> to the community--that is, to the bourgeois Zemstvo
> self-government, with the leading role given to the medical
> corporation.[10]

Having eliminated the roadblocks presented by an organized but reluctant medical body, the Soviet regime proceeded to build its own national health service as an integral part of its governmental structure. Indeed, the organization of that service and the basic principles undergirding it were established before the launching of the industrialization and collectivization drives. By the end of the twenties, there were about three times as many physicians as before the Revolution. Although the establishment of a national health service cannot be said to be a sine qua non for the process of modernization and industrialization, it is difficult to conceive that the Soviet drive would have proceeded at the rate it did with a population afflicted by epidemic and other diseases, untreated trauma, a high level of mortality, and consequently a low life expectancy.

Identifying and isolating the precise contribution of the health system to the health and the energy of a population is difficult, if not impossible, because of the complex and interrelated nature of social systems and because of the effect of such factors as nutrition, housing, environmental conditions, and economic levels. Commenting on Myrdal's general view that one of the reasons health and education have had a low priority in planning national development resulted from a philosophy that regarded investments in physical elements (roads and dams, for example) as overriding, John Bryant adds: "More recent evidence suggests that physical investment may not be the primary engine of development, and that investment in human resources, such as health and education, plays an important role in the development process. A reasonable view is that health is an essential factor in the development process being both an instrument for and a product of development."[11] Were it not so, the Soviets, in the light of many pressing needs and scarcity of resources, most likely would not have supported the establishment and the rapid development of a national health service on the scale they did. It could be argued, of course, that providing health services to the population is inherent in the Soviet blueprint and is an expression of the regime's concern with the welfare and the well-being of the population per se. But given the hard-nosed attitude traditionally exhibited by Soviet leaders (beginning with Lenin) toward the wishes and wants of the population, this is not convincing, nor, in my opinion is it more than a partial explanation. Perhaps more convincing (although still a partial explanation) is the public relations or propagandistic aspect of that service, to which I will return later. This then leads me to a closer examination of the concept of the health system itself.

The Health System[12]

The "health system"[13] of any society is that societal mechanism which has arisen or has been devised specifically to deal with the problems caused by the incapacitating nature of illness, trauma, and (to some degree) premature mortality. These problems have sometimes been defined as the five Ds: Death, Disease, Disability, Discomfort, and Dissatisfaction.[14]

These constitute, in the aggregate, the major target to which the health system must address itself. As such that system may be further defined as the aggregate of resources, commitments, and personnel the society is willing to put aside or "invest" in the health concern as opposed to other concerns and problems. This it does through a series of activities and services that can be grouped into at least six different categories or modalities: Prevention, Diagnosis, Treatment, Rehabilitation, Custody, and Health Education.

The totality of these activities and services I call the Gross Medical Product (GMP) of the society. The GMP for any time period consists of the aggregate of decisions (including the decision not to act),acts, and procedures performed by health personnel. These acts are transactions that go from the health system to the health problem of the population. Thus the physician who gives a physical checkup, establishes a diagnosis, or removes an inflamed appendix contributes to the GMP. So does the nurse who cares for a patient and gives medications; the X-ray technician who takes a picture of a broken bone; and even the hospital cook who prepares food for the patients and staff. The determination of the precise boundaries of the health system is empirical and to some degree is definitional or arbitrary. Is the American pharmacist who dispenses prescription drugs, as well as sells many other items, a part of the American health system? Is the mother who nurses a sick child, or who indeed decides whether to call a physician, a part of the health system? Is animal husbandry a part of that system, not so much because of the food it provides but because of the use of the pancreas of cattle in the production of insulin?

Whatever the answer, one must decide what to include and exclude, otherwise the very concept of an identifiable and differentiated health system becomes meaningless. I might suggest that the American pharmacist is part of that system only insofar as he formally dispenses drugs prescribed by a licensed physician, though some would argue that he has other "medical" functions, such as advice and referral. The mother who nurses a sick child is not a part of that system, because she is not involved in it formally and occupationally. The failure to set up fairly strict boundaries and to stick to them would be self-defeating, since in the last analysis everything is connected with everything else. One might argue, for example, that the farmer is part of the health system since food is essential to maintaining life and health.

Two other components of the health system must be included, however, because they are indispensable for the functioning and the survival of that system. I call these components "internal" to the health system primarily because their outputs do not go from that system directly to health problems but remain within the system; one component provides education and training (or socialization) for future health personnel (physicians, nurses, feldshers, X-ray technicians, and so on) to replace those who drop out of the system through retirement, disability, death, or other causes; the other internal component is research aimed at discovering or elaborating new knowledge, new techniques, or new technologies to improve the functioning of the health system.

As a differentiated and specialized subsystem of the society, the health system can be neither self-supporting nor autonomous but must, by its very nature, rely on the availability of supports and resources from the society it serves. Such structural supports should not be taken for granted and must remain problematic, particularly since resources are usually finite and other subsystems constantly compete for them, as we shall later see. Thus, the elimination of such support, or its substantial diminution, would affect the ability of the health system to function and would eventually deprive the social system of health services or a significant portion of them. To use a very simple illustration, the physician, as a specialist, typically provides medical services fulltime. As such, he cannot attend directly to his own needs, such as raising his own food, building his own house, making his own clothes, or educating his own children. Some mechanism must be devised for the exchange of medical time--that is, medical services for nonmedical time, for example, the components of his standard of living; in other words, he must be compensated. This compensation may be either on a fee-for-service basis or a salary paid from taxes and other revenues (as is the case in the Soviet Union) or from a designated fund to which the patient has contributed; in some instances the compensation may be in the form of room and board and an allowance. Thus, although one might quibble ad infinitum as to what should be the proper income of physicians relative to the income of other occupations within the health system (that of nurses, for instance) or in the society at large, the necessity of some compensation is not debatable; even the most devoted and ascetic physician, Western or Soviet, cannot survive (and practice medicine) solely from the gratitude of his patients or from a sense of having done his duty.

There are at least four (and probably more) distinct structural supports for the health system:

1. The health system must have both legitimacy and a mandate, and these must be congruent with the value system and the culture of the society. They define the functions of the health system as proper and desirable and, indeed, impose a responsibility on it. Society, so to speak, enters into a contract with the health system and gives it an often monopolistic character in providing health services.

2. The health system requires a supply of knowledge and technology, an accumulated "state of the art." This state of the art, wherever a medical system is based on verifiable knowledge, excludes external truths or sacred revelations, since every aspect of it is open to challenge and modification through research and experience. This is in sharp contrast, for example, to religion (or ideology), where the basic principles or laws are held to be universal, immutable, and "sacred" and where the function of the religious specialist is to uphold these principles, to remind people of their absolute truth and validity, to guard against heresy, and, when necessary, to interpret or reinterpret them so that they will continue to be relevant under changed circumstances. The scientific method has been shown to be most effective in dealing with health problems, and it claims universal validity. It should be noted that scientific knowledge as a cultural entity is the only input to the medical system that is essentially nonfinite. Knowledge per se, once acquired, or techniques once developed are not diminished when used. On the other hand, as the development of modern medicine has clearly shown, the very availability of new knowledge and technology has immensely increased the pressures for manpower and financial resources.

3. The health system needs personnel who are especially motivated, screened, trained, and deployed within the occupational roles of the system. This is a scarce resource since educated manpower in any society is finite and costly, and other subsystems in the society usually compete for it. Society thus "invests" or "immobilizes" a portion of its available labor force in the health system, that is, those who become physicians, nurses, orderlies, technicians, and so on. Within limits, one society may import trained manpower from another society (as does the United States), but at any one time the supply of such man-**power** in the world is finite.

4. The health system must have economic resources to pay health personnel, purchase land, build hospitals and clinics, buy medicines and equipment, and pay for maintenance. Any society thus devotes a certain percentage of its Gross National Product or its budget to medicine and health care, whether this allocation is the result of a planned political administrative decision, as in the Soviet Union, or the result of the expenditure of tax monies and private funds affected by a mixture of market mechanisms and governmental disbursements, as in the United States.

Insofar as personnel and funds or capital are the prime scarce and quantifiable resources, one may possibly analyze their use in each case on two levels:

a. the proportion of the total available active manpower and the proportion of the Gross National Product (or the total national budget) that goes to the health system in contrast to all other systems;

b. the proportion of total manpower and economic resources that go to the different internal components of the health system, to the different types of services, or to different groups of the population.

By so analyzing over time, one might determine how a specific society first allocated its scarce resources to health as against other areas of concern; then one could examine the shifts of allocations within the health system, for example, in response to a change in the structure of morbidity that accompanies modernization. The word "allocation" does not necessarily connote a conscious and planned administrative decision on investments. In the United States, for example, no agency decides to "allocate" 8 percent of the Gross National Product to health: this allocation is the aggregate result of a myriad of individual and collective decisions and other factors such as those noted earlier.

This conceptual model yields a formal definition: the health system of any society is that societal mechanism that transforms generalized inputs (legitimacy-mandate, knowledge, personnel, and economic resources) into specialized outputs in the form of health services aimed at the health problems of the society. An important element in metabolizing these inputs into outputs is the structure, the organization, the management, the internal integration, and the rationalization of the health system in its totality. We shall examine the framework within which that system operates shortly, but one additional point must be made here: the health system in any society, and in the Soviet Union in particular, must necessarily operate within the constraints of other societal needs, resources, tasks, and priorities.

The existence of competing claims for support from other subsystems indeed permits us to transcend the rather narrow "health framework" and move to a societal framework, and to identify another important question: What kind of balance or equilibrium does a society achieve as it attempts to reconcile the different claims for resources, and what mechanisms operate to resolve these claims, by allocating weights or priorities, particularly when resources are very scarce? In Soviet society such an allocation results from conscious decisions reached at the apex of society, that is, within the highest councils of the Communist party. In a country like the United States, the process is much more decentralized, spontaneous, unplanned, and uncoordinated. But both societies must satisfy the resource needs of their other subsystems: for example, the general education of their young people; the provision of social welfare services to their needy, disabled, or older citizens; investment capital for industrial expansion; the maintenance of a defense establishment; communications, roads, housing, and so on.

We now turn more particularly to the Soviet health system, first specifying the nature and the flow of resources into it, then briefly examining the structure of the health system itself. This is followed by an assessment of that health system's performance or its functional contribution to Soviet society, as measured from certain statistical indexes. Although I shall not attempt this systematically here, such an analytical framework might then permit us to compare the Soviet health system with those of other communist countries in the process of modernization, and with those of noncommunist societies.

Resource Inputs

The four types of supports outlined earlier operate in Soviet society in the following manner:

1. Legitimacy-Mandate: At the most general level, this principle holds that society has a responsibility to supply preventive, clinical, and allied health services consonant with the state of the art, provided by qualified physicians and other personnel, to all its citizens regardless of their ability to pay. The Soviet health system is thus officially described as a socialist system of governmental and community measures whose major aims are the prevention and treatment of disease, the provision of healthful working and living conditions, and the achievement of a high level of work capacity and long life expectancy for the individual. The system operates by means of the following principles:

a. Public health and personal medical care are a responsibility of the state and a function of the government.

b. The development of all public health and medical measures takes place within the framework of a single plan.

c. The entire health service is centralized; health facilities, for example, are organized in tiers of increasing sophistication as one moves from local facilities to those that serve larger areas, up to those at the national level.

d. Health and allied services are available at no direct cost at time of use. They are underwritten through general revenues and taxation and are part of the different governmental (Soviet) budgets (all-union, republican, regional, and local),[15] with a few exceptions: for example, the patient must pay for drugs prescribed for outpatient use (except for a specified list of conditions--mostly chronic).

e. Preventive medicine stands, in theory at least, at the center of the Soviet health system and is said to guide most of its activities.

f. The principle of the unity of theory and practice, derived from Marxism, rejects the idea of knowledge for its own sake. Thus medical research must be oriented primarily to the solution of practical problems such as industrial absenteeism due to illness.

g. The efforts of medical personnel by themselves will not be sufficient to improve the health of the population unless they secure popular support in so-called voluntary community work. This idea is derived from Soviet (and socialist) ideology regarding the active and participatory role the masses should play in socialist society, in running their "own affairs."

h. As long as medical services remain a scarce resource, those who perform the more important jobs in society (and often their immediate families) must have priority over those whose jobs are not so critical. Access to health services is thus stratified as a perquisite of rank and and occupation.

2. Knowledge: Generally speaking, the knowledge input is not problematic in that it is accepted, more or less universally, as a principle of scientific medicine. Indeed, Marxist doctrine requires that the health system provide services in accordance with scientific knowledge and root out the superstitions of traditional medicine. To some degree, Soviet medical science has been affected first by the isolation in which the regime has kept the Soviet Union, making the exchange of personnel and experience difficult, if not sometimes impossible. Second, for a period after the Second World War, the campaign for Russian priorities and for the exaltation of the superiority of Russian science did have some impact on medicine and medical research. This campaign--which must be viewed within the framework of reactive nationalism and of a search in the past for national identity and moral superiority over a more technologically advanced West--has by now largely been dismantled. Soviet scientists and medical historians are no longer required to establish the priority of Russian (medical) science. But while it existed, the campaign was couched in scientific terms: in other words, Russian scientists, using canons of science and the inherent wisdom of the great Russian people, had discovered the scientific truth before their foreign colleagues, but they had kowtowed to a mendacious West which had appropriated the credit.

Some of the campaign focused on folk medicine and folk remedies and the superiority of certain medicinal herbs used by the Russian peasants over pharmaceutical compounds (one might suspect because of the perennial shortage of the latter). But even there, the injunction was to examine the merits of these remedies in order to separate what was scientifically valid from what was spurious. As might be expected, charlatans, quacks, faith healers, and native practitioners have not completely disappeared from such a vast country, where a sizable portion of the population still lives in villages. These practitioners are stigmatized in official publications as the last remnants of superstition and ignorance which an enlightened and scientific approach to disease will eventually eliminate, rather than as a valuable heritage of the national culture. Thus the Soviet Union, unlike China, has not developed a parallel medical system based on traditional native medicine, with two separate streams of practitioners and with the native one receiving the bulk of ideological support. No Russian equivalent of acupuncture or the barefoot doctor seems to exist in the Soviet Union.

Since knowledge is a cultural resource that once discovered or developed can be transmitted, shared, and learned, and since medical research is usually costly (and rarely classified), one can understand why the Soviet health system has emphasized the application of universally available knowledge and the delivery of health services rather than the very costly generation of new knowledge. I would thus presume that a partial reason why Western scientists and physicians lack interest in Soviet medicine has been the relatively modest performance of Soviet medical research compared with that of many other nations in the West. Thus, as I shall suggest later, the Soviet contribution, in a comparative perspective, has been in administrative mechanisms for the application of knowledge toward the health needs of the population rather than in basic research.

3. Personnel: In absolute and comparative terms, the Soviet Union certainly has
made the most impressive progress in number of personnel. Between 1913 and 1970
the number of physicians in the Soviet Union increased 24 times, and the proportion of physicians to the population moved from 1.5 per 10,000 to 23.9 per
10,000, or an increase of almost 16 times. Table 1 charts this development and
compares it with the United States. On the basis of available figures, the
Soviet Union has at present about the highest proportion of physicians to the
population of any country in the world (table 2). Such an increase in the number
of physicians would not have been possible without a massive influx of women into
the profession, reaching a high of more than 75 percent in the postwar years
(table 3). Recently, however, that proportion has tended to decline. There is
reason to believe that the regime is not entirely satisfied with such an extreme
feminization. According to Bowers[16] (who unfortunately does not give the source
of his information), the percentage of women admitted into medical schools was
officially reduced by decree from 85 to 65 percent in 1966 or 1967. If this
trend were to continue, it is possible that within a generation the proportion of
women could fall back to 65 percent or even less. Given what we know of Soviet
society and the general position of women,[17] it is quite possible that recent
Soviet efforts to raise the quality of medical education and services might be accompanied by a deliberate effort to increase the proportion of male physicians.
During a visit to the Soviet Union in the summer of 1975 I was told, on several
occasions, that the aim was a profession about evenly divided between male and
female physicians. The high proportion of women in the medical profession, plus
the fact that they average (both in the United States and the USSR) a considerably smaller number of work hours per week or year than their male colleagues
(about 40 percent), must be considered in any comparative examination of the
number of physicians, the availability of services, and the number of medical
acts produced by the two medical contingents.[18]

The distribution of physicians is uneven from republic to republic (see
table 4) and by area. Thus large cities have many more physicians per capita
than smaller areas, and the countryside still suffers from a grievous shortage of
physicians.[19] In 1970, the number of Soviet physicians (including stomatologists
and dental physicians) per 100,000 of the population for the Soviet Union as a
whole was 274. Some republics had well over 300 physicians per 100,000 (Georgia,
362; Latvia, 356) whereas other republics had about 200 or fewer physicians per
100,000 (Tadzhikistan, 159; Uzbekistan, 200). Thus, not even a centralized system of the politically monolithic type has been completely successful in deploy-
ing its professional personnel to undesirable or understaffed areas of its territory. In light of this, feldshers still play an important role in providing
health services to the rural population.[20] The deployment situation is not different in the United States. For example, in 1969 the number of physicians per
100,000 for the United States as a whole was 163. In the Northeast that figure
was 192.3, whereas in the South it was 113.7. The discrepancies are even more
marked if the states are compared. Thus Mississippi's figure was 78, whereas
New York's was 234 (table 5). At the same time, in modern medicine the expansion of health personnel has been much more rapid among nonphysicians than among
physicians. By 1970, in both the Soviet Union and the United States, physicians
represented no more than 10 to 12 percent of all those working in the health
system (table 6). Finally, the percentage of the active Soviet labor force
(excluding collective farmers) engaged in the health service has increased from
1.6 percent in 1932 to 3.3 percent in 1970, or has about doubled in the last
forty years. In the United States that figure has tripled over the same period
(table 7).

4. Economic Resources: I have not been able to obtain estimates of the proportion of the Gross National Product invested in the health sector of Soviet
society, and I have had to satisfy myself with budget figures. However, since the
overwhelming majority of health and other human services are financed through the
budget and aggregated to give a national figure, I think that such figures give us
a relatively accurate reflection of investments and priorities. The proportion of
the national budget of the USSR devoted to health and its protection in the past

Table 1

Physicians, United States and USSR 1910-70

| | United States | | | USSR | |
Year	Physicians (absolute numbers)	Physicians per 10,000 Persons	Year	Physicians (absolute numbers)	Physicians per 10,000 Persons
1910	135,000	15.7	1913	23,200	1.5
1921	145,404	13.4	1920	18-20,000[1]	N.A.
1931	156,405	14.1	1928	63,900	4.0
1942	180,496	13.4	1940	134,900	7.2
1950	219,997	14.3	1950	236,900	13.6
1960	260,484[2]	13.2[3]	1960	385,400	20.0
1970	340,000+	16.3	1970	577,249	23.8

Sources: United States: Statistical Abstract of the United States, 1958 (Washington, D.C.: U.S. Government Printing Office, 1959), p. 75, table 84.

Statistical Abstract of the United States, 1967 (Washington, D.C.: U.S. Government Printing Office, 1968), p. 66, table 80.

Statistical Abstract of the United States, 1970 (Washington, D.C.: U.S. Government Printing Office, 1971), p. 67, table 94.

USSR: Zdravookhranenie v SSSR: Statisticheskii Sbornik (Moscow, 1960), p. 50. Narodnoe khoziaistvo SSSR v 1968 g. (Moscow, 1969), pp. 729-31.

"The Soviet Health System: Statistical Materials," in Sovetskoe zdravookhranenie 31 (1972):31 ff. Narodnoe khoziaistvo SSSR v 1970 g. (Moscow, 1971), p. 689.

NOTE: Stomatologists and dental physicians (zubnie vrachi) and the military are not included for the USSR.

1. Estimate   2. Without osteopaths and physicians in the federal service.   3. Figure for 1967.

245

Table 2

Number of Physicians in Selected Countries, 1970

Country	Physicians per 10,000 Persons	Country	Physicians per 10,000 Persons
Austria	18.5	Portugal	9.1
Belgium	15.4	Romania	11.9
Bulgaria	18.6	Spain	13.4
Czechoslovakia	21.0	Sweden	13.6
Denmark	14.4	Switzerland	14.2
Finland	10.2	United Kingdom: England and Wales	12.2
France	13.4	United Kingdom: Northern Ireland	13.3
Germany, Federal Republic and West Berlin	17.2	United Kingdom: Scotland	13.0
Germany, Democratic Republic and East Berlin	16.0	United States	15.8
		USSR	23.8
Hungary	19.8	Yugoslavia	9.9
Iceland	14.5		
Italy	18.1		
Japan	11.3		
Luxemburg	10.6		
Netherlands	12.5		
Norway	13.8		
Poland	15.2		

SOURCE: World Health Statistical Annual, 1970 (Geneva: World Health Organization, 1974) pp. 41, 42, 43, 44.

Table 3

Women in Medicine, USSR and United States, 1913-70
(as percentage of all physicians)

USSR		UNITED STATES			
Year	Women in Medicine	Year	Women in Medicine	Women Admitted to Medical Schools	Women Graduating from Medical Schools
1913	10	1930	n.a.	n.a.	4.5
1920	n.a.	1940	n.a.	n.a.	5.0
1928	45	1950	6.0	n.a.	10.7
1940	62	1960	7.0	9.9[1]	5.5
1950	77	1970	7.0	11.1	n.a.
1960	76				
1970	72				

SOURCES: United States: World Sanitary Statistics Annual, 1966. Vol. 3. Health Personnel and Hospital Establishments (Geneva: World Health Organization, 1970), p. 36. Datagrams (Association of American Medical Colleges), vol. 7, no. 8 (February 1966), table 2.

USSR: Zdravookhranenie v SSSR: Statisticheskii Sbornik (Moscow, 1960), p. 50
Narodnoe khoziaistvo SSSR v 1959 g. (Moscow, 1960), p. 787.
Narodnoe khoziaistvo SSSR v 1961 g. (Moscow, 1962), pp. 743-44.
Narodnoe khoziaistvo SSSR v 1969 g. (Moscow, 1969), pp. 729-31.

NOTE: Figures for the USSR include stomatologists and dental physicians (zubnie vrachi).

[1]Figure for 1968.

Table 4

Medical Density in the USSR, by Republic, 1913-70
(physicians per 100,000 persons)

Republics	1913	1940	1950	1960	1968	1970
Total USSR	15	72	136	200	259	274
Russian	15	74	145	209	273	290
Ukrainian	19	80	131	199	261	276
White Russian	13	47	80	164	239	258
Uzbekistan	3	42	95	138	181	200
Kazakhstan	3	39	90	139	201	219
Georgian	13	128	263	330	359	362
Azerbaidzhan	12	92	201	237	243	250
Lithuanian	12	67	106	173	252	274
Moldavian	12	40	98	143	192	205
Latvian	21	109	146	265	339	356
Kirghizian	2	34	95	154	195	207
Tadzhikistan	1	38	77	127	154	159
Armenian	6	68	172	242	301	288
Turkmenistan	5	67	124	187	211	214
Estonian	45	83	127	239	320	331

Source: Zdravookhranenie v SSSR: Statisticheskii Sbornik (Moscow, 1960), pp. 81-82; Narodnoe khoziaistvo SSSR v 1959 g. (Moscow, 1960), p. 788; Narodnoe khoziaistvo SSSR v 1961 g. (Moscow, 1962), p. 743; Narodnoe khoziaistvo SSSR v 1968 g., p. 730 (Moscow, 1969); Narodnoe khoziaistvo SSR v 1970 (Moscow, 1971), p. 690.

Note: Excluding the military, including stomatologists and dental physicians.

248

Table 5

Medical Density in the United States, by State, 1969
(physicians per 100,000 persons)

State	Number of Physicians	Density	State	Number of Physicians	Density
Alabama	3,008	86	Nebraska	1,705	119
Alaska	195	78	Nevada	529	118
Arizona	2,680	161	New Hampshire	1,025	144
Arkansas	1,745	88	New Jersey	10,765	152
California	37,032	194	New Mexico	1,170	120
Colorado	3,968	194	New York	42,824	234
Connecticut	5,673	190	North Carolina	5,417	107
Delaware	737	138	North Dakota	587	97
Dist. of Columbia	2,905	371	Ohio	14,922	139
Florida	10,576	169	Oklahoma	2,989	118
Georgia	4,811	106	Oregon	3,087	152
Hawaii	1,130	153	Pennsylvania	19,190	163
Idaho	677	95	Rhode Island	1,482	168
Illinois	15,314	139	South Carolina	2,232	85
Indiana	5,328	104	South Dakota	568	87
Iowa	3,282	118	Tennessee	4,605	117
Kansas	2,736	120	Texas	13,391	122
Kentucky	3,290	103	Utah	1,423	137
Louisiana	4,256	115	Vermont	862	197
Maine	1,262	131	Virginia	5,120	121
Maryland	6,811	184	Washington	5,023	151
Massachusetts	11,634	214	West Virginia	1,925	106
Michigan	13,076	149	Wisconsin	5,325	126
Minnesota	5,725	155	Wyoming	324	102
Mississippi	1,807	78	Puerto Rico	2,313	84
Missouri	7,019	152	Possessions [1]	142	43
Montana	721	105			

Total Physicians 338,379
Average Density 163

Source: Statistical Abstract of the United States, 1970 (Washington, D.C.: Government Printing Office, 1970), p. 67, table 89.

Note: Excluding non-federal physicians with temporary foreign addresses (3,784), including 29,650 federal physicians assigned by state and 2,081 physicians with unknown addresses. These figures are for medical doctors (324,942) and osteopaths (13,437).

[1] American Samoa, Canal Zone, Guam, Virgin Islands, and island territories of the Pacific.

Table 6

Health Workers, Physicians, and Dentists, USSR and United States,
1960, 1966, 1970

	1960	1966	1970
USSR			
Total health workers[1]	3,461,000	4,427,000	5,080,000
Physicians and stomatologists	361,600[2]	531,600	616,900
Physicians and stomatologists as percentage of total	10	12	12
United States			
Total health workers	2,642,300	3,672,000	4,043,000
Physicians and doctors of ostheopathy	274,834	305,115	348,328
Dentists	82,630	86,317	116,280
Total, M.D.s, D.O.s, and dentists	357,464	391,432	464,608
Physicians, D.O.s and dentists as percentage of total	14	11	10.6

Sources: USSR: Narodnoe khoziaistvo SSSR v 1967 g. (Moscow, 1968), pp. 71, 72. Narodnoe khoziaistvo SSSR v 1970 g. (Moscow, 1971), pp. 514,689.

United States: Statistical Abstract of the United States, 1970 (Washington, D.C.: U.S. Government Printing Office, 1970), pp. 64, 67.

Statistical Abstract of the United States, 1973 (Washington, D.C.: U.S. Government Printing Office, 1973), pp. 71, 72.

Health Manpower, U.S. 1965-67, ser. 14, no. 1, National Center for Health Statistics, U.S. Dept. of Health, Education, and Welfare (Washington, D.C.: U.S. Government Printing Office, 1968), p. 53, table 17.

[1]Includes social security and physical culture.
[2]1958.

Table 7

Health Workers as Percentage of Total Labor Force, United States and USSR, 1930-70

United States				USSR			
Year	Total Labor Force	Health Workers	%	Year	Total Labor Force	Health Workers	%
1930	48,686,000	900,000	1.8	1932	24,200,000	399,000	1.6
1940	51,742,000	1,090,000	2.1	1940	33,926,000	673,000	2.0
1950	62,208,000	1,440,000	2.3	1950	40,400,000	1,041,100	2.6
1960	69,628,000	2,040,000	2.9	1960	62,032,000	1,920,500	3.1
1970	82,715,000	4,403,000	5.32	1970	90,186,000	2,952,200	3.3

Sources: USA: Estimates and Projections of the Labor Force and Civilian Employment in the USSR: 1950-75, U.S. Dept. of Commerce, Bureau of the Census (Washington, D.C.: U.S. Government Printing Office, 1967), International Population Reports, series P-91, no. 15, p. 26. Health Manpower Perspective: 1967, U.S. Dept. of Health, Education, and Welfare, Public Health Service, Bureau of Health Manpower (Washington, D.C.: U.S. Government Printing Office, 1967), p. 5, table 1. Health Manpower Source Book: Allied Health Manpower 1950-1980 (Washington, D.C.: Public Health Service Publication no. 263, 1970) p. 48, sec. 21. Statistical Abstract of the United States 1973 U.S. Government Printing Office, Washington, D.C., 1973), p. 71, table 103.

USSR: Narodnoe khoziaistvo SSSR v 1969 g. (Moscow, 1970) pp. 529, 530, 531. Narodnoe Khoziaistvo SSSR v 1970 g. (Moscow, 1971) pp. 509, 511, 689.

Note: Figures for the USSR exclude members of collective farms.

thirty years has tended to stabilize around 6 percent. This is less than the proportion allocated to education (about 16 percent in 1963) and to social welfare (between 9 and 10 percent). On the other hand, the 6 percent figure seems--although not strictly comparable--quite in line with the average percentage figures of GNP devoted to health in countries where such figures are available, as is seen, for example, from Brian Abel-Smith's pioneering studies on the subject.[21] In the United States this figure stands at about 8 percent, having doubled within the past forty years.

In addition to paying the salaries of the health manpower mentioned, the budget permits building health facilities. For example, the number of hospital beds has increased from 207,300 to 2,567,300, or more than twelve times, between 1913 and 1970, and more significantly, the number of hospital beds per constant units of population has increased eightfold in that period. The corresponding growth in hospital beds for the United States has not been as impressive, if only because at the beginning of the period examined the per capita supply was more than three and a half times greater in the United States than in Russia. Indeed, at present, the number of hospital beds per constant unit of population is more than 20 percent greater in the Soviet Union than in the United States (table 8). It would take us too far afield to speculate about the reasons for the differences except to observe that in some industrial nations (the United States, England and Wales, and Sweden, for example) either the supply of hospital beds per capita has fallen or its growth has begun to decline, some of the major reasons probably being costs, the fact that many conditions could be treated more efficiently and economically on an outpatient basis, and (at least in the United States) a sizable reduction in beds for psychiatric patients.

Figure 1 summarizes the flow and amount of resources to the health system in the USSR and the United States.

Structure of the Soviet Health Service

Protecting the health of the Soviet population and providing health services, allied services, and education for all health personnel, as well as research, fall within the overall purview of the Ministry of Health or, more literally, the Ministry of Health Protection USSR (Ministerstvo zdravookhranenia SSSR). In one sense, that ministry has been vested with the mandate of organizing and operating the health system of the entire Soviet society except the armed forces. The health minister of the USSR is a member of the Council of Ministers and has "cabinet" rank. The ministry is of the union-republican type (rather than all-union) and therefore operates through counterpart health ministries of the republics and autonomous republics. These in turn direct and supervise the activities of health departments attached to the different administrative levels of the soviets, down to the localities. In actuality, this structure is designed to provide a fair amount of centralization, integration, and standardization as well as latitude and flexibility for republican health ministries and their subordinate units in adapting their services to local health conditions and needs.

Planning and financial allocations regarding the health ministries (all-union and republican) must consider the needs and priorities of other ministries and be consonant with the general directives of the Communist party and with available resources. One can also argue that both making and implementing such decisions are facilitated by the existence of a health service in which personnel are employees of that service and the facilities are all owned and controlled by it. The regime is thus enabled to determine ahead of time, within gross limits of course, what the medical bill for Soviet society will be for health personnel services, since such services are paid on nationally tariffed salaries

Table 8

Hospital Beds, United States and USSR, 1909-70

UNITED STATES			USSR		
Year	Total Number of Beds	Beds per 1,000 Persons	Year	Total Number of Beds	Beds per 1,000 Persons
1909	421,065	4.7	1913	207,300	1.3
1920	817,020	7.7	1917	149,300	1.0
1930	955,869	7.8	1928	246,500	1.6
1940	1,226,245	9.3	1940	790,900	4.0
1950	1,455,825	9.6	1950	1,010,700	5.6
1960	1,657,970	9.2	1960	1,739,200	8.1
1970	1,649,663	8.2	1970	2,567,300	10.6

Sources: United States: Statistical Abstract of the United States, 1949 (Washington, D.C.: Government Printing Office, 1950), p. 83.

Statistical Abstract of the United States, 1970 (Washington, D.C.: Government Printing Office, 1971), p. 68.

USSR: Central Statistical Board of the USSR Council of Ministers, Forty Years of Soviet Power (Moscow, 1958), p. 309.

Narodnoe khoziaistvo SSSR v 1969 g. (Moscow, 1970), p. 732.

253

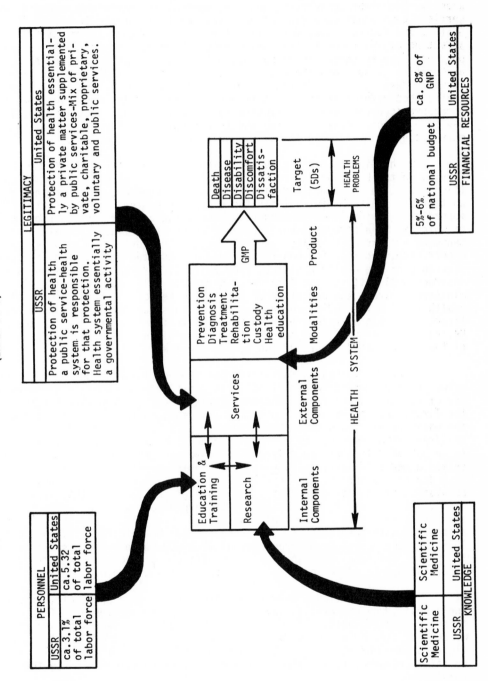

RESOURCES INPUTS
USSR AND UNITED STATES OF AMERICA

(EARLY 70'S)

FIG. 1

and since the interplay of market mechanisms is reduced to a minimum. Under present conditions, for example, it would be next to impossible to determine and to control the bill the American people pay for medical services by physicians, since these services do not fall, in the great majority of cases, under the jurisdiction, the responsibility, and the financing of a central national (or federal) agency. One might conjecture, however, that as an increasing number of medical services come under some kind of national health insurance scheme in the United States, the federal government will play an increasingly important role in affecting expenditures in the health area. Moreover, in the USSR the government does not have to negotiate or bargain with a powerful medical profession or association as has been the case, for example, in Great Britain and Japan, or as it would have to in the United States. That such a structure is heavily bureaucratic goes without saying; that it embodies many of the negative aspects of bureaucratic organization everywhere cannot be gainsaid. But it does provide one way to a national health service and to control expenditures, and as such it deserves more attentive study than it has hitherto received in the West.

The diagram below provides a scheme of the structure of the health service in the USSR and its connection with the Soviets and the Communist party (figure 2). In the administrative structure diagrammed, every administrative unit of the Health Ministry (with the exception of the Health Ministry USSR) is subordinate to two lines of authority: one, the appropriate organ of the soviets of which it is a component part and from which it derives its tasks or assignments as well as most of its required logistic support (including, in the countryside, lodgings for health personnel); and, two, the next higher unit in the structure of the Health Ministry, from which it derives its modus operandi, instructional letters, and other necessary methodological supports. That the ministry controls the education of the future personnel who will work within the health service (including the number of students admitted) and supervises and finances a whole structure of research institutions (beginning with the Academy of Medical Sciences USSR, the major research arm of the ministry) is further evidence of the "integrated" nature of the health service.

Access to health facilities for the population is provided through two networks of primary care facilities that constitute the portals of entry into Soviet socialized medicine: the territorial and the occupational network. In the first, the individual is automatically assigned to an outpatient facility on the basis of his residence. Four thousand persons (about 3,000 adults and 1,000 children) form a medical microdistrict panel (uchastok). Primary care is given in an outpatient clinic that typically serves the population of ten microdistricts, called a medical district (raion). Two physicians (terapevti) and one pediatrician, plus one or two nurses, are usually directly and personally responsible for the population of one microdistrict. They have office hours at the clinic and also visit patients at home. Specialists are also available in the clinic, but each one serves more than one microdistrict. Several polyclinics, in turn, are affiliated with hospitals to which patients can be referred. (I was told in 1975 that the uchastok had been reduced to 2,000 persons and was entrusted to one terapevt. This does not, in my mind, constitute a major change, particularly since the number of persons per physician remains the same.)

The occupational network operates on the same principle, except that individuals, who are usually industrial workers, are assigned to facilities maintained by their plants. In addition, a whole gamut of facilities are reserved for members of the Soviet political and cultural élite and their families, thus reflecting the general stratification of Soviet society. These facilities are sometimes referred to as "closed" (zakritie), that is, not open to the general population.

Private practice still remains, although it is frowned upon as the remnant of a bourgeois past. A few "paying polyclinics" (platnie polikliniki) exist in which, for a relatively modest fee, a patient can have the services of a consultant or specialist. As far as I know, the Soviet Union has no private

Figure 2:

STRUCTURE OF THE HEALTH MINISTRY AND SUPERVISING ORGANS

(All levels)

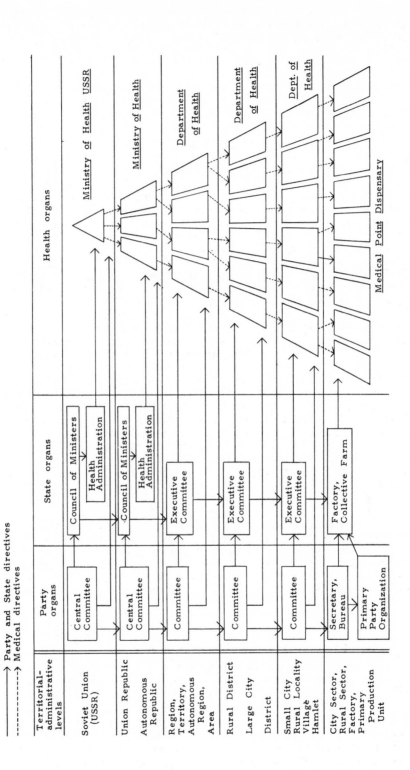

Mark G. Field, Doctor and Patient in Soviet Russia (Cambridge: Harvard University Press, 1957). Reprinted with permission.

medical facilities, although the special facilities reserved for the elite must be considered a functional equivalent (for example, the Kremlin hospital or the medical facilities reserved for members of the Academy of Sciences).

The Impact of the Health System: Psychological and Statistical

As mentioned earlier, evaluating precisely the specific impact of the health system on the human resources of society is difficult since a variety of other factors (nutrition, housing, sanitation, etc.) also affect the state of that resource. On the other hand, the Soviet regime and its leaders are realistic enough and their resources are scarce enough that they would not decide to allocate more than 3 percent of their labor force (more than 3,000,000 persons at the present time) to a sector of society that is useless or a luxury or frill. In its propaganda, the health service is repeatedly presented to the population as still another aspect of the party's and government's care for the individual (zabota o cheloveke) and an expression of the view, as Stalin used to say, that man is the most precious capital. A study conducted some years ago with Soviet refugees, who presumably would be hostile to the regime, indicated widespread approval of the concept of socialized medicine as expressed in the Soviet Union and equally vehement rejection of a system patterned on the American model, where the medical care of the individual was not expressed as a constitutional right and was often financially inaccessible. The refugees' quarrel with the Soviet health system centered on the manner of implementation, its bureaucratic nature, its frequent impersonality, and the shortage of equipment and pharmaceuticals.[22] Thus, psychologically the Soviet system of socialized medicine provides a modicum of security and reassurance that Soviet citizens take for granted as much as American citizens take it for granted that the state must provide their children with an education. The system of socialized medicine is undoubtedly one of the better-liked features of the Soviet institutional structure. Soviet propaganda rarely fails to remind Soviet citizens that in capitalist countries the medical system is primarily for the benefit of the rich, that physicians shamelessly exploit patients to enrich themselves, and that the poor and the members of ethnic and racial minorities suffer and die because they cannot afford medical or hospital care or medicines.

Regarding the "maintenance of capacity," whatever statistical materials we have--and admittedly they are scant--indicate a sizable reduction in the incidence and the prevalence of morbidity relating to infectious diseases (table 9). Furthermore, indications are that, in its morbidity and mortality pattern, the Soviet Union is catching up with the developed nations of the West, cancer and heart disease being the major causes of concern (and death) rather than infectious diseases.

The crude death rate declined from 30.2 per 1,000 immediately before World War I to 8.5 per 1,000 in 1972--that is, by a factor of more than 3.5. If we assume that the Soviet Union has about 250 million persons today, this means a reduction of roughly five and a half million in the number who would be dying annually had the 1913 rates prevailed in the early seventies (2,050,000 instead of 7,550,000--a far from negligible figure). It is noteworthy that the natural increase of the population had reached about the same level in Soviet and American societies by the early seventies (less than 1 percent), and that birth and death rates exhibited the same general declining trend, leading to a decidedly more rational and economical use of human and other resources (table 10). It is also generally accepted that when general living, economic, and health conditions are favorable, infant mortality rates are lower, whether one looks at a single country over time or at a number of countries at the same point in time.[23] In 1913 the infant mortality in Russia was 269 per 1,000 or 273 per 1,000 within the boundaries before September 1939 (table 11). This meant that more than a

Table 9

Incidence of Individual Infectious Diseases among the Population, USSR, 1940-69

	1940	1950	1960	1965	1966	1967	1968	1969
Thousand Cases								
Typhoid and paratyphoid fever A, B, and C[1]	121.3	48.3	47.3	25.5	27.5	23.9	23.3	22.8
Scarlet fever	251.5	596.1	671.2	530.8	691.6	597.3	502.0	434.9
Diphtheria	177.0	83.9	53.2	4.7	3.1	2.6	2.2	1.7
Whooping cough	453.3	315.1	554.1	190.0	145.7	114.7	119.4	52.7
Tetanus	...	2.1	2.3	1.4	1.3	1.1	0.9	0.7
Acute poliomyelitis	1.3	2.6	7.2	0.30	0.29	0.14	0.12	0.19
Measles	1,181.9	1,045.9	2,083.3	2,128.7	1,747.2	1,798.1	1,579.8	510.4
Infectious hepatitis (Botkin's disease)[2]	...	...	513.1	470.1	465.2	372.9	371.4	339.1
Epidemic typhus, including Brill's disease[3]	48.0	16.4	6.2	3.7	3.4	3.3	3.1	2.8
Malaria	3,198.6	781.3	0.4	0.3	0.3	0.3	0.3	0.3
Number of Cases per One Hundred Thousand of Population								
Typhoid and paratyphoid fever A, B, and C	62	27	22	11	12	10	10	9
Scarlet fever	129	331	313	230	297	254	211	181
Diphtheria	91	47	25	2	1.3	1.1	0.9	0.7
Whooping cough	232	175	259	82	63	49	50	22
Tetanus	...	1.2	1.1	0.6	0.6	0.5	0.4	0.3
Acute poliomyelitis	0.7	1.4	3.3	0.13	0.12	0.06	0.05	0.08
Measles	605	581	972	923	750	763	663	212
Infectious hepatitis (Botkin's disease)	...	...	239	204	200	158	156	141
Epidemic typhus, including Brill's disease	25	9.1	2.9	1.6	1.5	1.4	1.3	1.2
Malaria	1,637	434	0.17	0.14	0.13	0.11	0.11	0.14

[1] Only cases of paratyphoid A and B were recorded before June 1965.
[2] Including parenteral hepatitis.
[3] Beginning in 1953 cases of Brill's disease were most often encountered.

Table 10

Crude Birth Rate, Crude Death Rate, and Natural Increase of the Population,
United States and USSR, 1910-72
(per 1,000 persons)

	United States				USSR		
Year	Birth Rate	Death Rate	Natural Increase	Year	Birth Rate	Death Rate	Natural Increase
1910	30.1	14.7	15.4	1913	47.0	30.2	16.8
1920	27.7	13.0	14.7	1926	44.0	20.3	23.7
1930	21.3	11.3	10.0	1937	38.7	18.9	19.8
1940	19.4	10.8	8.6	1940	31.7	18.3	13.4
1950	24.1	9.6	14.5	1950	26.5	9.6	16.9
1960	23.7	9.5	14.2	1960	24.9	7.1	17.8
1970	18.2	9.4	8.8	1970	17.4	8.2	9.2
1971	17.3	9.3	8.0	1971	17.8	8.2	9.6
1972	15.6	9.4	6.2	1972	17.8	8.5	9.3

Sources: United States: Statistical Abstract of the United States, 1968 (Washington, D.C.: Government Printing Office, 1969), p. 55; ibid., 1971, p. 47; ibid., 1974, pp. 53, 60.

USSR: Narodnoe khoziaistvo SSSR v 1972 g. (Moscow, 1973), p. 47.

Table 11

Infant Mortality, United States and USSR, 1913-71
(number per 1,000 born alive but dying within one year of birth)

	United States				USSR		
Year	Total Deaths	Male	Female	Year	Total Deaths	Male	Female
1915	99.1	109.9	89.4	1913	269[1]	---	---
1920	85.8	95.1	76.1	1920-22	334	---	---
1930	64.6	71.3	57.5	1926-27	187[2]	201	172
1940	47.0	52.5	41.3	1940	182	---	---
1950	29.2	32.8	25.5	1950	81	---	---
1960	26.0	29.3	22.6	1959	40.6	44.2	36.7
1970	19.8	----	----	1969	26	---	---
1970	19.02	{ 19.06[3] { 32.33[4]	14.55[3] 26.19[4]	1970	25	---	---
				1971	23	---	---

Sources: United States: Statistical Abstract of the United States, 1950 (Washington, D.C.: Government Printing Office, 1951), p. 77; ibid., 1971, p. 55; ibid., 1974, p. 59.

Vital Statistics Rates for the United States, 1940-1960, Public Health Service publication no. 1677 (Washington, D.C.: National Center for Health Statistics, 1968), p. 206.

USSR: Narodnoe khoziaistvo SSSR v 1969 g. (Moscow, 1970), p. 31.
Narodnoe khoziaistvo SSSR v 1972 g. (Moscow, 1973), p. 46.
World Health Statistics Report, vol. 24, no. 6 (1971).

[1] For USSR within boundaries prior to 17 September 1939, the figure is 273.
[2] European part of the USSR only.
[3] White.
[4] Negro and other.

quarter of all children born alive died within one year of their birth. This figure declined to 187 in 1926 (European part of the USSR alone) and to 182 by 1940. In 1950 the infant mortality rate was 81 per 1,000; this figure declined by another 50 percent by 1959, reaching the level of 23 by 1971 or less than one-tenth of the corresponding figure for 1913 (table 11).

These are, of course, aggregated national rates. I would presume that there are substantial differences in Soviet infant mortality rates between the European part of the USSR and, let us say, the Central Asian republics, and between urban and rural areas. The rate, incidentally, was still higher than that of the United States and of fourteen other advanced nations with the lowest rates in the world (Sweden placed first and the United States placed last of the fifteen). On the other hand, nonwhite infant mortality in the United States for 1970 was higher than the Soviet national rate. Just as the gap between the Soviet Union and other developed countries in infant mortality is closing, so is the one in life expectancy at birth. Indeed statistics reveal that the gap between the United States and the Soviet Union has almost been closed (table 12), though here again neither the Soviet Union nor for that matter the United States compares favorably with such nations as the Federal Republic of Germany, France, England and Wales, and Sweden to name a few.

Conclusions

This paper is a preliminary statement on the manner in which the Soviet Union, having decided that health is an important resource and, indeed, a public utility, has gone about managing the conservation, the repair, and the preservation of that resource. More conceptual and statistical sophistication is needed before we can attempt more precise measurements of the impact of the health system on the "capacity" of the population. It is imperative to compare that performance with performances in other socialist countries and with those in the developed countries of the West in order to gain a more meaningful perspective, although Soviet progress in terms of Soviet society alone has been impressive, particularly compared with the situation in the early twenties.

The Soviet Union has mounted, in the course of its half-century history, a national health service operating as a public service, employing about three million persons, using a relatively sizable portion of the available budget, and providing a gamut of health services to almost a quarter of a billion persons spreading over two continents. As such, I submit that it is an important element in understanding the nature of that society and in appraising its stability, continuity, and functioning as a social system. And this is apart from the intrinsic interest in the sociological aspects of medicine and health institutions, and from the lessons that might be garnered for other societies facing the same range of problems.

Undoubtedly the question of "convergence" arises in connection with a comparative examination in this area. As was mentioned earlier, the process of modernization has been accompanied by a shift in the morbidity structure both in the United States and the USSR and in other similarly developed societies; vital indexes such as infant mortality, life expectancy at birth, and changes in the age structure have also tended to move in the same directions, although any comparison between the United States and the USSR must take into account how the demographic catastrophe of the Second World War affected the Soviet Union. Furthermore, the size and the nature of the resource inputs in the two societies are in about the same range. Some clearly etched differences are perhaps more visible in the general mandate and legitimacy. Yet in the United States the role that the polity is assuming and will continue to assume concerning a health insurance scheme, perhaps to be followed by a national health service, is

Table 12

Average Life Expectancy at Birth, United States and USSR 1920-71

	United States				USSR		
Year	Total	Male	Female	Year	Total	Male	Female
1920	54.1	53.6	54.6	1926-27	44[1]	42[1]	47[1]
1930	59.7	58.1	61.6	1930	---	---	---
1940	62.9	60.8	65.2	1938-40	48.4	46.7	50.2
1950	68.2	65.6	71.1	1950	68	64	71
1960	69.7	66.6	73.1	1960	70	65	73
1968	70.2	66.6	74.0				
1971	n.a.	68.3	75.6	1970-71	70	65	-

Sources: United States: Statistical Abstract of the United States, 1971 (Washington, D.C.: Government Printing Office, 1972), p. 53; ibid., 1974, p. 58.

USSR: Narodnoe khoziaistvo SSSR v 1956 g. (Moscow, 1957), p. 271.
Narodnoe khoziaistvo SSSR v 1969 g. (Moscow, 1970), p. 588.
Narodnoe khoziaistvo SSSR v 1972 g. (Moscow, 1973), p. 126.

[1]European part of the USSR only.

undoubtedly not fundamentally too different from the Soviet one. Indeed, one might argue that the number of available options in this area within modern society is not particularly great, and that these choices tend to narrow with time, increased demand for services, increased costs, and the increased application of biomedical technology in medicine.

I would assume, looking at the medical scene in the United States and the Soviet Union, that the United States will need to concentrate its efforts in the future on the distribution of health services. Such an effort will require more governmental intervention, a greater need for rationalization and planning, and decreased autonomy for the medical profession and hospitals. I would assume that in the Soviet Union the direction will be toward increasing the quality of health services and of medical research; this may lead to an increase in the overall status of the medical profession and to increased autonomy in professional matters. Whether one wants to call this convergence, coincidence, or resemblance, I would argue that the differences are decreasing and the similarities increasing.

Notes

[1] In addition to my own work, such as Doctor and Patient in Soviet Society (Cambridge: Harvard University Press, 1957), Soviet Socialized Medicine: An Introduction (New York: Free Press, 1967), and a fair number of articles and chapters in books, the list is small. Henry E. Sigerist was the major pioneer, if we exclude the earlier reports of W.Horsley Gantt, A Medical Review of Soviet Russia (London: British Medical Society, 1928) and Sir Arthur Newsholme and John Adams Kingsbury, Red Medicine: Socialized Health in Soviet Russia, (New York: Doubleday, Doran and Co. 1933). Sigerist's work in this area, such as Socialized Medicine in the Soviet Union (New York: W. W. Norton, 1937) and Medicine and Health in the Soviet Union (New York: Citadel Press, 1947) was, in my opinion, flawed by his enthusiasm for the principle of socialized medicine and the Soviet version of it, as well as by his silent support of a Stalinist-type of regime which blunted his otherwise sharp critical judgment. One could also mention a rather disorganized book by Irène Lazarévitch, La médecine en U.R.S.S. (Paris: Iles d'Or, 1953) and an even worse one by George A. Tabakov, Medicine in the United States and the Soviet Union, (Boston: Christopher Publishing House, 1962). Max Brandt, Osteuropa Institute of the Free University of Berlin, has written a few papers and monographs on the subject, and so has Heinrich Schultz, a former Soviet physician who edited the now defunct Review of Soviet Medical Sciences (earlier Review of Eastern Medical Science). Also in Germany Heinz Müller-Dietz has kept a close watch on Soviet medicine for several years, has written several studies on the subject, and edits the Medizinische Literatur Dienst, a monthly series of translations of important articles in medicine from the USSR and Eastern Europe. For a few years, Medical Reports published by the Institute of Contemporary Russian Studies at Fordham University tried to keep a Western public briefed on development in Soviet medicine, but it also succumbed to indifference. Professor Hans Harmsen's group at the Academy of State Medicine in Hamburg has published several studies on the development and the organization of health institutions in the Soviet Union, the People's Democracies, and East Germany. In the late sixties E. Richard Weinerman wrote a survey of Hungarian, Polish, and Czech medical systems, Social Medicine in Eastern Europe (Cambridge: Harvard University Press, 1969). John Fry wrote a cursory study, Medicine in Three Societies (New York: American Elsevier Publishing Co., 1970), in which he compared Soviet, American, and British medicine. Ralph Croizier has enlightened us on the cultural sources behind the revival of traditional medicine in Communist China, and particularly the barefoot doctors and the reawakened interest in acupuncture and, to a lesser degree, moxibustion, Traditional Medicine in Modern China (Cambridge: Harvard University Press, 1968). See also his "Traditional Medicine as a Basis for Chinese Medical Practice," in

Medicine and Public Health in the People's Republic of China ed. Joseph R. Quinn, Publication no. NIH 72-67 (Washington: U.S.D.H.E.W., June 1972). Incidentally this recent publication contains other interesting papers on different aspects of Chinese medicine. The publication in 1974 of The Soviet Health Service: A Historical and Comparative Study, by Gordon Hyde (London: Lawrence and Wishart), is in the Sigerist tradition: a well-meaning but almost totally uncritical study of the system, adding little to our knowledge. There have also been a few articles scattered in the professional medical literature, primarily travel notes and observations, such as Pierre Rentchnick, Esculape au pays des soviets, (Geneva: Médecine et Hygiène, 1955). For an example of one of the latest, see James E. Muller, Faye G. Abdellah, F. T. Billings, Arthur E. Hess, Donald E. Petit, and Roger O. Egeberg, "The Soviet Health System: Aspects of Relevance for Medicine in the United States," New England Journal of Medicine 286 (March 1972): 693-702; J. A. Cooper, "USSR and US Health Policies," New England Journal of Medicine 286 (March 1972): 722-4. There are also official reports of the several medical delegations that went from the United States to the Soviet Union, the publications of the John E. Fogarty International Center for Advanced Study in the Health Sciences, and reports from the World Health Organization. Add to these Victor W. Sidel's paper on "Feldshers and 'feldsherism,'" New England Journal of Medicine 278 (1968): 934-92; Patrick B. Storey and Russell B. Roth "Emergency Medical Care in the Soviet Union," Journal of the American Medical Association 217 (2 August 1971): 588-92; and P. B. Storey, "Continuing Medical Education in the Soviet Union," New England Journal of Medicine 265 (August 1971): 437-42. This list represents a fair proportion of the work done on this topic in the last fifty years or so. One could also add the few references to Soviet and East European medicine in The American Bibliography of Slavic (or Russian) and East European Studies published at Indiana University from 1957 through 1966, and by the Ohio State University Press thereafter. The record is neither extensive, systematic, nor particularly impressive.

[2]There are of course other mechanisms that are important for the functioning of social systems: the institutionalization of behavioral patterns, which introduces an element of social pressure and predictability without which social systems might quickly fall apart; the maintenance and reinforcement of learned and institutionalized behavioral patterns; and the control of deviance.

[3]For a review of the main events in medicine that preceded the Revolution, see Field, Doctor and Patient in Soviet Russia, particularly pp. 1-13; Soviet Socialized Medicine, particularly pp. 15-29; also, "Medical Organization and the Medical Profession," in Cyril E. Black, ed., The Transformation of Russian Society (Cambridge: Harvard University Press, 1960), pp. 541-52, and "Taming a Profession: Early Phases of Soviet Socialized Medicine," Bulletin of the New York Academy of Medicine, 48, no. 1 (2d ser.): 83-92 (January 1972).

[4]Field, Doctor and Patient p. 15.

[5]Ibid.

[6]Ibid.

[7]Ibid. For a collection of essays regarding Lenin's view on health see Lenin o zdravookhranenii (Lenin on Health Protection) (Moscow, 1969).

[8]Field, Doctor and Patient; idem., Soviet Socialized Medicine.

[9]There is a degree to which, in any society, an individual's body and thus its condition (i.e., its health) is considered public property; the individual is not free to neglect or freely dispose of that piece of property. To take extreme but illustrative cases, self-inflicted injuries or venereal diseases are often

punishable offenses in military organizations because they deprive the organization of the individual's services. Suicide, of course, is frequently considered a legal or moral offense or both.

[10]M. I. Barsukov, Velikaia oktiabrskaia sotsialisticheskaia revolutsia i organizatsia sovetskogo zdravookhranenia (The Great October Revolution and the organization of soviet health protection (Moscow, 1951), p. 27.

[11]John Bryant, Health and the Developing World (Ithaca: Cornell University Press, 1969), p. 312.

[12]The basic conceptual scheme I am using here is one that I have developed over the last few years and is certainly not original with this paper. For a more comprehensive statement of that scheme at the theoretical level, see, for example, "The Concept of the 'Health System' at the Macrosociological Level," Social Science and Medicine 7 (1973): 763-85, and "Prospects for the comparative sociology of medicine: An effort at conceptualization," in Current Research in Sociology-Current Sociology (The Hague: Mouton, 1974) pp. 147-83.

[13]I use the word "system" in a generic sense as that segment or sector of society concerned with the health problems of the population. The health "service," as I have used it here to describe Soviet medicine, is one type of health system.

[14]Jack Elinson, "Methods of Sociomedical Research," in Howard E. Freeman, Sol Levine, and Leo G. Reader, eds., Handbook of Medical Sociology (Englewood Cliffs, N. J.: Prentice-Hall, 1972),2d ed. p. 488.

[15]In some instances collective farms finance part of their health services from their own funds.

[16]John C. Bowers, "Special Problems of Women Medical Students," Journal of Medical Education 43 (May 1968): 532-37.

[17]Mark G. Field and Karin I. Flynn, "Worker, Mother, Housewife: Soviet Woman Today," in George H. Seward and Robert C. Williamson, Sex Roles in Changing Society, pp. 257-84 (New York: Random House, 1970).

[18]See Field, "American and Soviet Medical Manpower: Growth and Evolution 1910-1970," International Journal of Health Services, 5, 3 (1975): 455-74.

[19]See, for example, Mark G. Field, "Health Personnel in the Soviet Union," American Journal of Public Health 56 (1969): 1904-1920; and Field, "Evolutions Structurelles de la profession médicale aux USA et en USSR," Cahiers de Démographie et Sociologie Médicales 11 (1971):104-19.

[20]Sidel, "Feldshers and 'feldsherism.'"

[21]Brian Abel-Smith, Paying for Health Services: A Study of the Costs and Sources of Finances in Six Countries, Public Health Paper no. 17 (Geneva: World Health Organization 1963), and An International Study of Health Expenditures, Public Health Paper no. 32 (Geneva: World Health Organization, 1967).

[22]See Mark G. Field, "Former Soviet Citizens' Attitudes toward the Soviet, the German and the American Medical Systems," American Sociological Review 20 (1955): 674-79.

[23]Helen C. Chase, "The Position of the United States in International Comparisons of Health Status," American Journal of Public Health 62 (April 1972): 583.

POSTFACE

Mark G. Field

A collection of essays like this is apt to invite about as many new questions as it has tried to raise. And in the final analysis no definitive answers can be given, at any one time, to many of the issues examined here. Furthermore, several areas (which I will mention below) could not be examined and discussed within the compass available to the symposium. As the list of papers originally presented at the symposium indicates, I have had the painful task (with the help of a small committee) of eliminating several worthy contributions because the volume would otherwise have been much larger, and its publication would have become problematic.

This volume must thus be seen as part of a continuing effort on the part of specialists in several of the social sciences disciplines to understand the nature of contemporary social structures, especially those that have arisen, or are emerging, in communist societies around the world. As I have stated earlier, my hope (as well as that of my colleagues in this endeavor) is therefore that the effort represented by this volume will be but one link in the long chain of scholarly discussion and debate about this complex matter. Progress is admittedly slow, and definite or final answers impossible--only approximations, often quickly eroded by time and events, can now be made.

One of the distinguishing features of communist societies, as pointed out earlier, is a "party" that guides the destinies of these societies. I often wish that another name could be invented to eliminate the semantic confusion that exists between a "party" in the Western sense (one of several groups competing for power) and the "party" in the communist or Leninist sense (a single party that rules society and does not permit the existence of other parties). This party claims legitimacy from its assertion that it is the embodiment, in the real world, of a body of scientific doctrine derived from Marxism and Leninism. It directs the development of communist societies in the name of that doctrine but, as is quite clear, very often not in accord with that doctrine. After all, Communist Russia and Communist China have each interpreted the sacred texts in a different, and sometimes conflicting, way.

A major question, which Lowenthal has discussed at some length in this volume, is how long the party will retain this leading role and what the costs will be in general efficiency and modernity. The existence of such a body, its retention through time, its functionality, and its ability--as a power-maintaining bureaucracy--to deal with the many problems brought about by modernization are some of the critical issues of modern times. Some scholars argue that in the long run the internal differentiation that accompanies and characterizes advanced modern societies is incompatible with a single, all-encompassing ruling authority or body that takes upon itself the awesome (and impossible) task of directing and monitoring all processes within the society. This task is to become the function of both decentralized and democratized participation by the population and of the existence of procedures (legal norms, contracts, etc.). On the other hand, one might argue that societies that do not have a body such as the party will eventually develop one (or its functional equivalent) precisely because the differentiation and the fragmentation process of modern life will have gone too far and, unaccompanied by a parallel process of integration, will have become destructive. The image of the organized, purposeful party that promises to "clean house," make the trains run on time, and forcibly integrate the disruptive elements of society often has an irresistible allure, just like the "man on horseback" in the nineteenth century.

Thus it seems to me that the analysis presented here has a bearing not only on the understanding of communist societies and their variations around the world, but also on the nature of modern society however one interprets that term Sociology and Marxism are both products of a nineteenth century that was baffled by the enormous and rapid changes taking place in industrializing societies: the breakdown of primary groups, the changes in family structure, the rise of new elites and the formation of new socioeconomic classes and groupings. For example, it was the phenomenon of differential suicide rates among different social groupings that so intrigued Durkheim and propelled him on the road to formation of a new discipline and field of inquiry. And, as I mentioned in the Introduction, some of the more baffling aspects of industrialization and its consequences, phenomena which at that time "did not make any sense," were undoubtedly what impelled Marx and Engels to seek an understanding of what was taking place.

Thus, in light of the general malaise and concern about industrial, urban, and mechanical or impersonal societies, one must cast a comparative look at those systems that claim they have a solution because they are inspired by a "scientific" vision of the world. Have they been able to develop and modernize with less trauma and fewer dislocations and with less destruction of basic values and social fibers than those societies that modernized under the fierce competitive whip of private capitalism? The best answer I can get is largely no. The very process of modernization, and the accumulation of the necessary capital, has its rules (perhaps not ironclad rules, but still rules) that transcend ideology and politics, and that impose themselves and their consequences, particularly when time is a critical dimension. One might argue that were these societies able to transform themselves in isolation from the rest of the world, that transformation would have been less traumatic. But this argument is largely invalid, for no society in the world today is an entity in and of itself. Thus, as I mentioned earlier, the time dimension looms as critical here. Remember, for example, Stalin's 1931 statement, quoted in the Introduction, that the Soviet Union had just ten years to become a mighty industrial state or fall victim to the attacks of its enemies abroad: "We are fifty to a hundred years behind the advanced countries. We must make good this distance in ten years. Either we do it, or we shall be crushed." Whatever one may think of Stalin, his crystal ball in this case turned out to be correct, almost to the day (the Germans attacked in June 1941). But compressing an industrialization program into a decade instead of, say fifty years, carried its own consequences and almost unendurable strains.

As modern societies move toward the twenty-first century, the "private" ownership of land and capital in the sense in which Marx understood it, seems to become less important, while control of these resources--the essentially political power to decide in which manner and for what purposes these will be utilized--and the ability to manage them (including the ability to control and utilize labor) become strategically significant.

Clearly only some aspects of modernization and its consequences could be examined within the compass of the symposium. Many other issues need more intensive investigation and analysis as they relate to modern communist societies. One of these, barely touched upon either in the symposium itself or in the papers, is that of ethnicity and nationality, of the survival and significance of these groupings, and indeed of their resistance to the homogenization predicted to be a consequence of industrialization and modernization. Another is the role of women, as affected by modernization in communist and noncommunist societies. Sokolowska's paper touched on that question with particular reference to Polish society, but she declined to have it considered for inclusion in this volume. Another most important topic is the changing role of the peasantry in communist societies, as examined in the paper by Sanders. Further work also needs to be done on the emergence in these societies of a variety of interest groups and the problem of articulating them with each other as well as with the ruling bodies of the party. Also at question (discussed at the symposium, but left without resolution) are "inclusion" and "citizenship," or the degree to which modernization in communist countries has been accompanied by greater participation of the population in social and political processes; this is one aspect of the all-important problem of "legitimating" the role of the party (touched on to some extent by Lowenthal). Future attention also must be given to the decline of the work ethic and the rise of the consumer ethic in communist society; the quite specific differences in the prestige of various occupations that arise with modernization and their feedback into the aspirations and motivations of youth; the increasing importance, for any modern or modernizing society, of science and technology and consequently of professional occupations and professional groups; the importance of the "welfare" aspects of modern society; and a quest for new community. These constitute, so to speak, an agenda for the future. Our hope collectively, was that the symposium and this volume should be considered only as part of an ongoing important enterprise. The problems and the "costs" of modern society are so enormous and formidable that they should occupy the attention of scholars, whichever side of whichever "curtain" they reside and work on.

Participants at the Symposium at Salzburg

R. V. Burks*	United States
Walter D. Connor	United States
Ralf Dahrendorf	Federal Republic of Germany
Mark G. Field	United States
B. Michael Frolic	Canada
Sung-Chick Hong	South Korea
Alex Inkeles	United States
Kenneth Jowitt	United States
T. Anthony Jones	United States
Zev Katz	United States
György Konrád**	Hungary
Richard Lowenthal	Federal Republic of Germany
Mervyn Matthews	England
John Montias	United States
Talcott Parsons	United States
Eugen Pusic	Yugoslavia
Seymour M. Rosen	United States
Magdalena Sokolowska	Poland
Peter H. Solomon	Canada
Robert C. Tucker*	United States
Ezra F. Vogel	United States
Wlodzimierz Weselowski	Poland
Irwin T. Sanders**	United States
Ivan Szelenyi**	Hungary

Rapporteuses:

Ms. Doris Katz	United States
Ms. Beverley Fisher	England

* Representing the Planning Group on Comparative Communism
**Prepared papers but were unable to attend.

Papers Prepared for the Symposium

Salzburg, Austria

5-10 September 1972

1. Walter B. Connor, "Deviance, Stress and Modernization in Eastern Europe"

2. Mark G. Field, "Health as a 'Public Utility' or the 'Maintenance of Capacity' in the Soviet Union"

3. Mark G. Field and T. Anthony Jones, "Modernization Theory and Some Tasks of the Symposium: A Background Paper"

4. B. Michael Frolic, "Non-Comparative Communism: Soviet and Chinese Cities"

5. Sung-Chick Hong, "The Processes and Consequences of Industrialization in North Korea"

6. Alex Inkeles, "The Modernization of Man in Socialist and Non-Socialist Societies"

7. Kenneth Jowitt, "Modernization and Mobilization in Marxist-Leninist Systems"

8. Zev Katz, "Patterns of Social Stratification in the U.S.S.R."

9. György Konrád and Iván Szelényi, "Social Conflicts of Under-Urbanization"

10. Richard Lowenthal, "The Ruling Party in a Mature Society"

11. Mervyn Matthews, "Educational Growth and Social Structure in the U.S.S.R."

12. John M. Montias, "Methodological Remarks on the Study of Modernization in Communist Countries"

13. Eugen Pusić, "The Yugoslav System of Participation and Self-Management"

14. Seymour M. Rosen, "Education, Modernization and Career Development in the U.S.S.R."

15. Irwin T. Sanders, "The Balkan Peasant Moves toward Industrialization"

16. Magdalena Sokolowska, "The Role of Women in Eastern Europe: The Case of Poland"

17. Peter H. Solomon, "Soviet Industrialization and Technological Innovation"

18. Robert C. Tucker, "Culture, Political Culture, Communism"

19. Ezra F. Vogel, "The Chinese Model of Development"

List of Contributors

Walter D. Connor is assistant professor of sociology and an associate of the Center for Russian and East European Studies at the University of Michigan. His publications include Deviance in Soviet Society: Crime, Delinquency, and Alcoholism (1972) and articles in Law and Society Review, Journal of Criminal Law, Criminology and Police Science, and American Sociological Review.

Mark G. Field is professor of sociology at Boston University and an associate of the Russian Research Center at Harvard University. He recently served as a lecturer in sociology at the Harvard Medical School and is now visiting lecturer at the Harvard School of Public Health. His publications include Doctor and Patient in Soviet Russia (1957), Social Approaches to Mental Patient Care (1964), Soviet Socialized Medicine: An Introduction (1967), and Evaluating Health Program Impact (1974).

B. Michael Frolic is an associate professor of political science at York University and was formerly a research fellow at Harvard University. His publications include Soviet Urban Government in Transition (in press) and "Moscow: The Socialist Alternative" in World Capitals, ed. H. Wentworth Eldridge (1975). He served as First Secretary, Canadian Embassy, Peking, 1974-75.

Alex Inkeles is the Margaret Jacks Professor of Education and professor of sociology at Stanford University and continues to hold an appointment as a research fellow at the Center for International Affairs at Harvard University. His publications include Public Opinion in Soviet Russia (1950), How the Soviet System Works (1959), What Is Sociology? (1964), Social Change in Soviet Russia (1968) and Becoming Modern (with David H. Smith) (1974).

T. Anthony Jones is assistant professor of sociology at the University of North Carolina at Chapel Hill. His interests include the effects of higher education on the new Soviet intelligentsia, development of planning systems in the USSR, patterns of modernization in the USSR and Eastern Europe, and relationship between societal change and reactions to deviance.

György Konrád is a Hungarian writer and sociologist and has been working with juvenile delinquents. He is a prolific writer on literary and sociological topics. His best-known work is The Case Worker, published first in Hungary (1969) and translated into many languages. The English edition was published in 1974.

Richard Lowenthal is professor emeritus of international relations at the Free University of Berlin. His publications include World Communism: The Disintegration of a Secular Faith (1964) and numerous essays in periodicals and scholarly journals.

Mervyn Matthews is a lecturer at the University of Surrey in England. He has written Class and Society in Soviet Russia (1972) and has edited Soviet Government: A Selection of Official Documents on Internal Policies (1974).

Peter H. Solomon, Jr., is assistant professor of political economy and sociology at the University of Toronto. His articles have appeared in Journal of Criminal Law, Criminology and Police Science, and Soviet Union. He has recently completed a book entitled Soviet Criminologists and Criminal Policy: Specialists in Soviet Policy Making (forthcoming).

Iván Szelényi formerly with the Sociological Institute of the Hungarian Academy of Sciences is now at the University of Kent, at Canterbury, England. He has taught and done research in the United States. His publications include Housing Systems and Social Structure and Reader in Urban Sociology.

Ezra F. Vogel is director of the East Asian Research Center at Harvard University and professor of sociology. His publications include A Modern Introduction to the Family (1960, 1968), Japan's New Middle Class (1963; revised edition, 1971), Canton under Communism (1969), Social Change: The Case of Rural China (1971) and Modern Japanese Organization and Decision Making (1975).

INDEX

LIBRARY OF CONGRESS CATALOGING IN PUBLICATION DATA
Main entry under title:

Social consequences of modernization in Communist
   societies.

   Based on a selection of papers presented at a symposium in Salzburg, Austria, in Sept. 1972, sponsored
by the American Council of Learned Societies under the
general auspices of its Planning Group on Comparative
Communist Studies.
   1. Communist countries—Social conditions—Congresses. I. Field, Mark G. II. American Council of
Learned Societies Devoted to Humanistic Studies. Planning
Group on Comparative Communist Studies.
HN960.S63   309.1'171'7   76—169
ISBN 0—8018—1786—2